D0071691

SHAKESPEARE *and* JONSON

SHAKESPEARE *and* JONSON

THEIR REPUTATIONS IN THE
SEVENTEENTH CENTURY COMPARED

GERALD EADES
BENTLEY

Two Volumes in One

THE UNIVERSITY OF CHICAGO PRESS
CHICAGO & LONDON

Standard Book Number: 226-04269-3

THE UNIVERSITY OF CHICAGO PRESS, CHICAGO 60637
The University of Chicago Press, Ltd., London

PREFACE

THIS STUDY IS VERY MUCH A BY-PRODUCT OF MY research for *The Jacobean and Caroline Stage*. While reading seventeenth-century documents, I kept track of all mentions of Jacobean and Caroline plays and playwrights in order that I might have solid evidence for later remarks on the reputations of the various dramatists. At first I assumed that I would not have to bother about Shakespeare and Jonson because practically all references to them had been collected in the two allusion books. After noting a number of omissions, however, I began to check each passage I came across against the collections and to transcribe those not found there.

As my file of transcriptions grew, I came to realize that the two allusion books gave a misleading picture of the respective reputations of their subjects. Of course, I knew in a general way, without adding up the evidence, that Jonson's reputation before the closing of the theaters was greater than Shakespeare's, and I assumed that the chronological distribution of the passages in *The Jonson Allusion-Book* gave a fairly accurate picture of the situation, with about five-eighths of the allusions falling in the forty-six years 1597–1642 and three-eighths in the fifty-eight years 1643–1700. Apparently Jonson's reputation declined rapidly in the last three-fifths of the century while Shakespeare's, on the contrary, rose.

At this stage I dropped the whole project for a month or so, and, for a quite unrelated reason, checked all the early editions of seventeenth-century plays in the University of Chicago Libraries. In going through the front matter of a large number of Restoration plays I noted, somewhat to my surprise, that Jonson was mentioned at least as often as Shakespeare and that a goodly number of the allusions were unrecorded. It appeared that my assumption about the falling-off of Jonson's reputation was all wrong. Then there was nothing for it but to have a look at the publications of the second half of the century. Half-reluctantly and half-eagerly, I went through as many likely volumes from 1650 to 1700 as I could get my hands on and found new Jonson allusions by the hundreds.

In the meantime, as I checked passages in *The Shakspere Allusion-Book*, I could not fail to note how very many of the extracts printed there were not really allusions at all and how far out of their true chronological position many of them were placed. By this time I had enough evidence to suggest, though not to establish, several conclusions: (*a*) The relative number of allusions by seventeenth-century writers to Shakespeare and to Jonson was not what the two allusion books indicated. (*b*) The apparent decline in Jonson's reputation after his death as suggested by the chronological distribution of the passages in *The Jonson-Allusion Book* was illusory. (*c*) There were far fewer valid allusions to Shakespeare and his works in the seventeenth century than *The Shakspere Allusion-Book* suggested.

These conclusions were simply general impressions; as yet I had not gone far enough to be able to make any precise statements. I needed to know just how many allusions, judged by the same standard of validity, had been reported for each man. I needed to know how these allusions were distributed chronologically when all were dated by the same standards. And I needed to know what different kinds of allusions there were and the comparative number of each type. Obviously a passage which simply named Shakespeare, without distinction, in a list of a dozen other authors was much less significant than a poem to his memory which said that his writings could not be praised too much.

Having got this far more or less by accident, I found myself driven to continue the investigation and to collect and sift the material which might resolve the problems raised by my harmless curiosity. This book is the result.

In the course of this somewhat tortuous process of tracing down allusions, of transcribing, classifying, counting, checking, and rechecking, I have encountered the friendly interest and assistance of a number of institutions and individuals—an interest I am flattered to acknowledge. The resources of the Henry E. Huntington Library, the Newberry Library, the University of Chicago Library, the Widener and Houghton libraries of Harvard, and the kindness of their custodians have greatly facilitated my search for and checking of allusions. The Research Committee of the Modern Language Association made a grant toward the expenses of typing and mounting the thousands of passages I have had to use. Research in the humanities is heavily indebted to such institutions—often more than to the universities themselves.

Miss Bertha Hensman and Mr. James Merrin have helped with mounting, checking, and collating and have given of their time far beyond the requirement of the bond. Miss Hensman also brought four new allusions to my attention, voluntarily submitting herself to the curse of "allusion consciousness." Professor Hallett Smith criticized the manuscript, greatly to my profit. (Reviewers of the book might well begin that cherished last paragraph, "In spite of the efforts of Professor Smith, Bentley's native awkwardness and inaccuracy still appear on pages . . . . .") Professor Arthur Friedman read the galleys for Volume I in an attempt to bring the accuracy of those pages up to the high standard of *Modern Philology*.

Constant assistance at all stages of the project, from my first ludicrously inadequate conception of the task to the last line of the Index, has come from my collaborator-assistant. Research has never been a lonely job for me.

G. E. B.

December 12, 1944

CONTENTS

VOLUME I: *Discussion*

VOLUME II: *Allusions*

SHAKESPEARE *and* JONSON

VOLUME I

Discussion

CHAPTER I

THE PROBLEM OF UNDERSTANDING
LITERARY REPUTATIONS

THIS BOOK IS AN ATTEMPT TO UNDERSTAND THE RE-
gard in which Shakespeare and Ben Jonson were held
by their contemporaries and successors in the seventeenth century. Such an understanding, in the complete
sense in which we desire it, is, of course, unattainable,
for the vast majority of Englishmen who witnessed or
read the plays of the two masters left no record of their
pleasure or pain. Many records have no doubt been destroyed, and presumably many others are still unprinted
or unnoted. Yet there remains a sizable body of recorded opinion which has already been collected or which
is here set forth for the first time. With this recorded
opinion I propose to deal.

At the very outset it is well to remember the obvious
fact that writers who seem literary giants to us were
often pigmies in the eyes of their contemporaries, that
phrases which ring unforgettably in our ears tinkled
very small in the ears for which they were written.
Nineteenth-century critics and historians were often
hero-worshipers, and they not infrequently attributed
to a sixteenth- or seventeenth-century masterpiece a
contemporary fame and influence which it certainly
never had in its own age.

This tendency to foist our own critical standards and
literary judgments upon the public of Marlowe or

Milton or Shakespeare is no doubt perfectly natural, but it is nonetheless a gross and dangerous distortion. A devoted and enthusiastic admirer of a great artist of the past can easily mislead generations of students. Such has been the fate, in at least one aspect of his work, of the great Milton scholar, David Masson. Masson, like most readers of Milton, was deeply impressed by *Areopagitica* and sought in the pamphlet literature of the time evidence of the influence of this noble document. His findings may be fairly summarized by some of his own statements.

The effect of Milton's *Areopagitica*, immediately after its publication in November 1644, and throughout the year 1645, seems to have been very considerable. Parliament, indeed, took no formal notice of the eloquent pleading for a repeal of their Licensing Ordinance of June 1643. . . . . But public opinion was affected, and the general agitation for Toleration took more and more the precise and practical form into which Milton's treatise had directed it. . . . . There can be no doubt, however, that as Milton, in his *Areopagitica*, had tried to make the official licensers of books, and especially those of them who were ministers, ashamed of their office, so his reasons and sarcasms, conjoined with the irksomeness of the office itself, did produce an immediate effect among those gentlemen, and modify their official conduct.[1]

For example, one finds that John Lilburne had been a reader of the *Areopagitica*, and had imbibed its lesson, and even its phraseology. . . . . There is proof, in the writings of other Independents and Sectaries, that Milton's jocular specimens of the *imprimaturs* in old books had taken hold of the popular fancy. . . . . On the whole, then, Milton's position among his countrymen from the beginning of 1645 onwards may be defined most accurately by conceiving him to have been, in the special field of letters, or pamphleteering, very much what Cromwell was in the broader and harder field of Army action, and what the younger Vane was, in Cromwell's absence, in the House of Commons.[2]

Now this statement of the great Milton scholar accords well with what a modern reader of Milton's

[1] David Masson, *The Life of John Milton* (1873), III, 431–32.

[2] *Ibid.*, pp. 433–34.

sonorous periods would naturally think their influence must have been. Furthermore, Masson cites evidence of a sort from contemporary documents for his conclusions. Yet a fuller examination of the extant pamphlets of these years has shown how wrong Masson was. William Haller, after extensive reading in the thousands of tracts of the Puritan Revolution preserved in the Thomason Collection at the British Museum and in the McAlpin Collection at Union Theological Seminary, makes a very different and much better-grounded statement about the reception and influence of Milton's work.

It appears incredible that Milton's great plea for freedom of the press should have failed of any mention whatever in the thousands of pages printed at the time and abounding in specific references to hundreds of other publications, but the present writer is constrained to report that after a protracted search he has failed to find a single one. . . . . In the light of these facts, we must dismiss the notion that *Areopagitica* had any appreciable effect on the situation in 1644. Masson surmises that Lilburne had imbibed Milton's lesson and very phraseology, but we have seen Lilburne defending free speech on the pillory as early as 1637, and he might have learned what else he needed to know about liberty from many other publications prior to *Areopagitica*. Masson also thinks that the mock order from the Westminster Assembly, prefixed to *The Arraignment of Mr. Persecution*, was suggested by specimen imprimaturs jocularly cited by Milton. But Overton was modeling his mockery on the Marprelate tracts. Masson's most serious misapprehension is, however, of the effect of *Areopagitica* upon enforcement of the printing ordinance. He would have us believe that by Milton's persuasion the licensers grew more lax. The fact is that from the Adoption of the printing ordinance in 1643, directed against royalists and prelatists, the licensers differed among themselves in their attitude toward the issues that arose between the Presbyterians and their various opponents. As the controversy developed, some naturally leaned further to one side and some to the other, and the pamphleteers meanwhile grew bolder and more numerous. The whole system of censorship in fact tended to break down.[3]

The evidence of contemporary pamphlets points, therefore, to the fol-

[3] William Haller (ed.), *Tracts on Liberty in the Puritan Revolution, 1638-1647* (1934), I, 135-36.

lowing conclusions concerning Milton's reputation and influence in the years immediately following 1643. (1) Little or nothing was known of him to the pamphleteers and the general public, save as the author of a scandalous book [*The Doctrine and Discipline of Divorce*] which was widely condemned but not widely read. (2) Since none of the critics of the divorce tract seems to have had any personal knowledge of Milton, even of his marital difficulties, we are led to infer that he refrained from association with any recognized groups of Independents, sectaries or Levellers. (3) *Areopagitica* . . . . seems to have attracted no contemporary attention, and to have had no discernible effect.[4]

If Milton idolatry can so distort the place of the man in his time, what can be expected of Shakespeare idolatry? For one hundred and fifty years it has flourished like the bay tree in the land.[5] Many reasons might be cited for thinking that Shakespeare would have had a wider appeal in the seventeenth century than Milton, and certainly some of them are valid; but the surest way to attain any understanding of his contemporary reputation, as of Milton's or Jonson's, is to examine the surviving records of the time.

These records will not, of course, give us Shakespeare's —or any other man's—reputation just as it stood in the years 1601–1700, for we know that many records have been destroyed or lost and that even more comments were never written down. To understand fully the standing of any dramatist in the seventeenth century we should need, for every year in the century, complete records of attendance at public performances of his plays in London and in the provinces, the number of command performances at court, the number of private performances, the number of copies of his works sold and

<hr/>

[4] *Ibid.*, p. 139.

[5] See, e.g., R.W. Babcock, *The Genesis of Shakespeare Idolatry, 1766–1799* (1931); Charles Knight, *A History of Opinion on the Writings of Shakespeare* (1866); D. Nichol Smith, *Shakespeare in the Eighteenth Century* (1929); Augustus Ralli, *A History of Shakespearian Criticism* (1933).

the number of readers for each copy, all printed statements about the man or his works, all written comments in private papers like letters and commonplace books and diaries, and, finally, records of all unwritten conversations about him. Even such fantastically complete records as these would need others to complement them —weather records and public health records to discount performance figures; printing and literacy records to discount reading and private-papers figures; and a vast amount of biographical and personality records to discount private conversation. Such an impossible mass of evidence would require corresponding figures on other contemporary dramatists for interpretation. Every scholar who writes of the reputation of any figure in the past must be conscious of how far his evidence falls short of such ideal completeness.

Yet some Shakespearean records of all these types do exist—a number surprisingly large considering the remoteness of the time and the status of the drama in the minds of most literate men in the seventeenth century. Similar records exist for Ben Jonson, the contemporary dramatist nearest Shakespeare in stature. A comparison of the numbers and types of these records, decade by decade, ought to give us a clearer picture of Shakespeare's reputation in the seventeenth century than we can now reach by any other means, and the same comparison would display Jonson's standing as well.

A good part of the extant records in these various classes mentioned above have been collected at one time and another into allusion books.[6] A certain num-

---

[6] The various collections of allusions to Shakespeare and Jonson are discussed in chap. iii.

ber of new allusions to Shakspeare and Jonson and their works are here set forth for the first time.[7] If we test all these allusions by a single standard of validity and distribute them into decades and types, we have a body of material, reliable though incomplete, upon which we can base a sounder estimate of the reputations of Shakespeare and Jonson than any other which has been offered. Such testing, distribution, and analysis of the results is the purpose of the succeeding chapters.

[7] See Vol. II, Parts I and II.

CHAPTER II

WHAT IS AN ALLUSION?

THE FIRST PROBLEM TO CONFRONT THE ALLUSION-chaser is the necessity for a definition sufficiently exact to enable him to identify his quarry. Unfortunately, collectors of allusions have not always faced this problem. *The Shakspere Allusion-Book* reprints as allusions scores of passages from the works of sixteenth- and seventeenth-century writers which have seemed to some readers to echo Shakespeare's words, his ideas, or situations in his plays. To take these passages as allusions to Shakespeare is in many cases a highly dubious procedure and in some patently absurd.[1] There are,

---

[1] It is suggested, for instance, that when Webster had his Cornelia say

> "Will you make mee such a foole? heere's a white hand:
> Can bloud so soone bee washt out?" (*The White Devil*, V, 4, 76–77)

he was imitating Shakespeare's

> "Will all great Neptune's ocean wash this blood
> Clean from my hand? No. This my hand will rather
> The multitudinous seas incarnadine,
> Making the green one red" (*Macbeth*, II, 2, 60–64);

and that Middleton's

> "MISTRESS PURGE: Husband, I see you are hoodwinked in the right use of feeling and knowledge,—as if I knew you not then as well as the child knows his own father!" (*The Family of Love*, V, 3)

is an imitation of Falstaff's

> "By the Lord, I knew ye as well as he that made ye"
>   (*Henry IV, Part I*, II, 4, 295–96).

There are equally dubious examples from Dekker (*The Shakspere Allusion-Book*, I, 106), from Marston (I, 108, 131, 153), from Webster (I, 115–19), from Middleton (I, 110, 141–44), from Heywood (I, 146, 165, 232; II, 40), from Beaumont and Fletcher (I, 196–203, 283), from Massinger (I, 296–304, 359), from Chapman (I, 170), from Jonson (I, 333), and from Shirley (I, 357).

for instance, many stock situations and characters in the Elizabethan drama which were used over and over again by most of the dramatists of the time, including William Shakespeare.[2] There is no reason to think that Fletcher or Massinger imitated Shakespeare whenever he used one of these stock situations, or even that he imitated Edwards or Kyd or Greene or Lyly, who used them before Shakespeare did. One might even hazard the generalization that Elizabethan playwrights, like modern ones, were much less self-conscious in their use of sources than scholars are likely to think.

Many passages in *The Shakspere Allusion-Book* alleged to be deliberate echoes of Shakespeare's words or sentiments are just as dubious as some said to reflect his situations and characters. Shakespeare, like other Elizabethan dramatists, made constant use of proverbial expressions. When a later dramatist employs one of the same proverbial expressions or comparisons which Shakespeare has put into the mouth of a character, there is no evidence of imitation of Shakespeare, and therefore no allusion.[3]

[2] See the tracing of a number of these situations and characters through many plays in Robert Stanley Forsythe's *The Relations of Shirley's Plays to the Elizabethan Drama* (1914).

[3] Massinger need never have seen or read *As You Like It* to have written

"Are you on the stage,
You talk so boldly?
PARIS: The whole world being one
This place is not exempted"
(*The Roman Actor*, I, 3; see *The Shakspere Allusion-Book*, I, 302).

Edwards had made the same comparison in *Damon and Pythias* (II, 3) some thirty years before Shakespeare did, and Edwards attributed the comparison to Pythagoras.

In the same way Massinger's passage of the gods smiling at lovers' perjuries (*The Parliament of Love*, V, 1; *The Shakspere Allusion-Book*, I, 301) probably did not come from *Romeo and Juliet*; for Robert Greene had used it, as well as various

This difficulty of allusions which do not allude is, of course, particularly acute in the case of Shakespeare. The situations, characters, and lines of his plays have long been more familiar than any others in English literature except, perhaps, those of the King James translation of the Bible. Consequently, similarities to his work are more frequently noted and commented upon than similarities to any others. All too often readers of Shakespeare are not content simply to point out the resemblances but must insist that they have found clear-cut allusions to Shakespeare or imitations of his lines. A number of these dubious allusions have, unfortunately, found their way into *The Shakspere Allusion-Book*.

As for Jonson, far fewer readers have found themselves sufficiently conversant with his lines to note similarities in the works of other writers.[4] Moreover, there has been no modern idolatry and no jealous pressing of admirers' claims that he was all things to all men in all times. Consequently, the parallel passages printed in *The Jonson Allusion-Book* are very few. This is not to say that only genuine Jonson allusions appear in that collection. Jonson's familiar pugnacity and the known number of his enemies have made scholars overeager to identify him with any unnamed object of satirical

---

classic writers. Even *The Shakspere Allusion-Book* itself notes at another point (I,189 n.) that the proverb is found in Ovid. For other examples see Morris Palmer Tilley, *Elizabethan Proverb Lore in Lyly's Euphues and in Pettie's Petite Pallace with Parallels from Shakespeare* (1926); see also *The Shakspere Allusion-Book*, II, 39, 70.

[4] The most familiar extended list of Jonsonian parallels is that found in William Dinsmore Briggs's "The Influence of Jonson's Tragedy in the Seventeenth Century," *Anglia*, XXXV (1912), 277-337. The great majority of these parallels are not sufficiently close or distinctive to be called allusions. Only 4 of the 174 have been counted in my totals of Jonson allusions.

attack. Occasionally, as in the case of Dekker's *Satiro-mastix*, there is abundant external evidence to prove that Jonson was indeed the object of the attack; but more often the unspecified victim might equally well, or better, have been someone else.[5]

After much puzzling over passages which have been printed as Shakespeare or Jonson allusions but which actually present no evidence that the authors had either of the great dramatists in mind, I have settled on a series of tests for allusions. On the one hand, an acceptable allusion must mention the name of Jonson or Shakespeare or the name of one of their compositions or characters, or it must contain at least one line quoted from their works.[6] About 98 per cent of the 3,269 Shake-

[5] A good instance in point is Thomas Heywood's sneer in the "Epistle to the Reader" of the 1633 quarto of *The English Traveller*: "*True it is, that my Playes are not exposed vnto the world in Volumes, to beare the title of* Workes, (*as others*)" (*The Jonson Allusion-Book*, p. 175). Now the ridicule of Jonson for calling the 1616 edition of his plays, epigrams, poems, entertainments, and masques *The Workes of Beniamin Jonson* is endless (see *The Jonson Allusion-Book*, pp. 119, 196, 271, 319, 486–87, and Vol. II, pp. 35, 108, 111). In any year before 1633 such ridicule necessarily applies to Jonson, for before that year no collection of English plays except his had been called "*Works*." But in the year of Heywood's complaint two other collections of plays which used the pretentious title had appeared: *Certaine Learned and Elegant Workes of the Right Honorable Fulke Lord Brooke* (1633) and *The Workes of Mr. Iohn Marston* (1633). Since the Greville volume had been licensed in the Stationers' Register eight months before *The English Traveller*, Heywood very probably had seen it, and he may well have known of the Marston collection, too. His sneer, therefore, is not certainly aimed at Jonson; indeed, considering the recency of the other publications, it is rather more likely to refer to them. For other doubtful satiric references see *The Jonson Allusion-Book*, pp. 9–10, 11, 29–32, 33, 54.

[6] To be really meticulous, of course, one must refrain from calling any passage a quotation from Shakespeare or Jonson unless the writer specifically acknowledges that he is quoting from one of them (I am speaking here of passages too brief to be absolutely and infallibly identified as coming from either of the two great dramatists), for in spite of a teasingly close similarity to Shakespeare's or Jonson's lines the passage may be completely original or even an echo or lifting from the work of another author. The strict application of this principle, however, would be sheer pedantry; and, though I have longed for strict rules and uncontrovertible principles in setting up the tests for validity, I have been sufficiently indiscriminate to accept as a quotation any passage of one full line or more which first appeared, so far as we know, in a work of Shakespeare or Jonson, whether credited to him or not.

speare and Jonson allusions which I have accepted and classified conform to these requirements. In the other 2 per cent, exceptions have been allowed because external evidence makes it clear that one of the dramatists or his work is referred to, even though no names are mentioned. Most of these exceptions are descriptions of Horace in *Satiromastix* or descriptions of preparations for or performances of masques not named but known from external evidence to have been Jonson's.

On the other hand, certain types of passages which specifically mention the playwrights have been systematically excluded. Title-pages of a man's own works, Stationers' Register entries of those works, publishers' advertisements, and sale catalogues have all been eliminated. These are publishing records and not allusions; and, though they are assuredly evidence of popularity, they belong in bibliographical studies— where they have all been competently treated—and not in allusion books. Publication records of apocryphal plays, on the other hand, are allusions, because a false attribution on a title-page is an attempt to sell a book, usually fraudulently, by an appeal to the public which recognizes the author. Such an appeal goes beyond a mere publishing record; like a quotation it is an attempt to exploit the reputation of Shakespeare or Jonson. It is therefore in the nature of an allusion and has been counted as such.[7]

There are, of course, a number of cases in which special precautions have to be observed in the application of these standards. Restoration revisions of Shake-

[7] By the same token, the mention of Shakespeare or Jonson on title-pages but not as author constitutes an allusion, e.g, the title-pages of *Jonsonus Virbius* (1638) or of *The Poems of Ben Jonson Junior* (1672).

speare's plays and drolls have been treated as if they were canonical works; that is, publication records have not been counted as allusions, but other references to these works have been counted as allusions to the plays from which they are derived.[8] Again, there are a number of passages which mention mythological or historical characters appearing in Shakespeare's or Jonson's plays but by no means in these plays alone. Such figures as Venus, Adonis, Caesar, Brutus, Antony, Cleopatra, Troilus, Cressida, Portia, Sejanus, Catiline, Richard III, Henry VIII, etc., may be referred to as historical or legendary personages without any trace of an allusion to a play. Usually it is perfectly clear that no reference to creations of Shakespeare or Jonson is involved, and no one has claimed the passage as an allusion; but several such references have been included in *The Shakspere Allusion-Book* which probably do not refer to Shakespeare.[9] On this point I have followed the principle that when there is reasonable doubt about the passage it must be eliminated.

Finally, I have restricted allusions to those found in English books and manuscripts.

In the matter of chronological limits, I have maintained narrower restrictions than some of the allusion collections have set up. All allusions considered in this study must have been published (if in printed books) or written (if extant only in manuscript) between the years 1601 and 1700 inclusive. The year 1700 as a terminal date has been generally used and needs no defense.

[8] In many cases it is not possible to tell whether an allusion refers to a Restoration revision of a Shakespearean play or to the folio text (see below, pp. 108–11).

[9] See, e.g., the passages mentioning Lucrece (I, 96; II, 295), Cressida (I, 128), Venus and Adonis (I, 178, 256), Cleopatra (I, 262), and Timon (II, 416).

The elimination of sixteenth-century allusions perhaps requires some explanation as being less familiar. The first and least defensible reason is the concentration of my own interest in the seventeenth century. The second and more considerable is the fact that this study is intended primarily as a comparison of two great literary reputations. Since Shakespeare was born ten years before Jonson and began writing several years before him, it is very difficult to assess the significance of the difference in the Shakespeare and Jonson allusions in the sixteenth century. How much is due to the fact that Jonson probably had not written anything except school exercises by the date of the first Shakespeare allusion? How much is due to the fact that when Francis Meres published *Palladis Tamia* he might have seen nearly half the plays of the currently accepted Shakespeare canon, but very little of Jonson, since 95 per cent of the Jonson canon was still unwritten? Furthermore, in Renaissance society courtly groups were the most articulate. In comparing carly allusions, then, how can one allow for the fact that most of Shakespeare's work appealing to the courtly group was written in the sixteenth century, nearly all of Jonson's in the seventeenth?

These and similar difficulties of comparison are for the most part avoided by eliminating sixteenth-century allusions from consideration. Even at the beginning of the seventeenth century, certain of the difficulties still exist, for reputations are cumulative. In the last year of Elizabeth, Shakespeare's writing career was more than half-finished; none of Jonson's greatest comedies and none of his masques had yet been written. A com-

parison of the allusions to the two men between 1601
and 1700, then, only minimizes and does not wholly
obviate the difficulty posed by the earlier date of Shakespeare's work.

The chronological restrictions placed on allusions
sometimes raise a problem of dating. What is the proper
date for an allusion—date of composition, date of
licensing for the stage in the case of a play, date of
licensing for the press, or date of printing? Obviously,
the date of composition is the real date of the occurrence
of the allusion; but in the great majority of cases, probably nine-tenths, there is no generally accepted date
of composition. The date of licensing for the stage or the
press, being nearest to the date of composition, would be
second choice; but for perhaps half the allusions there is
no recorded date of licensing for the press and for four-
fifths of them no date of licensing for the stage. A con-
sistent attempt, therefore, to organize a mass of allusions on the basis of composition or licensing dates
leads to chaos. Thus in *The Shakspere Allusion-Book*,
in which all three methods of dating are used with a
fine impartiality,[10] one can never tell how many of a
group of allusions dated in the third decade of the century were printed then. If Shakespeare allusions so
dated are compared, as in this study, with Jonson allusions of the same decade, the comparison goes very
much askew because of the variety in the dating methods employed.

[10] As well as a wholly indefensible practice of occasionally abandoning the classi-
fication-by-date system entirely and grouping allusions by author, as for example,
Webster (I, 115–19), Beaumont and Fletcher (I, 196–203), Burton (I, 281–82),
Herbert (I, 321–24), Massinger (I, 296–304), Pepys (II, 89–97), Dryden (II, 174–
80), Lee (II, 264); or even by subject (I, 32–40).

Faced with this difficulty, I have revised the dating of the entire body of Shakespeare and Jonson allusions used and have classified each allusion by the date of its first printing, with two exceptions. First, in the case of manuscript allusions, where no printing date, of course, is available, I have had to fall back upon the date assigned to the manuscript by its editor or cataloguer. Second, in the very few instances in which an author has himself given the precise date of composition—mostly dated letters—that date has been accepted.

These principles of dating and classification have occasionally led to the inclusion of passages not given seventeenth-century dates in the allusion collections and to the exclusion of others which have been so dated. For instance, Richard Carew's praise of English writers, including Shakespeare, in his *Excellencie of the English Tongue*, which is dated 1595–96 in *The Shakspere Allusion-Book*, is considered here as a seventeenth-century allusion, for it was first published when Camden included it in the second edition of his *Remaines concerning Britaine* in 1614. On the other hand, the account of the conversation between Ben Jonson, Mr. Hales of Eton, and others, which *The Jonson Allusion-Book* prints under the date "about 1633," is excluded entirely; for, though it concerns an event of the early seventeenth century, it was first printed by Nicholas Rowe in the life of Shakespeare published in his edition of 1709.

I hope that this all does not sound like wilful juggling. For a study of this sort it was necessary to have exact and rigid rules by which to consider the thousands of passages, and I have arrived at the above system only after considering and trying a great many others; I believe the criteria here set forth to be the strictest and most defensible of all those I examined. They are not whimsical, but utilitarian, though occasionally their exact application, as in the Rowe quotation just instanced, leads to decisions which are, at first blush, puzzling. I have tried to wander through the maze of allusions with the jewel of consistency to guide me; I hope the reader can follow with confidence and comprehension.

CHAPTER III

THE COLLECTIONS OF SHAKESPEARE
AND JONSON ALLUSIONS

IN THE SEVENTY YEARS SINCE C. M. INGLEBY PUBLISHED
his *Shakspere Allusion-Books*, Part I, a number of collections of allusions to Shakespeare and Jonson have
appeared. Anyone reviewing these collections is most
forcibly struck by the number and particularly by the
diversity of readers—historians, librarians, public officials, English scholars, publishers, clergymen, lawyers,
booksellers, general readers—who have reported Shakespeare allusions, as compared with the handful of professional scholars who have been concerned with references to Jonson. One hundred and twenty-seven individuals have contributed Shakespeare allusions to the
ten principal collections used for this study, while all
the Jonson allusions are the results of the observations
of nine scholars, and all but about 200 of the 2,225
Jonson allusions examined for this book have been reported by only three searchers.[1]

[1] The various collections of Shakespeare allusions acknowledge contributions by
the following readers: C. R. Baskervill, E. F. Bates, Thomas Bayne, Edward Bensly,
G. E. Bentley, "Bibliothecary," G. Binz, Thomas Birch, A. C. Bradley, John Brant,
Rudolph Brotanek, H. Brown, Rawdon Brown, C. Elliot Browne, John Bruce, A.
H. Bullen, George Bullen, D. B. Brightwell, C. B. Carew, George Chalmers, Sir
Edmund Chambers, W. Chappell, William Chetwood, Andrew Clark, Charles
Crawford, Peter Cunningham, J. P. Collier, G. L. Craik, P. A. Daniel, R. K. Dent,
Bertrand Dobell, Edward Dowden, Alexander Dyce, J. W. Ebsworth, C. Edmonds,
Karl Elze, Arundell Esdaile, Herbert Evans, C. H. Firth, F. G. Fleay, E. Fox, P. S.
Furness, F. J. Furnivall, R. Garnett, Mr. Gilson, Sir Israel Gollancz, A. B. Grosart,
C. Haines, J. W. Hales, J. O. Halliwell-Phillipps, H. C. Hart, C. S. Harris, Edward B.
Harris, W. C. Hazlitt, Bertha Hensman, Charles S. Herpich, J. N. Hetherington,

One sure conclusion is to be drawn from a comparison of the size and variety of these two groups, namely, that a much higher proportion of all the existing allusions to Shakespeare written before 1701 has now been found, collected, and published than of the Jonson allusions. Considering the tremendous interest in Shakespeare in the nineteenth and twentieth centuries, one sees at once that this was inevitable. Whatever the primary interests of a student reading the printed books or manuscript remains of the sixteenth and seventeenth centuries, he is sure to have read or at least heard of Shakespeare and to be brought up short by a mention of his name. And the less literary the character of the text, the more likely the reader is to stop and comment upon the allusion and report it—generally, it would appear from the annotations in the allusions books, to some member of the New Shakspere Society. And not only is Shakespeare's name arresting, but his works have

---

E. H. Hickey, H. A. Holden, Joseph Hunter, Alfred H. Huth, C. M. Ingleby, William Jaggard, Maurice Jones, J. J. Jusserand, W. P. Ker, Joseph Knight, Emil Koppel, Maria Latrielle, Sir Sidney Lee, H. Littledale, P. A. Lyons, W. D. Macray, Margaret Macalister, R. B. McKerrow, Edmund Malone, John M. Manly, Mr. Massey, Paul Meyer, John Munro, Brinsley Nicholson, A. C. P., W. G. P., Sir T. Philips, Emma Phipson, Bernard Quaritch, R. R., Isaac Reed, R. Roberts, T. Rodd, Hyder E. Rollins, A. S. W. Rosenbach, F. J. Routledge, Nicholas Rowe, T. Rundall, Walter Rye, H. E. S., R. Savage, Edward J. L. Scott, W. D. Selby, C. Severn, Richard Simpson, Richard Sims, G. C. Moore Smith, Lucy Toulmin Smith, Teena Rochfort Smith, J. Spedding, Caroline Spurgeon, Howard Staunton, George Steevens, Leslie Stephen, W. H. Stevenson, H. P. Stokes, W. G. Stone, Mrs. C. C. Stopes, D. L. Thomas, G. Thorn-Drury, Morris Tilley, Samuel Timmins, W. S. W. Vaux, E. Viles, C. W. Wallace, Joseph Warton, P. Whatley, F. P. Wilson, Aldis Wright, and E. Yardley.

The nine collectors of Jonson allusions are J. Q. Adams, Jesse Franklin Bradley, W. D. Briggs, C. B. Graham, Thornton Shirley Graves, Howard P. Vincent, Bernard Wagner, Miss Bertha Hensman, who has brought two Jonson and two Shakespeare allusions to my attention, and myself. The two passages published by Arthur Melville Clark and Don Cameron Allen (see p. 36, n. 32) have not been accepted as valid allusions, and I have therefore not counted them.

grown so familiar that all his titles, many of his characters, and hundreds of his lines are widely recognized; general readers have consequently been able to identify them in commonplace books, correspondence, sermons, songbooks, histories, diaries, newspapers, and treatises.

Jonson, on the other hand, has had no such public. The unexpected appearance of his name tingles no spine except that of an occasional overly enthusiastic student of the drama; the very commonness of his patronymic helps to obscure him. The titles of many of his works are little known. The literate reader who thinks "Shakespeare!" at once when he sees mention of *The Two Gentlemen of Verona* or *Measure for Measure*, *Coriolanus* or *All's Well That Ends Well*, is merely puzzled at the sight of *The Case Is Altered* or *A Tale of a Tub*, *Cynthia's Revels* or *The Magnetic Lady*. The names of Jonsonian characters casually mentioned in seventeenth-century documents are even less familiar to the modern general reader. It might be amusing to make an academic parlor game of the demonstration of this fact. In the allusions so far recorded from the seventeenth century, the following characters—half Jonson's, half Shakespeare's— are each mentioned from two to seven times. In that century they were apparently about equally familiar, though the total number of allusions to the seven Jonson characters adds up to more than the total for the seven Shakespeare characters. The object of the demonstration-game would be to see how many of these characters can be adequately identified by any well-read individual and then to compare the familiarity of the two groups. The characters in ascending order of seventeenth-century popularity are Shylock, King

Lear, Mercutio, Fly, Romeo, Pug, Bottom, Ursula, Asper, Adam Overdo, Juliet, Crispinus, Polonius, Captain Otter.[2]

In the comparative familiarity of the lines of the two writers, the discrepancy is greatest of all. Most readers have committed to memory at least a few lines of Shakespeare; and they can recognize, if they cannot repeat, scores of passages from the plays and the sonnets. Probably the same readers could recognize or even repeat any stanza of "To Celia" and possibly a few other lines from Jonson's most popular poems, but who knows the lines from his plays? Of all forms of seventeenth-century allusion to Jonson, quotations from his works are the most likely to go unnoted unless they are identified in the text.[3] This fact is of great importance in considering the significance of the comparative number of quotations from Jonson and from Shakespeare recorded in the collections of seventeenth-century allusions.[4]

There can be no doubt, then, that many more allusions to Jonson than to Shakespeare remain to be discovered and recorded.[5] All comparisons of the number of allusions to the two dramatists must discount the figures accordingly. In any category which now shows

[2] Complete figures on the number of seventeenth-century allusions to the characters of the two dramatists are given below, pp. 120 ff.

[3] The comparative popular familiarity of the lines of the two dramatists is well illustrated by the selections in the last (1939) edition of Bartlett's *Familiar Quotations*, which devotes 77 pages to 1,849 quotations from Shakespeare, 2 pages to 41 quotations from Jonson.

[4] See below, pp. 73-80.

[5] Especially in the last three decades of the century, where a much smaller proportion of the extant literature has been examined for Jonson allusions than in the earlier decades.

more allusions to Jonson than to Shakespeare, the preponderance is probably actually greater than the present figures indicate; in categories in which there is little present difference in the figures, allusions yet to be found would probably push Jonson into the lead; in categories in which there are now a great many more Shakespeare allusions, the undiscovered references would probably cut down Shakespeare's dominance.

SHAKESPEARE COLLECTIONS

A little less than two-thirds of the seventeenth-century allusions to Shakespeare and to Jonson which form the basis of this study have appeared in various gatherings of my predecessors. The collections of Shakespeare allusions I have used are as follows:

C. M. INGLEBY. *Shakspere Allusion-Books*, Part I. "New Shakspere Society Publications." London, 1874.

————. *Shakespeare's Centurie of Prayse*. 2d ed. "New Shakspere Society Publications." London, 1879.

FREDERICK J. FURNIVALL. *Some 300 Fresh Allusions to Shakspere.* "New Shakspere Society Publications." London, 1886.

JOHN MUNRO. *The Shakspere Allusion-Book . . . . Reissued with a Preface by Sir Edmund Chambers.* Oxford, 1932.

————. "More Shakspere Allusions," *Modern Philology*, XIII (January, 1916), 129–76.

[G. THORN-DRURY]. *Some Seventeenth Century Allusions to Shakespeare and His Works Not Hitherto Collected.* London, 1920.

HYDER E. ROLLINS. "Shakespeare Allusions," *Notes and Queries: Twelfth Series*, X (1922), 224–25.

[G. THORN-DRURY]. *More Seventeenth Century Allusions to Shakespeare and His Works Not Hitherto Collected.* London, 1924.

SIR EDMUND CHAMBERS. *William Shakespeare*, Vol. II (Oxford, 1930), Appens. A, B, and C.

These collections contain many passages which I have not used at all because, according to my definition,[6]

---

[6] See above, pp. 10–16.

they are not allusions—that is, they are parallel passages or publication records or common sayings—or they do not properly fall within the limits of the seventeenth century. It is therefore necessary to consider each collection in turn and to indicate the number of allusions accepted and the number rejected, with the reasons for the rejections.

"THE SHAKSPERE ALLUSION-BOOK"

All the valid passages of the first three collections were reprinted in *The Shakspere Allusion-Book* of 1909, and all that volume, in turn, was reprinted without revision in the last edition of 1932. A discussion of *The Shakspere Allusion-Book* of 1932, therefore, covers all the other four; that collection, furthermore, is the standard familiar one.

The principal defects of the collection are the natural results of the method of its compilation. As John Munro pointed out in his Preface to the edition of 1909, "These volumes were not made in a day. Thirty years have passed in their compilation, and the thousands of books from which their contents have been drawn stretch over three hundred years. Many willing hands, too, have lent assistance. Antiquaries, scholars, and friendly readers, have all most kindly helped." Unfortunately, the many willing hands had many different standards of what constituted an allusion, of what constituted a proper reference, and of what system of dating was to be used; and the editors made no very thorough attempt to reduce them all to order. Consequently, the collection is somewhat chaotic, even printing a number of its passages in more than one place.[7] For the purposes of this study, each passage in *The Shakspere Allusion-Book* has been examined according to the standards set up for a valid seventeenth-century allusion to Shakespeare or Jonson. The valid allusions have been redated where necessary, and all have been classified according to type by decades.

The examination has resulted in the rejection of a great many of the passages in this standard collection of Shakespeare allusions. The group most easily eliminated is the one made up of those passages first printed before 1601 or after 1700, and of those found in manuscripts dated outside the period by their editors. Five hundred and three of the passages in *The Shakspere Allusion-Book* have been eliminated by the date test; some of them are dated within the seventeenth century in the collection but fall outside that period when redated according to the principles set up here.[8] Most of the passages in this rather large group of rejections are one- or two-line quotations from Shakespeare's works reprinted in early anthologies like *England's Parnassus* and *Belvedere* and presented in Appendixes B, C, and D of *The Shakspere Allusion-Book*.

Another large number of passages has been rejected because they are not allusions but mere parallel passages, usually very far-fetched parallels. They have

---

[7] See *The Shakspere Allusion-Book*, I, 198 and 328, 291 and 345, 466 and 526; I, 73, and II, 494; I, 72, and II, 478; II, 180 and 393; I, 418 and II, 468; II, 33 and 469; II, 121 and 469.

[8] A large number of these passages are not true allusions anyhow, but if they fall outside the seventeenth century no attempt has been made to classify them further.

been discarded, as in the case of Jonson, unless there is as much as one line quoted or a mention of the author's name or the name of one of his works or characters. Two hundred and seventy-two passages have been rejected, the great majority of them, 229, from Volume I.[9]

A number of passages have been eliminated because, though they do mention the names of Shakespeare's characters or works, the names are too common to refer certainly to his creations and there is no other indication that the writer of the passage had Shakespeare in mind. This standard is a difficult one to apply. Unfortunately, there are more than a hundred characters, plays, or poems of Shakespeare which bear the names of familiar historical or mythological figures. When a writer mentions Julius Caesar or Richard III or Venus and Adonis, he does not necessarily have Shakespeare in mind. Even when a title is mentioned as that of a play, the allusion is not always clear, especially in the case of *Richard III* and *Hamlet*, where other plays of the name are known. On the whole, I have tended to exclude in case of doubt, though I suspect myself of having been overindulgent in the case of *Hamlet*. Altogether, 44 passages mentioning the names of Shakespearean creations have been discarded because reference to Shakespeare seemed doubtful.

A number of the passages in *The Shakspere Allusion-Book* are what I have called publishing records and not allusions—title-pages of Shakespeare's own works, Stationers' Register entries, publishers' advertisements, and sale catalogues. If such records use the name of the dramatist incidentally or inaccurately, as in the title

[9] See above, p. 7, n. 1, and p. 8, n. 3.

The Poems of Ben Jonson Junior (1672), or refer to apocryphal plays, then there is an allusion; but ordinary publishing and advertising records have been eliminated. Two hundred and ninety-three passages in *The Shakspere Allusion-Book* have been eliminated on these grounds.[10]

Twenty-six passages have been eliminated because, though they do use Shakespeare's words, Shakespeare himself was quoting a proverbial saying. Such passages are adequately illustrated in chapter ii.[11]

Another group of passages has gone into the discard because, though they do not fall exactly into any of the foregoing classifications, they are still too vague and uncertain to be accepted as genuine allusions. The title-page of *The True Chronicle Historie of the Whole Life and Death of Thomas Lord Cromwell*, which says that the play was "Written by W. S.," is an example, for "W. S." may refer to a number of men other than William Shakespeare.[12] Similarly, the satiric passages about Studioso in *The Return from Parnassus*[13] are not sufficiently clear to be accepted as certain references to Shakespeare. Twenty-one such passages in *The Shakspere Allusion-Book* have been rejected.

Finally, a small group of passages has been discarded because they were duplicates or foreign, not English,

[10] In this figure are included the title-pages and other publishing records of drolls and Restoration adaptations of Shakespeare's plays. On the other hand, literary passages referring to these drolls and adaptations have been accepted as genuine allusions to Shakespeare.

[11] See also below, p. 28, n. 17.

[12] On the other hand, the title-page of another apocryphal play, *A Yorkshire Tragedy*, does contain an allusion, for it says that the play was "*Written by* W. Shakspeare."

[13] *The Shakspere Allusion-Book*, I, 155.

allusions or because they were Restoration adaptations of Shakespeare's plays. This last category is the only confusing one. As we have noted, these adaptations have been considered as part of the Shakespeare canon; therefore, any reference to the adaptation is a Shakespeare allusion, but the publication records of the recensions are not, and the adaptation itself is not an allusion. In this miscellaneous group are 16 discarded passages, 11 of them duplicates.

A supplement to *The Shakspere Allusion-Book* is provided in the Preface to the reprint of 1932 written by Sir Edmund Chambers. This Preface presents 14 new allusions[14] not found in the body of the book, most of them taken from the author's own *William Shakespeare*. Of these 14 passages in the Preface, 3 have been rejected because they are sixteenth- rather than seventeenth-century allusions. One other is discarded because it had been printed by Munro in his article, "More Shakspere Allusions," and is here counted as from that source. A fifth passage comes from G. Thorn-Drury's *More Seventeenth Century Allusions to Shakespeare and His Works Not Hitherto Collected* and is counted among Thorn-Drury's valid allusions. Altogether, then, only 9 of the 14 passages in the Preface can be added to the collection of valid allusions.

When all these figures on *The Shakspere Allusion-Book* are assembled, we find a grand total of 2,216 passages presented in that volume as allusions to Shakespeare,[15]

[14] Chambers numbers the passages I–XII, but his No. IV contains 3 separate allusions.

[15] Several hundred of these passages come from the appendixes, the Preface, and the notes on other passages. Often the passages cited in the notes are clearer allusions to Shakespeare than those in the body of the work.

of which 1,180 have been rejected for the various reasons assigned. The 1,036 remaining passages constitute the bulk of the valid seventeenth-century allusions to Shakespeare which have been used for this study.

After *The Shakspere Allusion-Book*, the largest collection of passages referring to Shakespeare is that gathered over a number of years by George Thorn-Drury and assembled in two pamphlets, *Some Seventeenth Century Allusions to Shakespeare and His Works Not Hitherto Collected* (London, 1920) and *More Seventeenth Century Allusions to Shakespeare and His Works Not Hitherto Collected* (London, 1924). In these two pamphlets, 254 passages presumably referring to Shakespeare but not found in *The Shakspere Allusion-Book* are set forth. The chronological limits indicated in the titles are strictly observed, and therefore only 1 passage[16] has had to be discarded because of the date of the first edition or manuscript in which it occurs. Publishing records are generally eschewed in these collections, and only one passage—a bookseller's advertisement of *Lucrece*—has been rejected because it falls into this class. A rather large number of passages have been thrown out, however, because they are alleged parallel passages, which really show no clear allusions to Shakespeare's work. Notable are the proverbial expressions quoted from seventeenth-century writers and supposed to derive from Shakespeare, when, as a matter of fact,

---

[16] *More Seventeenth Century Allusions*, p. 20. The passage was first printed in 1704 and therefore could not be accepted, even though it does refer to events before Monmouth's death.

others had used them long before the Swan of Avon.[17]
A total of 25 passages has been eliminated from the
total of 254 because they are quotations of proverbial
expressions rather than quotations of Shakespeare's
work or because they are mere parallel passages whose
parallelism may be doubted. Two further passages
refer to Portia and to Venus, but not necessarily to
Shakespeare's characters of these names. Altogether,
29 passages have been rejected from Thorn-Drury's
total of 254, leaving 225 allusions which may be accepted as valid.

JOHN MUNRO'S "MORE SHAKSPERE ALLUSIONS"

After *The Shakspere Allusion-Book* and Thorn-
Drury's gatherings, the most extensive collection of
allusions is that published by John Munro,[18] the editor
of the 1909 *Allusion-Book*, as a supplement to that
volume. The first source of confusion in this collection
is Munro's reprinting of a number of allusions which
had been published by Thorn-Drury in *Notes and
Queries* and which Thorn-Drury later gathered into his
own two pamphlets.[19] A few of Munro's allusions had
already appeared in *The Shakspere Allusion-Book* but
escaped Munro's attention because they had been

[17] Thorn-Drury found three passages using the proverb "Love will creep where
it cannot go" and attributed them all to imitations of Shakespeare's line in *Two
Gentlemen of Verona* (IV, 2, 19–20). Proteus in this speech actually calls attention
to the fact that he is using a common expression by prefacing the proverbial remark
with the words "for you know that." The proverb, of course, is the old one, "Kynde
[in the sense of 'kindness' or 'love'] will creep where it may not go." *The Oxford Dictionary of English Proverbs* ([Oxford, 1935], pp. 250–51) quotes examples in 1350,
1460, 1500, 1546, and 1548, as well as 1614, 1635, and 1641.

[18] "More Shakspere Allusions," *Modern Philology*, XIII (January, 1916), 497–
544.

[19] A perfectly legitimate procedure on Munro's part, for he published in 1916, and
Thorn-Drury did not collect his allusions until 1920 and 1924.

taken from other editions and were differently dated. Altogether, 63 of Munro's 130[20] have been eliminated because they appeared in other collections. Of the 67 remaining, 4 are dated before the year 1601 and have been thrown out for that reason. Twelve others are mere parallel passages, at best using only three or four of Shakespeare's words. Nine more use the names of characters in Shakespeare's plays and poems—Brutus, Antony, Venus, Adonis, Troilus, Hotspur, Cleopatra— but use them in such a way as to make it unlikely or at best uncertain that the authors had Shakespeare's creations in mind. One is simply the old proverb, "Love will creep where it cannot go," again. Thus of Munro's total of 130 passages, 89 have had to be discarded for one reason or another, leaving only 41 which are valid additions to the collections in *The Shakspere Allusion-Book* and Thorn-Drury's pamphlets.

HYDER ROLLINS' "SHAKESPEARE ALLUSIONS"

Rollins' collection contains 18 passages, 15 of which are valid allusions. Of the other 3, 1 had already appeared in *The Shakspere Allusion-Book*, and 1 is a line which does appear in Shakespeare but which Shakespeare himself had quoted from Marlowe.[21] The other rejected passage is another example of the all-the-world's-a-stage figure used by many poets long before Shakespeare as well as after.

SIR EDMUND CHAMBERS' "WILLIAM SHAKESPEARE"

Appendixes A, B, and C of this monumental work contain allusions to Shakespeare of various kinds.

[20] Munro numbers the items 1–86; but his numbers refer to sources, not individual allusions; a number of the books furnished several references.

[21] "Who ever lov'd, that lov'd not at first sight" (*Hero and Leander*, l. 176).

Those in Appendix A are records, mostly from parish registers and legal documents, of the activities of Shakespeare, his ancestors, his friends, and his descendants. Though there are not many references of this type in *The Shakspere Allusion-Book*, those mentioning Shakespeare by name are certainly allusions. Since the passages in this appendix are all biographical records, none naming Shakespeare has been rejected because it was a parallel passage, a publishing record, or a proverbial saying. Only those references failing to mention Shakespeare or dated after 1700 or before 1601 (112 of them) have had to be rejected. There remain 50 valid allusions in Appendix A which are not found in any of the other allusion collections.

The passages in Appendixes B and C are limited to personal references and to contributions to the "Shakespeare-Mythos"; and, since they are not offered as a collection of new allusions, it is not surprising that these two appendixes add very few to the grand total of Shakespeare allusions. There are 203 passages in Appendixes B and C,[22] of which 31 are earlier than 1601 and 78 are later than 1700. Of the remainder, 83 had appeared in previous collections.[23] Seven more are vague and uncertain references to Shakespeare—like those in Jonson's *Poetaster*—or are references to common names, like Sir John Oldcastle, which may or may not be intended for Shakespeare's character. There remain only 4 valid new allusions of the seventeenth

[22] The passages are numbered I–LVIII in one appendix and I–LVIII (*sic*) in the other, but a number contain several distinct allusions.

[23] Really, only 78 had appeared in collections dated before 1930, but 5 of Sir Edmund's new allusions were used by him in his Preface for the reprint of *The Shakspere Allusion-Book* in 1932 and have here been counted as part of that collection.

century to be added to the total from these two appendixes, or 54 from all three.

In these various gatherings a total of 2,983 passages has been presented. Many of them are duplications, others fall outside the selected period 1601–1700, and largest of all is the group which cannot be counted as valid allusions according to the standards set up in chapter ii. For one or another of these reasons, 1,612 passages have been discarded, leaving 1,371 valid allusions. This very large number of passages in the familiar collections which has been rejected after testing by a well-defined standard is significant. Here we have one of the reasons for the frequent overestimation of Shakespeare's influence in his own century. The bulk of the two volumes of *The Shakspere Allusion-Book* is not what it seems.

JONSON ALLUSIONS

The collections of Jonson allusions are fewer and smaller than those of Shakespeare, and from them fewer allusions have had to be discarded. Both facts are indirect reflections of Shakespeare's popularity in the last one hundred years. Because of the interest in Shakespeare, more people have collected allusions to him than to Jonson; because of the avid interest in and extensive knowledge of Shakespeare, more people have wanted to see allusions to him where none exist. No doubt a further reason for the comparatively small number of unacceptable Jonson allusions printed has been the warning example of the Shakespeare collections. The first four, and the largest, Shakespeare gatherings were printed some years before the first Jonson collection, and no one can examine the earlier publications without noting the uncertainty of their standards.

The previously printed collections of Jonson allusions here used are as follows:

JESSE FRANKLIN BRADLEY and JOSEPH QUINCY ADAMS. *The Jonson Allusion-Book*. New Haven, 1922.

THORNTON SHIRLEY GRAVES. "Jonson in the Jest Books," in *Manly Anniversary Studies*. Chicago, 1923.

W. D. BRIGGS. "The Influence of Jonson's Tragedy in the Seventeenth Century," *Anglia*, XXXV (1912), 277–337.

BERNARD WAGNER. "A Jonson Allusion and Others," *Philological Quarterly*, VII (1928), 306–8.

C. B. GRAHAM. "Jonson Allusions in Restoration Comedy," *Review of English Studies*, XV (1939), 200–204.

HOWARD P. VINCENT. "Ben Jonson Allusions," *Notes and Queries*, CLXXVII (1939), 26.

The foremost collection is, of course, *The Jonson Allusion-Book*. This volume contains 861[24] statements about Jonson and his works which have all been tested by the same standards applied to the Shakespeare allusions. Under these tests, 55 of them have been discarded because they do not fall within the period 1601–1700.[25] Fifty-three more have been thrown out because they are what I have called publishing records rather than allusions. Twenty-one others are descriptive passages, generally satiric, which someone has thought

[24] There are not 861 separate entries in the volume, but many of the passages, like those in *The Shakspere Allusion-Book*, are really comprised of several different Jonson allusions, though the printing of the extracts sometimes obscures this fact; note, e.g., the three separate allusions in the lines taken from the Preface to *The Womens Conquest*, pp. 363–64; and the two distinct allusions in the Preface to *Momus triumphans*, p. 418. All passages have been compared with the original to determine whether the references to Jonson are all part of one discussion or independent allusions.

[25] Forty passages appeared before 1601; 14 were not first printed until after 1700, though they have been given seventeenth-century dates in the collection. One is eliminated because it is printed twice under two different dates (pp. 258 and 313). Sixty-nine other passages have been redated, but in these cases both Bradley and Adams' date and mine fall within the seventeenth century.

might have been aimed at Jonson but which do not mention his name or the name of any of his creations and which may equally well refer to various other individuals of the time. Two further passages are references to Beaumont and Fletcher's *The Scornful Lady* from Sir Henry Herbert's office-book, which cannot be allowed as Jonson allusions. Only one extract has been eliminated because it is a parallel passage or situation.

This last figure is most illuminating as evidence of an important fact bearing on the usual estimates of the comparative reputations of Shakespeare and Jonson in their own times. Much of the supposed great reputation of Shakespeare in the seventeenth century is a simple matter of the modern familiarity with his lines. When we read one of the various Jacobean or Caroline or Restoration repetitions of an idea or a figure or a situation, Jonson or Lyly or Heywood never comes to mind, though they may all have used it; but if it ever appeared in however modified a form in any of the thirty-seven plays or poems of Shakespeare, someone is sure to note it and to call attention to the allusion, though more often than not there is no allusion at all. It seems to me that a comparison of the number of parallel passages discarded by precisely the same standards from *The Shakspere Allusion-Book* (272) and from *The Jonson Allusion-Book* (1) is a striking illustration of this fact.

After the passages enumerated have been discarded for the reasons assigned, there remain in *The Jonson Allusion-Book* 729 allusions in the period 1601–1700 which are valid according to the standards set up in chapter ii. These 729 passages are the only Jonson allusions used in the following chapters which will not be found printed in Volume II, Part II. Other Jonson allusions which have been previously published are very few and for convenient reference have been reprinted in Volume II.

After *The Jonson Allusion-Book*, the next largest collection of valid allusions from seventeenth-century sources referring to Jonson and his works[26] is that of C. B. Graham. None of the passages in his collection had appeared in *The Jonson Allusion-Book*. The 16 allusions are all drawn from Restoration comedies printed between 1661 and 1695, though Graham has used production instead of printing dates, and all, accordingly, fall within the chronological limits which have been set up. Since all the passages, moreover, mention Jonson's name or the name of one of his accepted works or characters, the entire collection has been used in this study. All the passages are reprinted in Volume II, each with acknowledgments of Professor Graham's prior claim.

Thornton Shirley Graves's interesting article in *The Manly Anniversary Studies*, "Jonson and the Jest Books," treats Ben as the subject of popular stories— an illuminating phase of his reputation and one in which he completely overshadows Shakespeare.[27] Since Professor Graves's purpose was primarily to trace and classify jokes, the bulk of his passages are drawn from eighteenth- and nineteenth-century publications which fall outside our chronological limits. Of the 89 passages about Jonson which he prints or alludes to, only 8 come

[26] I am ignoring my own collection of 152 allusions, which appeared in the *Huntington Library Quarterly*, V (October, 1941), 65–113. This collection was just a preliminary sketch for the present volume—though I did not know it at the time—and the allusions have been distributed where they belong in Vol. II.

[27] See below, pp. 94–98.

from seventeenth-century sources and are not found in *The Jonson Allusion-Book*. Since each of the 8 mentions Jonson by name, they are all valid allusions and are reprinted in Volume II.

W. D. Briggs's survey, "The Influence of Jonson's Tragedy in the Seventeenth Century,"[28] is the only one of the six Jonson studies used which is not intended to be a collection of allusions. In the 174 passages cited, Jonson's name is never mentioned, nor is the name of any of his works or characters. The extracts are all parallel passages intended to show indebtedness to Jonson rather than frank allusion to him. Four of the passages are, however, sufficiently exact quotations of Jonson's own lines to fulfil the requirements of a genuine allusion, and they have been reprinted in Volume II, Part II.[29]

The last two articles used have contributed 1 and 2 allusions, respectively. Bernard Wagner included only 1 passage about Jonson in his article, "A Jonson Allusion and Others,"[30] and this one meets all the requirements which have been set up here. Of the 3 ex-

---

[28] *Anglia*, XXXV (1912), 277–337.

[29] These rather surprising figures—4 valid allusions in 174 passages—are, it must be pointed out, by no means a refutation of Professor Briggs's contention that Jonson greatly influenced the tragedy of the century. There can be no doubt that the influence of *Catiline* and *Sejanus* was much greater than has been commonly recognized. My own figures on the specific allusions to the two plays are enough to demonstrate this fact (see below, pp. 109–12). My purpose and method and Professor Briggs's are simply different. I am presenting evidence that Jonson was so widely known and admired that hundreds of seventeenth-century writers took it for granted that their readers would be impressed or illuminated by unquestionable allusions to the man and his work; Professor Briggs was trying to show that when seventeenth-century dramatists wrote tragedies they were often instructed by particular scenes and speeches in *Catiline* and *Sejanus*. Our investigations are complementary; the results are not contradictory.

[30] *Philological Quarterly*, VII (1928), 306–8.

tracts in Howard P. Vincent's, "Ben Jonson Allusions,"[31] 2 fall in the seventeenth century; both of
them mention Jonson by name.[32]

Altogether, 1,146 passages have been printed in the
various collections.[33] Three hundred and eighty-six
of them have been eliminated for the reasons specified,
and 760 have been accepted as valid allusions according
to the standards set up.[34] These 760 acceptable Jonson
allusions and the 1,371 valid Shakespeare allusions,
together with the new seventeenth-century allusions
to both poets which I have found,[35] comprise the materials upon which the following discussions of Shakespeare and Jonson's seventeenth-century reputations
are based.

[31] *Notes and Queries*, CLXXVII (1939), 26.

[32] Perhaps mention should be made here of two other passages which have been
printed as Jonson allusions: A. M. Clark's "Jonson Allusion in Jeremy Taylor,"
Notes and Queries, CXLVIII (1925), 459; and Don Cameron Allen's "A Jonson Allusion," *Times Literary Supplement*, April 18, 1936. The passage from Jeremy Taylor
is not really a Jonson allusion, but a Senecan one, as Edward Bensly pointed out
(*Notes and Queries*, CXLIX [1925], 31). The passage in Allen's note, though suggestive, is much too uncertain to be accepted as an allusion to *The Alchemist* according
to the standards used here.

[33] Including Clark's and Allen's single passages which are not in collections.

[34] This rejection of 33 per cent is not quite comparable to the rejection of 54 per
cent of the Shakespeare allusions, for the second and third largest Jonson collections
do not pretend to be gatherings of allusions before 1700. Briggs's passages were not
intended as allusions; Graves's jokes had no chronological limits. Excluding these
two collections entirely, only 15 per cent of the passages in the other gatherings
have been rejected.

[35] See Vol. II, Parts I and II.

CHAPTER IV

THE DISTRIBUTION OF ALLUSIONS BY DECADES

The familiar collections of shakespeare and Jonson allusions analyzed in the last chapter provide us with 1,371 valid seventeenth-century allusions to Shakespeare and 760 valid seventeenth-century allusions to Jonson. To these totals must be added the new allusions to the two dramatists which I have found and which are printed in Volume II, Parts I and II. These collections contain 59 new allusions to Shakespeare and 1,079 to Jonson, all of them tested by the standards which have been applied to the allusions of the earlier collections.

Judged by the mere number of allusions, then, Jonson's reputation was greater in the seventeenth century, taken as a whole, than Shakespeare's, for there are 1,839 recorded allusions to him and 1,430 to Shakespeare, and certainly many Jonson allusions are still unrecorded. The impression conveyed by the bulk of *The Shakspere Allusion-Book* is misleading; equally misleading is the impression conveyed by the greater number of supplementary collections of allusions to Shakespeare which have appeared.

Chiefly responsible for these erroneous impressions are the large number of false allusions in the Shakespeare collections and the large number of Jonson allusions which have hitherto escaped publication. It is well to remember at this point that there are doubtless many allusions to both men which are still unknown. It cannot be pointed out too often, however, that unquestionably far more allusions to Jonson than to Shakespeare remain to be discovered.

If Jonson's reputation, as indicated by collected allusions, seems greater than Shakespeare's in the seventeenth century as a whole, may it not be that the overall figures are misleading? A great preponderance of Jonson allusions in one decade of the century could obscure the fact that in most decades writers referred more often to Shakespeare. It will be further enlightening, therefore, on this and other scores to examine the distribution of allusions by decades.

1601–10

In the first decade of the seventeenth century one would expect to find more allusions to Shakespeare than to Jonson, because Shakespeare had been before the London audience longer. Nearly all his plays had been performed before 1610; furthermore, by that year all his poems and sixteen of his plays had been presented to the reading public, and some of the favorites had gone through several editions—*Venus and Adonis*, ten; *The Rape of Lucrece*, five; *Richard III*, four; *Henry IV*, *Part 1*, four; *Richard II*, three; *Romeo and Juliet*, three. In contrast, much of Jonson's work had not yet been written, and more was unpublished. Only eight of his plays, six of his masques and entertainments, and none of his poems[1] had been seen in print in the first decade of the century. In spite of the greater advancement of Shakespeare's career in this decade, there are 119 al-

---

[1] Except songs in plays and occasional pieces in anthologies like *Love's Martyr*.

lusions to Jonson in the period as compared to 81 to Shakespeare.

The much greater number of allusions to Jonson is most surprising. It is due in large part to the mention of Jonson in connections in which Shakespeare seldom or never figures. Most noteworthy are the references to the performances or preparations for performances of Jonson's masques. Letters of ambassadors and paid correspondents are full of this subject. Not only were masque performances spectacular occasions patronized by the most conspicuous people in London and therefore widely talked about, but almost all the spectators were literate. The high rate of literacy in Jonson's peculiar audience is a constant factor in the establishment of his reputation.

The next most noteworthy group of Jonson allusions in this decade comes from *Satiromastix* and other satiric jibes at Jonson. Here again is a connection in which Shakespeare is seldom found. Throughout his career, Jonson's sturdy, not to say bellicose, personality made enemies and attracted attention. Before the days of newspapers he was always "good copy," and long after his death he was still referred to in terms half of irritation, half of indulgence. Jonson made an impression both through his genius and through his personality; there are very few contemporary records of the impression made by the personality of "gentle Shakespeare."

Finally, nearly a score of the allusions from this decade are concerned with the performance or the publication of *Sejanus* and *Volpone*. There is no clear evidence that any of the plays of Shakespeare ever made such an impression on his contemporaries as did these two.[2] The significance of the number of references to *Sejanus* and *Volpone* in this particular decade becomes the greater when one remembers that *Hamlet, Othello, Lear,* and *Macbeth* are all products of the same period. Most of the allusions to the two Jonson plays are entire poems praising them in the highest terms,[3] and a number of them are written by poets of renown. Certainly, this group of allusions is most suggestive of Jonson's great distinction in the first decade of the century.

The Shakespeare allusions in the first decade of the century give no such clear dominance in any type of literary allusion. Most notable are the 17 records of Shakespeare's business and professional activities—his career as a player shown in casts and patents; his connection with property transactions, mostly in and around Stratford; and the appearance of his name in wills. Since there are only 1 or 2 records of this type for Jonson,[4] the discrepancy is marked. The difference seems due to two facts: (1) Shakespeare was obviously (for our general knowledge of Jonson confirms the judgment) more interested in the accumulation of property

[2] Throughout the century these plays were more frequently referred to than any of Shakespeare's (see below, pp. 109 ff.).

[3] Most of the poems appeared in the 1605 quarto of *Sejanus* and the 1607 quarto of *Volpone*. This fact brings up the important consideration that Jonson published his own plays, while Shakespeare did not—a distinction which cannot be overemphasized; it colors all phases of the study of the two dramatists. Certainly, much of the difference between the reputations of the two poets in their own century, as well as much of the difference in the study of their works since, has been due to this fact.

[4] In the first decade there are 24 allusions to Jonson in Class 17 (see below, pp. 96–98), but most of them are satirical digs or anecdotes or records of Jonson's unfortunate encounters with the law. Only one can, strictly speaking, be called a business or professional record.

than Jonson was, and (2) C. W. Wallace, Halliwell-Phillipps, Leslie Hotson, and others have ransacked millions of records seeking any barest mention of Shakespeare. There has been no search even remotely comparable for references to Jonson; consequently, more examples of Jonson's contact with legal affairs probably remain undiscovered. (No doubt such records are more likely to concern breaches of the peace, libel, and recusancy than property transactions.) One cannot fail to remark that Shakespeare's lead in records of this type has nothing to do with his literary reputation, though it may be taken as some indication of his repute as a solid man of property.

There are a number of references to Shakespeare's plays and characters in this decade, a few more than to Jonson's. The work most frequently mentioned (5 times) is *Venus and Adonis*, probably Shakespeare's best-known composition between 1590 and 1616; the character most popular in this, as in all other decades of the century,[5] is Falstaff.

1611–20

In the second decade of the century one might expect the Jonson allusions to outnumber the Shakespeare ones, for it was in this period that the first Jonson folio appeared.[6] Indeed, Jonson would not have ventured to publish this collection of his own works had not his reputation been very high. Even as it was, there were

---

[5] See below, pp. 109 ff.

[6] The obscurity of Shakespeare's death in 1616 has been so often remarked upon that no one will be surprised at the lack of allusion to it. One cannot help noting, however, the sharp contrast with the great outpouring of comment after Jonson's death in 1637.

many sneers at a man who would collect his own plays and who presumed to call them "Works."[7] Never before had such a collection appeared in English.

Between 1611 and 1620 there are recorded 88 allusions to Shakespeare and 103 to Jonson. When these references are sorted, surprisingly few of them seem to be related to the publication of the folio. Once more the largest group of Jonson allusions is made up of references of one kind and another to the masques. Another sizable group consists of allusions to Jonson's characters, which in this decade alone seem more popular than Shakespeare's. The only large group of Jonson allusions peculiar to this decade are those referring to his trip to Edinburgh, but even these are greatly outnumbered by allusions to the masques.

The Shakespeare allusions again are dominated by the business references—records of stock in the Blackfriars and the Globe, of ownership of London and Stratford houses and lands, of concern with the Mountjoy dowry. In this decade, again, there are several times as many such business records of Shakespeare as of Jonson and for the same reasons as before. Other types of allusion are less numerous than the 30-odd business and professional records. There are 11 records of payments for performances of Shakespeare's plays; 7 records of the presence of copies of his plays in private libraries; 4 allusions to Falstaff; 9 quotations from his works; and 4 accounts of the burning of the Globe which mention *Henry VIII* as the play being performed at the time. Characteristically, none of the authors of the fire stories

---

[7] The volume was entitled *The Workes of Beniamin Jonson*. For some of the many jibes at Jonson for his presumption see Vol. II, pp. 111, 123, 243.

which name the play being performed—Wotton or
Howes or Lorkins or the anonymous writer of the ballad—thought it worth while to mention the fact that the
play was written by William Shakespeare.

1621–30

The third decade is the period of the issue of the
famous First Folio of 1623. The modern reader would
expect that this, of all events connected with Shakespeare's career, must surely have called forth comments
in the literary world. It did, of course; there are more
passages praising Shakespeare and poems directed to
him in this decade than in the two previous ones together. Yet, even so, the discrepancy between the Jonson and Shakespeare allusions is greater than ever before. There are 108 to Jonson and only 43 to Shakespeare.

Nearly one-third of the Shakespeare allusions is made
up of poems or long prose passages in his memory, half
of this third printed in the Folio itself. Half a dozen are
records of performances of his plays, and about an equal
number are quotations from his works. The rest are
scattered.

In the case of Jonson, there is, because of his dimin-
ished output, a falling-off in the records of performances
of his masques and plays—only about one-third as
many as in the previous decade. But there is a striking
increase in the number of transcripts of his works appearing in commonplace books and manuscript anthologies—nearly twice as many as in the two preceding
decades together, and more than for Shakespeare in the
whole first half of the century. Other common types of

allusions to Jonson in the decade are lines or poems in his praise and personal records.

The situation with regard to Shakespeare and Jonson allusions in this third decade of the seventeenth century is for the modern student of literature the most arresting of all. When the book embodying the greatest achievement of any single volume in all literature appeared, the literate public for which it was issued talked mostly about a fellow named Jonson.

1631–40

The period of the 1630's includes the death of Jonson, and here one might reasonably anticipate that allusions to him would be more numerous than to Shakespeare, as they are. The comparative esteem in which their contemporaries held these two great dramatists is most vividly reflected by the fact that in the five years after Shakespeare's death not a single poem commemorative of that great passing appeared, while in the four years after Jonson's death there were more than fifty.

Altogether, there are 189 allusions to Jonson in this decade and 93 to Shakespeare. The Jonson allusions are, of course, dominated by the poems of the 1638 volume to his memory, *Jonsonus Virbius*, to which most of the distinguished poets of the time contributed. But there are numerous testimonials to him outside that volume in lines alluding to his greatness, though not always devoted primarily to it. There are 22 quotations from his work, as well as 17 records of performances of his plays.

The Shakespeare allusions in this decade are more numerous than in any previous one, even though there are only half as many as to Jonson. A number of verses in his praise are printed in the Second Folio of 1632 and in the *Poems* of 1640. Half a dozen of the poems in *Jonsonus Virbius* also mention Shakespeare, most of them with praise. There are 22 quotations from his works and 10 records of performances of his plays, as well as the usual allusions—this time 6—to Falstaff. The increasing frequency of literary allusions to Shakespeare in this period would be quite notable if he were not so completely overshadowed by Jonson.

1641–50

The fifth decade encompasses the terrible period of civil war. In such a time of national travail one might expect literary allusions almost to cease, especially in Puritan London. They do fall off from the preceding decade, but both the Shakespeare and the Jonson allusions are more numerous than in any of the three periods before the fruitful 1630's: 94 to Shakespeare and 125 to Jonson.

The great restriction of the wars on literary publication came in 1643, 1644, and 1645; and the allusions are correspondingly few in these years, but in 1646 they begin to increase. A large number is found in 1646, 1647, and 1648 in the Shirley, Beaumont and Fletcher, Suckling, Herrick, and Baron publications alone. Most productive of allusions, as one might expect, is the great parade of contemporary poets turned out to honor Beaumont and Fletcher in commendatory verses for the Folio of 1647. There are 20 allusions to the two earlier dramatists in these poems, 13 to Jonson and 7 to Shakespeare. It is significant that the 13:7 ratio in this collection of verses by play-conscious writers is very close to the ratio of all allusions in the previous four decades—519:305.

When the entire body of allusions of the fifth decade of the century is classified according to type, we find that the largest group referring to Shakespeare is made up of those mentioning his characters by name. There are 30 of them, half again as many as in any previous decade. The most popular character, as usual, is Falstaff, with 15 references; no other character of Shakespeare's is mentioned more than twice. Thirty-one of the allusions to Shakespeare in the decade quote from his works, and 3 praise him as a great, or the greatest, English dramatist.

The praise of Jonson as a ranking literary figure is even more common—28 passages offering homage to him. Thirty-nine passages quote from his work, and 36 refer to his plays by name, usually for purposes of illustration. This last group is surprisingly large, considering that the theaters were closed for eight of the ten years in the decade. Perhaps men thought more about particular plays when they could no longer see any in the theaters. Certainly, the publishing records make it clear that play-reading flourished in these years.[8]

1651–60

The decade of the Protectorate is the most astonishing of the century from the point of view of allusions. In this period, when the great outpouring of tracts and pamphlets suggests that every literate man in England took his pen in hand with a stern resolve to reform the

[8] See Louis B. Wright, "The Reading of Plays during the Puritan Revolution," *Huntington Library Bulletin*, No. 6 (November, 1934), pp. 73–108.

world, one might expect to find mere playwrights like Shakespeare and Jonson impatiently brushed aside. Yet from 1651 to 1660 there are more allusions to them than in any other decade of the century—630, as compared with the 495 of the articulate 1690's. In a time of stress and avid social and political planning, Englishmen remembered the great poets of their fathers. The allusions to Shakespeare (301) more than triple those of any preceding decade, and those to Jonson (329) double the number in any earlier period except that of his death.

The greatest single factor in this increase is the anthology of passages from plays published by John Cotgrave in 1655 under the title *The English Treasury of Wit and Language*,[9] a book containing 154 extracts from Shakespeare's plays and 111 from Jonson's. But even without Cotgrave there are more allusions in this decade than in any previous one. The highly allusive Gayton has 26, mostly to Jonson, in his *Pleasant Notes on Don Quixote;* there are 37, mostly to Shakespeare, in Poole's *England's Parnassus;* 27, mostly to Jonson, in Cotgrave's *Wits Interpreter;* and about 10 apiece in Cokayne's *Small Poems of Divers Sorts* and *Parnassus Biceps.* A remarkable proportion of these allusions is in the form of quotations published, generally without attribution, in the various anthologies.

Aside from the quotations, the allusions fall in fairly normal numbers into about the usual types. There are 41 praising Jonson as a great, or the greatest, play-

---

[9] For a discussion of this remarkable anthology see my article, "John Cotgrave's *English Treasury of Wit and Language* and the Elizabethan Drama," *Studies in Philology*, XL (April, 1943), 186–203.

wright, and 7 so designating Shakespeare. Particular plays of the two dramatists are mentioned 66 times— Shakespeare's 25 and Jonson's 41; Shakespeare's characters are named 43 times and Jonson's 38. Sixteen of the Shakespeare allusions concern apocryphal plays printed under his name in this decade, and 9 Jonson allusions are found in belated descriptions of his masques in *Finetti Philoxenis*. Other allusions are a scattering of various types, none particularly notable.

1661–70

After the great outburst of the 1650's, the allusions of the first decade of the Restoration seem meager; yet the 339 references of the time are really more numerous than those of any preceding decade except the fifties. Of that number, 196 refer to Jonson and 143 to Shakespeare. The bulk of them are of familiar types. Jonson is praised as a great, or the greatest, poet 24 times, Shakespeare 9. There are 137 references to particular plays of Jonson's, 60 to Shakespeare's. Shakespeare's characters, however, are mentioned 60 times to Jonson's 47. The really notable development of the time is found in the increase in the number of references to performances of plays—112, several such references often occurring in one passage. Inevitably there would be a greater number of such allusions than under the Protectorate, but it is surprising to find more than in any other decade of the century, before or after. It is highly improbable that there were actually more performances of Shakespeare's and Jonson's plays at this time than in the decade 1601–10, say, but there was certainly more writing about them. No doubt the relief at the removal of Commonwealth restrictions contributed to the popularity of writings about plays, but the character of the audience was probably even more significant. Most of Pepys's fellow-patrons at the Theatre Royal could write, and many did; neither literacy nor critical dramatic interest was so common at the Globe.

A large part of these references to performances—59 out of 112[10]—come from the diary of that inveterate but uneasy playgoer, the Clerk of the King's Ships.[11] He mentions 37 Shakespearean performances and 22 Jonsonian ones, all but 6 or 8 of which he attended himself. Though he saw more Shakespeare, in the original or a revised form, he had more praise for Jonson. The plays of Shakespeare which he saw in one form or another were *Hamlet*, *Henry IV, Part 1*, *Henry VIII*, *Macbeth*, *The Merry Wives of Windsor*, *A Midsummer-Night's Dream*, *Othello*, *Romeo and Juliet*, *The Taming of the Shrew*, *The Tempest*, and *Twelfth Night*; some of them he saw several times. The Jonson plays were *The Silent Woman*, *Bartholomew Fair*, *The Alchemist*, *Catiline*, and *Volpone*.

For many of Shakespeare's masterpieces Pepys had nothing good to say. Of *Twelfth Night* he opines: "It be but a silly play" (January 6, 1662/63) and "one of the weakest plays that ever I saw on the stage" (January 20, 1668/69). *Romeo and Juliet* "is a play of itself the worst that ever I heard in my life" (March 1, 1661/62).

---

[10] There are 15 or more other Shakespeare and Jonson allusions in Pepys, but they do not refer to performances.

[11] Even without Pepys's records there would be many more references to performances of plays in this decade than in any other, for in the first two decades of the century when there are 47 and 66 records of performances, respectively, a large number of the allusions concern Jonson's masques, not his plays.

A Midsummer-Night's Dream "is the most insipid ridiculous play that ever I saw in my life" (September 29, 1662). *The Merry Wives of Windsor* "did not please me at all, in no part of it" (August 15, 1667). *The Taming of the Shrew* "hath some very good pieces in it, but generally is but a mean play" (April 9, 1667) and is "a silly play and an old one" (November 1, 1667).

No play of Jonson is ever so roundly condemned. The worst he ever says is found in his remarks on *Catiline*, which he had called "a very excellent piece" when he read it on December 18, 1664. But when he saw a performance of the play on December 19, 1668, he said: "A play of much good sense and words to read, but that do appear the worst upon the stage, I mean, the least diverting, that ever I saw any. . . . . But the play is only to be read." It is most illuminating to note his qualification of his condemnation of Jonson in comparison with his categorical dismissal of *Twelfth Night*, *Romeo and Juliet*, *A Midsummer-Night's Dream*, and *The Merry Wives of Windsor*. Obviously, Pepys felt that Jonson was a classic presumably to be admired, but Shakespeare was not much different from any other dramatist.

This same attitude is apparent in his praise of Jonson and Shakespeare where the effect is reversed: the praise of Shakespeare is qualified, but of Jonson it is categorical. Moreover, it is quite clear that in certain instances the features of the Shakespearean play which he singles out for praise are Restoration additions, while the admirable Jonsonian characteristics are all parts of the original plays. His remarks on *The Tempest* are a case in point; he says it is "the most innocent play that ever

I saw; and a curious piece of musique in an echo of half sentences, the echo repeating the former half, while the man goes on to the latter; which is mighty pretty. The play [has] no great wit, but yet good, above ordinary plays" (November 7, 1667); "saw the Tempest again, which is very pleasant, and full of so good variety that I cannot be more pleased almost in a comedy, only the seamen's part a little too tedious" (November 13, 1667); "which, as often as I have seen it, I do like very well" (December 12, 1667); "which we have often seen, but yet I was pleased again, and shall be again to see it, it is so full of variety, and particularly this day I took pleasure to learn the tune of the seaman's dance, which I have much desired to be perfect in, and have made myself so" (February 3, 1667/68).

His comments on *Macbeth* are similarly mixed. It is "a pretty good play, but admirably acted" (November 5, 1664); "most excellently acted, and a most excellent play for variety" (December 28, 1666); "a most excellent play in all respects, but especially in divertisement, though it be a deep tragedy; which is a strange perfection in a tragedy, it being most proper here, and suitable" (January 7, 1666/67); "it is one of the best plays for a stage, and variety of dancing and musique, that ever I saw" (April 19, 1667); "which we still like mightily, though mighty short of the content we used to have when Betterton acted" (November 6, 1667).

Of *Henry VIII* Pepys says: "Saw the so much cried-up play of 'Henry the Eighth'; which, though I went with resolution to like it, is so simple a thing made up of a great many patches, that, besides the shows and processions in it, there is nothing in the world good or well done. Thence mightily dissatisfied" (January 1, 1663/64); "did see 'King Harry the Eighth'; and was mightily pleased, better than I ever expected, with the history and shows of it" (December 30, 1668).

Hamlet appealed to Pepys as an actor's vehicle. He writes of his attendance at five performances of the great tragedy; but four of the passages say nothing whatsoever about the play, though they contain the highest praise for Betterton, and two say that the whole play was "well performed." In one instance his praise of the acting is so stated as almost to imply that Betterton contributed more than Shakespeare: "Saw 'Hamlett' done, giving us fresh reason never to think enough of Betterton" (May 28, 1663). Only in his last record does Pepys ever hint that the play itself may have been good: "Saw 'Hamlet,' which we have not seen this year before, or more; and mightily pleased with it; but, above all, with Betterton, the best part, I believe, that ever man acted" (August 31, 1668).

After reading all this qualified praise of Shakespeare, one cannot but be impressed with Pepys's wholehearted enthusiasm for *Volpone*, *The Alchemist*, *Epicoene*, and *Every Man in His Humour*, and his only half-qualified praise for *Bartholomew Fair*.

Of *Volpone* he says: "A most excellent play; the best I think I ever saw, and well acted" (January 14, 1664/65). *The Alchemist* "is a most incomparable play" (June 22, 1661); "it is still a good play, having not been acted for two or three years before" (April 17, 1669). Of *Epicoene:* "Saw 'The Silent Woman.' The first time that ever I did see it, and it is an excellent play" (January 7, 1660/61); "to the Theatre, where I saw a piece of 'The Silent Woman,' which pleased me" (May 25, 1661); "saw 'The Silent Woman'; but methought not so well done or so good a play as I formerly thought it to be, or else I am now-a-days out of humour" (June 1, 1664); "I never was more taken with a play than I am with this 'Silent Woman,' as old as it is, and as often as I have seen it. There is more wit in it than goes to ten new plays" (April 16, 1667); "saw 'The Silent Woman'; the best comedy, I think, that was ever wrote; and sitting by Shadwell the poet, he was big with admiration of it" (September 19, 1668).

After reading *Every Man in His Humour*, he says that the play has "the greatest propriety of speech that ever I read in my life" (February 9, 1666/67).

Finally, Pepys's comments on *Bartholomew Fair* show a little of the qualifications with which he tempered his praise of Shakespeare; but the praise is more resounding, and the qualifications seem traceable to the relics of his youthful Puritanism. He says: "Saw 'Bartholomew Faire,' the first time it was acted now-a-days. It is a most admirable play and well acted, but too much prophane and abusive" (June 8, 1661); "and here was 'Bartholomew Fayre,' with the puppet-show, acted to-day, which had not been these forty years . . . . but I do never a whit like it the better for the puppets, but rather the worse" (September 7, 1661); "saw 'Bartholomew Fayre,' which do still please me; and is, as it is acted, the best comedy in the world, I believe" (August 2, 1664); "it is an excellent play; the more I see it, the more I love the wit of it; only the business of abusing the Puritans begins to grow stale, and of no use, they being the people that, at last, will be found the wisest" (September 4, 1668).[12]

Pepys is always winning in his lavish use of superlatives. It is noteworthy that in these passages most of the superlatives are used to express the unexampled badness of Shakespeare's plays and the unexampled excellence of Jonson's. The little man from the Admiralty was not an unusually perceptive or judicious critic, but his comments ought not to be explained away if we seek to understand the reputation of Shakespeare and Jonson in his time.

1671–80

In the eighth decade of the century the allusions to the two poets are more nearly equal than in any other period, except the last: Shakespeare, 173; Jonson, 183. This equality, furthermore, is not a matter of a great spurt in the allusions of one type to counterbalance the usual inequality in others; in most of the common types the distribution is more even than usual. The only exception is the very significant one of allusions calling the poet great, or the greatest of his kind. In this type Jonson holds his usual lead, 43, to 18 for Shakespeare. Thus, in spite of the near equality of the total number of allusions, most of the writers of the decade still acknowledge Jonson's pre-eminence.

In the other types the over-all equality is reflected. There are 39 quotations of Shakespeare to 27 of Jonson. Most of the Shakespearean quotations are found in

---

[12] All the passages in Pepys relating to the drama and theater have been conveniently collected, if not very well discussed, in Miss Helen McAfee's *Pepys on the Restoration Stage* (1916).

commonplace books and anthologies,[13] but most of the Jonson ones are quotations used as illustrations in a connected discourse. There are 48 references to Shakespeare's plays by name and 72 to Jonson's. Shakespeare's characters are alluded to 70 times, Jonson's 68. Even the casual references to the two dramatists by name but without particular significance are about the same—13 to Jonson, 11 to Shakespeare.

As might be expected, more of the allusions in this decade are made by John Dryden than by any other writer. Even Dryden contributed to the even-handed distribution of allusions by referring just 33 times to each dramatist. His great pronouncements of the previous decade probably had much to do with the gradual ascendancy of Shakespeare's reputation, but in this period he shows his preference less clearly.

1681–90

In the decade of the Glorious Revolution the number of allusions falls off somewhat, possibly because of the absorbing character of political events. There are 151 references to Shakespeare and 175 to Jonson. Upon breaking these figures down into types, one finds certain tendencies becoming apparent—tendencies carrying over into the last decade of the century and clearly indicating the rising tide of Shakespeare allusions, which, one would assume, will far surpass the Jonson allusions in the eighteenth century. First, we can notice the principal classes of allusions and then the tendency which they indicate. There are still, in the 1680's, more refer-

---

[13] The largest group of Shakespeare quotations is provided by the collection called *The New Academy of Compliments* (1671). This volume contains 15 songs from Shakespeare's plays, but I can spot only 2 of Jonson's songs in it.

ences which speak of Jonson as a great poet than of Shakespeare—37 to 22. The number of quotations from the two men are about equal—35 passages from Shakespeare and 29 from Jonson. In references to apocryphal plays, Shakespeare leads, as usual; the 20 Shakespeare references (mostly from Langbaine) in this class to 2 for Jonson are a fair index of the larger number of plays in the Shakespeare apocrypha. The significant change is seen in the comparative number of allusions to the plays and the characters of the two playwrights. There are 120 references to particular plays of Shakespeare as compared to 137 for Jonson, but 78 character references as compared to Jonson's 26. Of casual unclassifiable references to the two poets, there are 34 to Jonson, 9 to Shakespeare.

Before any conclusions are drawn from these figures, another set should be noted. In this decade fall the allusions from John Aubrey's *Brief Lives*, a manuscript which grew from 1669 to 1696. According to my practice, I have considered it in the year which falls midway between these terminal dates, or 1682. In Aubrey's biographies there are 40 allusions to Jonson, 3 to Shakespeare, including the lives of both the dramatists; that is, when Aubrey wrote the lives of their contemporaries and successors, he took occasion to mention Jonson or his works 39 times, Shakespeare's only twice. In another collection of the period similar in method to Aubrey's—William Winstanley's *Lives of the Poets* (1687)—there are 10 allusions to Jonson outside his own life, 3 to Shakespeare.

These facts about Aubrey and Winstanley's references and the figures on the allusions calling the poet great are interestingly and, I think, significantly in contrast with those of the allusions to the characters of the two dramatists. When Aubrey and Winstanley collected material on the lives of great English writers, scientists, and political figures, they found occasion to associate these men with Jonson or his works nine times as often as with Shakespeare. When men like Oldham, Shadwell, Roscommon, Tate, Gould, Crowne, Lee—to name a few of them—spoke of the greatest English poets, they chose Jonson almost twice as often as Shakespeare. Obviously, Jonson was still thought of as the great English dramatist. Yet when writers—some of these included—sought an effective illustration from literature, they chose Shakespeare's characters three times as often as Jonson's.

Since this same situation in regard to characters is found to an even more marked degree in the next decade, though it had not prevailed in earlier ones, the period 1681–90 apparently marks the beginning of a general recognition and acknowledgment of Shakespeare's unequaled powers of characterization[14]—a recognition which to the modern taste seems so natural as to be inevitable. Though in the 1680's Shakespeare's creations were not yet universally known, or Jonson's almost forgotten—as now—the movement toward the estimate of our day had clearly begun.

1691–1700

The last decade of the century is the only one in which more Shakespeare than Jonson allusions have been found, 251 to 244. Though this difference is not great—

[14] See below, pp. 84–86 and 126.

about 50.75–49.25 per cent—and though unnoted Jonson allusions in the numerous unexamined publications of the period would undoubtedly number more than the 7 which this 1.5 per cent represents, nevertheless, the rise of Shakespeare in general critical esteem is clearly evident.

When the allusions in various classifications are compared, the growth of Shakespeare's reputation becomes clearer. Significant is the fact that Jonson, though still called great more often than Shakespeare, leads by only 48 allusions to 34. This is a far cry from Jonson's dominance of the fourth, fifth, and sixth decades of the century in allusions of this type—63 to 10, 28 to 3, 41 to 7. Equally notable is the increased tendency to quote Shakespeare rather than Jonson: 71 quotations to 28. Most striking of all are the allusions to Shakespeare's characters: 352 to 75 for Jonson.

The casual references to the two dramatists are about equal, 31 to Shakespeare, 29 to Jonson. The references to apocryphal plays are mostly to Shakespeare, 28 to 7; but, as noticed before, this figure is not very significant because of the much greater number of apocryphal plays in the Shakespeare canon.

With all this evidence of increased deference to Shakespeare, the serious considerations of England's poetic past generally give Jonson greater attention. Gerard Langbaine's *Account of the English Dramatic Poets* (1691) refers to Jonson 53 times outside the account of his own life, to Shakespeare 44; Wood's *Athenae Oxonienses* (1691–92), 24 times to Jonson, 14 to Shakespeare. The differences here are not so great as in the accounts of Aubrey and Winstanley in the previous decade; nevertheless, the custom of literary historians is still to keep Jonson more constantly in mind than Shakespeare.

UNDATED ALLUSIONS

When all the printed and manuscript allusions of the seventeenth century have been assigned to the decade in which the text was published or in which the manuscript was written, there still remain a number of references in texts which, though clearly seventeenth century, have not so far been dated with sufficient precision to justify their classification in any particular decade. Most of them, of course, come from unprinted manuscripts. These undated allusions have been filed together, and, though they cannot be made to contribute to an understanding of the decade-by-decade development of the dramatists' reputations, they do suggest certain interesting inferences.

There are 68 of these undated references to Jonson, 13 to Shakespeare. Sixty-three of the Jonson allusions and 7 of the Shakespeare are from manuscript commonplace books,[15] a ratio which is most suggestive, for a large number of the commonplace books from which allusions have been reported fall into this undated

[15] Actually, the number of Jonson allusions in the undated commonplace books reported is greater than 63, though just how much greater one cannot tell. The uncertainty is caused by the fact that several of the reports on commonplace books say merely "the poems are by Ben Jonson, Carew, &c.," or "there are poems by Ben Jonson on folios. . . . ." According to the principles I have used, each poem constitutes an allusion, but from such indefinite reports I can count only 1 allusion for the volume or 1 for each page cited where nonconsecutive pages are given. Even in the second case one often finds on investigation that there is more than 1 short poem on a page. Thus an unascertainable number of Jonson allusions in these incompletely reported commonplace books remain uncounted.

In the case of the Shakespeare allusions in the commonplace books, there is never any such uncertainty. Passages referring to Shakespeare are reported in detail. Whenever his work is quoted, the precise number of quotations and their length are

group. The incomplete evidence which we have on commonplace books, then, suggests that in these private
repositories of gentlemen of literary tastes the preponderance of Jonsonian over Shakespearean selections
is about 9 to 1, whereas in the total number of allusions
of all kinds in the century it is only about 9 to 7. From
these figures we must infer that in the many commonplace books of the century yet unexamined or unre-
ported far more Jonson than Shakespeare allusions will
be found—a further reason for thinking that our present figures on quotations do a greater injustice to Jonson than to Shakespeare.[16]

These figures on the undated allusions provide further
evidence, it seems to me, for the conclusions already
suggested in considering the writings of Pepys, Aubrey,
Winstanley, Langbaine, Wood, *et al.*, namely, that
Jonson's prestige was greater than Shakespeare's even
in the periods in which one dramatist is referred to about
as often as the other. For commonplace books display
not only the lines the collector likes but the lines he
thinks he *ought* to like; they provide occasions not for
the casual references to plays and characters which will
be widely recognized but for the copying of whole
poems or passages from plays which have won the collector's approval. The extant commonplace books show
that this approval was bestowed on Jonson far more
often than on Shakespeare.

---

given, and often the texts are collated. This great difference in the precision of the
reporting of Shakespeare and Jonson allusions in the commonplace books is simply
another phase of the misleading picture of the reputations of the two dramatists
which we have inevitably acquired (see chap. iii).

[16] See above, pp. 18–21.

The classification of these undated allusions into types is not so illuminating as for the dated allusions, because there are too few to Shakespeare to make the figures for him mean very much. When the Jonson allusions are examined, one is somewhat surprised to note how often his nondramatic verse is quoted. Of course, epigrams, epitaphs, and short lyrics are much more suitable to commonplace books than passages from plays; but, even so, the disproportion is unexpectedly great. In the 64 quotations from his writings, not one comes from his plays, and only 7 from the masques. All the others represent Jonson the nondramatic poet.

CHAPTER V

THE DISTRIBUTION OF ALLUSIONS BY TYPES

In the preceding chapter some attention was paid to the *kinds* of allusions to Shakespeare and Jonson; but the primary emphasis has been upon chronological distribution. Further knowledge of the comparative reputations of the two great dramatists in the seventeenth century is to be gained, I think, from a more complete classification of the allusions into types. For this purpose twenty-two classes have been set up. These classes are not arbitrary, logical divisions into which all allusions to any author in any time must fall but are the result of a consideration of the 3,269 allusions to Shakespeare and Jonson which have been accepted for this study and of the variety they present. I have tried to devise classes which will reveal most about the terms in which seventeenth-century writers thought of the two poets and their works. A great many of the allusions fall into more than one class—a poem in praise of Shakespeare, for instance, may mention four of his plays and six of his characters and quote three lines; in such a case the allusion is put into several different classes, for it is much more revealing to note the various aspects of Shakespeare's reputation to which the author was contributing than to make an arbitrary decision as to which type is most fully represented. As a consequence of this method of multiple classification,

the total number of allusions by classes—over 5,000—
is much greater than the actual number of separate passages referring to Shakespeare and Jonson. Thus the
total number of allusions by classes is a meaningless
figure, but the number in any one class is significant.

The various classes into which the 3,269 allusions to
both dramatists have been divided follow.

CLASS I

Passages in which the name of the dramatist is used
alone as a standard of poetic or dramatic greatness.

> The World is busie now; and some dare say
> We have not seen of late one good New Play.
> And such believe Shakespear, long since in 's Grave,
> In Choicest Lybraries a place will have
> When not a modern Play will scape the fire.
>
> —NEVIL PAYNE, Epilogue, *The Morning Ramble* (1673)

> As twere the only office of a Friend
> To Rhyme, and 'gainst his Conscience to commend;
> And sweare like Poets of the Post, This Play
> Exceeds all Johnson's Works.
>
> —Commendatory verses by RICHARD WEST, prefixed to
> JAMES FERRAND'S EPΩTOMANIA (1640)[1]

Allusions in Class I are in some ways the most revealing of all, for each one of them specifically desig-
nates Shakespeare or Jonson as a standard of greatness.
In allusions of this type the evidence of Jonson's pre-
eminence in the estimates of the time is overwhelming.
In every single decade of the century he is praised more
often than Shakespeare, and his total is nearly three times
as great (p. 64). The greater reputation of Jonson is most
notable in the fourth, fifth, sixth, and seventh decades
of the century. The figures in these years really repre-

---

[1] For further examples of allusions in this class see Vol. II, pp. 11, 83, and 135.

sent Jonson's early posthumous reputation, for in the fourth decade, only 11 of 63 allusions offering Jonson the highest praise were published before his death in 1637. Such a growth in an artist's reputation in the years immediately following his death is, of course, a familiar phenomenon. These figures, however, afford clear evidence that this phenomenon did not occur in the growth of Shakespeare's reputation.

DISTRIBUTION OF ALLUSIONS
IN CLASS 1

	Shake-speare	Jonson
1601–1610	4	7
1611–1620	2	7
1621–1630	5	8
1631–1640	10	63
1641–1650	3	28
1651–1660	7	41
1661–1670	9	24
1671–1680	18	43
1681–1690	22	37
1691–1700	34	48
Undated	1	0
Totals	115	306

Another noteworthy fact demonstrated by the distribution of these allusions is to be seen in the comparative figures for Shakespeare and for Jonson in the last two decades of the century. As we have already noted,[2] these two decades seem to mark the beginning of the flood tide of Shakespeare's reputation, especially as seen in quotations from his works and references to his characters. In the nineties, indeed, the total number of allusions to Shakespeare for the first time outnumbers those to Jonson. Yet even in these two decades Jonson still clearly dominates the field when men of literary tastes speak of the greatest English dramatist.

[2] See above, pp. 55–57.

CLASS 2

A complete poem or a long passage (exclusive of biographical or bibliographical accounts) devoted wholly to the author or his works. The passage may be elaborate praise, or it may be an extended attack; concentration on Shakespeare or Jonson is the prime distinction. One illustration will suffice, since most of the passages in this class are too long to quote. Familiar examples are those in the front matter of the 1623 Folio or in *Jonsonus Virbius*.

TO THE MEMORY OF BEN JONSON

The Muses fairest light in no dark time;
The wonder of a learned age; the line
Which none can pass; the most proportion'd wit,
To nature, the best judge of what was fit;
The deepest, plainest, highest, clearest pen;
The voice most echo'd by consenting men
The soul which answer'd best to all well said
By others, and which most requital made.
—Anon., *Jonsonus Virbius* (1638)[3]

Allusions of this class are similar in their implication of the subject's reputation to those of Class 1. The composition of an extended passage about Shakespeare or Jonson is in itself evidence of the power of the name, even though the passage be a satiric attack rather than praise. There are more than three times as many allusions of this type to Jonson as to Shakespeare, with an unusual predominance of the Jonson allusions in the first and fourth decades (p. 66). The size of the collection in the first decade is largely accounted for by the numerous long passages about Jonson in Dekker's castigating

[3] The poem may have been written by Sidney Godolphin, since it is found in a manuscript collection of his poems (see John Drinkwater in the *Times Literary Supplement*, October 25, 1923). Other allusions of this class may be found in Vol. II, pp. 45–46, 52–53, 58–59, and 201.

Satiromastix and by the commendatory verses written for the first editions of *Sejanus* and *Volpone*. Twenty-six of the 30 passages come from these three sources. One is again reminded of the importance to Jonson's early reputation of the fact that his caustic tongue inspired articulate enemies and that he supervised careful editions of his plays.

The 5-to-1 predominance of verses on Jonson in the fourth decade is, of course, a result of the great out-

DISTRIBUTION OF ALLUSIONS
IN CLASS 2

	Shake-speare	Jonson
1601–1610	1	30
1611–1620	4	15
1621–1630	12	9
1631–1640	15	74
1641–1650	2	13
1651–1660	3	16
1661–1670	0	2
1671–1680	1	6
1681–1690	5	3
1691–1700	6	2
Undated	5	8
Totals	54	178

pouring of praise immediately after his death. About half the verses were printed in *Jonsonus Virbius* in 1638. In no decade of the century is the entire output of poems and long passages about Shakespeare ever half so great as the poems to Jonson in this single volume. Indeed, all the poems to Shakespeare in the first half of the century just about equal the number in *Jonsonus Virbius*, or half the number in the decade of Jonson's death.

It is also noteworthy that the poems and long passages to Shakespeare and Jonson fall off sharply after the Restoration. The passages to the two poets together are fewer in the last four decades than the Jonson allusions alone in the 1630's. It might be informative to collect Dryden allusions of this type in the last four decades and compare their number to the Shakespeare and Jonson ones.

Of the three decades in which Shakespeare allusions of this type outnumber the Jonson ones, the decade of the 1620's is to be explained by the appearance of the verses and prose passages in the Folio of 1623. In the last two decades, though the numbers are small, they may be said to represent the growing tendency to accept Shakespeare as the greatest English dramatist. The figures on allusions of Class 1 are, however, somewhat more conclusive evidence on the status of this movement, since the numbers there are much larger and the praise more uniform.

CLASS 3

The "great triumvirate"—Shakespeare, Jonson, and Beaumont and Fletcher—or any two of them, named as the standard of greatness or as the standard representatives of Elizabethan drama or literature. This type of allusion must be one of the most familiar to readers of all seventeenth-century and particularly Restoration literature. A good example is found in Owen Feltham's poem in *Jonsonus Virbius*:

> And should the Stage compose her selfe a Crowne
> Of all those *wits*, which hitherto sh'as knowne:
> Though there be many that about her brow
> Like sparkling stones, might a quick lustre throw:
> Yet *Shakespeare, Beaumont, Johnson*, these three shall
> Make up the Jem in the point Verticall.

Equally characteristic and somewhat more specific is Edward Phillips' statement in *Theatrum poetarum* (1675):

> *John Fletcher*, one of the happy *Triumvirat* (the other two being *Johnson* and *Shakespear*) of the Chief Dramatic Poets of our Nation, in the last

foregoing Age, among whom there might be said to be a symmetry of perfection, while each excelled in his peculiar way [p. 108].[4]

Since allusions of this class normally name both Shakespeare and Jonson, there is very little difference in the numbers for each. Occasionally, however, only two of the triumvirate, Shakespeare, Jonson, Beaumont and Fletcher, are named together. Usually when one is dropped it is Beaumont and Fletcher, especially early in the century, and only Shakespeare and Jonson are

DISTRIBUTION OF ALLUSIONS
IN CLASS 3

	Shakespeare	Jonson
1601–1610	0	0
1611–1620	0	0
1621–1630	0	1
1631–1640	12	8
1641–1650	13	9
1651–1660	14	16
1661–1670	23	23
1671–1680	37	36
1681–1690	30	30
1691–1700	45	49
Undated	1	0
Totals	175	172

named; but on several occasions it is Shakespeare or Jonson who is omitted. These figures indicate that Jonson is so dropped somewhat oftener than Shakespeare.

The figures of the frequency of allusions of this sort reveal practically nothing about the difference between the reputations of Shakespeare and Jonson. Usually the allusions do not distinguish among the members of the triumvirate. The steady increase of such allusions from decade to decade, except for the eighties, is suggestive of the growing tendency of writers to think of earlier English drama as the achievement of Shakespeare, Jonson, and Beaumont and Fletcher.

[4] Other examples may be examined in Vol. II, pp. 8–9, 12, and 232.

CLASS 3*a*

Shakespeare or Jonson and two or three other poets, not of the "triumvirate," named as a standard of greatness. This class is properly a corollary of the foregoing; it has little significance in itself, but it does serve to show how infrequently writers of the seventeenth century named Shakespeare or Jonson in a small group of great poets of the past other than the triumvirate. The class scarcely needs illustration. The most familiar example is William Basse's poem in memory of Shakespeare. Even in this poem it should be noted that Basse's selection of great poets is limited by place of burial and by the fact that Jonson and Fletcher were still alive when he wrote.

> Renowned Spencer lye a thought more nye
> To learned Chaucer, and rare Beaumond lye
> A little neerer Spenser, to make roome
> For Shakespeare in your threefold, fowerfold Tombe.[5]

—Lansdowne MSS 777

The figures on allusions of this class (p. 70) are useful chiefly for comparison with the figures of the preceding class. Such a comparison affords additional evidence that when seventeenth-century writers mentioned great dramatists of the past[6] they generally selected Shake-

---

[5] Among gentlemen of literary tastes in the seventeenth century this poem appears to have been the most popular tribute to Shakespeare. *The Shakspere Allusion-Book* records 10 manuscript and 5 printed examples. Other examples of allusions of this class may be found in Vol. II, pp. 83 and 106–7.

[6] One could almost say "great *poets* of the past," for in most of the allusions of Class 3*a* the name of Jonson or Shakespeare is coupled not with dramatists but with Chaucer, Spenser, or Sidney. Such a statement is not really warranted, however, for I have not collected the allusions to Chaucer, Spenser, and Sidney which mention neither Shakespeare nor Jonson; I do not know how many examples of such allusions there are. My impression from reading a good part of the literarily allusive passages of the century and from examining but not counting or classifying the collected Chaucer and Spenser allusions is that no group of nondramatic literary names is found half so often as Shakespeare, Jonson, Beaumont and Fletcher.

speare, Jonson, Beaumont and Fletcher, or some two of
the trio. Only infrequently did they select one member
of the triumvirate to group with two or three others not
of the triumvirate—Jonson about one-fourth as often as
he was included in the triumvirate, Shakespeare one-
eighth as often. Even here the preference for Jonson is
unequivocal.

DISTRIBUTION OF ALLUSIONS
IN CLASS 3*a*

	Shake-speare	Jonson
1601–1610	0	2
1611–1620	0	0
1621–1630	3	3
1631–1640	6	3
1641–1650	2	2
1651–1660	1	6
1661–1670	0	4
1671–1680	0	1
1681–1690	0	7
1691–1700	4	11
Undated	5	0
Totals	21	39

CLASS 4

Shakespeare or Jonson named in a list of literary men,
not confined to the triumvirate, but a list in which
Shakespeare or Jonson is given particular distinction.
Allusions of this and the following class are frequently
part of rather extended critical passages, like the As-
sizes-on-Parnassus compositions. Often both Shakespeare and Jonson are especially distinguished from the
other writers mentioned. When reasons for their distinction are given in passages of this type, Jonson is
generally admired for his learning. There seems to be
no clear consensus in the assignment of reasons for
Shakespeare's distinction.

And finally for Poetrie, 1 *Gower*, 2 Lidgate . . . . 3 the famous *Geofrie Chawcer* . . . . 4 Sir *Philip Sidney* . . . . 5 The renowned Spencer . . . . 6 Sam. Daniel . . . . 7 with Michael Draiton . . . . 8 Beaumount . . . . 9 Fletcher . . . . 10 My friend *Ben Iohnson*, equall to any of the Antients for the exactness of his Pen, and the decorum which he kept in *Dramatick* Poems, never before observed on the *English* Theatre.—PETER HEYLYN, *Cosmographie* (1652), Lib. I, p. 268.

> See how the Learned shades do meet,
> And like Aeriall shadowes fleet,
> More in number than were spide
> To flock 'bout the *Dulichian* Guide.
> The first, *Museus*, then *Catullus*,
> Then *Naso*, *Flaccus*, and *Tibullus;*
> Then *Petrarch*, *Sydney*, none can move
> *Shakespeare* out of Adonis Grove,
> There sullenly he sits.

—Verses by ANTHONY DAVENPORT, prefixed to SAMUEL
SHEPPARD'S *Loves of Amandus and Sophronia* (1650)[7]

Allusions of this type, comprising longer lists of great literary figures of the past, are not common early in the century. Probably the most familiar early list—and that too early for this study—is the one Francis Meres set forth in 1598 in his *Palladis Tamia*. Meres's long list of forty or fifty literary names and his undiscriminating praise are fairly characteristic of this type. Such lists are counted as allusions of Class 4 only when Shakespeare or Jonson is given special distinction. The two dramatists are so distinguished about an equal number of times, though Jonson, as usual, leads. The numbers are too small to make the comparison by decades very significant. It is not normal to find twice as many allusions to Jonson as to Shakespeare in the 1680's or to find three times as many allusions to Shakespeare as to Jonson in the 1660's.

[7] Other allusions of this type may be examined in Vol. II, pp. 82–83 and 235.

DISTRIBUTION OF ALLUSIONS
IN CLASS 4

	Shake-speare	Jonson
1601–1610	0	0
1611–1620	0	0
1621–1630	1	0
1631–1640	0	3
1641–1650	3	5
1651–1660	2	6
1661–1670	6	2
1671–1680	1	1
1681–1690	2	4
1691–1700	5	4
Undated	0	0
Totals	20	25

CLASS 5

Shakespeare or Jonson named in a list of three or more literary men, not the triumvirate, and without particular distinction. This class is just the residue of the lists-of-writers allusions after the passages of Classes 3, 3a, and 4 types have been segregated. Probably it does not need illustration, but examples may be found in Volume II, pp. 9, 135, 150, and 215–16.

Allusions of this class differ from those of the former only in that Shakespeare is not particularly distinguished in his lists or Jonson in his—usually nobody is distinguished in such lists. The fact that Jonson is named in half again as many lists as Shakespeare and that in every decade save one he is cited oftener is indicative of Jonson's reputation in nonliterary groups; for such lists, without discrimination among the poets, are usually found in works not primarily concerned with literature, like political histories. Not only did men of developed literary interests—men who talked about the distinctions of particular writers and who quoted from their works—prefer Jonson to Shakespeare in the seventeenth century; but men of less apparent literary interests, men who made a passing statement about literature in a political or social discussion, were also apparently more familiar with Jonson. Again the modern reader is given pause: in more than one-fourth of the seventeenth-century lists of literary men which distinguish or at least mention Jonson, Shakespeare is completely ignored.

DISTRIBUTION OF ALLUSIONS IN CLASS 5

	Shake-speare	Jonson
1601–1610	3	3
1611–1620	5	6
1621–1630	0	1
1631–1640	1	4
1641–1650	9	10
1651–1660	14	15
1661–1670	5	10
1671–1680	8	9
1681–1690	3	6
1691–1700	7	19
Undated	0	0
Totals	55	83

The numbers of allusions of this class taken by decades are again somewhat too small for illuminating comparison. The large number of lists-with-Jonson as compared to lists-with-Shakespeare in the last decade is not characteristic.

CLASS 6

Quotations from the works of Shakespeare or Jonson with or without acknowledgment as illustration or authority, i.e., quotations intended to be read in their context. This is the first of three classes of quotations, distinguished from the other two in that the Shakespearean or Jonsonian lines are frankly quoted, but not simply for their own sakes as in an anthology or commonplace book. Quotations of this type in the seventeenth century are more often from classic than from English authors, especially those intended not simply to illustrate but to exercise the weight of authority.

> Loyal all over! except one Knave, which I hope no body will take to himself; or if he do, I must e'en say with *Hamlet*,
>   . . . . *Then let the strucken Deer go weep*. . . . .
>   —APHRA BEHN, *The City-Heiress* (1682),
>   the Epistle Dedicatory

> And for my greater Authority I will adde these few excellent Verses of our Famous *Johnson* on this subject, which he calls a fit Rhime against Rhime.
>   Rhime the rack of finest Wits
>   .   .   .   .
> And as I doubt not well enough to wave any oblique exception that any man can throw on my Opinion (since patronized by his) so I do not detract from the deserts of any. . . . .—EDWARD HOWARD, Preface to *The Womens Conquest* (1671).[8]

These allusions are frankly quotations, though the author of them may not be named, and they are intended to impress the reader with their aptness or the weight of their authority. It is the second class so far noted in which the Shakespeare allusions outnumber the Jonson ones.

The greater Shakespearean total is due to the situation in the first three decades and the tenth. In the other six decades the numbers are about even: 56 quotations from Shakespeare, 61 from Jonson. In the first two decades the difference is evidently due to the earlier publication dates of Shakespeare's works, for 6 of the 8 quotations are from plays and poems of Shakespeare published in the sixteenth century before anything of

---

[8] Other examples of allusions in this class may be found in Vol. II, pp. 136, 228, and 254.

Jonson's was in print.[9] The other 2 quotations are from *Hamlet*, 1603 and 1604.

The situation in the last decade is the clearest example we have had so far of the evident rise of Shakespeare's reputation in the closing years of the century. For the first time in any decade in any class in which the numbers are large enough to have much meaning, the Shakespearean allusions are more than twice as numerous as the Jonsonian ones. This class is, further-

DISTRIBUTION OF ALLUSIONS
IN CLASS 6

	Shake-speare	Jonson
1601–1610	3	0
1611–1620	5	0
1621–1630	9	2
1631–1640	3	3
1641–1650	9	1
1651–1660	2	5
1661–1670	5	6
1671–1680	10	18
1681–1690	27	28
1691–1700	70	30
Undated	0	0
Totals	143	93

more, a significant one, for acknowledged quotations (as opposed to plagiarism) from an author are fairly good indications that his name or his lines can be expected to receive a respectful hearing. The first clear indications of anything like a general recognition of the unsurpassed quotableness of Shakespeare's lines is afforded by the figures for this decade. One would surmise that the number of Shakespearean quotations continued steadily to increase from the 1690's to the end of the nineteenth century.[10]

[9] *Venus and Adonis, Richard III, Romeo and Juliet.*

[10] The 1939 edition of Bartlett's *Familiar Quotations* has 1,849 quotations from Shakespeare, 41 from Jonson.

CLASS 7

Quotations of one or more lines from the works of
Shakespeare or Jonson or quotations of passages about
them or independent transcripts of their works, in commonplace books, anthologies, and independent manuscripts; sometimes the author is identified and sometimes not. Passages in this class, unlike those in Class 6,
have little or no relation to their context. At most, they

DISTRIBUTION OF ALLUSIONS
IN CLASS 7

	Shake-speare	Jonson
1601–1610	2	16
1611–1620	1	7
1621–1630	0	40
1631–1640	11	18
1641–1650	16	36
1651–1660	172	147
1661–1670	1	4
1671–1680	25	8
1681–1690	1	0
1691–1700	1	4
Undated	0	64
Totals	230	344

appear in a section of an anthology devoted to a particular theme; generally they would be equally appropriate if moved several pages backward or forward in
the manuscript or book in which they occur. Allusions
of this type are quite numerous, but they require no
illustration.[11]

About nine-tenths of the allusions in this class come
from commonplace books and printed anthologies, in
which they have no relation to their context. At first
glance it seems unaccountable that Jonson should lead
in this class by an even larger number than Shakespeare

[11] Examples are printed in Vol. II, pp. 2–3, 38–40, and 142.

did in the similar Class 6. The explanation seems to be that a large number of these allusions—perhaps one-third—come from manuscript sources, especially commonplace books, and Jonson is overwhelmingly dominant in such sources. Every one of the allusions in the undated group comes from a manuscript, and there the Jonson domination is greater than at any other point in the entire study. The extant seventeenth-century manuscript commonplace books are largely the products of the pens of undergraduates at Oxford and Cambridge, college dons, and gentlemen of leisure; with these groups Jonson seems, throughout the century, to have been held in far greater respect than Shakespeare. Jonson's name and copies of his poems—often copies of several poems—are usually to be found in such books, Shakespeare's seldom. Though I have not separated all the manuscript allusions in this class from the printed ones, my impression is that of the printed allusions a few more quote Shakespeare than Jonson. In the manuscript sources, quotations from Jonson are usually acknowledged, quotations from Shakespeare usually are not.

This discrepancy between printed and manuscript allusions to Shakespeare and Jonson is rather challenging. To what extent is Shakespeare's rising reputation in the late seventeenth century due to social changes? To what extent is Shakespeare's reputation a London reputation and Jonson's an Oxford and Cambridge one? Had the introduction of printing into England been delayed two hundred years, what would the comparative bulk of extant Shakespeare and Jonson works have been, and what would their comparative reputations have been today?

CLASS 8

Quotations of one or more lines from the works of Shakespeare or Jonson lifted without acknowledgment. Allusions in this class, like those in Class 6, depend on their context, but they are not acknowledged, and they are not cited to bring to bear the weight of authority. Sometimes they are simple examples of plagiarism, but more often they are intended as burlesques of the original.

WIFE: . . . . Hold up thy head, Ralph; show the gentlemen what thou canst do; speak a huffing part; I warrant you the gentlemen will accept of it.
CIT: Do, Ralph, do.
RALPH: By heaven, methinks, it were an easy leap
To pluck bright honor from the pale-faced moon;
Or dive into the bottom of the sea,
Where never fathom-line touched any ground,
And pluck up drowned honor from the lake of hell.
—BEAUMONT and FLETCHER, Induction, *The Knight of the Burning Pestle* (1613)

How I shall hurle *Protesebastus'* panting brain
Into the Air in mites as small as Atomes.
—ANON., *The Unfortunate Usurper* (1663), I, 4[12]

In the recorded examples of this type of allusion, Shakespeare is clearly dominant; in only one decade are the quotations from Jonson more numerous. One hesitates, however, to be too sure of the evidence; for the completeness of the collection in this type is more doubtful than in any other. The recognition of such allusions as these depends wholly upon familiarity with the lines of Shakespeare and Jonson, for there is generally no sign of allusion except the quoted words themselves. This is precisely the area in which the Jonson-compe-

[12] The lines are Jonson's (*Sejanus*, I, 256–57, with "Protesebastus" substituted for "his"). Other examples will be found in Vol. II, pp. 13, 29, and 41–42.

tence of all investigators is most inferior to their Shake-
speare-competence.[13] Probably very few lines quoted
from Shakespeare in accessible texts are still undetected;
hundreds of lines from Jonson may be. Thus, in spite of
our modern feeling that Shakespeare's lines *must* have
impressed themselves on the minds of his contemporaries far more than Jonson's, we cannot be sure of the
facts. Such evidence as we have confirms the modern
assumption.

DISTRIBUTION OF ALLUSIONS
IN CLASS 8

	Shake-speare	Jonson
1601–1610	5	0
1611–1620	3	1
1621–1630	0	1
1631–1640	8	1
1641–1650	6	2
1651–1660	1	1
1661–1670	0	3
1671–1680	4	1
1681–1690	7	1
1691–1700	0	0
Undated	0	0
Totals	34	11

The total number of allusions in this group is small,
but it should be pointed out that this class has probably
suffered more from my rejection of dubious parallel
passages in the Shakespeare and Jonson allusion books
than any other. I have said that an alleged parallel passage is not an allusion unless one full line is quoted.[14]
While this test seems to me the best that can be applied
to parallel passages, it is, nevertheless, quite possible
that in various instances some seventeenth-century
writer may have had Shakespeare or Jonson clearly in
mind though he lifted less than one line. Such plagiarism,

[13] See above, pp. 20–21.   [14] See above, pp. 8–11.

which to my mind is too uncertain to try to deal with, would fall into this class.

Shakespeare's or Jonson's name connected with an apocryphal play, on the title-page, in an advertisement, or in any passage in which the name of the dramatist and a play outside the accepted canon are associated. Allusions of this type scarcely need illustration.

DISTRIBUTION OF ALLUSIONS
IN CLASS 9

	Shakespeare	Jonson
1601–1610	5	0
1611–1620	0	0
1621–1630	1	0
1631–1640	0	0
1641–1650	0	0
1651–1660	16	5
1661–1670	10	0
1671–1680	0	1
1681–1690	20	2
1691–1700	28	7
Undated	0	1
Totals	80	16

The comparative numbers of these allusions to apocryphal plays is a direct reflection of the state of the text and canon of Shakespeare and Jonson. The great majority of the allusions come from title-pages, advertisements, and bibliographies published by such men as Winstanley, Langbaine, and Gildon, so that the ratio of the allusions is close to the ratio of plays in the Shakespeare apocrypha to plays in the Jonson apocrypha. There are about ten plays which are added to the Shakespeare canon by several different bibliographers, and only one so added to the Jonson canon. Ten other plays are erroneously ascribed to Shakespeare by only one man or occasionally by two; only one to Jonson. These ratios are reflected in the numbers of allusions; very few of the references could be called literary allusions.

Shakespeare's notorious unconcern with his published text led inevitably to a swollen apocrypha. Jonson's equally notorious concern with the printing of his plays discouraged unauthorized additions to the canon.

The decades in which most allusions of this type appear are the decades of publishers' and bibliographers' activity. In the first decade of the century Shakespeare's name appears on the title-pages of several plays which, according to general agreement, he did not write. In the sixth and seventh decades the long publishers' lists like those of Archer and Rogers and Ley attribute apocryphal plays to him. In the ninth and tenth decades the bibliographers discuss the apocryphal plays along with the canonical ones. The only apocryphal plays which are connected with the names of Shakespeare or Jonson more than once outside these publishers' and bibliographers' records are *Sir John Oldcastle* and *The Widow*. They alone have left evidence that in the popular mind they were connected with the names of the dramatists to whom they were erroneously attributed.

CLASS 10

References to plays or poems or masques of Shakespeare's or Jonson's by name or unmistakable synopsis. Every sort of mention of such a work is counted in this class.

BOWDLER: I never read anything but *Venus and Adonis*.
CRIPPLE: Why thats the very quintessence of love,
　　　　If you remember but a verse or two,
　　　　Ile pawne my head, goods, lands, and all 'twill doe.

　　　　　　　　　　　—THOMAS HEYWOOD, *The Fair Maid*
　　　　　　　　　　　　　of the Exchange (1607), sig. G₃

An *Alchymist* vsually answers his deluded scholler with expectation of
Proiection, and tells him the more his *Materials* be multiplied, the stronger
will the *Proiection* be; especially if it come to the mountenance of an hundred pounds, *Vid*. The Play of the *Alchymist*.—JOHN GEE, *New Shreds of
the Old Snare* (1624), p. 22 n.[15]

DISTRIBUTION OF ALLUSIONS
IN CLASS 10

	Shake-speare	Jonson
1601–1610	32	29
1611–1620	30	20
1621–1630	18	19
1631–1640	27	62
1641–1650	12	36
1651–1660	25	41
1661–1670	60	137
1671–1680	48	72
1681–1690	120	137
1691–1700	192	208
Undated	3	6
Totals	567	767

The next three classes are concerned with allusions to
works and characters. Class 10 includes all specific references to any play, poem, or masque in the accepted
Shakespeare or Jonson canon. Each name is recorded
separately; thus, if a writer commends 5 tragedies of
Shakespeare, the passage is counted as 5 examples of
Class 10, but counted as only 1 allusion in the total
count. Sometimes, particularly in the eighties and nine-

[15] Other examples of the type will be found in Vol. II, pp. 87, 147, and 203–5.

ties, a single long allusion of a biographical or critical character will contain 40 or more allusions of Class 10. This fact should be kept in mind in considering allusions of Classes 10, 11, 11*a*, 12, and 13. The numbers are large because every mention of a play, masque, or poem by name is counted under Class 10, regardless of the other classes into which the allusion may fall.

The comparative figures here are somewhat misleading; actually, the dominance of Jonson is greater than it appears, because the number of plays in the Shakespeare canon is greater than that in the Jonson. For instance, in his account of Shakespeare, Winstanley lists 48 works, several apocryphal, of course, while his equally laudatory account of Jonson lists only 21. Winstanley does not really speak of Shakespeare's plays twice as often as he does of Jonson's, as the figures alone would imply. In fact, outside the biographies of the two men, he refers to Jonson 10 times, to Shakespeare only 3 times.

This difference in the size of the canon is responsible for the greater number of allusions to Shakespeare in the first and second decades. By the end of 1610 there were at least thirty-five Shakespearean works in existence to refer to, but not more than thirteen Jonsonian, excluding the masques. In every other decade of the century the allusions to Jonson's works by name are more numerous, in spite of the larger Shakespeare canon.

The character of the allusions to Jonson's masques presents another factor to be considered in comparing these figures. In the first and second decades of the century they are more frequently mentioned than the plays;[16] yet, since they are seldom referred to by name, very few of the allusions to them are counted in this class.[17] These factors—the size of the Shakespeare canon and the namelessness of Jonson's masques—make the comparative familiarity of Shakespeare's titles appear greater than it really was.

This specific preference of seventeenth-century writers for Jonson's plays over Shakespeare's as shown, though inadequately, by the table for Class 10 is perhaps even more shocking to the modern taste than the general praise of Jonson over Shakespeare. It is not too difficult to understand that to the critical and literary mind of the seventeenth century Jonson's learning and his superb structural skill might in the abstract have seemed more admirable than Shakespeare's lyric eloquence and matchless characterization. But when it came down to specific cases, did these seventeenth-century writers actually prefer *Volpone* and *Sejanus* and *Catiline* to *As You Like It* and *Macbeth* and *King Lear?* The figures indicate that they did, and the later figures on allusions to individual plays exhibit the preference beyond the shadow of a doubt. *O tempora! O mores!*

CLASS 11

Literary references to a character in the works of Shakespeare or Jonson. Such references are generally for purposes of illustration, and almost always the character is mentioned by name, though occasionally there is an unmistakable allusion of this type when no name is mentioned.

[16] See above, pp. 38–40.

[17] See below, pp. 87–88, 90–91, 109.

Our Keepers knew no hurt, unlesse 't had bin
Drinking of Sack, honest *Iack Falstaffes* sinne.

    —B. R., *The Cambridge Royallist Imprisoned*
    (July 31, 1643), sig. A₄

Thay Quakte at Iohnson as by hym thay pase
because of Trebulation Holsome and Annanias.

    —G. C. MOORE SMITH (ed.), *William Hemminge's El-
    egy on Randolph's Finger* (1923), lines 183–84[18]

DISTRIBUTION OF ALLUSIONS
IN CLASS 11

	Shakespeare	Jonson
1601–1610	14	9
1611–1620	9	31
1621–1630	14	12
1631–1640	21	20
1641–1650	30	2
1651–1660	40	39
1661–1670	48	44
1671–1680	67	67
1681–1690	78	26
1691–1700	341	70
Undated	34	0
Totals	696	320

The references to characters present an aspect of
Shakespeare's and Jonson's reputations more like the
modern situation than any other revealed in this classification of allusions. In every decade except the second
and eighth, Shakespeare's characters seem better known.
Again it is well to remember that Shakespeare created
several times as many characters as Jonson did, not
only because he wrote twice as many plays, but because his normal cast is about twice the size of Jonson's.
This fact does not, however, wholly account for the difference, for Shakespeare's twenty most familiar char-

---

[18] This type of allusion is one of the commonest. There are many examples in Vol.
II, a few of which will be found on pp. 2, 6, 135, and 203–5.

acters are mentioned nearly three times as often as Jonson's twenty most familiar.[19] Though writers of the seventeenth century praised Jonson more than Shakespeare, though they discussed him oftener, quoted him oftener, mentioned his plays oftener, and recorded more performances of his works, they were evidently more deeply impressed by Shakespeare's characterizations than by Jonson's. This particular aspect of Shakespeare's creative genius triumphed over the critical standards which generally blinded the men of his time to his superiority.

CLASS 11a

References to characters of Shakespeare or Jonson as acting roles. Such theatrical allusions are much less common than the literary ones; but they are of no little importance, for they furnish highly desirable but generally inaccessible data on the plays of Shakespeare and Jonson in the environment for which they were intended— the theater.

Decemb. 3. 1662.

. . . . only the other day, when Othello was play'd, the Doge of Venice and all his Senators came upon the Stage with Feathers in their Hats, which was like to have chang'd the Tragedy into a Comedy, but that the Moor and Desdemona acted their Parts well.[20]—CATHERINE PHILIPS, *Letters from Orinda to Paliarchus* (1705), p. 96.

April 17th [1669]

. . . . and there hearing that "The Alchymist" was acted, we did go, and took him with us to the King's house; and it is still a good play, having not been acted for two or three years before; but I do miss Clun, for the Doctor.—H. B. WHEATLEY (ed.), *The Diary of Samuel Pepys.*[21]

[19] See the analysis of allusions to particular characters below, pp. 120 ff.

[20] This is a good example of an allusion which is classified in two different groups; it is both 11<i>a</i> and 12.

[21] Other allusions of this type will be found in Vol. II, pp. 13, 14, and 109.

Though the number of allusions in this class is too small to be wholly reliable, there is little doubt that Shakespeare's acting roles made more of an impression in the theater than Jonson's, as one would expect from the greater familiarity of his characters as revealed by the allusions in the preceding class. It is not surprising that three-fourths of these references to acting roles

DISTRIBUTION OF ALLUSIONS
IN CLASS 11a

	Shake-speare	Jonson
1601–1610	4	0
1611–1620	3	0
1621–1630	0	0
1631–1640	0	0
1641–1650	0	0
1651–1660	3	0
1661–1670	12	3
1671–1680	3	1
1681–1690	0	0
1691–1700	11	5
Undated	1	0
Totals	37	9

come from the last four decades of the century, for one of the most exasperating aspects of the study of the great Elizabethan dramatic outburst is the paucity of literary references to the plays in the theatrical environment for which they were written. Even when Jonson's friends refer to the fate of his plays in the theater, as in the commendatory verses for *Sejanus* and *Volpone*, they seldom say anything specific about the performance of particular roles.

CLASS 12

Literary or social references to performances or preparations for performances of plays or masques by Shakespeare or Jonson. Theatrical allusions of this type are nearly always made by members of the audience, or potential members of the audience; they are distinguished from passages of the following type which are nearly always made by, or in dealings with, members of the producing group.

1635, May 6.
    not farre from home all day att the bla: ffryers & a play this day Called the More of Venice.—"The Records of Sir Humphrey Mildmay," *The Jacobean and Caroline Stage*, II, 677.

    The Masque [Jonson's *Masque of Beauty*] was as well performed as ever any was; and for the device of it, with the Speeches and Verses, I had sent it your Lordship ere this, if I could have gotten those of Ben Jonson. But no sooner had he made an end of these, but that he undertook a new charge for the Masque [*Lord Hadington's Masque* or *The Hue and Cry after Cupid*] that is to be at the Viscount Hadington's Mariage.[22]—Rowland Whyte to the Earl of Shrewsbury, January 29,1607/8, in J. B. NICHOLS, *The Progresses of James the First* (1828), II, 175.[23]

At first glance the dominance of Jonson in allusions of this class seems a contradiction of the evidence of Class 11*a* concerning the comparative familiarity of the acting roles of the two dramatists. Two facts largely explain the discrepancy. First, most of the allusions in the first and second decades refer to the performances of masques, and the characters in the masques are almost never mentioned in allusions of any type. In the masque performances the spectacle completely overshadowed the characters; on the few occasions when actors were mentioned, they were referred to for social and not for

    [22] Whyte's statement is a good example of a single passage which constitutes two separate allusions, for he records both the performance of one masque and the preparation for another. Note that, as usual, though both masques are clearly indicated, neither is actually named.

    [23] Other examples of allusions of this type will be found in Vol. II, pp. 22–24, 34, and 115.

DISTRIBUTION OF ALLUSIONS
IN CLASS 12

	Shake-speare	Jonson
1601–1610	10	27
1611–1620	9	29
1621–1630	2	8
1631–1640	1	7
1641–1650	0	0
1651–1660	3	12
1661–1670	41	43
1671–1680	3	3
1681–1690	1	0
1691–1700	5	5
Undated	0	0
Totals	75	134

theatrical reasons. The second relevant fact is the customary attitude toward Shakespeare and Jonson in the seventeenth-century theater. Shakespeare's plays were generally thought of as acting vehicles, Jonson's as presentations of the work of a master; in the former, acting roles are a relevant and important consideration, in the latter they are not. Pepys's remarks, as noted in chapter iv, clearly reveal this attitude.[24] An even more compelling illustration is the frequent revision and adaptation of Shakespeare's plays for the Restoration stage as compared with the fidelity to Jonson's own text. The frequent cries of pedantic anguish uttered by modern writers over the mutilation of Shakespeare's text in the "improved" Restoration versions of his plays, the indignant protests against the "vandalism" of Davenant, Dryden, Tate, and Crowne, reveal a singularly naïve attitude. These men were not vandals; they were intelligent men of the theater acting in accord with the tastes of the time and the standards of the theater, acting as William Shakespeare himself had acted in his

[24] See above, pp. 49–54.

own theater. He might have been puzzled or even annoyed at the new taste, but he would scarcely have attacked the competent dramatists who were trying to adapt the available material to meet it.

These allusions of Class 12, then, as compared with those of Classes 11 and 11*a*, are an interesting further example of the characteristic seventeenth-century way of viewing Shakespeare and Jonson. The chronological distribution of the allusions is notable chiefly as evidence of the great interest in Jonson's masques in the reign of James I and of the great eagerness with which performances were discussed in the first decade after the reopening of the theaters at the Restoration.

CLASS 13

Business records of performances of, or preparations for performances of, plays or masques by Shakespeare or Jonson.

Playes for the Kinge this present yeare of oʳ Lord God. 1630
    At   . . . .

[H]ampton Court   The 17 of October. Midsomers Night's Dreame
    . . . .

    —MS 2068.8, Folger Shakespeare Library, printed in
    The Jacobean and Caroline Stage, I, 27

The bill of account of the hole charges of the Queen's
Maᵗˢ Maske at Chrismas 1610 [*Love Freed from Ignorance and Folly*]
Inprimis, to Mr. Inigo Johnes, as apeareth by his byll . . 238 li. 16 s. 10 d.
. . . .

Item, for 3 yeardes of flesh collored satten for Cupides
coate and hose att 14s. the yeard . . . . 2 li. 2 s.
. . . .

    Rewardes to the persons imployed in the maske.
Inprimis, to Mr. Benjamin Johnson for his inventions . . 40 li.
. . . .

Item, to Mr. Johnson for setting the songes to the lutes   5 li.
Item, to Thomas Lupo for setting the dances to the vio-
  lens. . . . .   5 li.

. . . .

—Exchequer Papers, printed in *Proceedings of the Society
of Antiquaries of London* (1859–61), Ser. 2, I, 31–32[25]

DISTRIBUTION OF ALLUSIONS
IN CLASS 13

	Shake-speare	Jonson
1601–1610.	0	10
1611–1620.	11	17
1621–1630.	6	8
1631–1640.	9	10
1641–1650.	0	0
1651–1660.	3	2
1661–1670.	7	21
1671–1680.	1	6
1681–1690.	0	1
1691–1700.	0	3
Undated.	0	0
Totals.	37	78

The figures on these business records of performances
of Shakespeare's and Jonson's plays might be taken as
an indication that Jonson was performed oftener in the
seventeenth century than Shakespeare. I doubt if this
was true; but in any case these figures can scarcely be
accepted as evidence on the frequency of performance in
the commercial theaters. Nearly two-thirds of the allusions are dated before the closing of the theaters, and
allusions of this type in that period nearly all concern
court performances of plays or masques. Jonson's greater attraction for courtly audiences, particularly in the
masque, is common knowledge; and these figures only

[25] For other examples of allusions of this type see Vol. II, pp. 43, 119, and 137–38.

verify the conclusion suggested by other types of allusions.

After the Restoration, the records of performances in
the public theaters are about equal for Shakespeare and
Jonson, but Jonson again dominates in the allusions to
performances at court. In considering these Restoration
records it should be remembered that the most familiar
collection of allusions of this type—Downes, *Roscius
Anglicanus*—is ruled out because of its date of publication.

CLASS 14

Letters written to Shakespeare or Jonson. Though
there are no known allusions of this type to Shakespeare
in the seventeenth century, there are several to Jonson.[26]

DISTRIBUTION OF ALLUSIONS
IN CLASS 14

	Shake-speare	Jonson
1601–1610	0	0
1611–1620	0	7
1621–1630	0	5
1631–1640	0	3
1641–1650	0	1
1651–1660	0	0
1661–1670	0	0
1671–1680	0	0
1681–1690	0	0
1691–1700	0	0
Undated	0	1
Totals	0	17

The figures on allusions of this type simply under-
score the fulness of our biographical knowledge of Jonson and the scantiness of our knowledge of Shakespeare.
But this familiar situation is in itself a manifestation of

[26] Allusions of this class scarcely need illustration; examples may be found in Vol.
II, pp. 26–27 and 30–31.

the contemporary reputations of the two men. It is not simply Jonson's intercourse with courtly and learned groups or the later span of his life, important though they are, which have preserved for us our fuller knowledge of him. Jonson's contemporaries, as the above figures show, thought it important or interesting to preserve relics of him; Shakespeare's apparently did not. This fact is in itself a direct reflection of the higher repute in which Jonson was generally held.[27] It should be further noted that these allusions nearly all come from manuscript collections—a type of source in which Shakespeare is generally completely overshadowed by Jonson.

CLASS 15

Records of honors conferred on or proposed for Shakespeare or Jonson. Again there are no examples of allusions to Shakespeare of this type in the seventeenth century, but there are several to Jonson.

Precept	Vigesimo quinto Septembris J^m vj^c Decimo Oc-
Gild	tauo. Ordanis the Deyne of gild to mak Ben-
Jonsoun burges	jamyn Jonsoun inglisman burges and gildbrother
and gildbrother	in communi forma.

—Edinburgh Council Register, Vol. XIII, fol. 39, in HER-
FORD and SIMPSON, Ben Jonson, I, 233

19 July 1619

Johnson, Benjamin; "omni humana litteratura feliciter instructus et eo nominea serenissimo rege annua pensione eaque satis honorifiça honestatus."—ANDREW CLARK (ed.), Register of the University of Oxford, 1571–1622 (1887), II, 238.[28]

---

[27] The extant letters to or about Shakespeare are sixteenth-century documents and therefore not considered here (see E. K. Chambers, William Shakespeare [Oxford, 1930], II, 101-6). Even these letters are business rather than personal or literary documents, and they appear to have been preserved for economic reasons.

[28] Other examples will be found in Vol. II, pp. 28 and 33.

Though allusions of this type are not the same as those of the former, their implication is similar—the preservation of such records implies a greater concern for Jonson than for Shakespeare. The records themselves, however, imply a much greater contemporary reputation than mere letters do. The records of the nomination of Jonson for Bolton's Royal Academy, of his royal pen-

DISTRIBUTION OF ALLUSIONS
IN CLASS 15

	Shake-speare	Jonson
1601–1610	0	1
1611–1620	0	8
1621–1630	0	8
1631–1640	0	1
1641–1650	0	0
1651–1660	0	0
1661–1670	0	1
1671–1680	0	1
1681–1690	0	0
1691–1700	0	1
Undated	0	0
Totals	0	21

sion, of his appointment as City Chronologer, of his honors at the hands of the Council of the City of Edinburgh, of his honorary degree at Oxford, are all distinctions which not only are not recorded for Shakespeare but which, so far as we can tell, never would have been proposed for him. In our day of the wholesale distribution of honors—academic, civic, and national—no one needs to be reminded that the award of formal honors is not necessarily any proof of solid merit; but such awards in any time are clear evidence of popular reputation— deserved or undeserved.

CLASS 16

Biographical accounts of Shakespeare or Jonson. Most such accounts are too long for illustration here, but the biographical remarks about Shakespeare made by Edward Phillips in 1675 and by Charles Gildon in 1698 are typical and too familiar to require reprinting.[29]

DISTRIBUTION OF ALLUSIONS
IN CLASS 16

	Shake-speare	Jonson
1601–1610	0	0
1611–1620	0	1
1621–1630	0	0
1631–1640	0	0
1641–1650	0	0
1651–1660	0	1
1661–1670	3	1
1671–1680	0	1
1681–1690	4	3
1691–1700	4	4
Undated	0	0
Totals	11	11

The comparative number of allusions of this type is not very revealing, for most of the references come from collections of biographies like Fuller's *Worthies*, Winstanley's *Lives of the Most Famous English Poets*, and Aubrey's *Brief Lives*, which treat both Shakespeare and Jonson, as well as many of their contemporaries. A few come from collections of manuscript notes, like those of Fulman or the Reverend John Ward, and record facts about only one of the two poets. Such collections are really more like commonplace books than like the other dictionaries of biography; their Jonson material is likely to consist of anecdotes—which fall into the next class—while their Shakespeare material is sometimes a fragmentary biography, recorded, apparently, because the information was thought to be curious or out of the way.

---

[29] Examples of such accounts of Jonson will be found in *The Jonson Allusion-Book*, pp. 112–15 and 354–58.

CLASS 17

Personal anecdotes or records of Shakespeare or Jonson. Allusions of this type differ from those in Class 16 in that they make no pretense of biographical or bibliographical completeness.

m^r Ben: Johnson and m^r. W^m: Shake-speare Being Merrye att a Tauern, m^r Jonson haueing begune this for his Epitaph

Here lies Ben Johnson that was once one

he gives ytt to m^r Shakspear to make vpp who presently wrightes

Who while hee liu'de was a sloe things
and now being dead is Nothinge.

finis

—Bodleian Ashmolean MS 38, p. 181, printed in E. K.
CHAMBERS, *William Shakespeare*, II, 246

Beniaminu) Johnson Ste	Presented that he is by fame a seducer of
Anne in blackfriers	youthe to popishe religion/he was monished to
321.b 1	appear to see farther pceding herin he having

Beniaminu) Johnson Ste   Presented that he is by fame a seducer of
Anne in blackfriers   youthe to popishe religion/he was monished to
321.b 1   appeare to see farther pceding herin he having
                             denyed bothe the fact & the fame and the
                             Church Wardens weare decreed to be here to
                             specifie what pticulers they have to Charrdg him
                             wth continuat in hunc diem/

—*A Book of Correction, etc.*, Wednesday, May 14, 1606, printed
in HERFORD and SIMPSON, *Ben Jonson*, I, 222[30]

Since allusions of this type record both documented fact and popular stories, their numbers bear witness to the greater fulness of biographical source material on Jonson and to the fund of popular anecdotes about him as well. Though there are more Jonson allusions of this class in every decade except the second, the figures are really misleading, for Jonson's dominance is much greater than the figures show. The Shakespeare allusions mostly occur before 1620, three-fourths of them falling in the first two decades. These 50 allusions nearly all concern business transactions or births, deaths, and

[30] Other examples of allusions of this class will be found in Vol. II, pp. 29, 59, 120, and 226.

marriages, and all but 8 or 10 are products of the tireless search for Shakespeare records of any kind in the last seventy-five years. Such records, of course, have nothing to do with Shakespeare's literary reputation, for they were not cherished because of his distinction but merely preserved as legal records. A similar search for Jonson records in the parish registers, at Somerset House, the Public Records Office, and other record

DISTRIBUTION OF ALLUSIONS
IN CLASS 17

	Shake-speare	Jonson
1601–1610	17	24
1611–1620	33	11
1621–1630	2	10
1631–1640	2	13
1641–1650	3	4
1651–1660	4	16
1661–1670	1	12
1671–1680	0	1
1681–1690	2	10
1691–1700	4	9
Undated	1	0
Totals	69	110

repositories would probably turn up as many such Jonson allusions, though of a somewhat different type. If we discounted the allusions of this type to either Jonson or Shakespeare turned up by modern research in record repositories during the last seventy-five years, the Jonson allusions would outnumber the Shakespeare ones 3 or 4 to 1.

Perhaps the anecdotes in this class should have been distinguished from the biographical records, since the two offer different implications about the reputation of their subject. There are, of course, far more anecdotes about Jonson than about Shakespeare. Indeed, the most popular of the Shakespeare anecdotes is one which couples him with Jonson.[31] This greater fund of recorded anecdote about Jonson is to be attributed not alone to the greater interest in him in the century but to the strongly marked character of the man which led to the accretion of stories. The majority of the anecdotes about Jonson concern his drinking, his association with the Tribe of Ben, and his verbal encounters with his contemporaries. The impression of Jonson's bluff pugnacity is witnessed by the epithet which is most frequently applied to him: "honest Ben."

CLASS 18

Casual references to Shakespeare or Jonson in statements not primarily about the dramatist. Allusions of this type never involve praise of the author but sometimes imply unfavorable criticism. Often they are found in accounts of other dramatists in which Shakespeare or Jonson is merely mentioned as a contemporary.

He . . . . in a short time fitted him for the life of a Stage-player in a common society, from whence after venting his frothy inventions, he had a greater call to a higher promotion; namely to be the Jester, (or rather a Fool) in *Shakespears* Company of Players: *Omne simile est appetibile sui similis,* every like desires his like: There he so long sported himself with his own deceivings, till at last like an Infidel Jew, he conceived preaching to be but foolishness.—WILLIAM YONGE, *Englands Shame: . . . . Being a Full and Faithful Relation of the Life and Death of that Grand Imposter Hugh Peters* (1663), pp. 7–8.

November 17, 1621. . . . . Dr. Donne is to be Dean of St. Paul's, so that if Ben Jonson could be Dean of Westminster, St. Paul's, Westminster and Christchurch would each have a poetical Dean.—JOHN CHAMBERLAIN to SIR DUDLEY CARLETON, *Calendar of State Papers, Domestic, James I* (1621), p. 310.[32]

---

[31] See Vol. II, p. 101, for one of the several examples of this anecdote.

[32] Other allusions of this type may be found in Vol. II, pp. 6, 176, and 208.

This class is really the miscellaneous one into which allusions find their way if they do not properly belong in any of the others. The references say nothing significant about Shakespeare or Jonson; they merely use the names, frequently for purposes of identification. As

DISTRIBUTION OF ALLUSIONS
IN CLASS 18

	Shake-speare	Jonson
1601–1610	2	4
1611–1620	0	3
1621–1630	0	4
1631–1640	6	7
1641–1650	5	7
1651–1660	11	22
1661–1670	6	15
1671–1680	11	13
1681–1690	9	34
1691–1700	31	29
Undated	1	0
Totals	82	138

might be expected, there are more such casual references to Jonson than to Shakespeare in every decade of the century except the last. Though the individual allusions of this class are not important, their sums offer another good index of the popular familiarity of Shakespeare and Jonson among writers in the seventeenth century.

CLASS 19

Criticism of the works of Shakespeare or Jonson. Passages of this type are not simply passing condemnation or praise of the man's work in general, but a notation of particulars of excellence or inferiority. The most familiar allusions in this class are the numerous passages in Dryden's essays and prefaces, but most of them are too long for quotation.

The Friends too of our great Dramatick Writer, *Shakespear*, will not be perswaded, but that even his Monstrous Irregularities were Conducive to those Shining Beauties, which abound in most of his Plays; and that if he had been more a Critick, he had been less a Poet.[33]—T. R., *An Essay, concerning Critical and Curious Learning* (1698), pp. 30–31.

Our Poets, continued he, represent the Modern little Actions of Debauchees, as *Ben Johnson* presented the Humours of his Tankard Bearer, his Pauls Walkers, and his Collegiate Ladies, *&c.* things then known and familiar to every Bodies Notice; and so are these now, and consequently delightful to the times, as Pictures of Faces well known and remarkable. These, Answered *Julio*, were *Ben Johnsons* Weaknesses, and have been as such sufficiently exploded by our New fashion'd Wits, and therefore methinks they should not be imitated by them of all Men Living. Such Representations are like a Painters taking a Picture after the Life in the Apparel then Worn, which becomes Ungraceful or Ridiculous in the next Age, when the Fashion is out.—[JAMES WRIGHT], *Country Conversations* (1694), pp. 9–10.[34]

DISTRIBUTION OF ALLUSIONS
IN CLASS 19

	Shake-speare	Jonson
1601–1610	0	2
1611–1620	1	0
1621–1630	0	0
1631–1640	0	3
1641–1650	2	0
1651–1660	1	0
1661–1670	5	10
1671–1680	11	9
1681–1690	2	7
1691–1700	14	7
Undated	0	0
Totals	36	38

The Jonson majority in allusions of this type is smaller than might have been expected in the light of the figures for Classes 1 and 2, yet an examination of the distribution by decades gives a fairly clear indication of the reason for the difference. In the two former classes—the praise of Jonson and the poems and prose passages addressed to him—the allusions are very numerous in

[33] This passage is also classified as Class 1.

[34] Other examples will be found in Vol. II, pp. 62–63 and 235–36.

the first six decades of the century, outnumbering those to Shakespeare 5 to 1 and 4 to 1, respectively. Though in the decades after the Restoration there are also more allusions to Jonson than to Shakespeare in those two classes, the majority is much smaller, about 7 to 4 and 7 to 6. Now allusions of Class 19 are not characteristic of the first half of the century at all; writers of this period clearly preferred Jonson to Shakespeare, as the figures in Classes 1 and 2 demonstrate, but they rarely gave specific reasons for their preference. Not until after the Restoration did critics of English *drama* become sufficiently articulate to write the extended dramatic criticism in which allusions of this type are usually found. By that time Jonson's reputation, though still dominant, was not overwhelmingly greater than Shakespeare's.

A second important factor in the situation is John Dryden. His championing of Shakespeare in his essays and prefaces was probably the most important single influence in the burgeoning of Shakespeare's reputation after the Restoration; in allusions of this class his significance is very clear. In the two decades of the sixties and seventies, three-fourths of the allusions of this class to Shakespeare come from the pen of John Dryden, only about one-fourth of those to Jonson. Indeed, one might hazard the guess that Dryden was not only largely responsible for the rapid growth of Shakespeare's reputation after 1668 but that much of the modern misconception of the comparative reputations of Shakespeare and Jonson in Dryden's lifetime is also due to the author of *An Essay of Dramatick Poesie*. Dryden's critical writings are much more widely known now than those of any of his contemporaries; his remarks on Shakespeare and Jonson are remembered when those of Shadwell and Howard and Oldham are forgotten. It is not easy to remember that, though Dryden's dramatic criticism is the best of the period, it is not therefore the most characteristic.

CLASS 20

Criticism of a single work of Shakespeare or Jonson. This classification differs from the preceding in that only one work is discussed instead of the qualities or shortcomings of the dramatist's work as a whole. Dryden's "Examen of the *Silent Woman*" in his *Essay of Dramatick Poesie* is the most familiar example. Most of the passages of this type, like Dryden's "Examen," are too long to quote. Probably the shortest of all is one which barely qualifies—Jonson's comment on *The Winter's Tale* in 1618.

Sheakspear jn a play brought jn a number of men saying they had suffered Shipwrack jn Bohemia, wher y^r is no Sea neer by some 100 Miles.— "Ben Jonson's Conversations with William Drummond of Hawthornden," in HERFORD and SIMPSON, *Ben Jonson*, I, 138.[35]

Allusions of this class might have been expected to approximate in number and distribution those of the former. The difference in distribution is not very puzzling; the most abnormal aspect is the 8 allusions to Jonson in the first decade. These 8 allusions account not only for the unusual proportion before 1660 but also for most of the increased majority of Jonson allusions in the class as compared with Class 19. Six of the 8 allusions come from the commendatory poems written for the first edition of *Sejanus*. The criticism of the play they set forth is due not to an unusual development of critical

[35] Other examples will be found in Vol. II, pp. 222–23 and 240–42.

interest in the first decade but to the reception of the
play in the theater. Jonson's friends, George Chapman, Hugh Holland, William Strachey, and three other
anonymous contributors, felt called upon to defend his
tragedy against the hostile public which, as they point
out, had hissed it in the theater; and their defense in-

DISTRIBUTION OF ALLUSIONS
IN CLASS 20

	Shake-speare	Jonson
1601–1610	0	8
1611–1620	1	1
1621–1630	1	0
1631–1640	2	1
1641–1650	1	0
1651–1660	0	0
1661–1670	0	6
1671–1680	3	6
1681–1690	3	2
1691–1700	7	7
Undated	1	0
Totals	19	31

cludes comment upon particular virtues of the play—
or allusions of Class 20. Without these 6 allusions, the
number before 1650 is almost exactly the same as the
number in Class 19, and the ratio of Shakespeare to
Jonson allusions does not differ greatly.

Our consideration of the variety of classes into which
allusions to Shakespeare and to Jonson fall in the seventeenth century has high-lighted several aspects of their
reputations. Perhaps least significant is the fact that in
fifteen classes there are more references to Jonson than
to Shakespeare; in six, more to Shakespeare than to
Jonson; and in one an equal number to each. More significant is the particular kind of allusion in which each
poet's majority occurs and the extent of the majority.

In seven classes of allusions, Jonson's majority is overwhelming, i.e., more than five times as many in groups under 50, more than twice as many in the groups of 50–300, and a majority of more than 100 in the groups containing from 300 to 1,300 allusions. These types in which Jonson overwhelmingly dominates are allusions offering the highest praise, poems or long prose passages devoted wholly to him, commonplace books and anthologies quoting his works, references to his plays by name, business records of his performances, letters to him, and records of honors proposed or bestowed. The extent of the Jonson majorities in these classes suggests strongly the following general opinions among seventeenth-century writers: Jonson had no serious rival as the greatest English dramatist; Jonson's compositions were more suitable than Shakespeare's for the commonplace book of a gentleman; Jonson's individual plays were more widely known and admired than Shakespeare's; Jonson's pieces were far more suitable for presentation before a courtly audience than Shakespeare's; Jonson was not only much more widely honored in his lifetime than Shakespeare, but mementos of him were cherished, while those of Shakespeare were not.

In two classes of allusions the references are overwhelmingly greater to Shakespeare than to Jonson, namely, allusions to apocryphal plays and to individual characters. As we have noted, the first of these is not very significant, indicating only that there are about ten times as many plays in the Shakespearean apocrypha as in the Jonsonian—a fact sufficiently clear without recourse to allusions. The allusions in the second class are highly significant, however, especially when considered in conjunction with the number of references to Jonson as the greatest dramatist and to his individual plays. Though Jonson had the higher general reputation and though his plays were more widely known, Shakespeare's characters still made a much deeper impression than those of Jonson. Under the circumstances this wealth of allusion to Shakespeare's characters is much more impressive than a similar preference for Jonson's characters would have been, for writers are paying homage to Shakespeare's unequaled powers of characterization in spite of themselves. In this class of allusion only does Shakespeare's seventeenth-century general reputation approach his modern one.

In six classes of allusions Jonson has a clear majority, i.e., 70–80 per cent in groups under 50, 55–70 per cent in groups of 50–300. These classes are allusions naming Jonson or Shakespeare and two or three others not of the triumvirate as a standard of greatness; lists of literary men in which none is particularly distinguished from the others; literary or social references to performances of his plays or masques; criticism of individual plays; biographical records and anecdotes; and miscellaneous allusions. These majorities suggest, though not quite so emphatically as the others, that writers making lists of English poets generally thought of Jonson before Shakespeare; that performances of Jonson's plays and masques were more popular social topics than performances of Shakespeare's; that individual merits of Jonson's plays seemed a more deserving subject than the individual merits of Shakespeare's; that Jonson as a man was more widely cherished in records and anecdotes than Shakespeare; and that Jonson's name came more easily to mind for casual reference than Shakespeare's.

There are three classes in which the clear majority of the allusions is to Shakespeare: quotations for purposes of illustration; plagiarism from his works or burlesques of his lines; and references to his characters as acting roles. The first class is the most significant, because there are over 200 allusions in it, while the other two are so small that the discovery of 25 or 30 new allusions could change the situation completely. These majorities suggest that, in spite of Jonson's great reputation and the hundreds of copies of his works in anthologies and commonplace books, Shakespeare's single lines were recognized as more quotable than Jonson's. The same suggestion is made, though less clearly because of the small numbers involved, by the Shakespearean majority in the second class. The third class reiterates, somewhat faintly, the popularity of Shakespeare's characters already observed.

Finally, in four classes of allusions the numbers are so nearly equal that no clear preference is shown. These classes are allusions to Shakespeare and Jonson as members of the triumvirate, in which Shakespeare leads by 3; lists of literary men in which Shakespeare or Jonson is given especial distinction, in which Jonson leads by 5; biographical accounts, in which the numbers are even; and criticism of the dramatist's works in general, where Jonson leads by 2. In the last three classes the numbers are so small that the discovery of a dozen new allusions could completely change the proportions.

CHAPTER VI

THE COMPARATIVE POPULARITY OF
INDIVIDUAL PLAYS

THE PRECEDING CHAPTERS HAVE MADE IT REASONABLY clear that to writers of the seventeenth century Jonson was better known and more highly respected than Shakespeare. Not until the final decade were Shakespeare and his creations mentioned so often as Jonson and his, and even then they were not so frequently praised. Not only was Jonson mentioned oftener, quoted oftener,[1] and praised oftener, but his individual plays and poems were named more frequently than Shakespeare's, though his canon is smaller. Only in the references to his characters does Shakespeare have anything like the unquestioned acclaim which seems to us now so inevitably his.

A little study of the allusions to individual works and characters of the two great dramatists will throw still further light on their reputations in the seventeenth century. Did Shakespeare make a greater impression in the time with his comedies or with his tragedies? Was Jonson's reputation based entirely on his great comedies? Which particular plays were most frequently men-

---

[1] That is, Jonson's combined total in Classes 6, 7, and 8 is greater than Shakespeare's. Since, as we have noticed, Jonson is quoted in commonplace books and other manuscript sources many times as often as Shakespeare, and since such sources are the most inadequately explored of all allusion fields, we can be reasonably confident that in the future more new quotations from Jonson than from Shakespeare will be turned up.

tioned? Which characters? The answers to such questions as these are at least suggested by the accompanying summaries of allusions.

The first list shows the individual works of Shakespeare and Jonson ranked in the order of popularity in the seventeenth century as indicated by extant allusions. Plays and poems referred to less than 8 times have not been included in this list.[2]

The evidence of these collected allusions to individual works of Shakespeare and Jonson affords clear-cut proof that Jonson's plays were much the better known in the seventeenth century. Six of Jonson's plays, besides the masques and the poems, were more commonly referred to than anything of Shakespeare's; Jonson's best-known play was mentioned more than twice as often as Shakespeare's. Even this comparison is an understatement, for Jonson's most popular play was unadulterated Jonson, while a number of the allusions to *The Tempest* are to either the Dryden and Davenant version or the operatic version, and the most specific comments sometimes refer to elements in the play for which Shake-

---

[2] The plays and poems to which there are 7 allusions or less are, in order of popularity: *The Arraignment of Paris; Cromwell; Cymbeline; The Fall of Mortimer; King John,* Parts 1 and 2; *Coriolanus; The Merchant of Venice; The Birth of Merlin; Locrine; The Merry Devil of Edmonton; Mucedorus; The Puritan Widow; All's Well That Ends Well; Antony and Cleopatra; As You Like It; Grammar; Two Gentlemen of Verona; The Two Noble Kinsmen; The Case Is Altered; King John; Poems* (Shakespeare); *The Puritan; Richard Crookback; The Spanish Tragedy* Additions; *The Beggars' Bush* (attributed to Jonson); *The Chances* (attributed to Shakespeare); *Edward II; Edward III; Edward IV; Hieronimo* (attributed to Shakespeare); *Hoffman* (attributed to Shakespeare); *The Isle of Dogs; The Passionate Pilgrim; Thierry and Theodoret* (attributed to Jonson); *The Roman Actor* (attributed to Shakespeare); *A Trick To Catch the Old One* (attributed to Shakespeare).

When the number of allusions represented gets as small as for these plays, the order does not mean much; the discovery of a very few new allusions could change it completely.

ALLUSIONS TO INDIVIDUAL WORKS OF
SHAKESPEARE AND JONSON[3]

Masques[4]	112	Taming of the Shrew	15
Catiline	89	Much Ado about Nothing[9]	14
Volpone	73	Richard II	14
Alchemist	67	Winter's Tale	14
Silent Woman	62	Julius Caesar	13
Sejanus	59	Rape of Lucrece	12
Poems (Jonson)[5]	52	Measure for Measure	12
Bartholomew Fair	48	Richard III	12
Tempest[6]	40	King Lear	11
Othello	37	Love's Labour's Lost	11
Macbeth[6]	34	Sad Shepherd	11
Henry IV, 1 and 2[7]	30	Tale of a Tub	11
Poetaster	28	Timon of Athens	11
Every Man in His Humour	25	Troilus and Cressida[6]	11
Hamlet	25	Cynthia's Revels	10
Henry VI,[6] 1, 2, and 3[7]	24	Eastward Ho!	10
Pericles	24	Widow	10
Venus and Adonis	24	Discoveries	9
Henry VIII	23	Henry V	9
New Inn	23	Horace	9
Magnetic Lady	22	London Prodigal	9
Merry Wives of Windsor	22	Sir John Oldcastle	9
Comedy of Errors[8]	18	Twelfth Night	9
Devil Is an Ass	18	Yorkshire Tragedy	9
Midsummer-Night's Dream	18	Staple of News	8
Every Man Out of His Humour	15	Titus Andronicus	8
Romeo and Juliet	15		

[3] These allusion figures at once invite comparison with those given in *The Shakspere Allusion-Book*, II, 540. The first sixteen there are:

Hamlet	95	Richard III	36
Henry IV, 1 and 2	69	Richard II	35
Venus and Adonis	61	Midsummer-Night's Dream	35
Romeo and Juliet	61	Julius Caesar	35
Othello	56	Henry VI, 1, 2, and 3	32
Lucrece	41	Much Ado about Nothing	30
Tempest	40	Henry VIII	29
Macbeth	37	Pericles	28

Part of the difference between my figures and those in *The Shakspere Allusion-Book* is accounted for by the fact that Munro included sixteenth-century allusions, as I have not, and part by the hundreds of allusions brought forward since his collection; but most important is his counting of many allusions which have been re-

[Footnotes continued on following page]

speare was not responsible.[10] Though many of the allusions to *The Tempest* do not themselves contain statements showing definitely which version the writer had in mind, it is pretty clear that the revisions and not

---

jected here as parallel passages, proverbial expressions, publication data, or vague and uncertain statements. Most eloquent is the difference between his *Hamlet* figures and mine. Since *Hamlet* has long been our most familiar play, imaginary parallels to its lines and situations are most commonly reported.

[4] In a list like this it is awkward to have all Jonson's masques lumped together, but it is the most accurate reflection of the way in which men of the seventeenth century seem to have thought of them. Allusions generally do not distinguish them but say "as in Jonson's masques" or "the gipsy in Jonson's masque." Separate listings would eliminate a large number of the allusions and tend to conceal the place they had in references of the time.

[5] Like the masques, the poems are generally not particularized in allusions.

[6] In many instances it is impossible to tell whether Shakespeare's original or the Restoration recension is referred to; even when the revision is clearly intended, the allusion has been counted for Shakespeare's play.

[7] Since, in the majority of instances, it is impossible to tell which part is referred to, the fairest procedure is to count all together.

[8] I feel confident that this group of words was often used without thought of Shakespeare's play, just as it is today; but so long as I cannot prove that the expression is proverbial it seems fairest to accept all the allusions.

[9] "Much ado about nothing" seems to be used as a proverbial expression, just as "a comedy of errors" is, but I cannot prove that it antedates Shakespeare's play.

[10] A writer in the *Athenian Mercury* considers the question:

"*Suppose a Man and Woman were shut up in a room together, who had never seen nor heard of the difference of Sexes before, how d'ye think they'd behave themselves?—wou'd they—*

"ANSW.: We say .... that we *don't know what to say*. We are very unwilling to send the Ladies to *Daphnis* and *Chloe* for Information—that Book is too *waggish* in some places, and not *spiritual* enough for 'em: As for the *Tempest*, that don't come up to the Question, tho *Mirande* and *Hypolito* are pretty fair for't, who had never seen, tho' they had heard of *Man* and *Woman*" (*Athenian Mercury*, IV, No. 13 [Tuesday, November 10, 1691], 2, reported by John Munro, "More Shakspere Allusions," *Modern Philology*, XIII [January, 1916], 168).

In Durfey's *The Marriage-Hater Match'd* (1692), Darewell says (p. 50):

"I told ye she was a High Flyer too, that is, I have seen her upon a Machine in the *Tempest*.

"L. BRAIN: In the *Tempest*, why then I suppose I may seek her Fortune in the *Inchanted Island*."

Shakespeare's original are generally intended. The best evidence for this conclusion lies in the fact that 90 per cent of the seventeenth-century allusions to *The Tempest* occur in the period 1667–1700, i.e., after the first production of the Davenant-Dryden version;[11] and most of the allusions in the first two years of this period come from the pen of Samuel Pepys, who clearly alluded to the current stage version.

That *Catiline* was most familiar of all the plays of the two dramatists in the seventeenth century ought to surprise no student of the period. There are allusions to it in every decade of the century after its composition in 1611. Cotgrave quoted it nearly twice as often as any play of Shakespeare's.[12] Robert Hills wrote in his commendatory verses for Robert Baron's *Mirza* in 1647 (sig. A₄),

> Mean time, who'l number our best *Playes* aright
> First *CATALINE*, then let him *MIRZA* write,
> So mix your names: in the third place must be
> *SEIANUS*, or *the next* that comes from *thee*.

Baron himself says:

> . . . . not without the example of the matchless *Johnson*, who, in his *Catiline* (which miraculous *Poem* I propose as my pattern) makes *Sylla*'s Ghost perswade *Catiline* to do what *Hannibal* could not wish.—*Mirza* (1647), sig. M₁.

Edward Howard held a similar opinion in 1671:

> I do not find but the highest of our English Tragedies (as *Cataline*, *The Maids Tragedy*, *Rollo*, *The Cardinal and Traytor*) considerable enough to

---

[11] Arthur H. Nethercot, *Sir William D'avenant, Poet Laureate and Playwright-Manager* (1938), p. 399.

[12] Thirty-three times (see my "John Cotgrave's *English Treasury of Wit and Language* and the Elizabethan Drama," *Studies in Philology*, XL [April, 1943], 202). Such quotations without acknowledgment of source are not, of course, counted as allusions to the play, but to the dramatist only.

be rank'd with the best of these.—Preface, *The Womens Conquest* (1671), sig. A₃ᵛ.

There can be little doubt that not *Hamlet*, *Lear*, *Othello*, or *Macbeth*, but *Catiline* was the premier English tragedy in the minds of seventeenth-century writers.

Volpone's distinguished position as the ranking comedy, though it accords better with modern opinion than *Catiline*'s, is not quite so unchallenged. Pepys, indeed, had called it "a most excellent play, the best I think I ever saw," but Pepys was not niggardly with his superlatives; and other writers, though mentioning *Volpone* more frequently than other comedies, do not praise it so often as they do *Catiline*, *Sejanus*, *The Alchemist*, and *The Silent Woman*.

The Alchemist, in particular, receives more specific praise in the century than *Volpone* does. Shirley wrote a prologue for it when he was working for the Werburgh Street Theatre in Dublin, beginning

> The Alchemist, a play for strength of wit,
> And true art, made to shame what hath been writ
> In former ages; I except no worth
> Of what or Greek or Latins have brought forth;
> Is now to be presented to your ear,
> For which I wish each man were a Muse here,
> To know, and in his soul be fit to be
> Judge of this masterpiece of comedy.
> —*Poems* (1646), ed. GIFFORD, VI, 490–91

James Howell, in writing to Jonson of the poet's divine fury, says: "You were mad when you writ your *Fox*, and madder when you writ your *Alchymist*."[13] Robert Herrick in his epigram on Jonson speaks of the ignorance that came to the theater after Jonson's death:

[13] *Epistolae Ho-Elianae*, ed. Joseph Jacobs (1890), p. 267. The letter is dated June 27, 1629.

> and that monstrous sin
> Of deep and arrant ignorance came in:
> Such ignorance as theirs was who once hist
> At thy unequall'd play, the Alchemist:
> —*Hesperides* (1648), ed. ALFRED POLLARD (1891), p. 188

Edward Howard in a discussion of the methods of "learned *Johnson*" calls the play "that great work of his the Alchymist."[14] Robert Gale Noyes says: "Of all the comedies of Jonson *The Alchemist* had the most brilliant stage-history . . . . it was acted oftener than any other Jonsonian play."[15] Noyes is speaking of the entire period 1660–1776, but the popularity of *The Alchemist* was well developed before the beginning of the eighteenth century.

The reputation of *The Silent Woman* is sufficiently familiar from Dryden's *Examen* and the various comments of Pepys.[16] Both this play and *Bartholomew Fair* have a much higher proportion of their allusions after the Restoration than do the preceding three. In both cases the subject matter must have had a particular appeal for audiences under Charles II, Samuel Pepys in the case of *Bartholomew Fair* to the contrary notwithstanding.

The popularity of *The Tempest*, as already noted, is a somewhat dubious measure of Shakespeare's appeal. The *Othello* allusions are based on much more solidly Shakespearean material and are more evenly distributed through the century. Indeed, in the allusions up through

---

[14] *The Womens Conquest* (1671), Preface, sigs. b₂ᵛ–b₃.

[15] *Ben Jonson on the English Stage, 1660–1776* (1935), p. 103.

[16] See above, pp. 52–53.

1680, *Othello* is Shakespeare's most popular play.[17]
Samuel Sheppard ranked it with *Catiline* in 1651 in his
verses on Davenant's *Albovine:*

> *Shakespeares Othello, Johnsons Cataline,*
> Would lose their luster, were thy *Albovine*
> Placed betwixt them.
> —*Epigrams Theological, Philosophical, and*
> *Romantick* (1651), Book 4, Epigram 30

Thomas Rymer suggests its position in his *Tragedies of
the Last Age Considered* (1678):

> I provided me some of those *Master pieces* of Wit, so renown'd every-
> where, and so edifying to the *Stage:* I mean the choicest and most applaud-
> ed *English Tragedies* of this last age; as *Rollo; A King and no King;* the
> *Maids Tragedy* by *Beaumont* and *Fletcher: Othello,* and *Julius Cæsar,* by
> *Shakespear;* and *Cataline* by Worthy *Ben* [2d ed. (1692), pp. 1–2].

Though Rymer grew weary of the slaughter before he
came to his analysis of *Othello* in *The Tragedies of the
Last Age Considered,* he got around to it several years
later in *A Short View of Tragedy.*[18] His opening state-

---

[17] The number of allusions to the most popular plays in the first eight decades of
the century may have some general interest. They are as follows:

Catiline	67	Poetaster	14
Sejanus	47	Henry IV, 1 and 2	13
Volpone	47	Magnetic Lady	13
Alchemist	45	Merry Wives of Windsor	13
Silent Woman	41	Poems (Jonson)	13
Masques	31	Comedy of Errors	12
Bartholomew Fair	27	Every Man in His Humour	12
Othello	21	New Inn	12
Macbeth	20	Hamlet	11
Venus and Adonis	20	Every Man Out of His	
Tempest	17	Humour	8
Henry VIII	16	Romeo and Juliet	8
Pericles	15		

Except for the increase in popularity of *The Tempest* and the decline of *Venus and
Adonis,* the relative positions of the various plays is more like that for the century as
a whole than might have been expected. Particularly notable is the fact that in each
list the same six plays of Jonson outrank Shakespeare's most popular piece.

[18] (1693 [for 1692]), pp. 86–146. This long discussion of *Othello* with its reiteration
of the names of the characters gives Desdemona, Othello, Iago, Cassio, Roderigo,

ment (p. 86) again points to the popularity of the play: "From all the Tragedies acted on our English Stage, *Othello* is said to bear the Bell away." To Rymer, of course, this popularity is entirely undeserved; and he sneers his way through the play in the all too familiar fashion of the critic who relies on his dogma because he cannot trust his perceptions. In spite of his contempt, however, Rymer has testified to the popularity of *Othello* with sufficient positiveness to confirm the implications of the allusion count.

Macbeth and *Henry IV*, *Parts 1 and 2*, are both like *The Tempest* in that their position is not due solely to appreciation of Shakespeare's original play. The *Macbeth* allusions are mostly, it would appear, to Davenant's operatic version;[19] for less than 10 per cent of them occur before 1663, the presumed date of Davenant's revision. An examination of Pepys's comments on the play, which he saw nine times, suggests that his admiration was generally elicited by the contemporary additions rather than by Shakespeare's original. In the case of *Henry IV* the allusions are generally incidental to references to Falstaff, the most popular character of the century; it is seldom mentioned for itself alone. The fact that there are more than four times as many allusions to the fat knight as to the play is a further suggestion that *Henry IV* appeared to the seventeenth century as the tail to Falstaff's kite.

Ludovico, and Brabantio positions misleadingly high in the ranks of Shakespearean and Jonsonian characters. Rymer's discussion does not, however, unduly affect the position of the piece in the play-allusions list, for his long analysis is counted as only one allusion to *Othello*.

[19] See Nethercot, *op. cit.*, pp. 391-95.

The familiarity of *Poetaster* is largely a result of the
War of the Theaters and of the appreciation of Jonson's jibe in introducing the play with an armed prologue. Few allusions express any great admiration for
the play itself.

Every Man in His Humour was really more widely
appreciated and more frequently acted than *Poetaster*.
Pepys's comment on *Every Man in His Humour*—
"wherein is the greatest propriety of speech that ever I
read in my life" (February 9, 1666/67)—is not un-
characteristic.

The position of *Hamlet*, fifteenth in the list, however
incredible it may seem in the twentieth century, is not
unsupported by other evidence. When John Cotgrave
collected quotations from contemporary drama for his
English Treasury of Wit and Language (1655), he selected more passages from fourteen other plays than from
Hamlet.[20] And though those fourteen plays, except for
Catiline and *Sejanus*, were not the same as the fourteen
which outrank *Hamlet* here, they are all by dramatists
whom we now consider inferior to Shakespeare—Greville, Webster, Jonson, Chapman, Dekker, Tourneur,
Daniel, Suckling, and Marston.

The positions of both the *Henry VI* plays and *Pericles*
are probably higher than seventeenth-century opinion
of Shakespeare's works would really warrant. The rank
of *Henry VI* above its betters is due to the fact that the
allusions to three different plays are all of necessity
lumped together here, and to the further fact that certain of the allusions may well refer to John Crowne's
Henry VI plays. Though *Pericles* undoubtedly ranked

[20] See *Studies in Philology*, XL (April, 1943), 202.

higher in the seventeenth century than it does now, I think its position here is probably due to the intrusion, in spite of my efforts, of certain allusions which really refer to fictional or historic accounts of Pericles.

Venus and Adonis falls lower in the list than one with a knowledge of the poem's early popularity and the editions it went through would expect. If all allusions to Shakespeare before 1701 had been included, *Venus and Adonis* would undoubtedly rank higher. These figures —which exclude all allusions before 1601—show that the poem's vogue was largely a sixteenth-century one. Though I have not counted the number of quotations from the various plays and poems, I have noted in checking them that there are more quotations from *Venus and Adonis* than from several of the works which rank above it in the list.

The rest of the works on the list are not sufficiently prominent to warrant individual discussion, but a few of them merit a remark or two.

Henry VIII owes its rank chiefly to Restoration performances; all but 2 or 3 of the allusions before the Restoration occur because it happened to be the play in performance when the first Globe burned.

The place of *The Magnetic Lady* and *The New Inn* again gives pause to the modern reader. Even Jonson's "dotages" are referred to more often than *King Lear*, *Antony and Cleopatra*, *As You Like It*, *Twelfth Night*, and *The Merchant of Venice*.

Romeo and Juliet, like *Venus and Adonis*, would have ranked much higher had sixteenth-century allusions been included, and so would *Richard II* and *Richard III*.

Finally, the low estimation of Shakespeare's comedies

is too conspicuous to ignore. Only one of them—*The Tempest*—ranks any higher than twentieth, and that play, as we have seen, appears to owe its position more to Dryden and Davenant than to Shakespeare. Some of the comedies most popular in modern times—*As You Like It*, *The Merchant of Venice*, and *Twelfth Night*— seem scarcely known at all in the seventeenth century. The reason is certainly not any contempt for comedy. The high rank of *Volpone*, *The Alchemist*, *The Silent Woman*, and *Bartholomew Fair* and the great achievement of Restoration comedy are clear proof of general interest in the form. It is Shakespearean comedy, or perhaps more accurately Shakespearean romantic comedy, which is ignored.

CHAPTER VII

THE COMPARATIVE POPULARITY OF IN-
DIVIDUAL CHARACTERS

THE ALLUSIONS TO THE CHARACTERS OF SHAKESPEARE and Jonson present a very different reputation-picture from that of the plays and poems, as has already been demonstrated by the summaries of allusions in Classes 10, 11, and 11*a*.[1] The numbers of allusions to individual characters throw further light on particular differences between the reputations of Shakespeare and of Jonson in the seventeenth century. The list on page 120 shows the characters ranked in order of the number of allusions to each. Characters mentioned less than 5 times have not been included in the list.[2]

Falstaff was clearly most famous of all the characters of Shakespeare and Jonson in the seventeenth century. This fact ought to surprise no reader familiar with the literature of the time, but the overwhelming dominance of his position has perhaps not been so obvious. It might have been guessed from Rowe's statement in 1709—"*Falstaff* is allow'd by every body to be a Master-

---

[1] See above, pp. 81–87.

[2] The characters named 3 or 4 times are, in order of popularity: Asper, Bolingbroke–Henry IV, Bottom, Mosca, Adam Overdo, Portia (*Caesar*), Tucca, Ursula, Wolsey, Beatrice, Bobadil, Buckingham (*Henry VIII*), Carlo Buffone, Christopher Sly, Cicero (*Catiline*), Crites, Dauphine, Doll Tearsheet, Epicoene, Hector, Hugh Evans, Littlewit, Lodovico, Miranda, Mrs. Ford, Mrs. Otter, Mrs. Page, Pug, Richard II, Romeo, Shallow, Tribulation Wholesome, Ann Page, and Apemantus. The characters named only once or twice do not seem worth recording.

ALLUSIONS TO CHARACTERS

[3] In many allusions it is impossible to tell whether the character in *Henry IV*, *Part 1*, *Henry IV*, *Part 2*, or *The Merry Wives of Windsor* is intended. Even when the particular play is indicated, however, all allusions have been counted together.

[4] Since most allusions do not name the play, all allusions to Prince Hal or Henry V from any of the plays containing the character have been counted together.

[5] Allusions to Antony in *Julius Caesar* and *Antony and Cleopatra* have been counted together.

[6] Allusions to Bardolph have all been counted together, whether they refer to the character in *Henry IV*, *Part 1*, *Henry IV*, *Part 2*, *Henry V*, or *The Merry Wives of Windsor*.

[7] Allusions to Pistol in *Henry IV*, *Part 2*, *Henry V*, and *The Merry Wives of Windsor* have been counted together.

[8] Allusions to the Hostess or Mistress Quickly in *Henry IV*, *Part 1*, *Henry IV*, *Part 2*, *Henry V*, and *The Merry Wives of Windsor* have been counted together.

[9] Sir John is the only character in the list from an apocryphal play, *Sir John Oldcastle*.

piece";[10] but Rowe was something of a special pleader, and his remarks about other Shakespearean characters are not borne out by seventeenth-century allusions. The typical allusions to Falstaff, furthermore, are not the self-conscious praise of the type usually bestowed upon *Catiline*. They are, for the most part, passing references obviously intended to enlighten the reader by a comparison or to amuse him by reminding him of the escapades or characteristics of Shakespeare's fat knight.

> Our Keepers knew no hurt, unlesse 't had bin
> Drinking of Sack, honest *Iack Falstaffes* sinne.[11]

> D'ye run away, b' *instinct* like Sir *John Falstaffe*,
> And *stare*, and *huffe*, and *puff*, as if y' had been
> Mauld, by th' *unluckie Rogues* in *Kendall Green*.[12]

> My brave comradoes, Knights of [the] tatter'd Fleece,
> Like Falstafs Regiment, you have one shirt among you.[13]

"Well," says he, "if this will not do, I will say, as Sir J. Falstaffe did to the Prince, 'Tell your father, that if he do not like this let him kill the next Piercy himself.' "[14]

I cannot but observe, Mr. *Bayes*, this admirable way (like fat *Sir John Falstaffe*'s singular dexterity in sinking) that you have of answering whole Books and Discourses, how pithy and knotty soever, in a line or two, nay sometimes with a word.[15]

[10] Nicholas Rowe, *The Works of Mr. William Shakespear in Six Volumes* (1709), I, xvii.

[11] *The Cambridge Royallist Imprisoned*, July 31, 1643, sig. A₄ (cited by Hyder E. Rollins, "Shakespeare Allusions," *Notes and Queries: Twelfth Series*, X [1922], 224).

[12] "On Oxford Visitors, 1648," in Henry Bold, *Poems* (1664), p. 164 (cited by John Munro, "More Shakspere Allusions," *Modern Philology*, XIII [January, 1916], 150).

[13] Thomas Randolph, *Hey for Honesty, Down with Knavery* (1651), Act III, scene I, p. 22.

[14] Samuel Pepys, *Diary*, August 29, 1666.

[15] Andrew Marvel, *The Rehearsal Transprosd* (1672), p. 190.

Fat *Falstaffe* was never set harder by the Prince for a *Reason*, when he answer'd, that *if* Reasons *grew as thick as* Blackberries, *he wou'd not give one.*[16]

I can answer for no body's palat but my own: and cannot help saying with the fat Knight in Henry the Fourth If sack and sugar is a sin, the Lord have mercy on the wicked.[17]

Such characteristic allusions as these reveal an affectionate familiarity with Falstaff which is not generally found in the allusions to other characters. There is no hint that the author feels he is displaying the impeccability of his own literary taste or the soundness of his training in the classics—suggestions which are frequently to be found in the Jonson allusions. Even before the Civil War Falstaff had become a part of the literary heritage of the language, and his words and deeds could be expected to have a wide enough familiarity to assist any author who chose to call upon him.

The five characters next in the list after Falstaff were all less familiar in the century than the figures would indicate. In each case a large number of the allusions come from a single long discussion in which the character is mentioned again and again. Othello, Desdemona, Iago, and Cassio, as well as Brabantio (twenty-second), Roderigo (twenty-fifth), and the Doge of Venice (forty-seventh) owe their positions to Thomas Rymer's analysis of *Othello* in his *A Short View of Tragedy*.[18] Rymer praises neither the characters nor the play in this discussion but vigorously ridicules both. Similarly, in

[16] John Dryden, *The Vindication of the Duke of Guise* (1683), p. 48 (cited by Munro, *op. cit.*, p. 163).

[17] Anonymous, *A Collection of Miscellany Poems, Letters, etc.* (1699), p. 327, letter dated "June 2 92" (cited by G. Thorn-Drury, *Some Seventeenth Century Allusions to Shakespeare and His Works Not Hitherto Collected* [1920], p. 46).

[18] (1693 [for 1692]), pp. 86–146.

the following chapter Rymer ridicules *Julius Caesar*,[19] though not at such length, with frequent allusions to characters and situations in *Othello*. Though all the references to plays and characters of Shakespeare and Jonson in these two chapters are bona fide allusions, the normal counting of them tends to give undue weight to Rymer in the consideration of Shakespeare's characters. In the play figures, Rymer's discussions count as only one allusion to each play, which gives a fairer estimate. No Jonson character is mentioned more than once in the discussion of *Catiline*, but the enthusiasm with which Rymer belabors *Othello* and *Julius Caesar* leads him to bring in the characters again and again.

A somewhat more accurate picture of the familiarity of these characters in the seventeenth century might be presented, therefore, if Rymer's *A Short View of Tragedy* were not considered and all the allusions there to characters of Shakespeare and Jonson subtracted from the above totals. Such a modification gives the standings shown in the list on page 124.

The most notable change in the altered figures is the enhanced prominence of Falstaff, who now has nearly four times as many allusions as the next character. Moreover, second place instead of fourth is taken by Brutus, and third instead of seventh by Hamlet. Probably no modern critic would hold Brutus in such high regard; but the fact that he is the leading character in Shakespeare's most familiar Roman play was more significant in the seventeenth century than it is now. Perhaps the fact that Brutus bears some likeness to the protagonists of heroic tragedy was also of significance,

---

[19] Chap. viii, pp. 147–59.

for the largest proportion of the Brutus allusions comes from the last two decades of the century. Indeed, a larger proportion of the Brutus allusions comes from these last two decades than of the allusions for any

CHARACTER ALLUSIONS EXCLUSIVE OF RYMER'S *SHORT VIEW*

Falstaff	131	Witches (*Macbeth*)	9
Brutus	34	Bartholomew Cokes	8
Hamlet	27	Hotspur	8
Doll Common	21	Sir John Daw	8
Julius Caesar	19	Collegiate Ladies	7
Othello	19	Otter	7
Morose	18	Bardolph	6
Trinculo	17	Catiline	6
Sir Politic	16	Cethegus	6
Prince Hal	15	Ghost (*Hamlet*)	6
Face	13	Pistol	6
Iago	12	Polonius	6
Caliban	11	Quickly	6
Cassio	11	Richard III	6
Cassius	11	Sycorax	6
Desdemona	10	Ananias	5
Macbeth	10	Cob	5
Sir Amorous La-Foole	10	Crispinus	5
Subtle	10	Dauphine	5
Volpone	10	Henry VIII	5
Ophelia	9	John of Wrotham	5
Rabbi Zeal-of-the-Land Busy	9	Juliet	5
Sylla's Ghost	9	Stephano	5
Truewit	9		

other leading character except Trinculo.[20] The new position of Hamlet is surprising only in that his popularity still falls so far short of Falstaff's. Since only about one-fourth of the references come before the Restoration, one is inclined to see in the Hamlet allusions as much Betterton as Shakespeare.

[20] See below, p. 126.

The most frequently named character of Jonson was Doll Common, and she ranks only fourth or eighth, depending on whether the Rymer allusions are counted or not. The marked difference between the relative popularity of Shakespeare's and Jonson's plays and their characters is most significant. In the play allusions, six creations of Jonson's (excluding the masques and poems) were more familiar than any of Shakespeare's; in character allusions Jonson ranks no higher than fourth or eighth. Again the evidence of the power of Shakespeare's characterization in spite of critical disapproval of the form of his plays is strikingly illustrated.

Why should Doll Common be more familiar than Face or Subtle or Sejanus, Volpone, Morose, or Rabbi Zeal-of-the-Land Busy? Two possible answers are suggested by the general character of the allusions to Doll. A number of them refer to her violence in the play, and several others use her name as a generic term for a prostitute. There is some implication here that Doll was more noteworthy on the stage than in the library, and a further suggestion that her name may have been a familiar one for a wanton before Jonson used it. I have found no such use antedating *The Alchemist*, however.

Considering the number of allusions to Brutus, it is not surprising that Caesar should be frequently named too, especially since the two are often mentioned together. Trinculo, on the other hand, seems a very minor character to be so familiar. Most of the references to him probably do not refer to the character Shakespeare created. A very few of them may refer to Trincalo in *Albumazar*. The popularity of this figure is indicated by Pepys's statement in his diary, February 22, 1667/68:

To the Duke's playhouse, and there saw "Albumazar," an old play, this second time of acting. It is said to have been the ground of B. Jonson's "Alchymist;" but, saving the ridiculousnesse of Angell's part, which is called Trinkilo, I do not see anything extraordinary in it, but was indeed weary of it before it was done. The King here, and, indeed all of us, pretty merry at the mimique tricks of Trinkilo.

Obviously, Tomkis' character was popularly discussed in the 1660's after the revival of *Albumazar;* and, though every effort has been made here to separate allusions to

ALLUSIONS TO CHARACTERS, 1601–80

Falstaff	93	Bartholomew Cokes	5
Doll Common	13	Cethegus	5
Sir Politic	13	Collegiate Ladies	5
Morose	12	Desdemona	5
Hamlet	11	Juliet	5
Subtle	9	Macbeth	5
Face	8	Quickly-Hostess	5
Sylla's Ghost	8	Rabbi Zeal-of-the-Land Busy	5
Othello	7	Richard III	5
Prince Hal	7	Sir John Daw	5
Bardolph	6	Truewit	5
Brutus	6	Volpone	5
Sir Amorous La-Foole	6		

the *Tempest* Trinculo from those to the *Albumazar* Trincalo, a few passages might refer equally well to either, and some errors may have been made.

Even without the *Albumazar* confusion, the Trinculo of *The Tempest* most often referred to is probably Dryden and Davenant's elaborated character rather than Shakespeare's original. Again, the fact that about 90 per cent of the allusions occur after the Dryden-Davenant revision is suggestive. As in the case of the play allusions, it is illuminating to note how the allusions to characters are distributed when the last two decades of the century are excluded.

The figures for the first eight decades show not only that Trinculo had no particular vogue before the eighties but that, except for Falstaff, Jonson's major characters were much more popular than Shakespeare's before 1681, that is, there are 62 allusions to the ten Shakespearean characters in the list and 104 allusions to the fourteen Jonsonian characters.[21] Again the evidence points to the fact that Shakespeare's reputation was largely a development of the last two decades of the century, and again the overwhelming popularity of Falstaff as Shakespeare's greatest creation is demonstrated.

To return to the list of all character allusions in the century, one is a bit puzzled at first glance by the vogue of Sir Politic Would-Be. The explanation is probably similar to that for Doll Common: the name came to be used as a generic one for pretenders to political knowledge.[22] As in the case of Doll Common, the aptness of the name may have been as influential as familiarity with the acting role.

The allusions to Prince Hal and those to Cassius are appendages to the reputations of Falstaff and Brutus. Most of the references to Prince Hal are found in Falstaff allusions; Hal is mentioned merely as the person Falstaff addressed or as his companion or the person whose questions elicited a famous reply. Cassius, similarly, is generally named in the Brutus allusions.

[21] These figures exclude all characters mentioned less than 5 times. When the allusions to these less popular characters are included, Jonson's characters are still more popular than Shakespeare's, though the ratio changes to about 22 to 17. These figures can be checked by adding the figures for the first eight decades in Classes 11 and 11a and subtracting the 93 Falstaff allusions from Shakespeare's total.

[22] See Vol. II, pp. 157, 184, and 229.

Of the other characters, only a few need comment or explanation. The Caliban allusions, like those to Trinculo, probably in most instances refer to the character in one of the revisions of *The Tempest* rather than in Shakespeare's original. I have found no references to the character before the Restoration. The same dictum applies to the Witches in *Macbeth* and to Sycorax and Stephano. The small number of allusions to characters from *Catiline* contrasts sharply with the popularity of the play.

Examining the list as a whole, one is at once struck with the obscurity of Shakespeare's heroines as compared with their vogue in the nineteenth and twentieth centuries. Only Desdemona and Ophelia seem to have made any impression worth mentioning. Lady Macbeth and Cleopatra, Beatrice, Portia, Rosalind, Miranda, Viola, Perdita, Imogen, and Cordelia are mentioned so seldom as to seem unknown. Clearly, the romantic comedies had very little appeal in the seventeenth century; and the same can be said with almost equal assurance of the romances, for the appeal of *The Tempest*—the only one with many allusions—lay in Dryden and Davenant's Trinculo and Caliban and their elaborate show, not in Shakespeare's play. The innocent heroine as Shakespeare conceived her had no charms for Caroline and Restoration audiences.

The ignoring of Lady Macbeth and Cleopatra, however, is not to be explained by their innocence. *Macbeth* in the version to which most references appear to be made had reduced the role of Lady Macbeth, while *Antony and Cleopatra* seems to have been seldom produced after the closing of the theaters, perhaps because it presented too many staging difficulties in the Restoration theater. Whatever the reasons for the situation, it is clear that the popularity of Shakespeare's characters in the seventeenth century is not due to the appeal of his heroines. They did not charm the writers of the seventeenth century as they have so many of the nineteenth and twentieth.

While Shakespeare received more recognition for his creation of character than for anything else, the characters which won him great acclaim were, first, Falstaff and then, far behind, the tragic heroes. There are more allusions to Falstaff than to Brutus, Hamlet, Othello, and Julius Caesar together, if we exclude, as we may reasonably do, the allusions in *A Short View of Tragedy*. Perhaps it is not surprising that the heroes of the romantic comedies—Orlando, Claudio, Bassanio, Antonio —are almost never mentioned, since modern readers find it difficult to believe that Shakespeare himself was very enthusiastic about them. More curious is the fact that men like Jacques, Touchstone, Benedick, Feste, and the Fool in *King Lear* seem no more familiar in the seventeenth century than the young lovers.

One cannot conclude, however, that only the astonishing vogue of Falstaff makes Shakespeare's seventeenth-century reputation as a creator of character greater than Jonson's. Even without the Falstaff allusions and even eliminating the characters generally mentioned with Falstaff—Prince Hal, Hotspur, Bardolph, Pistol, Mistress Quickly—the passages referring to Shakespeare's characters still outnumber those referring to Jonson's, 5 to 3. Clearly, the seventeenth-century writers thought that Shakespeare's one unquestioned superiority to Jonson was his characterization— and that his masterpiece was Falstaff.

CHAPTER VIII

CONCLUSIONS

A<small>FTER SUCH A TEDIOUS ANALYSIS OF THOUSANDS OF</small> allusions, what are we justified in concluding about the reputation which Shakespeare enjoyed in the seventeenth century? The question is not a fresh one, for various respected critics and scholars have declared themselves on the subject, often with notably slight reservations. Augustus Ralli said:

> The general average estimate of the century [1598–1694], however, was that Shakespeare was England's greatest, because most universal, poet—perhaps the world's greatest poet, because in drama he rivalled, if not surpassed, the Greek tragedians and the Latin comedians, and his stream of narrative verse flowed as smoothly as Ovid's. He is admitted to have excelled in "nature"—a word we should now replace by "realism": his readers or audience ascribing the tremendous impression on their minds from characters such as Hamlet, Lear, Macbeth to Shakespeare's literal rendering of external fact.[1]

Charles Knight asserted:

> Of the popularity of Shakspere in his own day the external evidence, such as it is, is more decisive than the testimony of any contemporary writer. He was at one and the same time the favourite of the people and of the Court.[2]

George Lyman Kittredge declared:

> In his own day, Shakspere was one of the best-known figures in England. He was held in high esteem, both as a man and as a poet, while in his capacity of dramatic author he was not only immensely popular, but was rated at something like his true value by most persons of taste and judgment.[3]

[1] *A History of Shakespearian Criticism* (2 vols.; Oxford, 1932), I, 10.

[2] *The Pictorial Edition of the Works of Shakspere* (1839–43), Suppl. Vol.: *A History of Opinion on the Writings of Shakspere*, p. 332.

[3] *Shakspere: An Address Delivered on April 23, 1916, in Sanders Theatre at the Request of the President and Fellows of Harvard College* (1916), p. 24.

These declarations on Shakespeare's reputation in his own time have been made by distinguished students of Shakespeare, men widely read in the literature of the seventeenth century. The assertions are evidently based on the tributes by well-known writers like Meres, Jonson, Harvey, Heminges, Condell, Milton, Hales, Benson, Digges, Margaret Cavendish, and Dryden. Yet the basis of these reputation estimates is obviously not broad enough; their authors have not considered the bulk of the statements about Shakespeare and his work in the seventeenth century, nor have they observed the precaution of comparing Shakespeare's reputation with the reputation of a contemporary dramatist of distinction like Jonson. The foregoing pages have demonstrated just how erroneous these three assertions are. Ralli's use of the comparisons with Greek and Latin drama and with Ovid is revealing, for such comparisons, though frequently used by the critics mentioned, are rare in the body of Shakespeare allusions taken as a whole. His statement about Shakespeare's rank as England's greatest dramatist is flatly contradicted by the allusion totals in Class I. Even more misleading is his statement about the effect of the characters Hamlet, Lear, and Macbeth. These are modern, not seventeenth-century, favorites; in their own century their rank among the popular characters of Shakespeare and Jonson was seventh, eighty-seventh,[4] and seventeenth, respectively.

The statements by Knight and Kittredge are less specific than Ralli's, but the contention that Shake-

[4] Lear's rank cannot be given exactly, for twenty other characters of Shakespeare and Jonson are mentioned the same number of times as he is. Specifically, he ranks between eighty-sixth and one hundred and seventh.

speare was at "the same time the favourite of the people and the Court" is completely overthrown by the evidence of the allusions. Kittredge's "immensely popular" must at least be reduced to "second most popular," while Shakespeare's "true value" is scarcely indicated by the allusions in Classes 1, 2, 10, 12, and 15 or by the rank of his individual plays or even his individual characters.

So far as mere popularity is concerned, Jonson was evidently more popular with writers in the century than Shakespeare; for, when all allusions are judged by the same standard, 1,839 passages alluding to Jonson have been recorded, as compared to 1,430 to Shakespeare; and we can be sure that there are many more still unnoted allusions to Jonson than to Shakespeare. The many erroneous assertions that Shakespeare was the most popular dramatist of the century are derived from a reading confined to only the better-known critical passages or from a consideration of the indiscriminately swollen *Shakspere Allusion-Book* and the incomplete *Jonson Allusion-Book*.

This greater popularity of Jonson is not simply a matter of the grand totals of all allusions in the century. When the allusions are distributed chronologically, we find that he is referred to more frequently than Shakespeare in every decade of the century except the last. In the third and fourth decades there are twice as many allusions to Jonson as to Shakespeare; in the sixth and eighth decades Jonson's majority is slight; in the last decade Shakespeare's majority is only 7 in nearly 500. Various factors affecting these totals have been noted, but none of them alters the conclusion that steadily throughout the century until the last decade Jonson was more often referred to than Shakespeare.

But a dramatist's reputation is not to be judged by the numbers of references to him alone: some allusions are much more significant than others. Accordingly, the seventeenth-century allusions to Jonson and Shakespeare have been classified into twenty-two types and considered for the additional light they throw on the esteem in which the two men were held. Since many of the allusions contain several different types of statements, they are counted in more than one class, sometimes in as many as six or eight different classes. Therefore, the total number of allusions in the various classes greatly exceeds the 1,430 passages referring to Shakespeare plus the 1,839 passages referring to Jonson.

Perhaps the most significant class is the first one, made up of allusions in which the name of the dramatist is used alone as a standard of greatness. There are nearly three times as many such allusions to Jonson as to Shakespeare, more in every decade of the century—in the fourth, fifth, and sixth decades more than six times as many. A second class of allusions is made up of complete poems or long passages devoted to the poet. There are between three and four times as many such allusions to Jonson as to Shakespeare, more than four times as many in the first five decades of the century. Only in the third, ninth, and tenth decades are such allusions to Shakespeare more numerous, and in each of these three periods the numbers are small.

These two classes of allusions, because of their direct statement of popular esteem, are among the most revealing of all evidence concerning Shakespeare's reputation in the seventeenth century. The evidence is emphatic that only in the third, ninth, and tenth decades of the century did Shakespeare seriously rival Jonson's reputation as the great dramatist of England; and even in those three exceptional decades the combined total of allusions elevating Jonson is greater than the combined total of such allusions to Shakespeare.

There are four classes of allusions which consist of lists of English writers named in seventeenth-century histories, criticisms, or the like. Jonson is named in 322 such lists, Shakespeare in 271. Most of these inventories do not particularly distinguish the poets listed, but Jonson's name quite evidently occurred more frequently to such writers than Shakespeare's. Thus Jonson was the most widely remembered as well as the most frequently praised.

The next three classes of allusions are made up of quotations from the two poets, acknowledged and unacknowledged. Here the figures are less reliable than in the other classes because Shakespearean quotations are so much more widely recognized and reported than Jonsonian ones. Even so, 442 Jonsonian quotations in the works of seventeenth-century writers have been reported, 407 Shakespearean ones. It should be noted, however, that Jonson's lead is greatest in quotations simply assembled for their own sakes, particularly in commonplace books. Shakespeare leads in quotations used in context for their aptness or to bring to bear the weight of authority, especially in the last decade of the century. Evidently, at least by the end of the century, Shakespeare's unsurpassed ability to phrase effectively the popular truth was recognized. Jonson, as witness the commonplace books, throughout the century made the greatest appeal to the university student and the dilettante.

Allusions of Class 10 show that Jonson's plays are mentioned 767 times in the century to Shakespeare's 567—this in spite of the fact that there are about twice as many plays in the Shakespeare canon as in the Jonson. Not only was Jonson generally more admired and more familiar than Shakespeare, but Jonson's plays individually were more frequently discussed than Shakespeare's.

Only in the two classes of allusions referring to characters does Shakespeare's reputation approach the dominance which has been often asserted for him. His characters as literary creations or acting roles are referred to 733 times to Jonson's 329—a dominance all the more significant when compared to the relative number of allusions to the plays. Though the writers of the seventeenth century as a whole did not appreciate Shakespeare's unequaled genius, they evidently did see that he was the greatest creator of character among English dramatists.

Two classes of allusions are concerned with records of performances of the plays and masques of the two playwrights; nearly twice as many references to Jonson's productions were noted as compared to Shakespeare's. These allusions do not necessarily indicate that Jonson was performed more than Shakespeare in the century, but only that there was more discussion by literate persons of Jonsonian performances.

Allusions of Classes 14 and 15 are biographical but nonetheless significant evidence of reputation. Seventeen letters or copies of letters to Jonson in the seventeenth century have been thought significant and preserved; none of Shakespeare's has been so cherished. Similarly, there are 21 records of public honors conferred on Jonson or proposed for him; none for Shakespeare. These two groups of allusions, though small and significant chiefly for the first part of the century, seem to me eloquent of the great esteem which the century had for Jonson and of its comparative neglect of Shakespeare. Jonson was publicly and formally honored in his lifetime, and his relics were cherished after his death; Shakespeare enjoyed neither distinction.

Personal anecdotes and records of the two men make up Class 17, in which the Jonson allusions outnumber the Shakespeare ones about 3 to 2. But the evidence of Jonson's predominant reputation is greater than the figures suggest, for five-sevenths of the Shakespeare allusions of this class are business and legal records which would have been preserved for Shakespeare the man of property had he never written a line. The Jonson allusions are mostly personal anecdotes bearing witness to the impression made by the man's genius and his personality.

Two classes of allusions are composed of critical passages about the poets' work in general or about particular examples. Fifty-five such passages concern Shakespeare; 69 concern Jonson. Though the Jonson majority here is clear, it is misleadingly small. The reason is that such critical passages are not characteristic of the first half of the century when Jonson's dominance was greatest; before 1650 Jonson leads 15 to 8; after, only 54 to 47. Thus more critical attention was devoted in the century to Jonson than to Shakespeare, even though most such criticism was written after Shakespeare's reputation had begun to grow faster than Jonson's.

Finally, the miscellaneous passages alluding to the dramatists only incidentally and in none of the foregoing ways number 82 to Shakespeare and 138 to Jonson. Here again, though the writers show no particular interest in or knowledge of the two dramatists, the same preference for Jonson appears.

The totals in these various classes of allusions have indicated the general aspects of the two reputations fairly clearly, but further analysis was necessary to display the standing in the century of particular works and characters. Of the individual plays, the most frequently mentioned are all by Jonson—*Catiline*, *Volpone*, *The Alchemist*, *The Silent Woman*, *Sejanus*, and *Bartholomew Fair*. Each of these plays has more allusions in the century than any product of Shakespeare's pen. When ranked with Jonson's plays according to the number of seventeenth-century allusions, the modern favorites in the Shakespeare canon do not show up well. *Hamlet* is fifteenth, *Lear* thirty-sixth, *Othello* tenth, *Macbeth* eleventh, *As You Like It* sixty-eighth, *Twelfth Night* fiftieth, *The Merchant of Venice* sixtieth. Shakespeare's most frequently mentioned title is *The Tempest*, which ranks ninth, but an examination of the allusions shows that more than half of them probably refer to the Davenant-Dryden revision and not to Shakespeare's original. Next most popular are *Othello*, tenth; *Macbeth*, eleventh; and *Henry IV*, twelfth. The other histories and the comedies, particularly the romantic comedies, appear far down on the list.

Only in references to characters does Shakespeare hold a place anything like that which modern critics think rightfully his. Here the position of the two dramatists is the reverse of that in the play allusions. The seven most popular characters are Shakespeare's; and, though the characters from *Othello* are given an undue prominence by the elaborate discussion of the play in Rymer's *Short View of Tragedy*, even when the allusions from this analysis are omitted, five of the six most commonly mentioned characters are still Shakespeare's— Falstaff, Brutus, Hamlet, Julius Caesar, and Othello. Far and away the most popular is Falstaff, by all odds the most frequently mentioned play character of the century. He is mentioned three times as often as Brutus, five times as often as Hamlet, thirteen times as often as Macbeth, and six times as often as Jonson's most popular character, Doll Common. No other creation of Shakespeare's of any kind so captured the imaginations of seventeenth-century writers.

Altogether, the seventeenth-century allusions to Shakespeare and to Jonson when sifted and classified by the same standards give a reasonably clear picture of the comparative reputations of the two great dramatists between 1601 and 1700. Jonson's general popularity among writers was the greater from the beginning of the century to 1690; Shakespeare's reputation was growing more rapidly than Jonson's in the last two decades. Throughout the century Jonson was unchallenged in most critical writing as the greatest English dramatist, his popularity in critical writings being greater than his over-all popularity. This unchallenged rank is confirmed by the records of formal honors offered Jonson and the preservation of his relics—phenomena wholly absent in the records of Shakespeare. By and large, Jonson was quoted more often than Shakespeare, especially in gentlemen's commonplace books. Jonson's individual works were more widely known and praised than Shakespeare's, especially *Catiline*, *Volpone*, *The Alchemist*, *The Silent Woman*, and *Sejanus*. Performances of Jonson's plays and masques were discussed by writing people nearly twice as often as Shakespeare's. Shakespeare's greatest achievement was evidently thought to be his characters, and this aspect of his reputation alone clearly overshadowed Jonson's. Falstaff had no rival; but Brutus, Hamlet, and Othello also appear to have been more widely known than any character of Jonson's.

All these comparisons, we must bear in mind, lead to an underestimation of Jonson's seventeenth-century reputation. The same standards have been applied here to the allusions to both poets, but in the search for allusions and records over nearly three centuries, the man-hours devoted to Shakespeare have exceeded by many times those devoted to Jonson. Hence, far more still unnoted Jonson allusions than Shakespeare allusions can be expected in the future, still further enhancing Jonson's reputation.

Clearly, Jonson, and not Shakespeare, was the dramatist of the seventeenth century. Only the modern enthusiasm for Shakespeare and the consequent overemphasis upon such seventeenth-century passages praising his works as have been frequently reprinted have blinded literary students to the obvious fact. Jonson himself could see that Shakespeare's plays are such "as neither man nor Muse can praise too much," that "he was not of an age, but for all time"; yet most of Jonson's contemporaries had not so much understanding. Jonson, whose plays best exemplified the accepted critical dogma of the time and who most vigorously preached the dogma, could perceive the genius of the artist who defied the rules. But for lesser writers the "learned Jonson" was the man.

INDEX

Actors, 51, 52, 86, 89, 98, 124

Adams, J. Q., 17 (n. 1)

Allen, Don Cameron, 17 (n. 1); "A Jonson Allusion," 36 (nn. 32 and 33)

Allot, Robert, *England's Parnassus*, 23

Allusions: classification of, 62–63; dating, 14–15; types of: acting roles, 86–87, apocryphal play, 80–81, biographical accounts, 94–95, casual references, 98–99, character references, 84–87, criticism, 99–103, "great triumvirate," 67–68, groups not triumvirate, 69–73, letters to Shakespeare or Jonson, 92–93, performances of plays or masques, 87–92, personal anecdotes or records, 96–98, poem to Shakespeare or Jonson, 65–67, quotations, 73–80, records of honors, 93–94, standard of greatness, 63–64, summaries, 103–6, works mentioned by name, 82–84

Anonymous: *Edward II*, 108 (n. 2); *Edward III*, 108 (n. 2); *Edward IV*, 108 (n. 2); *Jonsonus Virbius*, 11 (n. 7), 44, 45, 65, 66, 67; *The London Prodigal*, 109; *The Merry Devil of Edmonton*, 108 (n. 2); *Mucedorus*, 108 (n. 2); *The New Academy of Compliments*, 55 (n. 13); *The Puritan*, 108 (n. 2); *The Puritan Widow*, 108 (n. 2); *The Return from Parnassus*, 25; *Richard Crookback*, 108 (n. 2); *The True Chronicle Historie of the Whole Life and Death of Thomas Lord Cromwell*, 25; *The Unfortunate Usurper*, 78 and n. 12; *The Yorkshire Tragedy*, 25 (n. 12), 109

Apocryphal plays, 11

Archer, Edward, 81

Athenian Mercury, 110 (n. 10)

Aubrey, John, *Brief Lives*, 56, 57, 58, 60, 95

Babcock, R. W., *The Genesis of Shakespeare Idolatry, 1766–1799*, 4 (n. 5)

Baron, Robert, 45; *Mirza*, 111

Bartlett, John, *Familiar Quotations*, 20 (n. 3), 75 (n. 10)

Baskervill, C. R., 17 (n. 1)

Basse, William, 69

Bates, E. F., 17 (n. 1)

Bayne, Thomas, 17 (n. 1)

Beaumont, Francis, 69

Beaumont and Fletcher, 7 (n. 1), 14 (n. 10), 45, 67–68, 70 and n. 6, 71; *The Beggar's Bush*, 108 (n. 2); *Chances*, 108 (n. 2); Folio 1647, 45; *A King and No King*, 114; *The Knight of the Burning Pestle*, 78; *The Maid's Tragedy*, 111, 114; *Rollo or The Bloody Brother*, 111, 114; *The Scornful Lady*, 33; *The Two Noble Kinsmen*, 108 (n. 2); *The Widow*, 81, 109

Behn, Aphra, *The City Heiress*, 74

Bensly, Edward, 17 (n. 1), 36 (nn. 32 and 33)

Benson, John, 131

Bentley, G. E., 17 (n. 1); *The Jacobean and Caroline Stage*, v, 88, 90; "John Cotgrave's *English Treasury of Wit and Language* and the Elizabethan Drama," 47 (n. 9), 111 (n. 12), 116 (n. 20); "Seventeenth-Century Allusions to Ben Jonson," 34 (n. 26)

Betterton, Thomas, 51, 52, 124

Bible, King James translation, 9

"Bibliothecary," 17 (n. 1)

Binz, G., 17 (n. 1)

Birch, Thomas, 17 (n. 1)

Blackfriars, 42

Bodenham, John, *Belvedere*, 23

Bodleian, 96

Bold, Henry, *Poems*, 121 and n. 12

Bolton's Royal Academy, 94

Bradley, A. C., 17 (n. 1)

SHAKESPEARE *and* JONSON

VOLUME II

Allusions

PART 1

NEW SHAKESPEARE ALLUSIONS

[SIR GEORGE BUC?], *ca.* 1619 OR 1620

The Tradgedy of Ham . . . .

[The title appears in a list of plays on p. 197ᵛ of some waste paper from the Revels Office. It has been plausibly suggested that the plays of the list were being considered for court performance. Frank Marcham, *The King's Office of the Revels, 1610–1622* (1925), p. 11. See also E. K. Chambers, *Review of English Studies*, I, 484.]

[SIR GEORGE BUC?], *ca.* 1619 OR 1620

The Winters Tale
The 2. Noble Kinesmen

[The titles appear in another list on another scrap of waste paper (p. 70ᵛ) from the Revels Office, probably dating about 1619 or 1620. See above. Marcham, *The King's Office of the Revels*, p. 13, and Chambers, *loc. cit.*]

[SIR GEORGE BUC?], *ca.* 1619 OR 1620

nd part of Falstaff
laid yᵉⁱˢ 7. yeres

[The title appears in still another list of plays on another scrap of waste paper (p. 211ᵛ) from the Revels Office, probably dating about 1619 or 1620. See above. Sir Edmund Chambers conjectures that the mutilated entry originally read,

"Second part of Falstaff
not plaid yᵉⁱˢ 7. yeres."

a particularly tempting emendation, since the last known court performance of *Henry IV, Part 2* occurred about seven years before, when both *Sir John ffalstaffe* and *The Hotspur* were presented in the season of 1612–13. See Marcham, *The King's Office of the Revels*, p. 33, and E. K. Chambers, *The Elizabethan Stage*, IV, 180, and *Review of English Studies*, I, 481, 482, and 484.]

PLAYERS' BILL, 1630

Playes for the Kinge this present
yeare of oʳ Lord God. 1630.

1

At   . . . .

[H]ampton Court   The 17 of October.   Midsomers Night's Dreame

. . . .

[*The Jacobean and Caroline Stage*, I, 27, from MS 2068.8, Folger Shakespeare Library.]

THOMAS RANDOLPH, 1651

Hig. My brave comradoes, Knights of tatter'd Fleece,
Like Falstafs Regiment, you have one shirt among you.
Well seen in plundring money for the Alehouse.
Such is the fruit of our Domestick broiles,
We are return'd to ancient Poverty
Yet (seeing we are lowsie) let us shew our breeding.
Come, though we shrug, yet lets not leave our calling:
Leiutenants Rampant, bravely all train'd up
At the well skil'd Artillery of *Bridewell;*
March on brave souldiers, you that neer turn'd back
To any terrour but the Beadles whip.

[*Hey for Honesty, Down with Knavery* (1651), III, 1, p. 22.]

JOHN COTGRAVE, 1655

[On the engraved title-page of Cotgrave's *Wits Interpreter* (1655) are ten small portraits of literary figures, one of which is labeled "Shakespeare."]

JOHN COTGRAVE, 1655

Although Authority be a stubborn beast,
Yet he is oft led by the Nose with Gold.

[*The English Treasury of Wit and Language* (1655), p. 20, from the section entitled "Of Authority." The lines are from *The Winter's Tale*, IV, 4, 830–32.]

JOHN COTGRAVE, 1655

There is a History in all mens lives;
Figuring the nature of the times deceas'd,
Which well observ'd, a man may prophesie
With a neer aim, of the main chance of things.
As yet not come to life, which in their seeds
And weak beginnings, lie intreasured.

[*Ibid.*, pp. 127–28, from the section entitled "Of History." The lines are from *Henry IV, Part 2*, III, 1, 80–85.]

John Cotgrave, 1655

Our remedies oft in our selves doe lie,
Which we ascribe to heaven; the fated skie
Gives us free scope, onely doth backward pull
Our slow designes, when we our selves are dull.

[*Ibid.*, p. 146, from the section entitled "Of Industry, Indeavour." The lines are taken from *All's Well That Ends Well*, I, 1, 231–34.]

John Cotgrave, 1655

Impossible be strange attempts to those
That weigh their paines in sence, and do suppose
Who hath been cannot be; who ever strove
To shew her merit, that did misse her love.

[*Ibid.*, p. 146, from the section entitled "Of Industry, Indeavour." The lines are taken from *All's Well That Ends Well*, I, 1, 239–42.]

John Cotgrave, 1655

Ignominy in ransome, and free pardon,
Are of two houses, lawfull mercy is
Nothing of kin to foul redemption.

[*Ibid.*, p. 193, from the section entitled "Of Mercy." The lines are taken from *Measure for Measure*, II, 4, 111–13.]

John Cotgrave, 1655

The art of our necessities is strange,
And can make vile things precious.

[*Ibid.*, p. 202, from the section entitled "Of Necessity." The lines are taken from *King Lear*, III, 2, 71–72.]

[John Phillips], 1656

.... and be it said of thee,
Shakespeare, thou hadst a smooth & comick vain,
Fitting the sock, and in thy naturall brain
As strange conception, and as clear a rage
As any one that traffiqu'd with the stage.

[*Sportive Wit*, Part II, p. 70.]

Joshua Poole, 1657

That hang upon the dusky cheekes of night
As a rich jewel in an Æthiops eare.

[*The English Parnassus: or, A Helpe to English Poesie* (1657), p. 500, in the section entitled "Stars." From *Romeo and Juliet*, I, 5, 47–48.]

Joshua Poole, 1657

The floore of heaven
Is thick inlaid with pattens of rich gold.

[*Ibid.*, p. 501. From *The Merchant of Venice*, V, 1, 58–59.]

Joshua Poole, 1657

The wounded steeds
Fret fetlock deepe in gore, and with wild rage,
Yerk out their armed heeles at their dead masters,
Killing them twice, and tread a quagmire made
Of mangled brains.

[*Ibid.*, p. 547, from the section entitled "War." From *Henry V*, IV, 7.]

Joshua Poole, 1657

Thrice the brinded cat hath mew'd,
Twice and once the hedge pigge whin'd,
Harpier cries, 'tis time, 'tis time.
Round about the cauldron goe,
In the poisoned intralls throw.

. . . .

Coole it with a baboones blood,
Then our charme is firme, and good.

[*Ibid.*, pp. 560–61, from the section entitled "Witch." From *Macbeth*, IV, 1, 1–35.]

Joshua Poole, 1657

V. *Dubartas. Trophies, Witch of Endor.*
Ovids Metam. lib. 7. Amorum 1. Eleg. 5.
Horace. Epod. 5. Virgil Eclog, 8.
Theocritus Pharmaceutria,

Skakespears Macbeth.
Ben. Johnsons mask out of the house of Fame.
Lucan. Lib. 6.

[*Ibid.*, pp. 561–62, from the section entitled "Witch."]

ANONYMOUS, 1662

[The engraved frontispiece of Kirkman's *The Wits, or, Sport upon Sport* (1662) represents a stage upon which appear seven famous characters, all but one of them from the drolls printed in the volume. Two of the characters in the foreground are labeled "Sᵣ: I. Falstafe" and "Hostes."]

ANONYMOUS, 1674

12 Jack Falstaff.

["Observations on January," *Poor Robin, 1674. An Almanack.* Under the heading "Observations" in the almanac there are lists of birthdays of various "sinners," mostly legendary and fictitious, but including many real persons as well.]

ANONYMOUS, 1674

5 Mer. wife of Wi.

["Observations on March," *ibid.*, sig. A₇.]

ANONYMOUS, 1674

.... if you ask me to what end I made this Scheme: I answer, for the same end that other Astrologers make Schemes, viz to get money by them, which is their end, my end, and every ones end; for money it is the Nobelmans Tutor, the Lawyers Littleton, the Maior and Aldermans Fur Gown, the Justices Warrant, the Constable and Bum-bailiffs Tip-Staff, the Astronomers blazing star, the Mathematicians Record, the Presbyterians Directory, the Independants ex tempore, the Quakers thee and thou, yea what not.

> Did not Will Summers break his wind for thee,
> And Shakespear therefore writ his Comedie?
> The German Princess for thee plaid her part,
> Though afterwards it brought her to the Cart.

[*Ibid.*, sig. C₅. The first two lines of verse are from Randolph's *Hey for Honesty*, I, 2. Munro notes (*Modern Philology*, XIII [1916], 520) that they are also quoted in an almanac of 1653.]

JOHN DRYDEN, 1677

Mr. Rymer sent me his booke, which has been my best entertainment hetherto: tis certainly very learned, & the best piece of Criticism in the English tongue; perhaps in any other of the modern. If I am not altogether of his opinion, I am so, in most of what he sayes: and thinke my selfe happy that he has not fallen upon me, as severely and as wittily as he has upon Shakespeare, and Fletcher. for he is the only man I know capable of finding out a poets blind sides:

[Charles E. Ward, *The Letters of John Dryden* (1942), pp. 13–14. The letter is dated by the appearance of Rymer's *Tragedies of the Last Age* in the summer of 1677.]

ANONYMOUS, 1681

The air is still sharp and piercing, which shall cause men to have such stout stomachs, that a great many people shall feed (according as Sir *John Falstaffe* used to fight) three hours together by *Shrewsbury* Clock.

[*Poor Robin, 1681. An Almanack of the Old and New Fashion*, sig. A₇, under the "Observations" for the month of March.]

ANONYMOUS, 1681

20 . Jack Felstaffe

[*Ibid.*, sig. A₅. The above appears in the list for January.]

THOMAS OTWAY, 1682

And Husband sounds so dull to a Town Bride,
You now a-days condemn him e'r he's try'd;
E'r in his office he's confirm'd Possessor,
Like Trincaloes you choose him a Successor.

[Epilogue "Written by a Person of Quality" to Aphra Behn's *City Heiress* (1682), in *Rare Prologues and Epilogues, 1642–1700*, ed. Autrey Nell Wiley (1940), p. 78.]

RICHARD HEAD, 1684

Have a care Mr. *Wheedle* how deeply you engage, or concern your self with this *Hot-spur*, or *Furioso*.

[*Proteus Redivivus: The Art of Wheedling or Insinuation* (1684), p. 50. I have not seen the first edition of 1675.]

CHARLES, EARL OF MIDDLETON, 1685

This you are to consider as an Instruction, and as for advice, Iagos is the best y^t can be given you by, S^r, Y^r most faithfull Servant, Middleton.

[Letter to George Etherege dated December 7, 1685, in H. F. B. Brett-Smith (ed.), *The Dramatic Works of Sir George Etherege* (1927), I, xlii. Miss Sybil Rosenfeld, *The Letterbook of Sir George Etherege* (1928), p. 345, reads the name Zago instead of Iago. Since her transcripts are modernized and Brett-Smith's are not, and since I can make no sense of Zago, I take it that the Rosenfeld transcript and not the Brett-Smith one is in error. Miss Bertha Hensman kindly called my attention to this allusion.]

N[ATHANIEL] T[HOMPSON], 1685

Though now he cuts his Capers high,
He may with *False-staff* one day cry,
(When Age hath set him in the *Stocks*)
A Pox on my Gout, a Gout of my Pox.

Yet that Fat Knight with all his Guts,
That were not then so sweet as Nuts,
Though oft he boldly fought and winkt,
Led *Harry M——* by Instinct;
Reveres a Buckram Prince of *Wales*,
His great Heart quops, his Courage quails.

The *Lyon Rampant* is too wise,
To touch a Prince, though in Disguise:
Much less a Prince so Kind and Civil,
To touch a *Kingdom* for *Kings-Evil.*

["A Canto upon the Miraculous Cure of the K's Evil, perform'd by the D. of M. in 80," *A Collection of 86 Loyal Poems* (1685), p. 23.]

N[ATHANIEL] T[HOMPSON], 1685

The stroaker *Graitrix* was a sot,
And all his Feat-tricks are forgot;
But *Duke Trinculo*, and *Tom Dory*,
Will be a famous Quack in *story.*

[*Ibid.*]

N[ATHANIEL] T[HOMPSON], 1685

The Solicitous Citizen: *Or* Much-ado about NOTHING.

[Title of a poem, *ibid.*, p. 130.]

George Etherege, 1686

If you flatter him the lion becomes a lamb, and, without examining anything you advance, will, like the Lord Chamberlain in *Hamlet*, cry, "Oh! very like a weasel."

[Letter to Lord Sunderland, September, 1686, in *The Letterbook of Sir George Etherege*, ed. Sybil Rosenfeld, p. 104. I owe this allusion to the kindness of Miss Bertha Hensman.]

Anonymous, *ca.* 1688

These were follow'd by some of a more modern stamp, whose only pride was a large pair of Boot-hose & a well starch'd Ruff, & whose Style, as well as their Habit was something more elegant & refin'd than that of those antique Reformers of our inconstant Language: in the head of these advanc'd Will. Shakespear, & Ben. Johnson, whose unparallel'd worth never mett with any Rivals, but such as did not understand it, & consequently could not equal it: these march'd forward with all the Modesty in their Garb, & the Majesty in their Deportment that befitted the Innocence & Learning of their Times.

[*A Journal from Parnassus*, ed. Hugh MacDonald (1937), pp. 5–6.]

Anonymous, *ca.* 1688

The next that appear'd after Bays was his Freind Tate, whose name Apollo searching for, & not finding it upon record, ask'd him what he had to say for himself; He reply'd that he was a Brother of the Quill that had been free of Tonson's Shop, had kept Company with Bays, had written three Plays, reviv'd two, & translated a Poetical History of the French Pox. Apollo told him, if that was all, his Plea was very weak, for his own Plays had been damn'd, Shakespear's wrong'd, and his Siphylis excell'd by every Mountebank's Bill.

[*Ibid.*, p. 16.]

Anonymous, *ca.* 1688

The humble Address of his Maties poor
Subjects the Company of Players.

. . . . We have exhausted Shakespear, Fletcher, & Johnson, are now plundering Terence, & must shortly be forc'd to go higher &

borrow Plots from Plautus & Aristophanes. Nay for the better maintaining the Trade we have not only reviv'd old Plays but acted our own, & cannot but blush while we boast that our Burlesque has succeeded better than many of our Poets labours.

[*Ibid.*, pp. 53 and 54.]

ANONYMOUS, *ca.* 1688

Hereupon their Address was form'd into a Bill, & referr'd to a Committee of Greivances, in which every Member nominated had his peculiar province of inspecting & licensing the severall Species of Poetry.

The Examination of Heroics was assign'd to Spencer: of Epics & Pindarics to Mr Cowley: of Panegyrics to Mr Waller: of Satyrs to Mr Oldham. For Stage-Poetry the supervising of Tragedies was committed to Shakespear; of Comedies to Ben. Johnson: of Tragic-Comedies to Beaumont & Fletcher: of Prologues, Songs & all the Garniture & Appurtenances of this sort of Poetry (especially Prefaces,) to Bays who it seems had been old Dog at them ever since Herringam hir'd him by the week to epistolize his Readers.

[*Ibid.*, pp. 37–38.]

ANONYMOUS, *ca.* 1688

[The Players] are grown so fine that nothing will suit with their Palate but Shakespear or Johnson, & a modern Author after nine Months labour to elevate & surprize, must be forc'd to stand to their Courtesy without Appeal.

[*Ibid.*, p. 56.]

ANONYMOUS, *ca.* 1688

. . . . when Shakespear in the behalf of himself and his Freinds the Ancient Play-wrights rose up & moved that some cognizance might be taken of the gross Abuses that had been put upon themselves & the Town in the dull Revival of those Plays of theirs which some ignorant Admirers under the pretence of liking them best, had render'd worse, & debas'd them from the general Applause of Readers to the just Censure of Auditors: but withal so lamentably patch'd so miserably disfigur'd, that the original Authors either

cou'd not, or wou'd not know them for their own; this they imputed
not to the poor Players, whose honest ignorance wou'd not presume
to make any Alterations (thô they were sometimes guilty of Omissions) but to the dull diligence of those profess'd Plagiaries, by
whom their Works might more justly be said to be mortify'd than
reviv'd. Nay, (added Shakespear) I cannot without Indignation
remember the unsufferable affront their very Laureat has put not
only upon my Writings but my Person in rudely disturbing my
Ashes & exposing my very Ghost in a Prologue upon the Stage, with
more pangs than ever returning Spirit suffer'd, to be the unhappy
deliverer of his Nonsense, & it may be after all these injurious Complements, to find my self rail'd at in his next Critical Preface.

[*Ibid.*, pp. 57–58.]

Thomas Shadwell, 1688

Belf. Jun. Oh no! Remember *Shakespear;* If Musick be the Food
of Love, Play on—There's nothing nourishes that soft passion like
it, it imps his Wings, and makes him fly a higher pitch.

[*The Squire of Alsatia* (1688), p. 15, ll. 20–23.]

[John Dunton], 1691

For it being the Fashion there for all the Puppies to be shav'd,
and have *Perukes* made of Shock-Dogs long Hair, our English
Spaniel, little *Fopling*, must needs be in the Fashion too, and gets
him a swinging Shock Wig, which made him look vary gracefully,
much like *Trinkala*'s Monster in the Tempest.

[*The Parable of the Puppies* (1691), p. 2.]

Anthony à Wood, 1691–92

He [Thomas Otway] was a man of good parts, but yet sometimes
fell[(+)] into plagiary, as well as his contemporaries, and made use
of *Shakespear*, to the advantage of his purse, at least, if not his
reputation.

(+) *Ger. Langbaine* in his *Account of the English Dramatick Poets*, &c. Oxon. 1691.
p. 396.

[*Athenae Oxonienses* (1691–92), Vol. II, col. 591.]

ANONYMOUS, 1693

Nay, the *wayward Sisters* who in *Macbeth* strove
Which shou'd best their Art in *reading Fortunes* prove,
Had yielded their *Rosin*, and *Beesoms*, and *Devils* to you,
Who twenty times stranger *Feats* can do.

[*Athenian Mercury*, Saturday, June 10, 1693.]

THOMAS RYMER, 1693

And on this occasion two Competitors have a juster occasion to work up, and shew the Muscles of their Passion, then *Shakespear's Cassius* and *Brutus*.

[*A Short View of Tragedy* (1693), p. 15.]

THOMAS RYMER, 1693

But it must not be forgotten in the Second Act, that there be some *Spanish-Fryar* or *Jesuit*, as St. *Xaviere* (for he may drop in by miracle, any where) to ring in their ears *the Northern Heresie;* like *Jago* in *Shakespear, Put Money in thy Purse*, I say, *Put Money in thy Purse*. So often may he repeat *the Northern Heresie*. Away with your Secular Advantages; *I say, the Northern Heresie;* there is Roast-meat for the Church; *Voto a Christo, the Northern Heresie*.

[*Ibid.*, p. 16.]

THOMAS RYMER, 1693

If Mr. *Dryden* might try his Pen on this Subject, doubtless, to an Audience that heartily love their Countrey, and glory in the Vertue of their Ancestors, his imitation of *Aschylus* would have better success, and would *Pit, Box*, and *Gallery*, far beyond any thing now in possession of the Stage, however wrought up by the unimitable *Shakespear*.

[*Ibid.*, p. 17.]

THOMAS RYMER, 1693

And after that were reckon'd for Comedy, *Edward* Earl of *Oxford;* for Tragedy amongst others, *Thomas* Lord of *Buchurst*, whose *Gorboduck* is a fable, doubtless, better turn'd for Tragedy, than any on this side the *Alps* in his time; and might have been a better direction to *Shakespear* and *Ben. Johnson* than any guide they have had the luck to follow.

[*Ibid.*, p. 84.]

THOMAS RYMER, 1693

The French confess they had nothing in this kind considerable till 1635. that the Academy Royal was founded. Long before which time we had from *Shakespear*, *Fletcher*, and *Ben. Johnson* whole Volumes; at this day in possession of the Stage, and acted with greater applause than ever.

[*Ibid.*, p. 85.]

THOMAS RYMER, 1693

One would not talk of rules, or what is regular with *Shakespear*, or any followers, in the Gang of the *Strouling* Fraternity; but it is lamentable that *Ben. Johnson*, his Stone and his Tymber, however otherwise of value, must lye a miserable heap of ruins, for want of Architecture, or some Son of *Vitruvius*, to joyn them together.

[*Ibid.*, p. 161.]

SIR THOMAS BLOUNT, 1694

Dryden says, That *Beaumont* and *Fletcher* had, with the advantage of *Shakespear*'s Wit, which was their *precedent*, great Natural Gifts, improv'd by Study. . . . . Their *Plots* were generally more regular than *Shakespear*'s, especially those which were made before *Beaumont*'s death; and they understood and imitated the Conversation of *Gentlemen* much better; whose wild Debaucheries, and quickness of Wit in *Repartees*, no Poet before them could paint as *they* have done. . . . . Their Plays are now the most pleasant and frequent Entertainments of the Stage; *two* of *theirs* being acted through the Year for *one* of *Shakespear*'s or *Johnson*'s: The reason is, says *Dryden*, because there is a certain *gayetie* in *their* Comedies, and *Pathos* in their more serious Plays, which suits generally with all Mens Humours. *Shakespear*'s Language is likewise a little obsolete, and *Ben. Johnson*'s Wit comes short of *theirs*. Dryd. *Essay* of *Dramatick Poesie, pag.* 34.

[*De re poetica: or, Remarks upon Poetry. With Characters and Censures of the Most Considerable Poets* (1694), "Characters and Censures," pp. 22–23.]

ANONYMOUS, 1698

The *Winter* Quarter beginneth at such time as our Earthly Globe hath volved its self to the greatest Northern Inclination, ... This Quarter, by reason of the Coldness of the Weather, is the most uncomfortable of all the four.

> *When Isicles hang by the Wall,*
> *And* Dick *the Shepherd blows his Nails,*
> *And* Tom *bears Logs unto the Hall,*
> *And Milk comes frozen home in Pails.*

[*Poor Robin, 1698,* sig. C₃ᵛ.]

ANONYMOUS, 1698

How often is the good Actor (as for Instance, the *Jago* in the *Moor of Venice*, or the Countess of *Notingham* in the Earl of *Essex*) little less than Curst for Acting an Ill Part? Such a Natural Affection and Commiseration of *Innocence* does Tragedy raise, and such an Abhorrence of *Villany*.

[*A Defence of Dramatick Poetry: Being a Review of Mr. Collier's View of the Immortality and Profaneness of the Stage* (1698), p. 72.]

JOHN DUNTON, 1699

Gentlemen,

Having now Sold the *Venture of Books I* brought into this Countrey (maugre all the Opposition *I* met with from *Patrick Campbel* and other Enemies) and being to Embark an Hour hence for *England, I* send this as my *Last Farewel to my Acquaintance in* Ireland (whether Friends or Enemies) and with this shall conclude the *Dublin Scuffle.*

Gentlemen!

I Told you in my *First Letter,* That I had brought into this Kingdom, *A General Collection of the most Valuable Books, Printed in* England, *since the Fire in* London *in 66. to this very time; to which, I told you, was added,—Great Variety of Scarce Books.* . . . . Ben Johnsons *Works*—Shakespears *Works*—Beaumont *and* Fletchers *Works*—Cowleys *Works*—Oldhams *Works*—Drydens *Works*—Congreves *Works*— . . . ."

[*The Dublin Scuffle* (1699), pp. 108–9.]

John Dunton, 1699

When we came to this Gentleman's House, his Scholars were acting *Henry* IV. and a Latin Play out of *Terence;* they were all Ingenious Lads, and perform'd their parts to a wonder; but one *Ellwood* (who acted *Falstaffe*) bore away the Bell from the whole School.

[*Ibid.*, p. 383.]

Charles Gildon, 1699

Tho. Dogget.

. . . . nor do I know of any remarkable Thefts from other Plays, unless the imitation of *Shakespear's Clowns*, in the character of *Hob*, which I look on as a praise to *Mr. Dgget* (*sic*) and no Fault.

[*The Lives and Characters of the English Dramatick Poets* (1699), p. 39.]

Charles Gildon, 1699

John Fletcher and Francis Beaumont

. . . . *Two Noble Kinsmen*, a Tragi-Comedy, *fol.* Mr. *Shakespear* assisted in the writing of this Play.

[*Ibid.*, p. 60.]

Charles Gildon, 1699

Christopher Marlow

A Famous Poet of Queen *Elizabeth* and King *James's* Time, contemporary with the Immortal *Shakespear*, was a Fellow-Actor with *Heywood*, and others. . . . .

[*Ibid.*, p. 92.]

Charles Gildon, 1699

The Arraignment of Paris, a Pastoral, supposed by *Kirkman* to be Mr. *William Shakespear's*.

[*Ibid.*, p. 157.]

[James Wright?], 1699

. . . . in my time, before the Wars, *Lowin* used to Act, with mighty Applause, *Falstaffe, Morose, Vulpone,* and *Mammon* in the *Alchymist.* . . . . *Tayler* acted *Hamlet* incomparably well, *Jago, Truewit* in the *Silent Woman,* and *Face* in the *Alchymist; Swanston* used to Play *Othello*.

[*Historia histrionica* (1699).]

PART II

NEW JONSON ALLUSIONS

ROBERT CHESTER, 1601

[At the end of *Love's Martyr* (1601) is a group of poems contributed by other poets on the same enigmatical subject of the Phoenix and the Turtledove. "Ben Iohnson" appears after "Επος," which is preceded by "Praeludium," and "Ben: Iohnson" after "Ode ἐνθουσιαστικὴ," which is preceded by "The Phoenix Analysde"; these are the last poems in the group. The first two were reprinted by Jonson in the *Forest* section of the 1616 folio; the latter were not reprinted but are accepted by Newdigate as Jonson's (*The Poems of Ben Jonson* [1936], pp. 365–66). Grosart in his edition of *Love's Martyr* (1878) ventures the opinion that the first two poems in the group signed "Vatum Chorus" are probably also by Jonson (p. lxi), and Newdigate is tempted by the same conjecture (*op. cit.*, p. 366), but I have not here considered them as his.

The *Jonson Allusion-Book* quotes the title-page of the appended section in *Love's Martyr*, but I have thought it necessary to give the additional information, since as I count Jonson allusions there are four in the section, whereas Bradley and Adams mention only "a poem." Jonson's name does not appear on the title-page.]

THOMAS DEKKER, 1602

[*Horace's Study.*]
Enter Horace in his true attyre, Asinius bearing his cloake.

Asinius. If you flye out, ningle, heer's your cloake; I thinke it raines too.

Horace. Hide my shoulders in't.

Asin. Troth so th'adst neede, for now thou art in thy pee and kue; thou hast such a villanous broad backe that I warrant th'art able to beare away any mans jestes in England.

. . . .

Asin. Yes, faith, I finde my wit a the mending hand, ningle; troth, I doe not thinke but to proceede poetaster next commencement, if I have my grace perfectlie; everie one that confer with me now, stop their nose in merriment, and sweare I smell somewhat of Horace; one calles me Horaces ape, another Horaces beagle, and such poeticall names it passes. I was but at barbers last day, and

15

when he was rencing my face, did but crie out, fellow, thou makst me *connive* too long, & sayes he, Master Asinius Bubo, you have eene Horaces wordes as right as if he had spit them into your mouth.

[*Satiromastix*, ed. Josiah H. Penniman (1913), II, 2, 1–25.]

THOMAS DEKKER, 1602

> *Horace* . . . .
> *That we to learned eares should sweetly sing,*
> *But to the vulger and adulterate braine*
> *Should loath to prostitute our virgin straine.*

[*Ibid.*, ll. 72–74. These are ll. 7, 8, and 11 of the Prologue to *Cynthia's Revels* transposed and slightly altered.]

ANONYMOUS, 1604/5

XXXI. Ben Johnson's Twelvth Nights Reuells. Pap. XVII.

[David Casley, *A Catalogue of the Manuscripts of the King's Library* (1734), p. 265. This manuscript (Royal MS 17.B.XXXI) is "the copy submitted to the Queen for the performance on 6 January 1605." It is not holograph but has been signed by Jonson at the end: "Hos ego versiculos feci. Ben: Jonson" (Herford and Simpson, *Ben Jonson*, VII, 164. The manuscript is reprinted in *ibid.*, pp. 195–201).]

ANONYMOUS, *ca.* 1605

Most honorable Lord:
    Although I cannot but know yo[r] Lo: to be busied wth far greater and higher affaires, etc.

Ben: Johnson.

[This letter of Jonson's to the Earl of Suffolk, written in 1605, was copied with eight others (see below) in a commonplace book, probably Chapman's, now in the possession of Mr. William Augustus White of New York. It was first reported by Bertram Dobell in "Newly Discovered Documents of the Elizabethan and Jacobean Periods," *Athenaeum*, Nos. 3830–33 (I [1901], 369–70, 403–4, 433–34, 465–67). Since this and the six letters immediately following concern imprisonment for certain passages in a play, almost certainly *Eastward Hoe*, Dobell conjectures that Chapman copied them for reference at or near the time of their imprisonment. The letter is reprinted from the manuscript in Herford and Simpson, *Ben Jonson*, I, 193–94.]

ANONYMOUS, *ca.* 1605

To the most nobly-vertuous and thrice-honor'd
Earle of Salisbury.

Most truely honorable, /

          / It hath still bene the Tyranny of my
Fortune so to oppresse my endeuors, that before I can shew my
selfe gratefull (in the least) for former benefitts, etc.

                    Yo^r Honors most deuoted
                    in heart as wordes./

                              Ben. Ionson

[A copy of this letter, written in 1605 and first printed by Gifford from the holograph copy in the Cecil Papers at Hatfield, is to be found in the Chapman manuscript (see above). Herford and Simpson point out (*Ben Jonson*, I, 190) that the
copy in the commonplace book was evidently a transcript of the first draft.]

ANONYMOUS, *ca.* 1605

Noble Lord,
     I haue so confirm'd Opinion of yor vertue, And am so fortified in
myne owne Innocence, etc.

                              Ben. Johnson.

[Another copied letter. See above. This letter, written in 1605 to an unnamed lord,
is reprinted from the manuscript in Herford and Simpson, *Ben Jonson*, I, 196–97.]

ANONYMOUS, *ca.* 1605

Excellentest of Ladies.
     And most honor'd of the Graces, Muses, and mee; if it be not
a sinne to prophane yor free hand with prison polluted Paper, etc.

                              Ben: Jhonson.

[Another copied letter. See above. This letter, written in 1605 to an unnamed
lady, probably the Countess of Bedford, is reprinted from the manuscript in *ibid.*,
pp. 197-98.]

ANONYMOUS, *ca.* 1605

The Noble fauoures you haue done vs, Most worthy Lord: can
not be so conceald or remou'd: but that they haue broke in vpon vs,
euen where we lye double bound to their Comforts, etc.

                              Ben: Johnson.

[Another copied letter. See above. This letter, directed probably to Lord D'Au-
bigny in 1605, is reprinted from the manuscript in *ibid.*, p. 198.]

ANONYMOUS, *ca.* 1605

Most worthely honor'd,

For mee not to solicite or call you to succoure in a tyme of such neede, were no lesse a sinne of dispaire, than a neglect of youre honor, etc.

Ben: Johnson.

[Another copied letter. See above. This letter, directed to the Earl of Montgomery in 1605, is reprinted from the manuscript in *ibid.*, p. 199.]

ANONYMOUS, *ca.* 1605

Most Noble
 Earle:

Neither am I or my cause so much vnknowne to youre Lordshipp, as it should driue mee to seeke a second meanes, or dispaire of this to youre fauoure, etc.

Ben: Johnson.

[Another copied letter. See above. This letter, written to the Earl of Pembroke in 1605, is reprinted from the manuscript in *ibid.*, pp. 199–200.]

ANONYMOUS, *ca.* 1605?

To my worthy & honord frend: M^r. Leech.

M^r. Leech

I do not offend vsually this way: and therefore one Importunacye may be the better suffred. I pray you to be careful of this Gent^s: necessitie, etc.

Your true louer & frend
Ben: Jonson.

[Another copied letter. See above. This letter and the following one are much more doubtful as to date. Reprinted from the manuscript in *ibid.*, p. 200.]

ANONYMOUS, *ca.* 1605?

To my honord & vertuous frend M^r· Tho: Bond Secretary to my ho: Lord the Lord Chauncellor of England.

S^r.

I am bold, out of my trust in your frendship, to request your help to the furdering this Gentleman's suite, etc.

Your poore vnprofitable louer
Ben: Jonson.

[Another copied letter. See above. Quoted in *ibid.*, p. 201.]

SIR GEORGE BUC, 1605

[There is an unspecified marginal reference to Jonson in Buc's Δαφνις πολυστεφανος, *An Eclog treating of Crownes, and of Garlandes, and to whom of right they appertaine* (1605). See Mark Eccles, "Sir George Buc, Master of the Revels," in *Thomas Lodge and Other Elizabethans*, ed. Charles J. Sisson (1933), p. 454.]

COURT RECORD, 1605/6

Beniaminu⁾ Iohnson et	Presented, that they refuse not to
vx⁾ dicte poᵉ	Come to divyne servis but have ab-
xijᵈ	sented them selves from the Coion
xijᵈ	beinge oftentymes admonished wᶜʰ
Pasch 4 & xviijᵈ	hathe Continued as farr as we Can
4 & xviijᵈ	learne ever since the kinge Came in
[2ᵃ sessione]	he is a poett and is by fame a se-
[Tē Pasch]	ducer of youthe to yᵉ popishe Re-
[Cl. Gard in Pasch./	ligion

[*A Book of Corrections or Presentments of the Consistory Court of London*, Book 1605–6, fol. 23ᵛ, entry for the Parish of St. Anne's, Blackfriars, under date of Friday, January 10, 1605/6, quoted in Herford and Simpson, *Ben Jonson*, I, 220.]

SIR JOHN SALUSBURY, ca. 1600–1612

[On fol. 40 of Sir John Salusbury's manuscript commonplace book (MS 184, Library of Christ Church, Oxford) appears the poem which was printed in the 1640 folio under the title "*An Ode to James Earle of* Desmond, *writ in Queene Elizabeths time, since lost, and recovered.*" It must have been written in the commonplace book between about 1600, when it was composed, and the death of Sir John Salusbury on July 24, 1612. See Carleton Brown, *Poems by Sir John Salusbury and Robert Chester* (1914), pp. xxvi and 5–7; Newdigate, *The Poems of Ben Jonson*, pp. 125–27 and 357–58.]

COURT RECORD, 1606

26 Aprilis 1606 Compᵒ dictus Beniamyn Iohnson . . . . bothe he and his wife doe goe ordinaryly to Churche and to his owne pshe Churche & so hath don this halfe yeare but for their receyving he sayethe he hathe refused to recyve the Coion vntill he shall be re- solved either by the minister of the pshe or som other in the scruple he maketh therin but his wife he sayethe for a[n]y thing he knowthe hathe gon to Churche & vsed alwayes to receyve the Coion and is appoynted to receyve the Coion to morow Towching the last pᵗ of the p⁾sentmᵗ for his seduceing of youthe he vtterly denyethe bothe

the fact & fame therof or eu⁾ going about to seduce or ᵱswade any
to the popishe religion. . . . .

[*A Book of Corrections or Presentments of the Consistory Court of London*, Book
1605–6, fol. 23ᵛ, quoted in Herford and Simpson, *Ben Jonson*, I, 220–21.]

COURT RECORD, 1606

To certify of their diligent going to Churche / And he

Beniaminu⁾ Johnson et
eius vx⁾ ste Anne black-
friers
23. b 1

Presented that he is by fame a seducer
of youthe to popishe religion / he was
monishd to appeare to see farther ᵱseed-
ing herein he having denyd bothe the
fact & the fame & the Churw: weare decreed to be here to specifie what pticulers they haue to Chardg him with.

[*Ibid.*, entry for Wednesday, May 7, 1606, fol. 321ᵛ, quoted in Herford and Simpson, *Ben Jonson*, I, 222.]

COURT RECORD, 1606

Beniaminu⁾ Johnson Ste
Anne in blackfriers
321. b 1

Presented that he is by fame a seducer
of youthe to popishe religion / he was
monished to appeare to see farther pceding herin he having denyed bothe the
fact & the fame and the Church Wardens
weare decreed to be here to specifie what
pticulers they have to Charrdg him wᵗʰ

px
continuat in hunc diem /

[*Ibid.*, entry for Wednesday, May 14, 1606, fol. 329, quoted in Herford and Simpson, *Ben Jonson*, I, 222.]

COURT RECORD, 1606

Beniaminu⁾ Johnson et
eius vx⁾ p̄o ste Anne in le
blackfriers
329. a 1
23. b 1

Presented that he is by fame a seducer
of youth to popishe Religion continuat in
hunc diem / he was monished to appeare
to see farther proseding herein he having
denyed both the fact & the fame. / They
are both to Certify of their diligent & ordinarie going to Churche / he is to Certify how he is satisfied in the scruple he

Cʳ Gard et Johnsō   made of his receyving the Coiōn by them
Dᵈ px stayᵈ at seale   he was referred vnto to conferr wᵗʰ.

[*Ibid.*, entry for Wednesday, June 2, 1606, fol. 334ᵛ, quoted in Herford and Simpson, *Ben Jonson*, I, 222.]

ANONYMOUS, 1608-9

[A summary of the action of Jonson's *Masque of Queens* is found in Brit. Mus. Harl. MS 6947, fol. 143. Simpson says of it: "It was the custom to submit to the Court before any performance a summary description, partly no doubt to suit the convenience of officials who had to prepare for it, partly, if it was a play, to enable the authorities to see if there was anything dangerous in the subject-matter. 'Have you heard the argument?' says the King to Hamlet. 'Is there no offence in it?'

"This particular argument was copied out by an illiterate clerk who writes 'Hil' for 'Hell,' calls Zenobia 'Tenobia,' Candace 'Cnidace,' Bonduca 'Bundrica,' and Amalasunta 'Amalasanta,' makes Camilla queen of the 'Voscians,' and occasionally misspells. It was made before the masque took its final form, for Atalanta appears in the list of queens. Inigo Jones made a design for her dress, but in the actual performance Hypsicratea was substituted for her" (Herford and Simpson, *Ben Jonson*, VII, 318).]

COURT RECORD, 1610

Beniamine Iohnson Iuꝛ 5° Maij 1610
Dña Aña Argall iuꝛ 8 Maij 1610   Mat. Carew
Cheigny Rowe iuꝛ 2° Octobꝛ 1610
Paul B⟨ur⟩cheer iuꝛ 19   Mat. Carew
Novēb 1610   Mat. Carew

[The names of the witnesses given in the margin of a Chancery document headed "Interrogatories to be ministred to witnesses to be examined on the pte and behaulfe of Willm Rowe gentleman Complᵗ against Walter Garland defᵗ," found in Chancery Town Depositions of James I's reign, Bundle 357, Public Record Office, and quoted by Herford and Simpson, *Ben Jonson*, I, 227.]

COURT RECORD, 1610

p Rowe queꝛ.

8 die Maij. 1610.
Aṅō 8, Ia: Regis./

     Beniamin Johnson of the Precinct of the blackffreers London gent. aged 37. yeers or theraboutes sworne &c. by direction vpon the 1. 12. 13. 14. 15. & 16ᵗʰ Interꝛ./

     1. That he doth know the pł: & defᵗ in this Suyte, and hath knowne Wᵐ Row gent. named for the compł: about 5. yeares, and Walter Garland named for the defᵗ, about 4. yeares./

12. That he hath knowne the def^t vse many word*es* &
meanes. . . . .

[The deposition of Jonson from Chancery Town Depositions, quoted in *ibid.*,
p. 228.]

HENRY JACKSON, 1610

-Postremis his diebus adfuerunt Regis Actores Scenici. Egerunt
cum applausu maximo, pleno theatro. Sed viris piis et doctis impii
merito visi sunt, quod non contenti Alcumistas perstringere, ipsas
sanctas Scripturas fœdissimè violarint. Anabaptistas scilicet velli-
cabant; ut sub hac persona lateret improbitas.- . . . .

—nusquam majori plausu theatra nostra sonuisse, quam cum
intraret personatus ille nebulo, qui, ut fictum Anabaptistarum
sanctitatem spectatoribus deridendam proponeret, scripturas im-
pie, et prodigiosè contaminavit. Habuerunt et Tragœdias, quas
decorè, et aptè agebant. In quibus non solùm dicendo, sed etiam
faciendo quædam lachrymas movebant.— . . . .

Sept. 1610.

[Fulman Papers, Vol. X, fols. 83^v and 84^r, in the library of Corpus Christi College, Oxford. The letter was written by Henry Jackson of Corpus Christi and copied
later by William Fulman, of Meysey Hampton. The passage is reported by Geoffrey
Tillotson in *"Othello* and *The Alchemist* at Oxford in 1610," *Times Literary Supplement*, July 20, 1933, p. 494.]

ANONYMOUS, 1610/11

A Short Account of the Masque Made by
the PRINCE OF WALES.

1611, Jan. 11.—The new hall of the palace was furnished as
usual with its galleries round about, a green carpet on the floor, a
dais at the top for the king and queen. At the bottom a very large
curtain painted with the kingdoms of England, Scotland and Ireland, with the legend above *Separata locis concordi pace figantur.*
When their Majesties entered accompanied by the princess and the
ambassadors of Spain and Venice, flageolets played and the curtain was drawn discovering a great rock with the moon showing
above through an aperture, so that its progress through the night
could be observed. Old Silenus mounted on this with some dozen
satyrs and fauns who had much to say about the coming of a great

prince to be followed by a thousand benefits, in the hope of which the fauns danced about joyfully, exciting great laughter. They then danced a ballet, with appropriate music with a thousand strange gestures, affording great pleasure. This done the rock opened discovering a great throne with countless lights and colours all shifting, a lovely thing to see. In the midst stood the prince with thirteen other gentlemen chosen as famous dancers of the Court. Before passing into the hall ten musicians appeared each with a lute and two boys who sang very well some sonnets in praise of the prince and his father. Then ten little pages dressed in green and silver with flat bonnets a l'antique danced another ballet with much grace. During this a cock crew ten times, standing on the rock, and then, according to the prophecy of Silenus, there came the gentlemen in short scarlet hose and white brodequins full of silver spangles coming half way to the calf, some wearing jackets with wide folds, as the Roman emperors are represented and the sleeves the same, all in gold and silver cloth, white and scarlet feathers on their heads and very high white plumes, and black masks. Each one wore a very rich blue band across the body, except that of the prince, whose band was scarlet to distinguish him from the rest. They entered dancing two ballets intermingled with varied figures and many leaps, extremely well done by most of them. The prince then took the queen to dance, the earl of Southampton the princess, and each of the rest his lady. They danced an English dance resembling a pavane. When the queen returned to her place the prince took her for a coranta which was continued by others and then the gallarda began, which was something to see and admire. The prince took the queen a third time for *los branles de Poitou*, followed by eleven others of the masque. As it was about midnight and the king somewhat tired he sent word that they should make an end. So the masqueraders danced the ballet of the sortie, in which the satyrs and fauns joined. With vocal and instrumental music the masqueraders approached the throne to make their reverence to their Majesties. The masques being laid aside, the king and queen with the ladies and gentlemen of the masque proceeded to the banqueting hall, going out after they had looked about and taken a turn round the table; and in a moment everything was thrown down with furious haste, according to the strange custom of the country. After this their Majesties withdrew and the ambassadors took leave. . . . .

Spanish.

[Historical Manuscripts Commission, *Report on the Manuscripts of the Marquess of Downshire*, Vol. III: *Papers of William Trumbull the Elder 1611–12* (1938), pp. 1–2. The masque this night was Jonson's *Oberon, the Fairy Prince.*]

WILLIAM DRUMMOND, 1612

Ben Jhonson's Epigrams.

[In the list of *"Bookes red be me, anno* 1612." David Laing, "A Brief Account of the Hawthornden Manuscripts," *Archaeologia Scotica*, IV (1857), 75.]

J. BEAULIEU, 1612/13

J. Beaulieu to William Trumbull

[1613–]13, March 3. Paris.—This gentleman, Mr. Ben. Johnson (who . . . . cannot but be well known unto you by his reputation) having spent some 12 months travel in this country, in Mr. Raughley's companie, who was committed to his charge by Sir Walter his father, hath now taken a resolution to pass by Sedan into your parts. . . . . He hath been desirous that I should add to the credit of his own merit that of my recommendation towards you, with whom he doth profess to have a great desire to make particular acquaintance, ... which will be sufficient to recommend him to your good estimation and entertainment besides the testimonial of his extraordinary and rare parts of knowledge and understanding which make his conversation to be honoured and beloved in all companies, specially for the commendation he hath not to abuse the power of his gifts, as commonly other overflowing wits use to do, to the prejudice of other men's honour. More I shall not need to add . . . . to recommend him unto you, since that his nature and known qualities, wch. by a few days' conversation wilbe better known unto you, wilbe more than sufficient a motive to your good affection. . . . . This only particular I must require in his behalf at your hands that in Mr. Russell's, Mr. Chandeler's (if he be there) and the rest of your most selected friends' company, you do charge him, by the authority of your place, with the best cup of claret that Brussels shall afford, to remember the healths of his friends here.

[Historical Manuscripts Commission, *Report on the Manuscripts of the Marquess of Downshire*, IV (1940), 54.]

J. BEAULIEU, 1612/13

J. Beaulieu to William Trumbull

1613, March 11. Paris.— . . . . At Mr. Johnson's entreaty I did accompany him with a letter of recommendation to you, which I suppose he was desirous to have to prevent the rumour of some cross business wherein he hath been interested here. What is good in him I was content to relate, and indeed he hath many worthy parts, for the rest you shall soon make a discovery thereof.

[*Ibid.*, p. 59.]

JOHN BROWNLOWE, 1613

John Brownlowe to William Trumbull

1613, April 3. Antwerp.— . . . . I return your letter to Monrs. Aenskombe and enclose one for Mr. Rawlegh and Mr. Jnoson's bills of exchange, who importuned me so earnestly for 10*l*. more that I could not refuse. I have entered 20*l*. upon your account, besides the 20*l*. charge of Sir Wm. Stanley. From hence is great store of calivers sent packed up towards Dunkirk.

[*Ibid.*, p. 81.]

WILLIAM DRUMMOND, 1613

Ben Jhonson's Epigrames

[In the list of books read by Drummond "*Anno* 1613." David Laing, "A Brief Account of the Hawthornden Manuscripts," *Archaeologia Scotica*, IV (1857), 76.]

THOMAS PORTER, 1614

436. Octavo, paper, 17th century.—Thomæ Porteri de Hemnall ministri Epigrammata. Latin poems dedicated to Sir John Heveningham.—On the last page is written "Per me Thomas Porterum ministrum de Hemnall 12 die Martii" mensis 1614. There are epigrams on (amongst other persons) Samuel Daniel, Ben Jonson, W. Shakespeare, Edm. Spenser. . . . . .

[Manuscripts of the Earl of Leicester at Holkham Hall, Norfolk, Historical Manuscripts Commission, *Ninth Report*, Part II, p. 362, col. 1.]

FRANCIS BEAUMONT, *ca.* 1615

To M^r B: J:.

Neither to follow fashion nor to showe
my witt against the State, nor that I knowe
any thing now, with which I am with childe
till I haue tould, nor hopeinge to bee stilde
a good Epist'ler through the towne, with which
I might bee famous, nor with any ytch
like these, wrote I this Letter but to showe
the Loue I carrie and mee thinkes do owe.
to you aboue the number, which [can] best
in something which I vse not, be exprest.
to write this I invoake none, but the post
of Douer, or some Carriers pist-ling ghost,
for if this equall but the stile, which men
send Cheese to towne with, and thankes downe agen,
tis all I seeke for: heere I would let slippe
(If I had any in mee) schollershippe,
And from all Learninge keepe these lines as [cl]eere
as Shakespeares best are, which our heires shall heare
Preachers apte to their auditors to showe
how farr sometimes a mortall man may goe
by the dimme light of Nature, tis to mee
an helpe to write of nothing; and as free,
As hee, whose text was, god made all that is,
I meane to speake: what do you thinke of his
state, who hath now the last that hee could make
in white and Orrenge tawny on his backe
at Windsor? is not this mans miserie more
then a fallen sharers, that now keepes a doore,
hath not his state almost as wretched beene
as [h]is, that is ordainde to write the [grinne]
after the fawne, and fleere shall bee? as sure
some one there is allotted to endure
that Cross. there are some, I could wish to knowe
to loue, and keepe with, if they woulde not showe

their studdies to me; or I wish to see
their workes to laugh at, if they suffer mee
not to knowe them: And thus I would Commerse
with honest Poets that make scuruie verse.
by this time you perceiue you did a misse
to leaue your worthier studies to see this,
which is more tedious to you, then to walke
in a Jews Church, or Bretons Comon talke.
but know I write not these lines to the end
to please Ben: Johnson but to please my frend: ffinis: FB:

[Printed from Holgate MS, fol. 110, and Add. MS 30982, fol. 75ᵛ, in the Pierpont
Morgan Library, New York, and the British Museum, respectively, in Chambers,
William Shakespeare, II, 224–25. The poem was first noted in the *Times Literary
Supplement* for September 15, 1921, p. 596, where the manuscript from which it was
taken was dated 1603–26.]

J. M., *ca.* 1615

Surrey & Sidney, honoʳ of oʳ age
were both of them of noble parentage
yet not their honoʳ makes them live so longe
as doth their poems & learned pleasinge songe
before their time Sʳ Jeffr'y Chaucer he
the first life giver to oʳ poesie
Phaër & Twyne, Harvy, Gaskoyne, Goldinge
Lydgate, Skelton, Grange, Googe & Fleminge
Warner & Watson, France, Churchyarde, Whetston
Monday, Lilly, Britton, Danyell, Draiton
Chapman & Jonson, Withers aunncient Tusser
w[i]th the divine soule-pleasinge Silvester
and noble Spencer. . . . .

[John Henry Hobart Lyon, *A Study of the Newe Metamorphosis* (1919), pp. 62–63.
On the date see *ibid.*, pp. 5–6.]

ANONYMOUS, 1603–26

[W. G. P., in a letter to the *Times Literary Supplement* of September 15, 1921, p.
596, describing the manuscript from which Beaumont's letter to Jonson is taken,
says: "The collection takes up about 250 closely written pages of a quarto bound in

contemporary vellum, and includes many of the shorter poems of Donne, Jonson, Richard Corbet, F. Beaumont and other well-known writers of the time. . . . . The poems appear to have been copied in at various dates between 1603 and 1626." How many poems by Jonson the author of the letter does not indicate.]

Anonymous, *ca.* 1616

["There is a contemporary manuscript of the masque [*Christmas His Masque*], showing an earlier state than the printed text, in the Folger Shakespeare Library at Washington, MS 2203.1., on folios 168–74. It gives a complete text of the speeches and songs, but not the descriptions of the characters, their dresses and properties, which Jonson supplied in the copy afterwards sent to press for the Folio. The title in the manuscript is 'Christmas his Showe,' which Jonson might have retained with advantage" (Herford and Simpson, *Ben Jonson*, VII, 433).]

Patent, 1615/16

D' conc⁾ ad vit'   Iames by the grace of god &c To all men to
Beniamino Iohnson   whome theis p[re]sent[es] shall come Greet-
                    ing. knowe yee that we . . . . in consideracion
of the good and aceptable service done and to be done vnto vs by
our welbeloved Servaunt Beniamyn Iohnson . . . . doe give and
graunt vnto the said Beniamyn Iohnson a certaine añuytie or
pençon of one hundred markes of lawfull money of England by the
yeare. To have hould and yerelie to receive the said Annuity or
pencion of one hundred markes by the yeare to the said Beniamyn
Iohnson and his Assignes from the ffeast of the birth of our lord
God laste past before the date hereof for and during the naturall
life of him the said Beniamyn Iohnson out of the Treasure of vs our
heires and successors in the Receipt of the Exchequer of vs our
heires and successors by the hand[es] of the Trēr and Chamblaines
of vs our heires and successors there for the tyme being att the
ffoure vsuall termes of the yere that is to say att the ffeast of Than-
nunciacion of the blessed virgin mary the Nativitie of St Iohn Bap-
tist St michaell Th'archangell and the Birth of our lord god
quartely by even porcions to be paid. . . . . Wittnes our selfe at
Westminster the first day of ffebruary.

                                        p bre de priuato Sigillo &c.

[Patent Roll, 13 James I, 29 (Roll 2084, No. 12), quoted in Herford and Simpson, *Ben Jonson*, I, 231–32.]

BEAUMONT AND FLETCHER, 1616

Tye your she Otter vp, good Lady Folly, she stinkes worse then a beare-bayting.

[Francis Beaumont and John Fletcher, *The Scornful Lady* (1616), IV, 1, sig. H₁. Elder Loveless is begging Lady Folly to call off her scolding woman, Abigail. As Gayley pointed out (*Beaumont the Dramatist*, p. 369), the line is a fairly obvious allusion to "The termagent Mrs. Otter and her husband of the Bear-garden" in *Epicoene*.]

WILLIAM DRUMMOND, 1617

Swell prowd my Billowes, faint not to declare
Your Ioyes, as ample as their Causes are:

[*Forth Feasting* (1617), in *The Poetical Works of William Drummond of Hawthornden*, ed. L. E. Kastner (1913), I, 143. W. D. Briggs in "The Influence of Jonson's Tragedy in the Seventeenth Century," *Anglia*, XXXV (1912), 331, pointed out that the lines are a slight adaptation of *Sejanus*, V, 1–2:

"Swell, swell, my ioyes: and faint not to declare
Your selues, as ample, as your causes are."]

EXCHEQUER RECORD, 1617

Mensis Decemb Aō Regni Reg[is] Iacobi quinto decimo
Thomas Henn one of the ordinarie groomes of the Prynces Chamber beinge sent in his highnes seruice . . . . with a messuage to Sʳ Charles Howard, and allsoe one other messuage from whithalle to Black fryers with a messuage to Benn Iohnson which seruises beinge done he returned with answeares to the places aforsaid. . . . .

Ro: Cary
W Alexander:

[Notices from the Exchequer of Receipt Miscellanea (Bundle 62), quoted in Herford and Simpson, *Ben Jonson*, I, 233.]

ANONYMOUS, *ca.* 1618

[There is at Chatsworth a manuscript of *Pleasure Reconciled to Virtue* belonging to the Duke of Devonshire which is earlier than the 1640 text and contemporary with the performance. "It was recorded in the Third Report of the Historical Manuscripts Commission, 1872, Appendix, page 43, with the extraordinary description 'A 12mo volume, paper, 16th century. Plenum reconciled to Kulum. (A Masque, 12 leaves).' . . . . It is a copy made for presentation to a courtier, either a performer

or a patron. . . . . The manuscript has valuable corrections of the Folio text. . . . .
The Manuscript is beautifully written with extreme care, and its lapses are trivial"
(Herford and Simpson, *Ben Jonson*, VII, 475–77).]

ANONYMOUS, 1619?

Sir Anthonie Ashley. ex gratiâ, 50*l.*; arrears, 112*l.* 10*s.* Duke of
Brunswick, 333*l.* 6*s.*, ex gratiâ; arrears, 416*l.* 13*s.* 4*d.* Alfonso Fera-
bosco, 50*l.* Instructor of the late Prince Henry in the art of Musick;
arrears, 12*l.* 10*s.* Benjamin Johnson, 66*l.* 13*s.* 4*d.*, for service; arrears, 150*l.* . . . .

[Manuscripts of the Earl de la Warr, Historical Manuscripts Commission,
Fourth Report, p. 310. The manuscript appears to be undated, but it is found with
others dated 1619.]

WILLIAM DRUMMOND, 1619

Sir,

Mr. Fenton shew mee a letter of yours, in which yee remember
your freinds heere, but I am particularly beholden to you for your
particular remembrance of mee. Other letters of yours I haue not
seene. The vncertaintye where to find you, hath made mee so negli-
gent in writing. When I haue vnderstood of your being at London, I
will not be so lazie. I haue sent you here the Oth of our Knights, as I
had it from Drysdale, haralt, if there be anay other such pieces wherein I can serue you, yee haue but to aduertise mee. Many in this coun-
trye of your friends haue trauelled with you in their thoughts, and
all in their good wishes place you well at home. What a losse were it
to vs if ought should haue befallen you but good. Because I doubte
if these come unto you, I shall commit you to the tuition of God,
and remaine

Your assured and loving freind.

[A first draft of the following letter to Jonson, preserved in the Hawthornden
MSS, Vol. IX, in the Library of the Society of Antiquaries of Scotland; quoted in
Herford and Simpson, *Ben Jonson*, I, 205.]

WILLIAM DRUMMOND, 1619

To my good freind BEN JONSON.

S^r.–after euen a longing to heare of your happy iourney, Mr Fenton shew mee a letter from you, remembring all your freinds heere,

and particularlie (such is your kyndnesse) mee. if euer prayers could haue made a voyage easie, your must haue beene, for your acquaintance heere in their thoughts did trauelle a long with you. The vncertaintye where to directe letters hath made mee this tyme past not to write, when I vnderstand of your being at London, I shall neuer (among my worthiest freinds) be forgetful of you. I haue sent you the oth of our knights, as it was giuen mee by Harald Drysdale, if I can serue you in any other matter, yee shall find mee most willing. [What a lose were it to vs if ought should haue befallen you but good.] Thus wishing that the successe of your fortunes may [answer our desires,] be equall [to the deserts of your many good parts,] to your deserts, I commite you to the tuition of God.

Edenbrough
30 of aprile. 619.

[From the autographs in the Hawthornden MSS, Vol. IX, in the Library of the Society of Antiquaries of Scotland, quoted in *ibid.*, p. 206.]

[SIR GEORGE BUC?] *ca.* 1619 OR 1620

[The Fox]

[This title has been canceled in a list of plays on a scrap of waste paper from the Revels Office, probably dating about 1619 or 1620. It has been plausibly suggested that the plays of the list were being considered for court performance. See Frank Marcham, *The King's Office of the Revels, 1610–1622* (1925), p. 13, and E. K. Chambers, *Review of English Studies*, I, 484.]

[SIR GEORGE BUC?] *ca.* 1619 OR 1620

the scilent Woeman:

[This title appears in another list of plays on another scrap of waste paper from the Revels Office, probably dating about 1619 or 1620. See above. Marcham, *The King's Office of the Revels*, p. 15, and Chambers, *loc. cit.*]

GIROLAMO LANDO, 1619/20

This night [January 17] the prince's masque took place, in which he and ten other cavaliers made a brave show. Among them Buckingham was first, and apparently he is as great a favourite with the prince as with his father. The ceremony lasted more than three hours, attended by an extraordinary number of ladies very richly dressed and laden with jewels. His Majesty took part with much gaiety and greatly enjoyed the agility and dancing of his son and of the marquis, who contended against each other for the favour and applause of the king and to give him pleasure.

[*Calendar of State Papers, Venetian, 1619-21*, p. 138. The masque was Jonson's *Pan's Anniversary*. See Herford and Simpson, *Ben Jonson*, VII, 528.]

Girolamo Lando, 1619/20

[March 6] They are preparing another representation of the masque given some days ago by the prince.

[*Calendar of State Papers, Venetian, 1619-21*, p. 190. The masque was Jonson's *Pan's Anniversary*. See Herford and Simpson, *Ben Jonson*, VII, 528.]

Anonymous, *ca.* 1620

[Brit. Mus. Harl. MS 4955, fols. 48-52, contains a masque of Jonson's described in *A Catalogue of the Harleian Manuscripts in the British Museum* (1808), III, 232, as "A Masque, not in his Works that I can find"; it "was made for the Newcastle family, probably for the Earl." The masque is "An Entertainment at the Blackfriars," which Jonson prepared for the christening of Charles Cavendish. See Herford and Simpson, *Ben Jonson*, VII, 767-78.]

Anonymous, 1620

A / Description / OF LOVE. / WITH / certain / *Epigrams*. / *Elegies*. / and / *Sonnets*. / AND / Also IOHNSONS Answer / to WITHERS. / *The Second Edition*, / With the Crie of LVDGATE. / AND / The Song of the BEGGER. / LONDON. / Printed by *Edw. Griffin*. / 1620.

[Jonson's "Answer to Master Withers," which is a parody of "Shall I wasting in despair, Die because a woman's fair," and printed in alternate verses with it, occupy sigs. D8-E1ᵛ. Newdigate reprints the poem from the edition of 1625 in his *Poems of Ben Jonson*, pp. 300-302. In his notes he points out (p. 372) that Sidgwick thought the lines were those of the poetaster Richard Johnson but that Richard Johnson's lines appeared in *The Garland of Princely Pleasures* (1620 [S.T.C. 14674])—a later edition of his *A Crowne Garland of Goulden Roses* (1612)—and are quite different from these, which may be presumed to be by Ben Jonson.]

ANONYMOUS, 1620

Ffor the Prince's Maske.

	£	s.	d.
Tooth Drewer, 1	02	07	04
Judgler, 2	01	01	10
Prophet, 3	00	09	07
Clocke Keeper, 4	00	09	08
Clarke, 5	01	03	08
	07	12	01
Ffor the Ffencer	05	00	06
Ffor the Bellowes Mender	01	17	00
Ffor the Tinker	01	04	02
Ffor the Mouse Trappman	00	19	00
Ffor the Jugler	00	10	02
Ffor the Cornecutter	00	05	00
Ffor the Tinder-box Man	00	03	06
Ffor the Clocke Keeper	00	06	06
Ffor the Scribe	00	02	10
Ffor the Prophett	00	02	04
For the Antick Maske at Xmas, 1620	38	12	10

[This is a digest of the accounts in "one of the Exchequer documents ordered to be destroyed," quoted by Hugh W. Diamond, *Notes and Queries: First Series*, XII (December 22, 1855), 485–86. The masque was Jonson's *Pan's Anniversary*.]

ANONYMOUS, 1620

1620. Last of March. Pressing payments on His Majesty's remove at the Annunciation pensions, &c. One pension was to Benjamin Johnson, the King's poett, 33*l.* Total amount, 22,301*l.*

[Manuscripts of the Earl de la Warr, Historical Manuscripts Commission, *Fourth Report*, p. 282.]

ANONYMOUS, *ca.* 1621

[The manuscript of *The Gypsies Metamorphosed* at the Huntington Library, H.M. 741, the best extant text of the masque, has often been said to be Jonson's autograph, but Simpson demonstrates that it is not (see Herford and Simpson, *Ben Jonson*, VII, 546–51).]

ANONYMOUS, *ca.* 1621

["In the Public Record Office there is a manuscript copy of the King's, the Prince's, and the Ladies' fortunes (from *The Gypsies Metamorphosed*). It is subscribed 'The Gipsies Maaske att Burley.' It contains the original, and shorter, form of the King's and Prince's fortunes. The text of the whole is bad; words are left out, misread, and misspelt. But it is valuable for giving us the names of some of the performers" (*ibid.*, p. 551).]

ANONYMOUS, *ca.* 1621

[Tanner MS 306 in the Bodleian on fols. 252–53 has a copy of parts of the fortune-telling in *The Gypsies Metamorphosed* (*ibid.*).]

ANONYMOUS, *ca.* 1621

[Bodleian MS Rawlinson poetry 172 on fol. 78 has a copy of parts of the fortune-telling in *The Gypsies Metamorphosed* (*ibid.*).]

JOHN CHAMBERLAIN, 1621

For lacke of better newes here is likewise a ballet or song of Ben Johnsons in the play or shew at the Lord Marquis at Burly, and repeated again at Windsor, for which and other goode service there don, he hath his pension from a 100 marks increased to 200^{li} *per annum*, besides the reversion of the mastership of the revells. There were other songs and devises of baser alay, but because this had the vogue and generall applause at court, I was willing to send yt.

[Letter to Sir Dudley Carleton, October 27, 1621, *The Letters of John Chamberlain* (1939), ed. Norman Egbert McClure, II, 404–5. Only the incomplete account in the *State Papers* is quoted in *The Jonson Allusion-Book*.]

DEED OF ASSIGNMENT, 1621

Beniamin Johnson his assignement to John Hull for his half yeares annuity at Michas. next, 33^{li} and 3^{li} more.

Memorandum that whereas by obligacon$^)$ of the date hereof I Beniamin Johnson am indebted to John Hull Cittizen & founder of London in Thirty and sixe pound[es]. . . . . I the sayd Beniamin haue Assigned John Hull to receiue and be payed his sayd debt out of my Anuall Pencon$^)$ . . . . (that is to say) to receiue the xxxiij^{li} to be due to me at Michas next for my halfe yeares Pencon$^)$ & thother iij^{li} of the sayd debt out of the residue of my sayd Pencon$^)$ when the same shalbe due, And to that end I doe desire and ap-

j° Junij 1621   pointe my frend Mr John Burgis to see the
sayd John Hull satisfyed his sayd debt. . . . .
In testimony hereof I haue hereto Subscribed
my name the first day of June, Anno dni$^)$
1621./

Teste	Signed
John Ewen	Ben: Johnson
Peter Bland	ffrend the last three pound[es]

                 by iust debt must be 4^{li}

                 Signed

                 Ben: Johnson

[Auditors' Patent Books, 1620-24 (E.403/2455/ fol. 51^v) preserved in the Public Record Office, quoted in Herford and Simpson, *Ben Jonson*, I, 236.]

JOHN BOYS, 1622?

The writing of the learned are called their works, *opera Hieronymi*, the works of *Hierome, Augustine, Gregory:* yea the very *playes* of a modern Poet, are called in print his *works.*

[*The Workes of Iohn Boys Doctor in Diuinitie and Deane of Canterburie* (1629), p. 921. I have not seen the 1622 edition of Boys's *Works*, but the 1629 edition seems to be merely a reprint without additions. This allusion in any case can refer only to Jonson, for his plays were the only ones printed as "*Works*" before 1629. The passage is noted in *The Shakspere Allusion-Book*, I, 258, but it cannot refer to Shakespeare, because the folio of 1623 was, of course, not entitled *Works.*]

JOHN GEE, 1624

An *Alchymist* vsually answers his deluded scholler with expectation of *Proiection*, and tells him the more his *Materials* be multiplied, the stronger will the *Proiection* be; especially if it come to the mountenance of an hundred pounds, *Vid.* The Play of the *Alchymist.*

[John Gee, *New Shreds of the Old Snare* (1624), p. 22 n.]

RICHARD JAMES, *ca.* 1625

He [Richard James] notices the severe strictures of some of the Fathers—Tertullian, Chrysostom, Cyprian—on the stage, and shows that these were just as applied to the indecencies then tolerated, but adds, that if these Fathers were now living they would willingly attend the representation of Ben Jonson's plays. These lines then follow:—

> Ede tuos tandem populo Jonsone libellos
> Et cultum docto pectore profer opus
> Quod nec Cecropiæ damnent Pandionis artes
> Nec sileant nostri præ tereantque senes
> Ante fores stantem dubitas admittere famam
> Teque piget famæ præmia ferre tuæ
> Post te victuræ per te quoque vivere chartæ
> Incipiant, cineri gloria sera venit.

[James MS No. 13, p. 25, quoted in *The Poems etc., of Richard James B.D.*, ed. Alexander B. Grosart (1880), p. 260.]

ANONYMOUS, 1603–49

Ode to Ben Jonson, by Jo. Earles, in *Latin*.

[Brit. Mus. Add. MS 15227, fol. 44, "List of Additions to the Department of Manuscripts. 1844," *Catalogue of Additions to the Manuscripts in the British Museum in the Years MDCCCXLI–MDCCCXLV* (1850), p. 115.]

ANONYMOUS, 1603–49

B. JOHNSON *in seipsum*.

> Here lies Johnson, who was ones sonne,
> Hee had a little hayre on his chin, his name
> was Benjamin.

[Brit. Mus. Add. MS 15227, fol. 45, quoted in Newdigate, *The Poems of Ben Jonson*, p. 341.]

DOCTOR J. WEBB, 1628/29

Letters to [Jonson], from Dr. J. Webb, 1628/9. *Engl.* and *Lat.* 1466, ff. 204–213, 354–372.

[Edward J. L. Scott, *Index to the Sloane Manuscripts* (1904), p. 284. The first letter is reprinted in *The Jonson Allusion-Book*, p. 142, but the second is not mentioned.]

HENRY BLOUNT, 1629

> Ovr stately Tragick Scene (whose high disdaines
> Slight humble Muses) courts thy lofty straines:

And with ambitious loue doth clime thy Bayes,
Whose ample branches her bright glory rayes:
Whence (as from Heauen) her spacious Eye doth view
Of storyed teares, and blood, the heauy crue,
How low they crawle, while she (farre more Diuine!)
Sides great *Seianus*, and fierce *Cateline:*
Where, in calme vertue, she more sweet doth shew
Then *Ioue*, when he in Golden drops did flow.

[Commendatory verses prefixed to William Davenant's *Tragedy of Albovine* (1629), sig. A.₂ʸ]

FRANCIS FANE, 1629

Here lyeth Ben Jhonson
Who was once one:
In his life a slow thinge
And now hee is dead nothinge.

[Newdigate, *The Poems of Ben Jonson*, p. 340, from the commonplace book of Sir Francis Fane (1629), now at Shakespeare's birthplace, Stratford-upon-Avon.]

ANONYMOUS, 1620–40

[A very bad text of the song of Christmas from *Christmas His Masque* (ll. 71–78, 93–101, 172–79, 182–245) is found in Harley MS 4955 in the British Museum, fols. 46–47. "This manuscript, being written for the Earl of Newcastle, is, in spite of its blunders, not without authority for important variants" (Herford and Simpson, *Ben Jonson*, VII, 434). W. D. Briggs, "Studies in Ben Jonson," *Anglia*, XXXVII (1913), 463–93, dates the manuscript and gives more details.]

ANONYMOUS, 1620–40

["The Newcastle manuscript (Harley 4955) ⟨of *The Vision of Delight*⟩ has on folios 40 and 41 without any heading the speeches of Phantasy (ll. 57–125). . . . . . From the use of the present tense in the stage-direction at lines 115–17, 'comes forth,' 'proceeds,' it appears to have been taken from a copy used for the performance and earlier than the printed text" (Herford and Simpson, *Ben Jonson*, VII, 462). See Briggs, *loc. cit.*, for a fuller description of the Jonson items in Harley 4955 and the date. The *Catalogue of the Harleian Manuscripts* does not mention these passages.]

ANONYMOUS, 1620–40

TO MR. BEN: JOHNSON IN HIS JORNEY
BY MR. CRAVEN.

WHEN witt, and learninge are so hardly sett
That from their needfull meanes they must be bard

Unless by going harde they mayntnance gett
Well maye Ben: Johnson say the world goes hard.

This was Mr Ben: Johnsons *Answer of the suddayne:*
IL may Ben Johnson slander so his feete
For when the profitt with the payne doth meete
Although the gate were hard the gayne is sweete.

[Brit. Mus. Harl. MS 4955, fol. 47*b*, quoted in Newdigate, *The Poems of Ben Jonson*, p. 336. See also Briggs, *loc. cit.*]

ANONYMOUS, 1620–40

18. Charles Cavendish to his Posterity, &c. an Epitaph.

[*A Catalogue of the Harleian Manuscripts*, III, 232, col. 1, MS 4955. Printed from a Bolsover Church MS by Newdigate in *The Poems of Ben Jonson*, p. 288, as Jonson's. The second item is printed in part by Newdigate, *The Poems of Ben Jonson*, p. 370. See Briggs, *loc. cit.*, pp. 463–64, on the date of the manuscript.]

ANONYMOUS, 1620–40

Epigramme. To my kind freind Mr Ben: Johnson upon his
Epigram to the Lo: Tresurer.

[Brit. Mus. Harl. MS 4955, fol. 173^v. The six lines of the epigram are printed by Newdigate, *The Poems of Ben Jonson*, p. 299. See Briggs, *loc. cit.*, pp. 463–64 and 473.]

ANONYMOUS, 1620–40

[A marginal note attributes to "Ben: Jonson" the following lines, which are the concluding ones to an epitaph on Charles Cavendish in Harl. MS 4955 entitled "His Posteritie of him to Strangers": "From which happiness, he was translated to the better on the 4th of Aprill, 1618. Yet not without the sad and weeping remembrance of his sorrowfull Lady, Katherine (second daughter to Cuthbert, late Lord Ogle, and sister to Jane present Countesse of Shrewsbury) who of her pietie, with her two surviving sonnes, have dedicated this humble monument to his memory, and doe all desire, in their tyme, to be gathered to his dust, expecting the happy howre of resurrection when these garments, here put of, shalbe put on glorified" (Newdigate, *The Poems of Ben Jonson*, p. 370). Briggs (*loc. cit.*, pp. 463–64 and 471) has a more meticulous transcript and a discussion of the date of the manuscript.]

ANONYMOUS, 1620–40

[The three poems on Katherine Lady Ogle printed by Newdigate in *The Poems of Ben Jonson*, pp. 289–90, are found in Brit. Mus. Harl. MS 4955, fol. 55. For a better description of the manuscript than Newdigate's and a discussion of the date, see Briggs, *loc. cit.*, pp. 463–64 and 472.]

ANONYMOUS, 1620–40

To the Right Honourable, the Lord Treasurer of England

[The epigram of which this is the title (from *Underwood;* see Newdigate, *The Poems of Ben Jonson*, p. 193) is found in Brit. Mus. Harl. MS 4955, fol. 173. The Harleian catalogue does not identify the poem, but the identification is made and the manuscript dated by Briggs, *loc. cit.*, pp. 463–64 and 473.]

ANONYMOUS, 1620–40

To My Detractor

[Jonson's poem, first printed in the quarto of 1640 (Newdigate, *The Poems of Ben Jonson*, p. 299), is found in Brit. Mus. Harl. MS 4955, fol. 173ᵛ. See Briggs, *loc. cit.*, pp. 463–64 and 473.]

ANONYMOUS, 1620–40

To my Lord Weston, Lo: Tresurer. A Letter.

[Jonson's poem, printed by Newdigate, *The Poems of Ben Jonson*, pp. 182–83, from *Underwood*, is found in Brit. Mus. Harl. MS 4955, fol. 174, under this title. See Briggs, *loc. cit.*, pp. 463–64 and 473.]

ANONYMOUS, 1620–40

AN EXPOSTULATION, WITH INIGO JONES.

[This poem, printed by Newdigate, *The Poems of Ben Jonson*, pp. 295–97, comes from Brit. Mus. Harl. MS 4955, fols. 174ᵛ–175ᵛ. See Briggs, *loc. cit.*, pp. 463–64 and 473.]

ANONYMOUS, 1620–40

TO INIGO MARQUESSE WOULD-BEE. *A Corollarie.*

[Newdigate prints the poem in *The Poems of Ben Jonson*, p. 298, from Brit. Mus. Harl. MS 4955; it is also in Harl. MS 6057. The more accurate Harleian reference, given by Briggs, *loc. cit.*, pp. 463–64 and 473, is MS 4955, fol. 176.]

ANONYMOUS, 1620–40

To Sʳ Lucius Carey, on the death of his Brother Morison

[Under this title is found in Brit. Mus. Harl. MS 4955, fols. 180–181ᵛ, Jonson's "Pindaric Ode" first printed in *Underwood* (Newdigate, *The Poems of Ben Jonson*, pp. 178–82). See Briggs, *loc. cit.*, pp. 463–64 and 474.]

ANONYMOUS, 1620–40

[The verse-letter to Jonson printed anonymously in *Wit Restored* (1658), pp. 79–81 (see *The Jonson Allusion-Book*, pp. 197–98), is found in Brit. Mus. Harl. MS 4955, fols. 185–185ᵛ, where it is said to be by Nicholas Oldisworth. See Briggs, *loc. cit.*, pp. 463–64 and 474.]

Anonymous, 1620–40

An other Lett. [i.e., from Ben Jonson to the Earl of Newcastle]

[This "begging request" (printed in Herford and Simpson, *Ben Jonson*, I, 211–12) is found transcribed in Brit. Mus. Harl. MS 4955, fol. 203. See Briggs, *loc. cit.*, pp. 463–64 and 485.]

Anonymous, 1620–40

2. Ben Jonson's Masque of the Metamorphosed Gipsies. See Whalley's Edit. vi. 69.

[*A Catalogue of the Harleian Manuscripts* (1808), III, 232, col. 1, MS 4955. According to Herford and Simpson, *Ben Jonson*, VII, 541 and 560–61, this is an inferior text related to that of the 1640 folio. See Briggs, *loc. cit.*, pp. 463–64, on the date.]

Anonymous, 1620–40

4955

A large Volume of Poems by various Authors, uniformly & fairly transcribed.

A great part by Ben Jonson & Dr. Donne. . . . .

    3. [Ben Jonson] to a friend.   31.

    4. ——— the Man. From the Underwoods, Celebration of Charis Art. IX.   34.   b.

    5. ——— the Body & Mind. From his Eupheme. 3 & 4.   35.   b.

    6. Ben Jonson, on a Country Life. From Horace Epod II.   37.   b.

    7. ——— Verses to the Erle of Newcastle inverted.   39.

    8. ——— To the Rt. Hon. Will. Viscount Mansfield.   40.

  10. ——— The Painter to the Poet, with the Answer.   41.   b.

  11. ——— To a Lady.   42.   b.

  12. ——— Execration on Vulcan.   43.

  16. Part of another Masque, apparently, with a Song of the Moon, by the same.   52.   b.

  17. ——— 'To the Memory of that most honoured Ladie, Jane, eldest daughter to Cuthbert Lord Ogle; and Countesse of Shrewsbury.'   54.

[*A Catalogue of the Harleian Manuscripts*, III, 232; see Briggs, *loc. cit.*, pp. 463–93, for a fuller description of the Jonson items in the manuscript and the date.]

Jo. Earles, *ca.* 1630

Ode ad B: J:

Sat est, si anili tradita de colo
Fabella lusit murcida Periclem.
Joco*que* semesos, et ipso
Dicta magis repetita mimo.

[From verses by "Jo: Earles" in Brit. Mus. Add. MS 15227, fol. 44ᵛ, quoted in
Shakspere Allusion-Book, I, 356 n.]

[Thomas Randolph?], *ca.* 1630

Bid: Come sirs pence a peece here is a new ballat a dainty new bal-
lat newly printed and newly come forth concerning his maies-
tyes subiects the bears in the palace garden and Vrcen ther
reuerend instructor the secund part to the same tune of the
life and death quene Dic.
Boy: Runne boyes runne a new ballat a new ballat
Bid: Tho it may seme rude for me to intrued
With thes my beares by chance-a
Twere sport for a king if they cold sing
As well as they can dance-a

. . . .

Bid: Then to put you out
Of feare or of doubt
Wee came from Sᵗ Katharins-a
Thes danceing three
By the help of me
That am the post of the signe-a

. . . .

Bid: We sel good ware
And we need not care
The cort and countrie know it.
Our ale is the best
And each good guest
Prays for ther soules that brue it.

. . . .

Bɪᴅ: ffor any ale house
     We care not a lowse
Nor tauerne in the twne-a
     Nor vintery cranes
     Nor S^t. Clements Daines
Nor the diuil can put vs downe-a.

. . . .

Bɪᴅ: Who has ther once bin
     Comes thether againe
The liquor is so mighty.
     Beare strong and Stale
     And so is our ale
And it burnes like aqua-vite.

. . . .

Bɪᴅ: ffrom morning til night
     And a bout day light
They'l sit and neuer grudg it.
     Til the fishwiues ioyne
     Ther single coine
And the tinker pownes his bug it.

[*The Drinking Academy or Cheaters Holy Day*, Huntington MS H.M. 91, pp. 20-22. As Rollins and Tannenbaum point out in the notes to their reprint of the play (Harvard University Press, 1930, p. 46), this ballad sung by Jack Bidstand is made up of stanzas 1–5 and 8 of the ballad sung by John Urson in Jonson's *Masque of Augurs*, performed at court on Twelfth Night, 1621/22, and printed in 1641.]

Tʜᴏᴍᴀs Rᴀɴᴅᴏʟᴘʜ, *ca.* 1630

. . . . yea the spring of the Muses is the fountaine of Sack, for to thinke *Helicon* a barrell of Beere, is as great a sin as to call *Pegasus* a Brewers Horse.

The divine Ben, the immortall Johnson knew this very well when he placed his oracle of Apollo at the Taverne of St. Dunstan and perhaps there he wrought his vulpone, the learned fox.

[The first passage comes from Randolph's *Aristippus* (1630), sig. C₁ᵛ. The second passage does not appear in printed editions of the play but is found immediately following the first in the manuscript of the play, Brit. Mus. Sloan MS 2531. See J. J. Parry, "A New Version of Randolph's *Aristippus*," *Modern Language Notes*, XXXII (1917), 351–54.]

COMPANY BILL, 1630

Playes for the Kinge this present yeare of o[u]r Lord God. 1630.

. . . .

The 19 of November . The Fox

[A bill for the presentation of plays by the King's men at court, September 30, 1630—February 21, 1630/31, Folger MS 2068.8. See *The Jacobean and Caroline Stage*, I, 27-29.]

THOMAS JAY, 1630

I know yon [you] would take it for an iniury,
(And 'tis a well becomming modesty)
To be paraleld with *Beaumont*, or to heare
Your name by some to partiall friend write neere
Vnequal'd *Ionson:* being men whose fire
At distance and with reuerence you admir'd.

[Commendatory verses prefixed to Philip Massinger's *The Picture* (1630), sig. A₄ᵛ.]

RICHARD BRATHWAITE, 1631

He [the decoy] ha's his varietie of Led suites: and can (if neede require) counterfeate the habit of *Grazier*, *Gallant*, or *Citizen* all in one day. With which habits he playes the cunning Impostor, and deludes those whose condition hee represents: He had neede bee one of *Volpone's* true-bred Cubbes that shall smell him out.

[*Whimzies* (1631), pp. 29-30.]

RICHARD BRATHWAITE, 1631

Hee [the gamester] seldome ha's time to take ayre, vnlesse it be to a Play; where if his pockets will giue leaue, you shall see him aspire to a *Box:* or like the *silent Woman*, sit demurely vpon the stage.

[*Ibid.*, p. 51.]

RICHARD BRATHWAITE, 1631

No season through all the yeere accounts hee [the zealous brother] more subiect to *abhomination* than *Bartholomew* faire: Their *Drums*, *Hobbihorses*, *Rattles*, *Babies*, *Iewtrumps*, nay *Pigs* and all

are wholly *Iudaicall*. The very *Booths* are *Brothells* of iniquity, and
distinguished by the stampe of the *Beast*. Yet under favour, hee will
authorize his *Sister* to eate of that uncleane and irruminating beast,
a *Pig*, provided, that this *Pig* bee fat, and that *himselfe* or some
other *zealous Brother* accompanie her: and all this is held for authentick and canonicall.

[*Ibid.*, pp. 200–201. Brathwaite so obviously summarizes the actions of Rabbi
Zeal-of-the-Land Busy in *Bartholomew Fair* that I include the allusion, though no
names are mentioned.]

R. H., 1631

Instance in others; to begin with the ambitious *man:* Is he not
ever swelling like the *Frog* in the *Fable:* till at last he breake and
burst? As did the *Israelitish*[k] *Absolom:* the *Roman*[k] *Seianus:* the
French Byron, and thousands moe?

[k]*Dion in vita Tiberij, et Gorl. in axiom. pollit. p.* 67 & *pag.* 409. his Tragedy is
also penned to the life, in English.

[*The Arraignement of the Whole Creature* (1631), p. 281, from the chapter entitled
"These Huskish Vanities, are never so fully and freely injoyed, but there is alwayes
something wanting to the Concupiscible, or rationall appetite."]

BEN JONSON, 1631

TATLE. . . . . The Play will tell vs that, sayes hee, wee'll goe see't
to-morrow, the *Diuell is an Asse*. Hee is an errant learn'd man, that
made it, and can write, they say, and I am fouly deceiu'd, but hee
can read too.

MIRTH. I remember it gossip, I went with you, by the same
token, *M*rs. *Trouble Truth* diswaded vs, and told vs, hee was a
prophane *Poet*, and all his Playes had *Diuels* in them. That he kept
schole vpo' the *Stage*, could coniure there, aboue the *Schole* of
Westminster, and *Doctor Lamb* too: not a Play he made, but had a
Diuell in it. And that he would learne vs all to make our husbands
Cuckolds at Playes: by another token, that a young married wife
i'the company, said, shee could finde in her heart to steale thither,
and see a little o'the vanity through her masque, and come practice at home.

["The first Intermeane after the first *Act*," *The Staple of Newes*, in Herford and
Simpson, *Ben Jonson*, VI, 303, ll. 43–56.]

BEN JONSON, 1631

CEN[SURE.] . . . . well, they talke, we shall haue no more Parliaments (God blesse vs) but an' wee haue, I hope, *Zeale-of-the-land Buzy*, and my Gossip, *Rabby Trouble-truth* will start vp, and see we shall haue painfull good Ministers to keepe Schoole, and *Catechise* our youth, and not teach 'hem to speake *Playes*, and act *Fables* of false newes. . . . .

["The third Intermeane after the third *Act*," *The Staple of Newes*, in *ibid.*, p. 345, ll. 50–55. The reference to the character from Jonson's own *Bartholomew Fair* may be simply another example of the author's assurance, or it may indicate some current acceptance of Jonson's character as a zealous Puritan type.]

JOHN POLWHELE (?), 1631

To the admired Ben Johnson to encourage him to write after his farewel to ye stage, 1631.

[Title of a poem in a manuscript, of about 1650, offered for sale by P. J. and A. E. Dobell, Tunbridge Wells, England, *Catalogue No. 44* (December, 1938), p. 355.]

ANONYMOUS, 1624–40

A Song at Court to invite the Ladies to Daunce.

[Under this title the next to the last song from *Neptune's Triumph* is copied in Brit. Mus. Harl. MS 4955, fol. 192. See W. D. Briggs, *Anglia*, XXXVII (1913), pp. 463–64 and 483.]

ROBERT BURTON, 1632

If he be rich, he is the man, a fine man, & a proper man, shel'e goe to *Iackatres* or *Tidore* with him; *Gelasimus de Monte aureo*, Sᵣ *Giles Goosecap*, Sᵣ *Amorous La-Foole*, shall haue her.

[*The Anatomy of Melancholy* (1632), Part 3, sec. 2, memb. 2, subs. 3, Ooo₃ᵛ. I owe this allusion to the kindness of Miss Bertha Hensman.]

MICHAEL OLDISWORTH, 1632

Behind the Abbey lives a man of fame;
With awe and reverence wee repeat his name,
Ben Johnson: him we saw, and thought to heare
From him some flashes and fantastique Geure;
But hee spake nothing lesse. His whole Discourse

Was how Mankinde grew daily worse and worse,
How God was disregarded, how Men went
Downe even to Hell, and neuer did repent,
With many such sadd Tales; as hee would teach
Vs Scholars, how herafter Wee should preach.
Great wearer of the baies, looke to thy lines,
Lest they chance to bee challeng'd by Divines:
Some future Times will, by a grosse Mistake,
Johnson a Bishop, not a Poët make.

[*Iter Australe* (1632), from the manuscript poems of Michael Oldisworth of Wotton-under-Edge, in the hands of P. J. Dobell. See Herford and Simpson, *Ben Jonson*, I, 113, n. 1.]

WILLIAM HEMMINGE, 1632–33

Instead of verse vppon his Coffine sittes
our Neotericall refined wyttes
whose magnitude of brayne has had the force
to Crye a play downe to hould vpp discourse,
Our Classicke pates, and such as had the Brayne
to make a Ceasar speake In Ceasars strayne,
Seianus Lyke Seianus, hee whose Lyne
reuyues A Cattalyn In Cattalyn,
(And myght the great Appollo pleased wth Benn
make the odd Number of the Muses ten),
The fluente Flettcher, Beaumonte riche In sence
for Complement and Courtshypes quintesence,
Ingenious Shakespeare, Messenger that knowes
the strength to wright or plott In verse or prose,
Whose easye pegasus Can Ambell ore
some threscore Myles of fancye In an hower,
Clowd grapling Chapman whose Aeriall mynde
Soares att philosophie and strickes ytt blynd,
Dauborne I had forgott, and lett ytt bee,
hee dyed Amphybion by thy Ministrye.

[*William Hemminge's Elegy on Randolph's Finger*, ed. G. C. Moore Smith (1923), ll. 43–62. The last twelve lines of this passage are quoted in *The Jonson Allusion-Book*, but they are taken from the inaccurate extracts from Hemminge's poem in *Choyce Drollery* (1656).]

WILLIAM HEMMINGE, 1632-33

Orderly thus disordred thay did goe,
true sorrowe knowes no Equipage In Woe:
for sent by Iohnson as some Authors say
Broome went before and kyndly sweept the way.

[*William Hemminge's Elegy on Randolph's Finger*, ed. Smith, ll. 109–12.]

WILLIAM HEMMINGE, 1632-33

Thay Quakte at Iohnson as by hym thay pase
because of Trebulation Holsome and Annanias.

[*Ibid.*, ll. 183–84.]

WILLIAM HEMMINGE, 1632-33

The muses morne; Minerva full of Ire
sett halfe a dozen Libraries on fier:
Such was the sight that ytt did seeme to bee
A Doomsday onlye framed for Poetrye.
Much of Ben Iohnson In her rage did fry
whilest hee deemd Vulcan for his enemye,
And manye learned pates as well as hee
weare sadly Martred for this Infamye.

[*Ibid.*, ll. 217–24.]

ANONYMOUS, *ca.* 1633

72. [Ben Jonson.] The King's Entertainment at Welbeck, 1663 [i.e., 1633].

[*A Catalogue of the Harleian Manuscripts* (1808), III, 233, col. 1, MS 4955. See Herford and Simpson, *Ben Jonson*, VII, 767 and 789.]

THOMAS NABBES, 1633

Sam. Shee's my Wife, Vncle.
Vnc. Yet more plots! sure the Parson of *Pancrace* hath beene here.
1. *Ten.* Indeed I have heard he is a notable joyner.
2. *Ten.* And *Totenham-Court* Ale pays him store of tith. It causeth questionlesse much unlawfull coupling.

[*Tottenham Court* (1638), V, 6, sig. K₂. The title-page of the play bears the statement "Acted in the Yeare MDCXXXIII." The "Parson of *Pancrace*" is obviously a reference to Chan. Hugh, vicar of Pancras, the matchmaker and intriguer of Jonson's *Tale of a Tub*, a play which was performed at the rival theater, the Phoenix, in the same year that Nabbes says his play was performed at the Salisbury Court theater.]

Aurelian Townshend, *ca.* 1633

Thow wert not borne, as other women be,
To need the help of heightning Poesie,
But to make Poets. Hee, that could present
Thee like thy glasse, were superexcellent.
Witnesse that Pen which, prompted by thy parts
Of minde and bodie, caught as many heartes
With euery line, as thou with euery looke;
Which wee conceiue was both his baite and hooke.
His Stile before, though it were perfect steele,
Strong, smooth, and sharp, and so could make us feele
His loue or anger, Witneses agree,
Could not attract, till it was toucht by thee.
Magneticke then, Hee was for heighth of style
Suppos'd in heauen; And so he was, the while
He sate and drewe thy beauties by the life,
Visible Angell, both as maide and wife.

[These lines, from Townshend's "An Elegie made by Mr Aurelian Townshend in remembrance of the Ladie Venetia Digby," refer to "of course, Ben Jonson," according to the note on p. 112 of E. K. Chambers, *Aurelian Townshend's Poems and Masks* (1912); they are to be found in *ibid.*, pp. 38–39. The poem is the last of a book of poems on Venetia Digby, constituting Add. MS 30259. The poem must have been written soon after her death (May 1, 1633).]

William Prynne, 1633

*Some Play-books since I first undertooke this subject, are growne from *Quarto* into *Folio;* which yet beare so good a price and sale, that I cannot but with griefe relate it, they are now (e) new-

---

* Ben-Iohnsons, Shackspeers, and others.

e Shackspeers Plaies are printed in the best Crowne paper, far better than most Bibles.

printed in farre better paper than most Octavo or Quarto *Bibles*, which hardly finde such vent as they.

[*Histrio-mastix* (1633), Preface, sig. **6ᵛ.]

ANONYMOUS, 1629–40

To the great and Gratious King Charles. On the Universary day of his Raigne 1629.

[Under this title the poem printed in *Underwood* (Newdigate, *The Poems of Ben Jonson,* pp. 173–74) is copied in Brit. Mus. Harl. MS 4955, fol. 192ᵛ. See W. D. Briggs, *Anglia,* XXXVII (1913), 463–64 and 483.]

ANONYMOUS, *ca.* 1634

73. [Ben Jonson.] The King & Queen's Entertainment at Boulsover, July 1634.

[*A Catalogue of the Harleian Manuscripts* (1808), III, 233, col. 1, MS 4955. See Herford and Simpson, *Ben Jonson,* VII, 767 and 806.]

ANONYMOUS, *ca.* 1634

An other Letter (i.e., from Ben Jonson to the Earl of Newcastle]

[This letter of thanks (printed in Herford and Simpson, *Ben Jonson,* I, 212) is found transcribed in Brit. Mus. Harl. MS 4955, fol. 203. See Briggs, *Anglia,* XXXVII (1913), 463–64 and 485.]

JAMES HOWELL, 1634

Howellus Johnsonio ευηρεμειν¹

Tempestiuè equidem (mî Johnsonî) in manus cecidit Dauisius, vt strenæ locum suppleat. Accipias eum, illo quo datur, anim[o]² felicissimum tibi annum exoptantem. Vale κεφαλὴ μοὶ προσφιλεσάτη & saluti consule, vt pergat amare

Tuum

Cal; Jan;   Ja Howell.

To THE poett
Mʳ Beniamin Johnson
vpon dʳ Dauis Welsh Gramar.

¹ Evidently meaning 'good luck'; it is Howell's attempt to reproduce εὐημερεῖν.

² One letter is cut off in the margin.

T'was a tough task, beleeue it, thus to tame
a wild and wealthy language, ...

[Written by James Howell on the flyleaf before the title of John Davis' *Welsh Grammar*, which he presented to Jonson. The poem itself makes no mention of Jonson. It was printed in a revised version in *Epistolae Ho-Elinae* (1645), sec. 5, xxvii, pp. 31–32. Quoted in Herford and Simpson, *Ben Jonson*, I, 258–60.]

SIR HUMPHREY MILDMAY, 1634

. . . . att nighte to the Courte wth a freinde to see Catteline Acted.

[Entry of November 9, 1634, in the diary of Sir Humphrey Mildmay. See *The Jacobean and Caroline Stage*, II, 676.]

ANONYMOUS, 1630–40

An Epigramme, to the Queenes Health

[This poem (printed in Newdigate, *The Poems of Ben Jonson*, p. 175, under the title "An Epigram to the Queene, then Lying in. 1630") is found in Brit. Mus. Harl. MS 4955, fol. 193, though it is not mentioned in the catalogue. See Briggs, *Anglia*, XXXVII (1913), 463–64 and 484.]

ANONYMOUS, 1630–40

Epigram
On the Prince's Birth, MDCXXX

[This poem (see Newdigate, *The Poems of Ben Jonson*, p. 174) is found in Brit. Mus. Harl. MS 4955, fol. 193, though it is not mentioned in the catalogue. See Briggs, *loc. cit.*]

CONSTANCE ASTON (?), *ca.* 1630–40

An Elegie on the Lady Jane Paulet marchionesse of winchester.

[A copy of Jonson's elegy, first printed in the folio of 1640, appears under this title in one of the Huntington Library's manuscript commonplace books (H.M. 904), said to have been that of Constance, daughter of Walter, first Lord Aston of Forfar. See B. H. Newdigate, "The Constant Lovers," *Times Literary Supplement*, April 18, 1942, p. 204, and April 25, 1942, p. 216.]

ANONYMOUS, 1631–40

A Letter to the Earle of Newcastle

[This letter concerning the printing of *The Devil Is an Ass* and *Bartholomew Fair* (printed in Herford and Simpson, *Ben Jonson*, I, 211) is found transcribed in Brit. Mus. Harl. MS 4955, fol. 202ᵛ. See Briggs, *loc. cit.*, pp. 463–64 and 485.]

An other Lr̃e [i.e., from Ben Jonson to the Earl of Newcastle]

[This letter (printed in Herford and Simpson, *Ben Jonson*, I, 213–14) is found transcribed in Brit. Mus. Harl. MS 4955, fols. 203ᵛ–204. See Briggs, *loc. cit.*, pp. 463–64 and 485.]

Anonymous, 1631–40

Mr. Thomas Carye:—To Ben Jonson upon occasion of his Ode.

[Carew's poem to Jonson has been transcribed in Brit. Mus. Harl. MS 4955, fols. 214–214ᵛ. See Briggs, *loc. cit.*, pp. 463–64 and 485.]

Anonymous, 1631–40

Mr Feltham:—in Ben Jonson.

[Under this title Feltham's reply to Jonson's ode, "Come leave this saucy way," is transcribed in Brit. Mus. Harl. MS 4955, fol. 216. See Briggs, *loc. cit.*, pp. 463–64 and 486.]

Anonymous, 1633–40

Epithalamion . . . . Celebrating the Nuptials of . . . .
Mr. Hierome Weston . . . . with the Lady Frances Stuart

[This epithalamium, first printed in *Underwood* (see Newdigate, *The Poems of Ben Jonson*, pp. 185–91), is found in Brit. Mus. Harl. MS 4955, fols. 176ᵛ–179ᵛ. See Briggs, *loc. cit.*, pp. 463–64 and 473.]

Thomas Morton, 1637

*Of the Baccanall Triumph of the nine
worthies of New Canaan*

. . . .

Master Ben: *I sing th' adventures of nine worthy wights*
Iohnson   *And pitty 't is I cannot call them Knights,*
      Since they had brawne and braine and were right able,
      To be installed of prince Arthures table.

[*New English Canaan* (Amsterdam, 1637), p. 146. As Newdigate points out (*The Poems of Ben Jonson*, p. 368), the whole poem is a clumsy parody of Jonson's "The Voyage It Self." The first five lines are Jonson's except for eight or ten altered words; thus Morton's marginal note is a simple acknowledgment of source.]

ANONYMOUS, 1634-40

An other Letter [i.e., from Ben Jonson to the Earl of Newcastle]

[This letter (printed by Herford and Simpson, *Ben Jonson*, I, 212) is found transcribed in Brit. Mus. Harl. MS 4955, fol. 203. See Briggs, *loc. cit.*, pp. 463–64 and 485. The manuscript dates before 1640, as Briggs shows, and Jonson's original letter cannot have been written before 1634 (Herford and Simpson, *loc. cit.*).]

SIR THOMAS SALUSBURY, *ca.* 1638

AN ELEGIE MEANT VPON
THE DEATH OF BEN: JOHNSON:

Shall I alone spare paper? in an age
when euerie pen shedds inke, to swell a page
in Johnsons Elegies, And ore his herse
(a sorrow worthie of him) dropp theire verse,
as plentie as the cheaper moisture falls
from duller braines, at common funeralls,
His death inspiringe richer witts, and more
then all the Auncient Hero's liues before
were Theme vnto: ye Spiritt of Poetrie
Like the Prophetique, keepes not companie
with the departted Soule in's flight; but falls
on those, whome Heauen to the succession calls.
And as the Tisbites, that from Jordans side
mounted in's flaminge Charriott, did abide
and cleaue vnto Elisha; Thine doth rest
not vpon one, but manie are possest
'mongst whome myselfe, though led like one of those
the prophetts children, that in zeale arose,
and cl[im]b'd the hills, as if in hope t' haue found
by the advantage of the higher ground
theyre ffather soar'd to Heauen; as much in vaine,
I find is my imployment, whilst I straine
my feeble Muse, to reach thy worth, and find
out language fitt to character thy mind;
or thy immortal gloryes to reherse
in deathles number, such as was thy verse.
    I might as well by contemplation make

my grosse empriss'ned soule to ouertake
thy free enlarged Spiritt, and expresse
thy not to be conceiued blessednes.
This were to doe like thee whose onelie penne
wrote things vnutt'rable by other men.

T. S.

[From "the Salusbury Manuscript in the National Library of Wales," printed by
Sir Israel Gollancz in "Ben Jonson's Ode to 'The Phoenix and the Turtle,'" *Times
Literary Supplement*, October 8, 1925, p. 655.]

Drv. Cooper, 1638

Shirley stand forth, and put thy Lawrell on,
Phoebus next heire, now *Ben* is dead and gone,
Truly legitimate, *Ireland* is so just
To say, you rise the Phenix of his dust.

[Commendatory verses prefixed to James Shirley's *The Royal Master* (1638),
sig. A₃ᵛ.]

Robert Cresswell, 1638

To yᵉ most Accomplish'tt his Honour'd Patron. yᵉ Lo:
Falkland. vpon yᵉ Receipt of a Booke, wᵗʰ a Lre, from his Loᵖ.

. . . .

In humane Writ, Wee Beggars turne & Fooles
To learne the Canting Language of yᵉ Schooles.
You haue Truth's Looking-Glasse, Expression! Tis
As cleere & faythfull as the Notion is:
You leade the Triumph of Immortall Ben
And fluent Sands, runs brighter from your Pen
This credits the Profession! . . . .

[Kurt Weber, *Lucius Cary Second Viscount Falkland* (1940), pp. 122, 124; quoted
from Hale MS XII, fols. 50ʳ–51ᵛ.]

George Daniel, 1638

. . . . Wee converse with Men,
Which setts new Edge on witt; the richest Pen
Of fancie here finds Inke; the glorious Names
Of Ionson, Beaumont, Fletcher, live with Thames,
And shall outlive his waters. Had they crept

In mudled remote Streams, their worth had slept;
And those great Fancies which all men Admire
Had flowen, but in the Smoake of their owne fire.
'Tis Fame gives Life; Iudgment gives Life to Fame;
Iudgment moves here; then be noe longer Shame
Vnto thy Genius; wast noe more thy witt
With Hinds, whose palats cannot relish it.

[From the first eclogue, ll. 59–70, in *Several Ecloges: The first revived; from some Papers formerlie written, 1.6.3.8. The rest, Written by the same Author; 1.6.4.8.*, *Poems of George Daniel* (1878), ed. A. Grosart, II, 139–40.]

WILLIAM DAVENANT, 1638

To Doctor *Duppa*, Deane of Christ-Church, and Tutor to the Prince. An acknowledgment for his collection, in Honour of *Ben. Iohnson's* memory.

How shall I sleepe to night, that am to pay
By a bold vow, a mighty Debt ere Day?
Which all the Poets of this Island owe:
Like Palmes,* neglected, it will greater grow.
How vainly from my single Stock of Wit,
(As small, as is my Art, to Husband it)
I have adventur'd what they durst not doe
With strong confed'rate Art, and Nature too.
This Debt hereditary is, and more
Than can be pay'd for such an Ancestor;
Who living, all the Muses Treasure spent,
As if they him, their Heire, not Steward meant.
Forrests of Mirtle, he disforrested,
That neere to Helicon their shades did spred;
Like Moderne Lords, w'are so of Rent bereft;
Poets, and they, have nought but Titles left:
He wasted all in Wreaths, for's conqu'ring Wit;
Which was so strong, as nought could conquer it
But's Judgment's force, and that more rul'd the sense
Of what he writ, than's Fancy's vaste expence.
Of that hee still was lavishly profuse;

* Misprinted "Palnes."

For joyne the remnant—Wealth of ev'ry Muse,
And t'will not pay the Debt wee owe to thee,
For honours done unto his Memory:
Thus then, he brought th'Estate into decay,
With which, this Debt, wee as his Heires should pay.

    As sullen Heires, when wastefull Fathers die,
Their old Debts leave for their Posteritie
To cleere; and the remaining Akers strive
T'enjoy, to keepe them pleasant whilst alive;
So I (alas!) were to my selfe unkinde,
If from that little Wit, he left behinde,
I simply should so great a debt defray;
I'le keepe it to maintaine mee, not to pay.
Yet, for my soul's last quiet when I die,
I will commend it to posteritie:
Although 'tis fear'd ('cause they are left so poore)
They'll but acknowledge, what they should restore:
However, since I now may erne my Bayes,
Without the taint of flatterie in prayse;
Since I've the luck, to make my prayses true,
I'le let them know, to whom this Debt is due:

    Due unto you, whose learning can direct
Why Faith must trust, what Reason would suspect:
Teach Faith to rule, but with such temp'rate law,
As Reason not destroys, yet keeps't in awe:
Wise you; the living-Volume, which containes
All that industrious Art, from Nature gaines;
The usefull, open-Booke, to all unty'd;
That knowes more, than halfe-Knowers seeme to hide:
And with an easie cheerefulnesse reveale,
What they, through want, not sullennesse conceale.
That, to great-faithlesse-Wits, can truth dispence
'Till't turne, their witty scorne, to reverence:
Make them confesse, their greatest error springs,
From curious gazing on the least of Things;
With reading smaller prints, they spoyle their Sight,
Darken themselves, then rave, for want of light:

Shew them, how full they are of subtle sinne,
When Faith's great Cable, they would nicely spinne
To Reason's slender Threads; then (falsely bold)
When they have weakned it, cry, t'wilt not hold!
   To him, that so victorious still doth grow,
In knowledge, and t'enforce others to know;
Humble in's strength; not cunning, to beguile,
Nor strong, to overcome, but reconcile:
To Arts Milde Conqueror; that is, to you,
Our sadly mention'd Debt, is justly due:
And now Posteritie is taught to know,
Why, and to whom, this mighty Summe they owe,
I safely may goe sleep; for they will pay
It at all times, although I breake my Day.

[*Madagascar; with Other Poems* (1638), pp. 138–41.]

SIR HUMPHREY MILDMAY, 1638

To see the foxe playe wth fra: Wortley.............. oo–o4–o6
. . . .
fayre & Cleere all this day I wente to Westmi: dined att Whitehall
& after dynner to the fox playe = att bl: fryers wth my Cozen fra.
Wortley & my Brother Anth,: & Came Jn Peace to Supper & bedd,
I bles god.

[Entries of October 27, 1638, in the account book and diary of Sir Humphrey. See *The Jacobean and Caroline Stage*, II, 678.]

RICHARD WEST, 1638

Read's flowry *Pastoralls*, and you will sweare
Hee was not *Iohnsons* only, but *Pans* Heire.

[Commendatory verses prefixed to Thomas Randolph's *Poems with the Muses Looking-Glasse: and Amyntas* (1638), sig. ***₄.]

MRS. ANN MERRICKE, 1638/39

I cu'd wish my selfe with you, to ease you of this trouble, and
with-all to see the Alchymist, which I heare this tearme is revis'd,
and the newe playe a freind of mine sent to Mr. John Sucklyn,

and Tom: Carew (the best witts of the time) to correct, but for
want of these gentile recreationes, I must content my selfe here,
with the studie of Shackspeare, and the historie of woemen, All
my countrie librarie.

[A manuscript letter in the Public Record Office, Mrs. Ann Merricke to Mrs.
Lydall, January 21, 1638/39. See *The Shakspere Allusion-Book*, I, 443.]

Thomas Bancroft, 1639

2. *To* the Reader.

Reader, till *Martial* thou hast well survey'd,
Or *Owens* Wit with *Ionsons* Learning weigh'd,
Forbeare with thankelesse censure to accuse
My Writ of errour, or condemne my Muse.

[*Two Bookes of Epigrammes, and Epitaphs* (1639), sig. A₃.]

George Daniel, 1639

Loe, this the Muse who variously did sing
And soar'd at Randome, with an Idle wing;
Told younger yeares the Passions of Love,
In broken Accents, as sick thoughts did prove;

. . . .

Hath wept the Funeralls of Buckingham,
And Herbert's Death, with some of lower Name,
Recorded vertuous; & hath paid a verse
To Iohnson's vrne, & wept vpon his Herse;
Ioyn'd with the Muses, Strongly to defend
The force of Numbers; . . . .

[*"Eclesiasticus: or The Wisedome of Iesus, the son of Syrach,"* *Poems of George
Daniel*, ed. A. Grosart, II, 209–10, ll. 1–4, 19–24.]

Sir Humphrey Mildmay, 1639

To the Alchemist eod [May 18, 1639]. oo–o5–oo

[Entry in Sir Humphrey's account book. See *The Jacobean and Caroline Stage*,
II, 678.]

ANONYMOUS, *ca.* 1640

[A commonplace book of about 1640, now in the possession of Professor J. Q. Adams, contains three poems by or about Jonson.

1. Carew's poem, "To Ben: Johnson Vpon occasion of his Ode to him selfe," which was first printed in Carew's works in 1640.

2. "Bens Answeare" (to Alexander Gill's "To B. Johnson on his Magnet ck Lady"), which appears in a version superior to that printed by Gifford.

3. "Ben: Johnsons Ode to himselfe."

(J. Q. Adams, "Notes on Ben Jonson, from a Seventeenth Century Common-Place Book," *Modern Language Review*, VII [1912], 296–99).]

CONSTANCE ASTON(?), *ca.* 1640

[In the Huntington Library manuscript commonplace book, H.M. 904, said to have belonged to Constance, daughter of Walter, first Lord Aston of Forfar (see B. H. Newdigate, "The Constant Lovers," *Times Literary Supplement*, April 18 and 25, 1942), appears a Jonson epitaph entitled "A Epitaph on ben: Johnson" and signed "M. S. C." The fourteen-line poem is the same as that printed on p. 272 of *The Jonson Allusion-Book* as Epitaph 191 in *Wits Recreations* (1640). This poem does not, however, appear in *Wits Recreations* but is Epitaph 175 in *Recreation for Ingenious Head-peeces* (1654), where it is entitled *"Another on Ben: J."* and is not signed.]

WILLIAM CAVENDISH, *ca.* 1640

To Ben: Ionson's Ghost

I would write of Thee, Ben; not to approue
My witt or Learneing; but my Iudgment, Loue.
But when I think or this, or that, to chuse;
Each part of Thee, is too big for my Muse.
Should I compare Thee to Romes dust, that's dead?
Their witt, to Thine's as heauy as thy lead:
Should I prophane Thee to our liueing Men?
Th'are light as strawes, and feathers to Thee, Ben.
Did wee want Ballads for these shallow tymes,
Or for our winter Nights, some sporting rhymes;
For such weake trifles, wee have witts great store;
Now thou art gone, there's not a Poet more.
Our Country's Glory! Wee must iustly boast
Thus much; more would but raise thy angry Ghost.
Wee may with sadder blackes behange thy hearse;
All els, were Libells on ourselues, if Verse.

Rest then, in Peace, in our vast Mothers wombe,
Thou art a Monument, without a Tombe.
Is any Infidel? Let him but looke
And read, Hee may be saued by thy Booke.

[From the Welbeck MS "in the hand of Newcastle's secretary, John Rollestone,"
A Collection of Poems, Welbeck Miscellany, No. 2 (1934), p. 43.]

ANONYMOUS, 1640

Rise *Synna*, *Sylla*, *Marius*, *Gracchus* Ghost,
With the rest of the whole Mechanick Host,
etc.

["Pyms *Juncto.* 1640," *Rump: or an Exact Collection of the Choycest Poems and
Songs Relating to the Late Times* (1662), p. 6. It is noteworthy that Sylla's Ghost in
the Prologue to *Catiline* names "the GRACCHI, CINNA, MARIVS" in l. 21.]

ANONYMOUS, 1640

121 *B. J. answer to a thiefe bidding him stand.*

Fly villaine hence or be thy coate of steele,
Ile make thy heart, my brazen bullet feele,
And send that thrice as thievish soul of thine,
To hell, to weare the Devils Valentine.

122 *The Theefe's replie.*

Art thou great *Ben?* or the revived ghost
Of famous *Shake-spear?* or som drunken host?
Who being tipsie with thy muddy beer,
Dost think thy rimes shall daunt my soul with fear
Nay know base slave, that I am one of those,
Can take a purse aswell in verse as prose,
And when th'art dead, write this upon thy herse;
Here lies a Poet that was robb'd in verse.

[*Wits Recreations* (1640), sigs. D₂ᵛ–D₃. Quoted in *The Jonson Allusion-Book*, p.
307, from *Musarum deliciae* (1655), and from a commonplace book of 1676, p. 382.
Apparently the lines were widely copied.]

John Benson, 1640

To the Right Honourable Thomas Lord Windsor, &c.

My Lord:

The assurance the Author of these Poems received of his Worth from your Honour, in his lifetime, was not rather a marke of his desert, than a perfect demonstration of your Noble love to him: Which consideration, has rais'd my bold desire to assume presumption, to present these to your Honour, in the person of one deceased; the forme whereof somewhat disperst, yet carry with them the Prerogative of truth to be Mr. *Ben: Jonsons;* and will so appeare to all, whose Eyes, and Spirits are rightly plac'd. You are (my Lord) a Person who is able to give value and true esteeme to things of themselves no lesse deserving: such were his, strong, and as farre transcendent ordinary imagination, as they are conformable to the sence of such who are of sound judgement: his Strenuous Lines, and sinewey Labours have rais'd such Piramydes to his lasting name, as shall out-last Time. And that these may, without any diminution to the glory of his greater Workes, enjoy the possession of publicke favour, (by your Honours permission) I shall be glad by this small Testimony account it a fit opportunity to assure your Honour, my Lord, that I am

Your most humble and affectionate Servant,

John Benson

[Dedication of *Ben: Ionson's Execration against Vulcan* (London, *J. O.* for *John Benson*, 1640), sigs. A₃–A₄.]

Richard Brathwaite, 1640

These [nice ones] will not grant admittance to their Suiters, to preferre their requests in their Chambers. No; they must be distanced by some Partition or Window; or else wooe by *Prospective Glasses:* or utter their thoughts (with the *Silent Lady)* through Canes or Trunks; as if *Affection* were an *Infection*.

[*Ar't asleepe Husband? A Boulster Lecture* . . . . By *Philogenes Panedonius* (1640), p. 256.]

Richard Brome, 1640

Stri. You may, you may; you have a wit sir *Hugh*, and a projective one; what, have you some new project a foot now, to out-goe

that of the Handbarrowes? what call you 'em the Sedams? oh cry
you mercy, cry you mercy; I heard you had put in for a share at
the *Asparagus Ga[r]den:* or that at least you have a Pension thence;
to be their Gather guest and bring 'em custome, and that you play
the fly of the new Inne there; and sip with all companies: am I
w'ye there sir?

[*The Sparagus Garden* (1640), I, iii, sig. B₄ᵛ. Jonson describes this character in the
1631 edition of *The New Inn:* "*Fly.* Is the Parasite of the Inne, *visiter* generall of
the house, one that had been a strolling *Gipsee,* but now is reclam'd, to be Inflamer
of the reckonings."]

RICHARD BROME, 1640

Mon. . . . . . yet thou and I *Iacke* have bin alwaies confident of
each other, and have wrought friendly and closely together, as ever
Subtle and his Lungs did; and shar'd the profit betwixt us, han't
we *Iacke:* ha?

[*Ibid.,* II, ii, sig. D₁ᵛ. In *The Alchemist* Face is nearly always called Lungs by
Mammon; see II, ii, iii, v; IV, i, v; V, iii.]

I. E., 1640

To Mr. *Ionson* upon these Verses.

[*I.e.,* Jonson's verses to the Right Honourable the L. Treasurer]

Your Verses were commended, as 'tis true,
That they were very good, I meane to you:
For they return'd you *Ben* I have beene told,
The seld seene summe of forty pound in gold.
These Verses then, being rightly understood,
His Lordship, not *Ben: Ionson,* made them good.
                                                    I. E.

[*Ben: Ionson's Execration against Vulcan* (1640), sig. E₃ᵛ.]

HENRY GLAPTHORNE, 1640

It starts our Authors confidence, who by me
Tels you thus much t'excuse the Comedy.
You shall not here be feasted with the sight
Of anticke showes; but Actions, such as might

And have beene reall, and in such a phrase,
As men should speake in: . . . .

[From the Prologue to *The Ladies Priviledge* (1640). The passage states, of course, the critical principles of comedy set out in the Prologue to *Every Man in His Humour* and even paraphrases Jonson's famous lines.]

BEN JONSON, 1640

Iro. Who made this EPIGRAMME, you? *Com.* No,
a great Clarke
As any'is of his bulke (*Ben: Ionson*) made it.

[*The Magnetic Lady*, Act I, scene 2, 1640 folio.]

LEWIS SHARPE, 1640

[Pupillus is fed passages from various poets to influence his style. The second passage he is offered is from the Epilogue to *Cynthia's Revels* and makes him assume the character of Jonson.]

Mer. . . . . now for the inspiration of a confident Poeticall wit.

Pup. Pray pick out the hard words, if there be any.

Mer. There's none in this—you shall heare it.

"This from our Author I was bid to say,
"By *Iove* 'tis good; and if you lik't you may.

Pup. Ile tell you how I like it presently.

Mer. Come sir, downe with it—

Fled. So, this past with ease—

Mer. How doe you find your selfe affected now?

Pup. Oh that I were in a Play-house—I wou'd tell the whole Audience of their pittifull, Hereticall, Criticall humours—Let a man, striving to enrich his labours, make himselfe as poore as a broken Citizen, that dares not so much as shew the tips on's Hornes: yet will these people crye it downe, they know not why: One loves high language, though he understands it not; another whats obscaene, to move the blood, not spleene: a third, whose wit lyes all in his gall, must have a Satyre: a fourth man all ridiculous: and the fift man not knowing what to have, grounds his opinion on the next man ith' formall Ruffe; and so many heads, so many severall humours; and yet the poor Poet must find waies to please 'hem all.

Mer. It workes strangely.

Pup. But when they shal come to feed on the Offalls of wit, have nothing for their money but a Drumme, a Fooles Coat, and Gunpowder; see Comedies, more ridiculous than a Morrice dance; and for their Tragedies, a bout at Cudgells were a brave Battalia to 'hem: Oh *Phoebus*, '*Phoebus*, what will this world come to?

[*The Noble Stranger* (1640), Act IV, sig. G₃ᵛ. Pointed out by Langbaine, *An Account of the English Dramatic Poets* (1691), p. 470.]

ANONYMOUS, 1641

First came the Poets, of each land, and tooke
Their place in order, learned *Virgill* struck
In for the first, *Ben Iohnson* cast a glout,
And swore a might [*sic*] oath hee'd pluck him out,
And wallowing towards him, with a cup of Wine,
He did so rattle him with *Catiline*,
That had not *Horace* him appeas'd, tis said
He had throwne great *Sejanus* at his head.

[*The Copie of a Letter sent from the Roaring Boyes in Elizium* (1641). Allusion recorded by Howard P. Vincent, *Notes and Queries*, CLXXVII (July 8, 1939), 26.]

ANONYMOUS, 1641

Neates tongues by thousands came; but most were taken
With salt gamon of Westphalia baken:
The Poets and the Soldiers slashing stood,
And great *Ben: Iohnson* swore that it was good.

[*Ibid.* Allusion recorded by Vincent, *loc. cit.*]

THOMAS BEEDOME, 1641

When *Johnson*, *Drayton*, and those happier men
That can drop wonders from their fluent Pen:
Have with their miracles of Poetry
Feasted thy eares and satisfi'd thy eye;
Then turne aside, and 'mongst the vulgar things,
Place what my new-borne Muse abruptly sings.

["The Author, To the Reader," *Poems* (1641), sig. B₈.]

Thomas Beedome, 1641

[In his *Poems* Thomas Beedome reprints Jonson's poem, "That Women Are But Mens Shaddows," with the refrain,

"Say, are not women truly then
Styl'd but the shadowes of us men?"

At the close Beedome prints *"Per Ben Johnson"* and then presents his own reply.]

Women are not mens shadowes.

E *Contra.*

1.

The sunne absented, shadowes then
Cease to put on the formes of men.
But wives, their husbands absent, may
Beare best their formes (they being away)
　　Say, are not women falsly then
　　Stil'd but the shadowes of us men.

2.

Shadowes at Morne and Even are strong,
At noone they are, or weake, or none:
Women at Noone are ever long,
At night so weake they fall along.
　　Say, are not women falsly then
　　Stil'd but the shadowes of us men?

3.

As bodies are contracted, shadowes so
Contract themselves to formes as bodies doe:
Let men be bounded neere so close: I wist,
Women will rove and ramble were they list.
　　Say, are not women falsly then
　　Stil'd but the shadowes of us men?

[*Poems* (1641), sig. E₇ᵛ.]

Thomas Beedome, 1641

Till* when (that I may come to speake our dayes)
Daniel thou livest circled with breath for bayes.

* Misprinted "Yill."

Nor Spencer to whose verse the world doth owe
Millions of thankes can unremembred goe:
Nor thou great Johnson, who knowst how to write
Such lines as equall profit with delight,
Whil'st thy untired readers wish each sheete
Had beene a volume, 'tis so neate, so sweete.
Next, fame seemes charily to spread her wings,
O're what the never dying Drayton sings,
Still lives the Muses Appollinean son,
The Phaenix of his age, rare Harrington,
Whose Epigrams when time shall be no more,
May die (perhaps) but never can before.

["Encomium Poetarum ad fratrem Galiel Scot," *ibid.*, sig. F₅.]

Io. BERMINGHAM, 1641

And, though thou *England* never saw'st: Yet, this
(Let others boast of their owne faculties,
Or being Sonne to *Iohnson*) I dare say,
That thou art farre more like to *Ben:* then they
That lay clayme as heires to him, wrongfully:
For he survives now only, but in thee
And his owne lines; the rest degenerate.
Nay, I can more affirme (and truly) that
In some things thou do'st passe him: being more sweet,
More modest, mylde, lesse tedious; Thy owne feet
Goe thou on stoutly then: if thou proceed,
Him (though't be much) in all points thou'lt exceed.

[Commendatory verses prefixed to Henry Burnell's *Landgartha* (1641), sig. A₃ᵛ.]

HENRY BURNELL, 1641

Prologue delivered by an Amazon
with a Battle-Axe in her hand.

The best of English Poets for the Stage
(Such was the envie, nicenesse, and the rage
Of pettish weakelings, and detracting fooles,
That could prayse no man; and, i' th' muddie pooles

Of their owne vices, were o'rwhelm'd) was faine
An armed Prologue to produce, on paine
Of being tongue-struck.

[*Landgartha* (1641), sig. A₄ᵛ. The Prologue referred to is Jonson's in *Poetaster*.]

SHACKERLEY MARMION, 1641

Joyn hands together, be wise, and use
Your dignities with a due reverence;
Tiberius Caesar joy'd not in the birth
Of great *Seianus* fortunes with that zeal,
As I shal to have rais'd you, though I hope; a
different fate attends you.

[*The Antiquary* (1641), sig. K₄.]

H. P., 1641

. . . . he's gone, whose muses early flight,
Gave hopes to th' world, we nere should see a night
Of Poetry, that th' Widdow of those rare men,
Spencer, and *Drayton*, admir'd *Donne*, great *Ben*,
Should now remarried be, but see th'ill lucke,
When just the match was made, oh the rude plucke!
Death snatch'd him hence.

[Commendatory verses prefixed to Thomas Beedome's *Poems* (1641), sig. A₇ᵛ.]

ANONYMOUS, 1642

That, old *Johnson*, the Poet, being dead, great Moan is made for
one of that Quality, to write the *Bishops Wars*.

[*The Scots Scouts Discoveries, by their London Intelligencer, And presented* . . . .
1639 (1642), from *Phœnix Britannicus*, ed. John Morgan (1732), I, 467.]

THOMAS FULLER, 1642

But princes have their grounds reared above the flats of common
men; and who will search the reasons of their actions must stand
on an equal basis with them.

[Thomas Fuller, *The Holy State. The Profane State* (1642). *The Holy State* (ed. 1841), Book IV, chap. i, Maxim vi. The lines are an inaccurate quotation of *Sejanus*, I, 537–40 (Herford and Simpson, *Ben Jonson*, IV, 372–73):

> "Princes haue still their grounds rear'd with themselues,
> Aboue the poore low flats of common men,
> And, who will search the reasons of their acts,
> Must stand on equall bases."

Pointed out by W. D. Briggs, "The Influence of Jonson's Tragedy in the Seventeenth Century," *Anglia*, XXXV (1912), 291.]

JOHN TAYLOR, 1643

Reader this tale upon Sir *Iohn* was framed at the *Staple of Newes*, to bring in the Quibble of *Winter*, and so I leave my pretty *Wit Harmophrodite* made up of Orator and Poet.

["Mercurius Aquaticus" (Taylor's answer to "Mercurius Britanicus") (1643), in *Works of John Taylor, the Water Poet, Fifth Collection* ("Publications of the Spenser Society," No. 25 [1878]), pp. 21–22.]

NICHOLAS OLDISWORTH, 1644

ON ABRAHAM COWLEY THE YONG POËT LAUREAT.

> Ben Johnson's wombe was great; and wee
> Did doubt, what might the issue bee:
> But now he brings forth to his praise,
> And loe, an Infant crown'd with Baies.

[From the Bodleian manuscript of Oldisworth's poems entitled "A Recollection of Certain Scattered Poems, Written Long Since by an Undergraduate, Being One of the Students of Christ Church in Oxford, and Now in the Year 1644 Transcribed by the Author and Dedicated to His Wife," reprinted by Arthur Nethercot, *Modern Language Notes*, XLIX (1934), 158.]

ANONYMOUS, ca. 1645

[A manuscript commonplace book, *ca.* 1645, headed *English Verses*, offered by Davis & Orioli, Wallingford, Berks. (Catalogue 105, Item 2), contains 108 poems by Jacobean and Caroline poets. "Among the poets represented are Sir Henry Wotton, Ben Jonson, Thomas Randolph, John Earle, Richard Corbet, Thomas Carew, William Strode, & Bishop Henry King. The names of the poets are not given, but many of the poems are identifiable. . . . . The collection has some slight affinity with the anthology, *Parnassus Biceps*, 1656, but on the other hand it contains very many poems not in that volume. . . . . There are two poems on Lady Digby (Ben Jonson & Randolph)."]

WILLIAM LEIGH, *ca.* 1640–50

"Withers paralel to Ben Jonson."

[From a commonplace book, *ca.* 1640–50, compiled by William Leigh and advertised for sale by Maggs, *Books Printed in England, 1640–1700* (London, 1940), Part I, Catalogue 696, Item 286. Only the title is given in the catalogue. Presumably it is followed in the commonplace book by Wither's "The Author's Resolution in a Sonnet." See Frank Sidgwick, *The Poetry of George Wither* (1902), I, 138–39.]

WILLIAM LEIGH, *ca.* 1640–50

"A Songe of BEN. JONSON'S

Shall I wastinge in despaire
Dye because another's faire,
etc.

[From a commonplace book, *ca.* 1640–50, compiled by William Leigh and advertised for sale by Maggs, *Books Printed in England, 1640–1700*, Part I, Catalogue 696, Item 286. The lines quoted were first printed under the title "Master Johnsons Answer to Master Wither" in the anonymous *A Description of Love* (1625). See Newdigate, *The Poems of Ben Jonson*, p. 300.]

ANONYMOUS, 1645

To his most loving Friend, the *Author.*

Deare Friend, you chid me when I said your *Pen*
Reviv'd *BEN: IOHNSON* from his grave agen.
Tell me you *Cricks*, I'le be judg'd by you,
Can there be lesse to CHARTAE SCRIPTAE due?
They all agree it, and with mee allow,
As large a *Laurell* to Empale thy *Brow.*
They thinke *Tom: Randall* (if alive) would be
Too weake a *Gamester*, for to play with *Thee.*
Since *Iustice* doth compell them grant so much,
Why should your *Hate*, to your owne *Fame* be such.
If you'le not be Commended, leave to write,
So you'le want *Praise*, your friends their chief delight.

[Commendatory verses prefixed to Edmund Gayton's (?) *Chartae scriptae: or a New Game at Cards, Call'd Play by the Booke* (1645), sig. A₃ᵛ.]

ANONYMOUS, 1645

[Some of Jonson's poems, among them "A fit of Rime against Rime" (*Underwood*, p. xxix), are printed in the third edition of *Wits Recreation*, published in 1645 with the title *Recreation for Ingenious Head-peeces*. "The extracts are badly printed copies of the Folio text" (Herford and Simpson, *Ben Jonson*, VII, 495). I have not seen this edition of *Wits Recreations*.]

ANONYMOUS, 1645

[Lines 121–232 and 1169–1243 of *The Gypsies Metamorphosed* are quoted from the 1640 folio in the third edition of *Wits Recreation*. See above.]

ANONYMOUS, 1645

["The Bearherds," ll. 166–225 of *The Masque of Augurs*, is quoted from the 1640 folio in the third edition of *Wits Recreation*. See above.]

ANONYMOUS, 1645

["The Welsh mans praise of Wales," ll. 217–84 of the masque *For the Honour of Wales*, is quoted from the 1640 folio in the third edition of *Wits Recreations*. See above. Simpson says: "This song was touched up in order to improve the Welsh wording and pronunciation."]

E. G., 1646

To the Author.

If ever I beleiv'd *Pythagoras*,
(My dearest freind) even now it was,
While the grosse Bodies of the *Poets* die,
Their Soule doe onely shift. And *Poesie*
Transmigrates, not by chance, or lucke; for so
Great *Virgils* soule into a *goose* might go.
But that is still the labour of *Joves* braine,
And hè divinely doth conveigh that veine:
So *Chaucers* learned soule in *Spencer* sung,
(*Edmund* the quaintest of the Fairy throng.)
And when that doubled Spirit quitted place,
It fill'd up *Ben:* and there it gained grace.
But this improved thing hath hover'd much,
And oft hath stoopt, and onely given a touch:
Not *rested* untill *now*, *Randall* it brush'd,

And with the fulnesse of its weight it crush'd,
It did thy *Cartwright* kisse, and *Masters* court,
Whose soules were both transfused in the sport.
Now more accomplish'd by those terse recruits,
It wooes thee (freind) with innocent salutes.

[M[artin] Ll[uelyn], *Men-Miracles with Other Poemes* (1646), sig. A₅.]

ANONYMOUS, 1640–54

31 *On an houre glasse.*

[Jonson's poem, "On a Lovers Dust. Made Sand for an Houre Glasse," is printed
under the above title in one or more of the editions of *Wits Recreations*. It is quoted
here from T. Park, *Musarum deliciae* (1874), II, 17. I have not seen the original editions of *Wits Recreations*—1640, 1641, 1645, 1654, and 1663—from which the
Musarum deliciae is compiled, and, since I cannot tell in which of these editions a
given passage was first quoted, I have been forced to date them all 1640–54 (which
places them in 1647, the mid-point between the two dates). The terminal date of
1654 instead of 1663 can be used because the editor of *Musarum deliciae* indicates
that the additions to the 1663 edition of *Wits Recreations* are all placed in one section which contains no Jonson quotations.]

ANONYMOUS, 1640–54

149. *On Giles and Ioane.*

[*Musarum deliciae*, II, 56–57. See above. The lines printed under this title in
Wits Recreations are the Jonson epigram "XLII. On Giles and Jone."]

ANONYMOUS, 1640–54

507. *On Banks the Vsurer.*

[*Ibid.*, p. 135. See above. The lines printed under this title in *Wits Recreations* are
the Jonson epigram "XXXI. On Banck the Usurer."]

ANONYMOUS, 1640–54

562. *On an English Ape.*

[*Ibid.*, p. 146. See above. The lines printed under this title in *Wits Recreations* are
ll. 1, 2, 7, 8, 11, 12, 15, and 16 of Jonson's epigram "LXXXVIII On English Mounsieur."]

ANONYMOUS, 1640–54

685. *Of Death.*

[*Ibid.*, p. 174. See above. The lines printed under this title in *Wits Recreations*
are Jonson's epigram "XXXIIII. Of Death."]

ANONYMOUS, 1640-54

104. *Another* [i.e., another epitaph on a child]

[*Ibid.*, p. 246. The epitaph printed under this title in *Wits Recreations* (see above) consists of the last four lines of Jonson's "An Epitaph to Prince Henry."]

ANONYMOUS, 1640-54

206. *On Prince Henry.*

[*Ibid.*, p. 284. The epitaph printed under this title in *Wits Recreations* (see above) consists of the first fourteen lines of Jonson's "An Epitaph to Prince Henry."]

ANONYMOUS, 1640-54

An Apologetique Song.

[*Ibid.*, pp. 353-54. See above. The lines printed under this title in *Wits Recreations* are the third part ("A Song Apologetique") of Jonson's "The Musicall Strife; in a Pastorall Dialogue."]

ANONYMOUS, 1640-54

Her supposed servant, described.

[*Ibid.*, pp. 364-66. See above. The verses printed under this title in *Wits Recreations* are Jonson's "9. *Her man described by her owne Dictamen*," with the first two lines omitted.]

ANONYMOUS, 1640-54

Another Ladyes exception.

[*Ibid.*, p. 366. See above. The lines printed under this title in *Wits Recreations* are Jonson's "10. *Another Ladyes exception present at the hearing.*"]

ANONYMOUS, 1640-54

The Good Fellow.

[*Ibid.*, pp. 419-20. See above. The lines printed under this title in *Wits Recreations* are Jonson's "The Good Wifes Ale," with minor variations. See Newdigate, *The Poems of Ben Jonson*, pp. 303 and 373.]

ANONYMOUS, 1640-54

A fit of Rime against Rime.

[*Ibid.*, pp. 433-35. See above. This poem of Jonson's from *Underwood* is reprinted in *Wits Recreations.*]

ANONYMOUS, 1640–54

THE GYPSIES.

The Captain Sings.

[*Ibid.*, pp. 439–40. See above. The verses printed under this head in *Wits Recreations* are Jackman's first song from *The Gypsies Metamorphos'd*.]

ANONYMOUS, 1640–54

Another Sings.

[*Ibid.*, pp. 440–41. See above. The verses printed under this head in *Wits Recreations* are Patrico's first song from *The Gypsies Metamorphos'd*.]

ANONYMOUS, 1640–54

To those that would be Gypsies too.

[*Ibid.*, pp. 443–45. The lines printed under this head in *Wits Recreations* (see above) are Patrico's speech in *The Gypsies Metamorphos'd*, ll. 1169–1243 in Herford and Simpson, *Ben Jonson*, VII, 604–7.]

JOHN FLETCHER, 1647

Fred. With Spels man?

John I with spoones as soone, dost thou thinke
The devill such an Asse as people make him?

[*The Chances* (folio of 1647), Act V, scene 2.]

JASPER MAYNE, 1647

Here, Sir, methinks, being a *Poet*, I see a piece of *Ben Johnson's* best *Comedy*, the *Fox*, presented to me; that is, *you*, a *Politique Would-be* the *second*, sheltring your self under a *capacious Tortoise-shell.*

[*A late Printed Sermon against False Prophets, Vindicated by Letter, from the Causeless Aspersions of Mr. Francis Cheynell* (1647), pp. 21–22.]

ANONYMOUS, 1647/48

But now farewell Playes for ever, for the Rebels are resolued to bee the onely Tragedians, none shall act *Cataline* but themselves; and therefore (they being angry) that their former Ordinance did no execution, have now mounted their roaring *Meg*, with which they intend to beat downe all the Stages, Galleries, and Boxes, in the severall Theaters.

[*Mercurius bellicus*, February 14–20, 1647/48, p. 7.]

ANONYMOUS, 1647/48

And therefore the better to *ingrosse* all *fooleries* within their own *Orbe*, they have made an Aditionall Order against *Stage-Playes* in *London* and *Middlesex*, and required the *Militia* to cause the *Benches* and *Boxes* in the *Play-houses* to be pull'd up by the Ropes: So that now no *Stages* must be *tollerated* but that at *Westminster:* None Act *Cataline* but themselves.

[*Mercurius elencticus*, January 19–26, 1647/48, quoted by Hyder E. Rollins, "A Contribution to the History of the English Commonwealth Drama," *Studies in Philology*, XVIII (1921), 286, n. 49.]

ANONYMOUS, 1648

"*Perfect Occurrences* [December 8–15, 1648] brought the news that the imprisoned King at Windsor Castle 'is most delighted with *Ben Johnson's* playes, of any bookes that are here.' "

[Rollins, *loc. cit.*, pp. 292–93.]

GEORGE DANIEL, 1648

Oh! he might Speake, or Ionson's numerous Soule
(Now great as Pindar's) might these Gests enroll;
But then, alas, the greife is where it lay;
They sing too high; wee know not what they Say;
For earth is dull, and may not comprehend
Those heights of wonder which they else have pen'd:

[From the fifth eclogue, ll. 107–12, in *Several Ecloges: The first revived; from some Papers formerlie written, 1.6.3.8. The rest, Written by the same Author; 1.6.4.8.*, *Poems of George Daniel*, ed. A. Grosart, II, 196.]

MERCURIUS PRAGMATICUS, 1648

Let the whole crowd of Poets, SENECA
SOPHOCLES, SHAKSPEARE, IOHNSON now in clay.

EVRIPIDES, with famous WEBSTER, and.
SVCKLIN, and Goffe, leave the Elizian Land.

["To the Readers of my former Peece," *The Second part of Crafty Crumwell, or Oliver in his Glory as King* (1648).]

WILLIAM CAVENDISH, 1649

. . . . thou hast lost thy complexion, by too much study. Why thou shalt bee an heire and rule the roaste of halfe a shire, if thy Father would but dye once, come to the Assises with a band of Ianisaries to equall the grand Signior, all thy tennants shall at their owne charge make them selfes fine & march, like Cavaliers with tyltinge feathers gaudy as *Agamemnons* in the playe after whom thou like a *St George* on horse back, or the high Sheriffe, shallt make the Country people fall downe in Adoration of thy crupper & silver sturrup, my right worshipfull. A pox on buckoram and the luggage in it, papers defild with court hand and long dashes or secretary lines, that straddle, more then Frenchmen, and lesse wholsome to the client! Is thy head to bee fild with *Proclamations** *Rejoyndere* & hard words beyond the *Alkemist?*

[*The Country Captaine* (1649), II, i, p. 22.]

WILLIAM CAVENDISH, 1649

Sing.

> Have you felt the wooll of Beaver?
> Man.—Or sheepes down ever?
> Sim.—Have you smelt of the bud of the Rose?
> Man.—In his pudding hose.
> Sim.—Or have tasted the bag of the Bee?
>   Oh so fine!
> Man.—Oh so fond!
> Sim.—Oh so brave!
> Man.—Such a knave!
> Sim.—Such a knave is he.

* Misprinted "Pcoclamations."

[*The Varietie* (1649), IV, i, p. 57. This is, of course, a parody of Jonson's well-known lines, "Have you seen but a bright lily grow, etc.," first published in *Underwood*, in *Works* (1641), though they were quoted by Wittipol in *The Devil Is an Ass* (1616), II, 6. Suckling also has a parody in "A song to a lute," published in *The Last Remains* (1659).]

W. G[RAY], 1649

BEN. JOHNSON. [ON ST. NICHOLAS' CHURCH AT NEWCASTLE UPON TINE.]

My Altitude high, my Body foure square,
My Foot in the Grave, my Head in the Ayre,
My Eyes in my sides, five Tongues in my Wombe,
Thirteen Heads upon my Body, foure Images alone;
I can direct you where the Winde doth stay,
And I Tune Gods Precepts thrice a Day.
I am seen where I am not, I am heard where I is not,
Tell me now what I am, and see that you misse not.

[*Chorographia, or a Survey of Newcastle upon Tine* (1649). Quoted by Newdigate, *The Poems of Ben Jonson*, p. 336.]

FRANCIS LENTON, 1649

For when I read thy much renowned Pen,
My Fancy there finds out another *Ben*
In thy brave language judgement, wit, & art,
Of every piece of thine, in every part:
Where thy seraphique *Sydneyan* fire is raised high,
In Valour, Vertue, Love, and Loyalty.

[Commendatory verses prefixed to Richard Lovelace's *Lucasta* (1649), sig. A₁ᵛ.]

ANONYMOUS, *ca.* 1650

Ben Jonson: on the birth of Pr. Charles, 1630, and "Still to be neat," *etc.* ff. 35, 105 b.

[Egerton MS 2725, "Poetical Miscellany with a few prose pieces .... *Circ.* 1650." *Catalogue of the Additions to the Manuscripts in the British Museum in the Years MDCCCLXXXVIII–MDCCCXCIII* (1894), p. 463. The song "Still to be neat" is from *The Silent Woman*, I, i.]

NICHOLAS BURGHE, *ca.* 1640–60

[The manuscript commonplace book of Nicholas Burghe, preserved among the Ashmolean manuscripts in the Bodleian, contains the following pieces by or about Jonson:]

21. 'Uppon Ben Jonson's Magnettick Ladye:' by 'ALEXANDER GILL.'

22. 'An invective wrighten by Mr GEORGE CHAPMAN against M^r. Ben Jonson. *Great learned wittie Ben, be pleas'd to light.*'

    After these words—*In vulgar praise had never bound thy*—the collector noted 'More then this never came to my handes, but lost in his sickenes.'

55. 'On M^r. Johnson's verses presented by hyme to the Lord Treasurer. *Your verses weare commended.*' (6 l.)

69. 'M^r. SOUCH TOWNLYE to M^r. Ben Johnson against M^r. Alexander Gill's verses wrighten by hym against the play called the Magnettick Ladye. *Itt cannott move.*'

79. 'On the right hono^ble. and vertuous Lord Weston, Lo: high Treasu. of England, uppon the day hee was made Earle of Portland. To the envious. *Look upp thou seed of envye.*' Subscribed 'by—BEN JOHNSON.'

83. 'An ode against Ben Johnson his playe of the New Inn. *Come leave this savige way.* (6 st. of 10.)

86. 'Uppon King Charles his birth-day. *This is Kinge Charles his day; speake ytt the Tower.*' (18 l.) By 'BEN JOHNSON.'

94. 'The cuntrys censure on Ben Jonson's New Inn. *Listen decaying Ben.*' (60 l.)

95. 'BEN JOHNSON'S ode to hymselfe. *Come leave the loathed stage.* (6 st. of 10.)

96. 'BEN JOHNSON to his detractor J. E. *My verses were comended thou dost say.*' (22 l.)

102. 'On begging a kiss of his M^ris. [by BEN JONSON.] *For love's sake kiss mee once againe.*' (2 st. of 6 and of 7.)

114. 'The Genius of the stage dep[l]oring the death of Ben Johnson. *How comes the world soe sad?* (74 l.) subscribed 'GEORGE STUTVILE.'

141. 'BEN JOHNSONS grace before Kinge James. *Our royall king and queene, God bless.*' (6 l.)

223. 'On a spruce ladye. *Still to bee neate, still to bee drest.*' By BEN JOHN[SON].

279. (21) 'Uppon Sal. Pavye, a boy of 13 years of age, and on of the companye of the revells to Queen Elizabeth. *Weepe wth me all yee that reade.*' (24 l.) By 'BEN JOHNSON:'

[William Henry Black, *A Descriptive, Analytical, and Critical Catalogue of the Manuscripts Bequeathed unto the University of Oxford by Elias Ashmole* (1845), No. 38, cols. 38–61. Nicholas Burghe was admitted a poor Knight of Windsor in 1660 and died June 22, 1670.]

ROBERT BARON, 1650

. . . .

With strenuous sinewie words that CAT'LINE swells
I reckon't not amongst th' Men-miracles.
How could that Poem heat and vigour lack
When each line oft cost BEN a glasse of sack?

. . . .

Go, forth, and live, great Master of thy Pen,
And share the Lawrell with thy namesake BEN,
Whose Genius thou hast as well as name,
And as your wits are equall, May your Fame.

["*To my Honour'd Friend* Benjamin Garfield *Esq; Vpon his excellent Tragi-comedy Entitled The Vnfortunate Fortunate,*" *Pocula Castalia* (1650), pp. 113–14.]

JO. BRADFORD, 1650

Poetrie's now grown Staple-Merchandize
Free from Old Custome or the New Excise.
Silvester, Spenser, Johnsonn, Draiton, Donn,
May see Verse measured by the Last and Tunn,
While Dutch, French, Spanish, English liquours use
T' adorn thy house, their learnings grace thy Muse.

[From a commendatory poem prefixed to Nicholas Murford's *Fragmenta poetica, or Miscelanies of Poetical Musings, Moral and Divine* (1650).]

ABRAHAM COWLEY, 1650

Dog. Go thy ways girl for one, and that's for *Puny* I hope; I see thou'lt ne'er turn Semstress, nor teach girls; thou'dst be a rare wife

for me, I should beget on thee *Donnes*, and *Johnsons:* but thou art
too witty.

[*The Guardian* (1650), III, i, sig. C₂ᵛ. The play was acted at Cambridge, March
12, 1641/42.]

ROBERT HEATH, 1650

Yes yes: And let our Ganymede nimbly flie
And fil us of the same Poetick sherrie
Ben-Iohnson us'd to quaffe to make him merrie.

["A sudden Phansie at Midnight," in *Occasional Poems*, p. 13, in *Clarastella*
(1650).]

ROBERT HEATH, 1650

*To one that asked me why I would write
an English Epigram after*
B. Johnson.

How! dost thou ask me why my ventrous pen
Durst write an English Ep'gram after Ben?
Oh! after him is manners, though it would
'Fore him, have writ, if how, it could have told.

[*Epigrams*, p. 33, in *Clarastella* (1650).]

[CLEMENT BARKSDALE], 1651

Johnson and *Fletcher! Davenant* and the *rest!*
Why have you so my *Fantasy* possest,
That I cann't chuse but *passe* away in Rime
What I must give a strict account for, *Time?*
What should I doe? My Head ak't and about
To break, hath much ease gotten, *now 'tis Out.*
Now I am fit being *freed* from this short paine,
To *translate* the wise *Grotius* againe.

[*Nympha Libethris or the Cotswold Muse* (1651), p. 47.]

[CLEMENT BARKSDALE], 1651
XIX *To the Reader.*

Blame not, that every *obvious* thing I take,
And on it presently do *verses* make.

To me alone a *Contumacy* i'st'
The manner of each *Epigrammatist*.
Thus *Harrington*, thus *Johnson;* and 'fore all,
The poet to be gelded, Martiall.

[*Ibid.*, p. 80.]

JOHN CLEVELAND, 1651

I look upon your letter as a spittle sermon, where I perceive your
ambition how you would prove your self a clean beast, because you
know how to chew the cud: For the first sentence, where you speak
of troubled spirits and sacred Oracles, you talk as if you were in
Doll Commons extasie, certainly your spirit is troubled, else your
expressions had not run so muddy: for never was Oracle more am-
biguous, if possible, to be reconciled to sense.

["Letters," *Poems by J. C.* (1651), p. 63.]

SAMUEL SHEPPARD, 1651

EPIG. 27.

Ben. Johnsons *Play, called the silent Woman.*
The reason why this play's not counted common
Is, 'cause it doth present the silent woman.

[*Epigrams, Theological, Philosophical, and Romantic* (1651), p. 31.]

SAMUEL SHEPPARD, 1651

EPIG. 6.

To the most excellent Poet, Sir William Davenant.

What though some shallow Sciolists dare prate,
And scoffing thee; *Apollo* nauseate:
What *Venus* hath snatch'd from thee, cruelly,
Minerva, with advantage doth supply:
Johnson is dead, let *Sherly* stoope to Fate,
And thou alone, art Poet Lawreate.

[*Ibid.*, p. 39.]

SAMUEL SHEPPARD, 1651

EPIG. 19.

The Poets invitation to Ben Johnsons *Ghost to appeare again.*

Reverend shade,
Since last I made
　　Survey of thee,
Mee thinks I find
A fresher mind
　　To Poesie.

Most honoured *Ben*
Appeare agen,
　　That so I may,
Embrace thy Ghost,
Although it cost
　　My lifes decay.

Sacred Spirit
Whose boundlesse merit
　　I Adore,
Upon thy Herse
I'le drop a Verse
　　And no more.

Thy Lawrell wreath
Doth lie beneath
　　Great *Phaebus* feet,
Hee askes of thee
Which way to be
　　A God more great.

Thou *Ben* shalt be
A Saint to me
　　Each Verse I make,
I'le censure it
By thy great Wit,
　　If it partake

The least of thine,
I will Divine
   It shall subsist,
Alas if not
The same I'le blot,
   'Twil not be mist.

[*Ibid.*, pp. 88–89.]

SAMUEL SHEPPARD, 1651

EPIG. 23.

On excellent strong Beere.

.   .   .   .

Had great *Johnson* had the hap
To taste of what flowes from this tap,
Nine muses had no number been
To contend 'gainst such *Hypocrene*,
And he (no doubt) had finish'd well
His *Mortimer*, and *Issabell*.

[*Ibid.*, p. 127.]

SAMUEL SHEPPARD, 1651

EPIG. 33.

Ben Jonson's *due Encomium.*

When he, with Verse to's pipe appli'd did sing,
The Rude *Woods listned to his caroling,
Scillas Doggs bark'd not, the harmonious spheares
Tooke paines to plant their Soules into their eares,
More excellent then he, no age e're saw,
More sacred, wonderfull, (by *Phaebus* Law)
His Verse Divinely fram'd, deserves alone,
The thrice three Sisters Benediction.

* *His excellent* Under-woods.

[*Ibid.*, p. 138.]

SAMUEL SHEPPARD, 1651

Yes *Coridon*, Ile tell thee then,
Not long agoe liv'd learned *Ben*,
He whose songs, they say, out-vie
All *Greek* and *Latine* Poesie,
Who chanted on his pipe Divine,
The overthrow of *Cataline*,
Both Kings and Princesses of might,
To heare his Layes did take delight,
The *Arcadian* Shepheards wonder all,
To heare him sing *Sejanus* fall,
O thou renowned Shepheard, we
Shall ne're have one againe like thee,
With him contemporary then,
(As *Naso*, and fam'd *Maro*, when
Our sole Redeemer took his birth)
Shakespeare trod on *English* earth,
His Muse doth merit more rewards
Then all the *Greek*, or *Latine* Bards,
What flowd from him, was purely rare,
As born to blesse the *Theater*,
He first refin'd the *Commick Lyre*,
His Wit all do, and shall admire,
The chiefest glory of the Stage,
Or when he sung of war and *Strage*,
Melpomene soon viewd the globe,
Invelop'd in her sanguine Robe,
He that his worth would truely sing,
Must quaffe the whole *Pierian* spring.
And now—(be gone ye gastfull feares
Alas I cannot speak for teares)
There is a Shepheard cag'd in stone
Destin'd unto destruction,
Worthy of all before him were,
Apollo him doth first preferre,
Renowned Lawreate be content,

Thy workes are thine own Monument.
Apollo still affords supply,
For the *Castalian* Fount's nere drie,
Two happy wits, late brightly shone,
The true sonnes of *Hyperion*,
Fletcher, and *Beaumont*, who so wrot,
Iohnsons Fame was soon forgot,
Shakespeare no glory was alow'd,
His Sun quite shrunk beneath a Cloud:
These had been solely of esteem,
Had not a *Sucklin* Rivald them.

["The Third Pastoral," in *ibid.*, pp. 249–51.]

Anonymous, 1652

For Courtly Phrases and Complements, I wanted none: For, Sir
Philip Sidney, and *Ben Johnson* can testifie, that I have so over-
burthened my Memory out of their Granaries, that it being too
weak to retain them lets them often drop here, and there to no
purpose.

[*A Hermeticall Banquet* (1652), pp. 126–27.]

Thomas Berney, 1652

Friend, did my fame and Muse shine forth as bright
As the renowned *Ben's*, then would that light
Like th' hour telling Sun, the Rectifier
Of Clocks and Watches, shine to the whole quire
Of common censu'rers, who would each correct
His peccant humor by my Dialect.

[Commendatory verses prefixed to Francis Goldsmith's *Sophompaneas, or Ioseph*
(1652), sig. B₁ᵛ.]

Francis Goldsmith, 1652

[In the notes to the first act of his translation of Hugo Grotius' *Sophompaneas, or
Ioseph*, p. 54, Goldsmith quotes eleven lines of Jonson's translation of Horace, as
they are found on pp. 13–15 of the translation in the 1640 folio. Goldsmith acknowledges the source of the translation by printing "B. Jonson" after the lines.]

Peter Heylyn, 1652

And finally for Poetrie, 1 *Gower*, 2 *Lidgate*, a Monk of *Burie*, 3 the famous *Geofrie Chawcer*, Brother in Law to *Iohn* of *Gaunt* the great Duke of *Lancaster;* of which last Sir *Philip Sidney* used to say, that *he marvelled how in those mistie times he could see so cleerly, and others in so cleer times go so blindly after him.* 4 Sir *Philip Sidney* himself, of whom and his *Arcadia*, more when we come to *Greece.* 5 The renowned *Spencer*, of whom and his *Fairie Queen* in another place. 6 *Sam. Daniel*, the *Lucan*, 7 with *Michael Draiton*, the *Ovid* of the *English* Nation. 8 *Beamount*, and 9 *Fletcher*, not inferiour unto *Terence* and *Plautus;* with 10 My friend *Ben. Iohnson*, equall to any of the antients for the exactness of his Pen, and the decorum which he kept in *Dramatick* Poems, never before observed on the *English* Theatre. Others there are as eminent both for Arts and Arms, as those here specified: of whom, as being still alive I forbear to speak: according to that caution of the Historian, saying, *Vivorum ut magna admiratio, ita* Censura *est difficilis.*

[*Cosmographie* (1652), Book I, p. 268.]

Richard Brome, 1653

Cras. Yes, yes, we must all agree, and be linckt in Covenant together.

Crac. By Indenture Tripartite, and't please you, like *Subtle, Doll*, and *Face.*

[*The City Wit, or, The Woman wears the Breeches*, III, i, sig. C₇ᵛ, in *Five New Playes* (1653).]

Richard Flecknoe, 1653

O *Smithfield*, thou that in Times of *yore*,
With thy *Ballets* didst make all *England* roar,
Whilst Goodwife *Ursuly* look'd so bigg,
At roasting of a *Bartholomew* Pig:
And so many Enormities every where
Were observ'd by *Justice Overdoe* there;
Full little (I wuse) didst thou thinke than
Thy mirth should be spoyld by the *Banbury* man:

And then too, he as little did thinke
How some in the world should make him stinke.

["A whimzey written from beyond Seas, about the end of the year, 52, to a Friend lately returned into England," *Miscellania, or, Poems of All Sorts* (1653), pp. 139–40. Ursula, the pig-woman, and Justice Overdo are, of course, characters in Jonson's *Bartholomew Fair*.]

JOHN HARDESTY, 1653

When this Play came first abroad into the World, it found the approbation of the most Excellent Persons, and best Masters of this Kind of Writing which were in that time, if there were ever better in any time; *Ben. Johnson* being then alive, who gave a Testimonie of this Piece even to be Envy'd.

["The Publisher to the Reader," prefixed to Henry Killigrew's *Pallantus and Eudora* (1653), a second edition of *The Conspiracy* (1638).]

IZAAK WALTON, 1653

. . . . and told them that old father Clause, whom Ben Jonson, in his Beggar's Bush, created King of their corporation, was to lodge at an alehouse, called "Catch-her-by-the-way," not far from Waltham Cross, and in the highroad towards London.

[*The Complete Angler*, ed. Sir Harris Nicolas (1903), p. 113. I owe this allusion to the kindness of Miss Bertha Hensman.]

EDMUND GAYTON, 1654

Besides, the Navall expedition of the *Gallyfoist*, and many other renowned workes, were all burnt to ashes, not so much as a line surviving or escaping, in that neverto be forgotten conflagration of Father *Benjaminos* study.

[*Pleasant Notes upon Don Quixot* (1654), p. 19.]

EDMUND GAYTON, 1654

Or if you will have our *Knight-Mummers* owne words, which like *Abel Druggers* ginger-bread, must melt out of his mouth before you can heare it, heare 'um e'n as good as mine Host mutter'd over him at the consecrating of him *Knight-Errant*, out of his provender book of Ceremonies.

[*Ibid.*, p. 56.]

EDMUND GAYTON, 1654

These were adventures of *A-jax*, which none but these two *Knight-Errants* (for they miss'd their way) ever attempted, except our Father *Ben* and his *Argonauts*, when they vent'red in an open an untilted whirrey, through the Common shores of a spring-tide; but how they escap'd the dangerous gulph of *Mala Speranzadel Arse-holo*, you may read at full, in that most celebrated Poem which is stil'd *A-jakes*.

[*Ibid.*, p. 74.]

EDMUND GAYTON, 1654

Such a shrill Note gave *Abel Drugger*, when after a nights expectation in the Privy-house (his gagge of Ginger-bread dissolv'd) he was to crave a blessing of his Mother the Queen of *Fairies*, and her *Ti-ti-ties*.

[*Ibid.*, pp. 78–79.]

EDMUND GAYTON, 1654

Besides these necessary Administrations, rare are the *Quedrums* of many of the houses of the *Barberino's;* like *A-bell* Drugger, you shall have one of them without a *Rebus* to his signe, which is as attractive as his Wife, or the adjacent pot of Ale, or his Plaister-box (if he be a *Chyron* too) or if not, as his Tweezer.

[*Ibid.*, p. 111.]

RICHARD WHITLOCK, 1654

THE LOAD-STONES *Touch-stone*, trying, who's
THE *MAGNETICK* LADY:

[Chapter heading in ZΩOTOMIA, *or Observations on the Present Manners of the English* (1654), p. 321.]

RICHARD WHITLOCK, 1654

But to view this *Magnetick Lady* in more general *Draughts*, be she *Maid* or *Wife:* she is of a naturall goodnesse. . . . .

[*Ibid.*, p. 348.]

ANONYMOUS, 1655

Shakespear, Johnson, Beumont, Fletcher,
Had each one his dainty Ducklin . . . .

["An Almanack, and no Almanack," *Merlinus Anonymus* (1655), sig. C₇. Quoted
by Hyder E. Rollins, "Shakespeare Allusions," *Notes and Queries: Twelfth Series*, X
(March 25, 1922), p. 224.]

ANONYMOUS, 1655

But what if *Will* a censure made-a
O' th' Poets? he but did as *Strada*.
So did old *Ben*, our grand Wits master,
In this Play called *Poetaster*.
The odds is ours, we are the higher,
We are *Knight Lauriat*, *Ben* the *Squire*.

[*The Incomparable Poem Gondibert, Vindicated from the Wit-Combats of Four Es-
quires* (1655), "On the Preface," p. 6.]

IMPRINT, 1655

Printed for *John Sweeting* at the *Angel* in *Popes-head* Alley, and
Robert Pollard at the *Ben Johnson's* Head behind the *Exchange*.
1655.

[Thomas Heywood and William Rowley's *Fortune by Land and Sea* (1655).]

IMPRINT, 1655

Printed for *Rob: Pollard* at *Ben-Jonsons* head behinde the *Exchange;* and *John Sweeting* at the Angel in *Popes-head* Alley. 1655.

[Robert Daborne's *The Poor Mans Comfort* (1655).]

IMPRINT, 1655

Printed by *Thomas Harper*, and are to be sold by *Robert Pollard*,
at his Shop behind the Old Exchange, at the signe of *Ben: Jonson*.
MDCLV.

[Sir Ralph Freeman's *Imperiale* (1655).]

IMPRINT, 1655

Printed for *Rob. Pollard* at the *Ben. Jonson*-head behind the Exchange, and *John Sweeting* at the Angel in Popes-head-Alley. 1655.

[Anthony Brewer's *The Love-sick King* (1655).]

IMPRINT, 1655

Printed for *Robert Pollard* at the *Ben Johnson's* Head behind the *Exchange*, and *John Sweeting* at the *Angel* in *Popes-head* Alley. 1655.

[William Rider's *The Twins* (1655).]

JOHN COTGRAVE, 1655

[John Cotgrave's *The English Treasury of Wit and Language Collected out of the most and best of our English Drammatick Poems* (1655) contains some 1,686 quotations from plays, of which 111 are quoted from the following plays by Ben Jonson:

Catiline: I, 191–99, 528–29; III, 42–45, 178–83, 183–86, 231–33, 247–52, 337–40, 368–69, 397–400, 433–35, 472–73, 479–80, 492–94, 504–9, 511–12, 647–55, 714–22, 746–54, 836–39; IV, 21–22, 29–32, 422–25, 637–39, 700–701, 758–61; V, 325–31, 373–75, 400–402, 414–18, 544–49

Cynthia's Revels: I, 2, 36–39, 42–44; V, 11, 2–27, 117–18, 169–74

The Devil Is an Ass: I, 2, 27–36; 5, 16–21, 22–23, 26; II, 4, 29–39

Eastward Hoe: I, 2, 31–33; III, 2, 193–96; IV, 2, 324–27; V, 1, 34–46

Every Man in His Humour: I, 1, 66–73; II, 3, 58–69; III, 5, 30–39

Every Man out of His Humour: II, 4, 133–34; III, 9, 10–20; IV, 4, 93–94

The New Inn: I, 4, 1–10; II, 1, 8–12; IV, 2, 14–16; 4, 265–76, 301–2

Poetaster: Prologue, 81–82; I, 2, 253–56; IV, 6, 62–73; V, 1, 61–67, 84–89, 92–93; 2, 26–27, 37–38, 75–97; 3, 61–67, 137–44, 629–30

Sejanus: I, 70–72, 299–301, 330–32, 381–83, 407–9, 410–20, 421–24, 498–502, 537–40, 578–79; II, 195–97, 208–9, 239–44, 254–59, 322–27; III, 302–15, 439–41, 659–60, 689–92, 715–17; IV, 89–92; V, 169–70, 383–90, 397–99, 701–4, 730–35, 836–38, 893–97, 898–903

The Staple of News: I, 3, 39–41; 6, 67–70; II, 1, 38–43; III, 4, 45–68; IV, 4, 150–59; V, 6, 60–66

Volpone: I, 1, 22–29; 2, 110–13; 4, 134–35; 5, 107–13; IV, 6, 51–53; V, 9, 19–20; 12, 99–101, 147–48, 150–51

For a further discussion of the book and its quotations see my article, "John Cotgrave's *English Treasury of Wit and Language* and the Elizabethan Drama," *Studies in Philology*, XL (April, 1943), 186–203.]

[JOHN COTGRAVE], 1655

[The engraved title-page of *The Wits' Interpreter, or the English Parnassus* (1655), bears the labeled portraits of ten wits: Spenser, Shakespeare, Jonson, Randolph, Richelieu, Dubartas, Strafford, Sidney, Bacon, and More. The same engraved title-page appears in the revised edition of 1662.]

JOHN COTGRAVE, 1655

SONG.

Come my *Celia* let us prove, *etc.*

[Jonson's "*Song.* To Celia" is printed on p. 141 (sig. I₇) of the "Love Songs, Epigrams, &c" section of *Wits Interpreter* (1655).]

JOHN COTGRAVE, 1655

To Madam Wouldbe.

Fine Madam *Wouldbe*, wherefore should you fear, *etc.*

[*Ibid.*, p. 304 (sig. Cc₆ᵛ). The epigram is Jonson's "LXII To Fine Lady Would-Bee.]

JOHN COTGRAVE, 1655

On Cob.

Cob, thou nor Souldier cheife, nor Fencer art,
Yet by thy weapon liv'st; th' hast one good part.

[*Ibid.* The epigram is Jonson's "LXIX To Pertinax Cob."]

JOHN COTGRAVE, 1655

On a Cheater.

Touch'd with the sin of false play in his punk, *etc.*

[*Ibid.* The epigram is Jonson's "LXXXVII On Captaine Hazard the Cheater."]

JOHN COTGRAVE, 1655

On a waiting Gentlewoman.

When *Mill* came first to Court, th' unprofiting soule, *etc.*

[*Ibid.*, p. 305 (sig. Cc₇). The epigram is Jonson's "XC On Mill. My Ladies Woman."]

JOHN COTGRAVE, 1655

On an English Mounsieur.

Would you believe when you this *Mounsieur* see, *etc.*

[*Ibid.* The epigram is Jonson's "LXXXVII On English Mounsieur."]

JOHN COTGRAVE, 1655

On a hungry Captain.

Do what you come for Captain with your news; *etc.*

[*Ibid.*, p. 306 (sig. Cc₇ᵛ). The epigram is Jonson's "CVII　To Captayne Hungry."]

JOHN COTGRAVE, 1655

On Groyn.

Groyn come of age, his state sold out of hand,
For his Whore *Groyn* doth still occupy the land.

[*Ibid.* The Epigram is Jonson's "CXVII　On Groyne."]

JOHN COTGRAVE, 1655

On a hot House.

Where lately harbour'd many a famous whore,
　　A purging bill now fixt upon the doore,
Tells you it is a hot house; so it may,
　　And still be a whore house, they're *Synonyma.*

[*Ibid.*, p. 308 (sig. Cc₈ᵛ). The epigram is Jonson's "VII　On the new Hot-House."]

JOHN COTGRAVE, 1655

On a Robbery.

Ridway rob'd *Duncote* of three hundred pound; *etc.*

[*Ibid.* The epigram is Jonson's "VIII　On a Robbery."]

JOHN COTGRAVE, 1655

On something that walks somewhere.

At Court *I* met in cloathes brave enough, *etc.*

[*Ibid.*, p. 309 (sig. Dd₁). The epigram is Jonson's "XI　On Some-thing, that walkes Some-where."]

JOHN COTGRAVE, 1655

On a Doctor.

When men a dangerous disease did scape,
　　Of old they gave a Cock to *Æsculape:*

> Let me give two that doubly am got free,
> From my diseases danger and from thee.

[*Ibid.* The epigram is Jonson's "XIII   To Doctor Empirick."]

JOHN COTGRAVE, 1655
On a Courtier.

> All men are wormes, but this no man in silk,
>   Twas brought to Court first raw, and white as milk;
> Where afterwards it grew a Butterflye,
>   Which was a Caterpiller, so will die.

[*Ibid.* The epigram is Jonson's "XV   *On Court-worme.*"]

JOHN COTGRAVE, 1655
On Brainhardy.

> *Hardy*, thy brain is valiant, tis confest, *etc.*

[*Ibid.* The epigram is Jonson's "XVI   To Brayne-Hardie."]

JOHN COTGRAVE, 1655
On a Lieutenant.

> Shift here in Town not meanest among Squires, *etc.*

[*Ibid.*, p. 314 (sig. Dd$_3$ᵛ). The epigram is Jonson's "XII   On Lieutenant Shift."]

JOHN COTGRAVE, 1655
On one perfum'd.

> Th' expence of odours is a most vain sin,
> Unlesse thou couldst Sir Cod wear them within.

[*Ibid.*, p. 315 (Dd$_4$). The epigram is Jonson's "XIX   On Sir Cod the Perfumed."]

JOHN COTGRAVE, 1655
On a Gamester reformd.

> Lord! here is a Gamester chang'd, his hair close cut, *etc.*

[*Ibid.* The epigram is Jonson's "XXI   On Reformed Gam'ster."]

JOHN COTGRAVE, 1655

Of a voluptuous Knight.

While *Beast* intrusts his fair and vertuous wife, *etc.*

[*Ibid.* The epigram is Jonson's "XXV On Sir Voluptuous Beast."]

JOHN COTGRAVE, 1655

On a Vsurer.

Bankes feels no lamenesse of his knotty gout,
His monies travel for him in and out.
Twere madness in thee to betray thy fame
And person to the world, ere *I* thy name.

[*Ibid.* The epigram is Jonson's "XXXI On Banck the Usurer."]

JOHN COTGRAVE, 1655

On a Lawyer.

No Cause nor Client fat will Cheveril lees,
    But as they come on both sides take their fees,
And pleaseth both, for while he melts his grease
    For this, that winnes for whom he holds his peace.

[*Ibid.*, p. 316 (sig. Dd₄ᵛ). The epigram is Jonson's "XXXVI On Chev'rill the Lawyer."]

JOHN COTGRAVE, 1655

On old Colt.

For all night sins with other wives unknown,
Colt now doth dayly penance in his own.

[*Ibid.* The epigram is Jonson's "XXXIX On Old Colt."]

JOHN COTGRAVE, 1655

On Gipsee.

Gypsee new bawd is turn'd Physitian,
    And gets more gold then all the Colledge can:
Such her quaint practice is, so it allures,
    That what she gave a whore, a Bawd she cures.

[*Ibid.* The epigram is Jonson's "XLI On Gypsee."]

John Cotgrave, 1655
On Giles and Jone.

Who says that Giles and Jone at discord be? *etc.*

[*Ibid.* The epigram is Jonson's "XLII   On Giles and Jone."]

John Cotgrave, 1655
To Wooall a Knight.

Is this the Knight, who some vast Wife to win, *etc.*

[*Ibid.*, p. 317 (sig. Dd₅). The epigram is Jonson's "XLVI   To Sir Lucklesse Wooall."]

John Cotgrave, 1655
Another.

Sir Lucklesse, troth for luck sake passe by one,
He that wooes every widow, will get none.

[*Ibid.* The epigram is Jonson's "XLVII   To the Same," i.e., Sir Luckless Wooall.]

John Cotgrave, 1655
On Spies.

Spies, you are lights in State, but of base stuff;
Who when y'ave burnt your selves down to snuff,
Stink, and are thrown away, end fair enough.

[*Ibid.* The epigram is Jonson's "LIX   On Spies."]

John Cotgrave, 1655
On Bawds and Vsurers.

Like as their ends, their fruits were so the same,
Bawdry and Usury were one kind of game.

[*Ibid.* The epigram is Jonson's "LVII   On Baudes, and Usurers."]

Henry Tubbe, 1655

[G. C. Moore Smith says that in the section of verse-epistles in Brit. Mus. Harl. MS 4126 (Tubbe's manuscripts) "the second is a paraphrase or adaptation of Suckling's lines 'To Master John Hales' (it is noticeable that, while Tubbe, like Suckling, invites his friend to see Jonson's plays, he says nothing of Shakespeare's, which Suckling clearly preferred)" (*Oxford Historical and Literary Studies*, Vol. V: *Henry Tubbe*, ed. G. C. Moore Smith [1915], pp. 56–57).]

HENRY TUBBE, 1655

Thence winged flie to the Elysian Groves,
Where, whilst wee still renew our constant Loves,
A Thousand Troops of Learned Ghosts shall meet
Us, and our coming thither gladly greet.
First the Great Shadow of Renowned BEN
Shall give us hearty, joyfull Wellcome: then
Ingenious *Randolph* from his lovely Arms
Shall entertaine us with such mighty charms
Of strict embraces, that wee cannot wish
For any comforts greater than this Blisse.

["When thou and I must part," *ibid.*, pp. 65–66. No others are named.]

HENRY TUBBE, 1655

But see! a brave Virago of Devotion
Is mounted next, swell'd wth the Spirit's Motion,
Like mad *Bes Broughton* in a learned Vaine,
Or Madam *Shipton* with prophetique Straine.

["Satyr. A Debate Concerning the Engagement," *ibid.*, p. 78. In the notes on p. 110 Moore Smith says: "Mr. Percy Simpson supplements the above in the following note:
'Tubbe has here confused two passages in Ben Jonson, viz. (i) the reference in *The Execration*, and (ii) the allusion to the Puritan divine, Hugh Broughton, in *The Alchemist* (Act II, sc. iii) where Dol Common is described to Sir Epicure as a lady who "is gone mad with studying Broughtons works":

"If you but name a word, touching the Hebrew,
    Shee falls into her fit."

The "fit" comes off in Act III, sc. v, and is a string of disconnected quotations from Broughton.' "]

HENRY TUBBE, 1655

The Quarrell is no more for Heart or Braine,
But for the Nose of Oliver *Tamberlaine!*
There's Valour, & Discretion too! enough
To farce a Brainlesse Tub with scribling Stuffe.

Sweare not feirce *Bobadill* (for Rime's sake *Bombell*)
The Foot of PHAROAH, but the Nose of CROMWELL.

["On the Dominical Nose of O[liver] C[romwell]," *ibid.*, p. 92. Note that the oath, "By the foot of Pharoah," is a favorite of Bobadill in *Every Man in His Humour.*]

HENRY TUBBE, 1655

Like an Huge *Hercules* in Poëtrie,
Whose roaring Bombards bellow to the Skie;
Like spruce Nasutus or wild Polyposus,
Who ever & anon wth nose doe pose us.

[*Ibid.*, p. 94. In the notes on p. 113 Moore Smith says: "Mr. Simpson writes: 'Cp. Jonson, *Poetaster* V. iii, where Tucca exclaims, after a parody of Marston's rant, "I mary, this was written like a HERCVLES in *poetrie.*" Tubbe had evidently been reading this play: "Nasutus" and "Polyposus" are taken from the "apologeticall Dialogue" added to it in the Folio of 1616.' "]

HENRY TUBBE, 1655

In a desperate Agonie his onely refuge is the Example of *Sampson*, whereby hee pretends the priviledge of an Extraordinarie Revelation to ruine others with himselfe; and though his ambition aimes at the bravery of *Cethegus*, to tread upon the World, when it falls, yet his malice is well apayd with so much honour, as may entitle him to the Power of perishing in a generall dissolution. Now the Eyes of his discretion are quite put out, hee will fall to 't blindly without sence or wit, and cares not how he injures his own person, or his freinds, so hee may but accomplish the destruction of his Enemyes. *Who would not fall with all the world about him?*

["Character: A Rebell," *ibid.*, p. 101. In the note on p. 115 Moore Smith says: "Tubbe . . . . as Professor Bensly points out, is clearly referring to Jonson's *Catiline* (III. i); *Cat.* 'That I could reach the axle, where the pins are Which bolt this frame; that I might pull them out, And pluck all into Chaos, with myself! *Cethegus:* What! are we wishing now? *Cat.* Yes, my Cethegus; Who would not fall with all the world about him? *Ceth.* Not I that would stand on it, when it falls.' "]

ANONYMOUS, 1656

["The 1656 edition of *Wit and Drollery* contained at page 79 a feeble poem entitled '*Verses written over the Chair of* Ben: Johnson, *now remaining at* Robert Wilsons, *at the Signe of* Johnson's *head in the Strand*' " (Herford and Simpson, *Ben Jonson*, I, 183).]

ANONYMOUS, 1656

[According to E. K. Chambers, *Aurelian Townshend's Poems and Masks* (1912), p. 113, Alexander Gill's attack on *The Magnetic Lady* beginning "Is this your Loadstone then that must attract" and Jonson's reply beginning "Shall the prosperity of a pardon still" are printed in *Wit and Drollery* (1656), a volume which I have not seen.]

ANONYMOUS, 1656

Mr. Townsends Verses to Ben Johnsons,
in answer to an Abusive Copie, crying down his Magnetick Lady.

It cannot move thy friend (firm Ben) that he
Whom the Star-Chamber censur'd, rimes at thee.
I gratulate the method of thy fate,
That joyn'd thee next in malice to the State.
So *Nero*, after paricidall guilt,
Brooks no delay till *Lucan's* blood be spilt;
Nor could his malice find a second crime,
Unlesse he slew the Poet of the time.
But (thanks to Hellicon) here are no blowes;
This Drone no more of sting then honey shewes.
His verses shall be counted Censure, when
Cast Malefactors are made Jury-men.
Mean while rejoyce, that so disgrac't a quill
'Tempted to wound that worth, time cannot kill.
And thou that darest to blast Fame fully blown,
Lye buried in the ruines of thy owne.
Vexe not thine ashes, open not the deep,
The Ghosts of thy slaine name had rather sleep.

[*Ibid.*, p. 49. In the note on pp. 113-14 Chambers says: "This is printed . . . . in *Wit and Drollery* (1656), 18, ... But it must be very doubtful whether it is rightly credited to Aurelian Townshend, for it occurs also in *Ashmolean MS*. 38, p. 58, and is thus headed, 'Mr. Zouch Townlye to m^r Ben Johnson against m^r Alexander Gills. Verses wrighten by hym against the play called the Magnettick Ladye.' At the end is 'finis Zouch Townlye.' "]

IMPRINT, 1656

Printed by *J. G.* for *Robert Pollard*, at the *Ben-Johnson's* head behind the Exchange, and *John Sweeting*, at the *Angel* in Popeshead Alley. 1656.

[⟨Anonymous,⟩ *Choyce Drollery* (1656).]

ABRAHAM COWLEY, 1656

With *Fate* what boots it to contend?
Such I *began*, such *am*, and so must *end*.
The *Star* that did my *Being* frame,
Was but a *Lambent Flame*,
And some small *Light* it did dispence,
But neither *Heat* nor *Influence*.
No matter, *Cowley*, let proud *Fortune* see,
That *thou* canst *her* despise no less than *she* does *Thee*.
Let all her gifts the portion be
Of Folly, Lust, and Flattery,
Fraud, Extortion, Calumnie,
Murder, Infidelitie,
Rebellion and Hypocrisie.
Do Thou nor *grieve* nor *blush* to be,
As all th' inspired *tuneful Men*,
And all thy great *Forefathers* were from *Homer* down to *Ben*.

["Destinie," in the section entitled "Pindarique Odes," p. 31, stanza 4, in *Poems* (1656).]

[JOHN PHILLIPS], 1656

Next these, learn'd *Johnson* in this List I bring,
Who had drunk deep of the *Pierian spring*,
Whose knowledge did him worthily prefer,
And long was Lord of the Theater,
Who in opinion made our learn'dst to stick,
Whether in Poems rightly dramatique:
Strong *Seneca* or *Plautus*, he or they,
Should bear the Buskin, or the Sock away.

["A Censure of the Poets," *Sportive Wit* (1656), Part II, p. 70.]

[JOHN PHILLIPS], 1656

Alas poor *Jack Taylor*, this 'tis to drink ale,
With nutmegs and ginger, with a toste, though *stale:*
It drencht thee in Rimes: hadst thou been of the pack,
With *Draiton* and *Johnson* to quaff off thy Sack,

They'd infus'd thee a *Genius* should nere expire
And have thawed thy Muse with Elemental fire.

["An Epitaph on John Taylor," *ibid.*, p. 130.]

[ABRAHAM WRIGHT,] 1656

BEN: JOHNSON | *To Burlace.*

[*Parnassus Biceps, or Severall Choice Pieces of Poetry Composed by the Best Wits that were in both the Universities before their Dissolution* (1656), p. 29. The poem which follows the title is Jonson's "My Answer. The Poet to the Painter." It is reprinted from the folio of 1640.]

[ABRAHAM WRIGHT,] 1656

To the Memory of | *BEN: JOHNSON.*

[*Ibid.*, p. 129. The poem printed under this title is Jasper Mayne's contribution to *Jonsonus Virbius* (1638).]

[ABRAHAM WRIGHT,] 1656

Against | *BEN: JOHNSON.*

[The title given to Owen Feltham's "An answer to the Ode, Come leave the loathed Stage" in *Parnassus Biceps* (1656), where it occupies pp. 154–56. Though Feltham's answer must have been written about the time of Jonson's ode (occasioned by events of 1629), it does not seem to have been published as his until it was included in *Lusoria* (1661). Apparently, the piece first appeared in print in *Parnassus Biceps.*]

[ABRAHAM WRIGHT,] 1656

A Song.

I Mean to sing of *Englands* fate
(God blesse in th' mean time the King and his Mate)
Thats rul'd by the *Antipodian* state,
                    Which no body can deny.
Had these seditious times been when
We had the life of our wise Poet *Ben,*
Apprentices had not been Parliament men,
                    Which no body can deny.

[*Parnassus Biceps* (1656), p. 159.]

GEORGE DANIEL, *ca.* 1657

Why may not wee better exempt his Name
Then vse it? adding nothing to our ffame;
And take the Radix of our Poesie
To honour more in this last Centurie,
The noble Sidney; Spencer liveing Still,
In an abundant fancie; Ionson's Qvill
Ever admir'd; these iustly wee may call
Fathers; high-placed in Apolloe's Hall.

["An Essay," *The Poems of George Daniel*, ed. A. Grosart (1878), I, 82.]

GEORGE DANIEL, *ca.* 1657

Or if he [Phoebus] be the nourisher of witt,
Why would he suffer Ice to smother it?
Noe! Phebus is my foe, or he has Swore,
Since Ionson Dyed, t'allow his Heirs, noe more:
I know not what to Iudge; but if I live,
Ile trye this Fancie fled, how to revive.

["Prevention," *ibid.*, p. 87.]

THOMAS PLUME, *ca.* 1657

Y^u Thing like a Thing, like a Man—s^d Ben Johnson to Sr Inigo Jones—who dairs not call him Jackanapes.

[Thomas Plume, MS 25 A, p. 123, Plume Library, Maldon, Essex. Quoted in Herford and Simpson, *Ben Jonson*, I, 184.]

THOMAS PLUME, *ca.* 1657

Ben Johnson borr. 50*l* & p^d it ag aft. w^{ld} h. borr. 100 ye gentl. told him—He h. dec^d him once & nev sh^d ag^n—

[MS 25 A, p. 95. Quoted in *ibid.*]

THOMAS PLUME, *ca.* 1657

Ben Johnson brings in his Gypsies dancing, who robd ye specta-to^{r}s—amongst ye rest there was one Xian, & he had lost (he said) his practise of piety. Y^e gypsies cleer thems[elves]—Yo^r book (or ballad) w^r you call it Is not here—o^r Society—dos not practise piety Y^e Autho^r y^t first undertook it Long agoe hims[elf] forsook it.

[MS 30, fol. 21^v. Quoted in *ibid.*, p. 185.]

THOMAS PLUME, *ca.* 1657

Searjant Noy was p[re]sented wth these verses frō Ben. Johnson while he was hims[elf] at his Comencem^t dinner for his degree of Searjant at law, y^t so he might take notice Ben stood w^thout expecting but a call to come to dinner,

> When ye w^ld was drowned, No venizon was found,
> bec: there was no park.
> Here Wee sit & get never a bitt,
> bec: Noy has all in his Arke.

[MS 30, fol. 6^v. Quoted in *ibid.*]

THOMAS PLUME, *ca.* 1657

B. Johnson was wth yong Wat Rawleigh in France & w^ld y^r be drunk—See you my gov^r s^d hee—

[MS 25 B, p. 82. Quoted in *ibid.*]

THOMAS PLUME, *ca.* 1657

B. Johns^n used to w^lk wth a Trunchion Cane & mt. an old Comrague in ye streets a long time absent fell a Bastinad. him—& chiding him—y^t he w^ld putt him to it, now he w. gr. old to discipl^n him—w^n not so abl as w^n he w. yong—

[MS 25 B, p. 78. Quoted in *ibid.*]

THOMAS PLUME, *ca.* 1657

One told Ben Johns^n—shakesp nev. studied for any th. he wrott. B. J. s^d—ye mō^e to blame He—[?he] s^d—Cesar never punishes any but for a just Cause & ar. time mk athyns in Bohemia—So Tom Goff brings in Etiocles & Polynices disc^ng of K. Rich. 2^d

[MS 25 B, p. 71. Quoted in *ibid.*]

THOMAS PLUME, *ca.* 1657

Here lies Ben Johnson Who once was one—h. own Epit.
Here lies Benjamin—wth little hair up. his chin
Who w^l he liued w. a slow th—& now he is bd is Noth
    Shakespr.
If y^u fall a galloping once s^d one—to An. yt w. thrown
    in a gallop
B Johsⁿ s^d h sh. rath. h. an Acr of witt yn of land—
      w^rup
      One called him—Wise Acre —

[MS 25 B, p. 51. Quoted in *ibid.*]

ANONYMOUS, 1657

"First [of the jests] in point of time is the rare one of the retort to
an impertinent inquisitive who asked on what passage out of Homer
the 'Father of our English Poets' was meditating. Ben replied that
he was meditating on a more worthy subject—'the 9 verse of the
39 Psalme which, as I remember,' says the author of the jest book,
'is to this purpose':

> For all the sinnes that I have done
> Lord quit me out of hand,
> And make me not a scorne to fooles
> That nothing understand."

[Thornton S. Graves, "Jonson in the Jest Books," in *Manly Anniversary Studies*,
pp. 128–29, from *A Banquet of Jests* (1657), p. 139.]

JOSHUA POOLE, 1657

Crafty.

The subtile fox.
Hyœna, Crocodile, and all beasts of craft,
Have been distil'd to make one nature up.
Volpone.

[*The English Parnassus: or, A Helpe to English Poesie. Containing A Collection Of
all Rhyming Monosyllables, The choicest Epithets, and Phrases* (1657), p. 240.]

Joshua Poole, 1657

v. Elegies on Dr. Donne, annexed to his Poems.
Quarles Emblems joynd with his divine Poems.
Habbingtons Castara, the third part.
Sr. John Beamounts Poems.
Johnsonus Virbius upon Ben. Johnson.
Upon Mr. Edw. King fellow of Chr. Coll. in Cambridge.

[*Ibid.*, p. 272. The above are listed as the sources or partial sources of the quotations illustrating "Elegy" in the section devoted to illustrative examples.]

Joshua Poole, 1657

A speaking Butterflie. Sober drunkards. Fastidious,
    Brisk, wise onely by inheritance.

["*Fantastick Gallant,*" *ibid.*, p. 301. Jonson's own characterization of Fastidious Briske in the front matter for *Every Man out of His Humour* is "A neat, spruce, affecting Courtier."]

Joshua Poole, 1657

Soft as the down of Swans.
Have you felt the wool of Beaver,
Or the nap of velvet ever,
Or the down of thistles?

["*Soft,*" *ibid.*, pp. 488–89. The lines are a misquotation of the song in *The Devi Is an Ass*, II, 6, ll. 108–9.]

Joshua Poole, 1657

Long winded monster, Crispinus, Hydra discourse.

["*Talkative,*" *ibid.*, p. 520.]

Joshua Poole, 1657

Truth.

Times eldest daughter. Times wonted off-spring.
Upon her head she wears a crown of stars,
Through which her orient haire waves to her wast,
By which believing mortals hold her fast.

[*Ibid.*, p. 533. The passage, except for the first line, is taken from the Angel's description of Truth in Jonson's *Hymenæi*, ll. 885–910 (Herford and Simpson, *Ben Jonson*, VII, 239–40).]

JOSHUA POOLE, 1657

Ingredients of witchcraft.
Peeces of dead carkases snatcht from ravenous beasts.
Wolves haire. Mad dogges foame. Adders eare.
Serpents slough. Spurging of a dead mans eyes.
Mandrake roote. Flesh, bones, and sculls from charnel
houses. Ropes, chains, raggs, bones, haire, sinews,
Marrow of men gibetted, blood and fat of slain infants.
Eggs and black feathers of a screech owle.
blood and back bone of a frogge.
Aconite, hemlock, henbane, adders tongue, night-shade,
Moon-wort, libbards bane, poppy, cypresse, wild fig-
trees growing on tombes, juyce of the larch tree, or A-
garicum. Basiliskes blood, vipers skin, the toad-eyes of
the owle, bats wings, young colts forehead.

[*The English Parnassus*, p. 561. This is a summary of the ingredients mentioned in the first eleven stanzas of the Hag's song in *Masque of Queens*.]

JOSHUA POOLE, 1657

Ben. Johnsons mask out of the house of Fame.

[*Ibid.*, p. 562. One of the sources of the quotations illustrating "Witches" in the section devoted to illustrative examples.]

ANONYMOUS, 1658

To his Noblest Friend Mr. Endimion Porter *upon Verses writ by* Ben. Johnson.

They that give wine to Poets, noble friend,
Verses receive, they need not verses send;
Onely your self that all men can out do,
Did send your Poet wine and verses too.

. . . .

The gift was rare, but there's a better thing,
You drew it from the bosome of a king;
For had you from the fountaine drawne a peece,
Pierced the Star, or squeez'd the golden fleece,
Or searcht the bowells of the Lyon, nay

Had you done more, sent a tall shipp a way,
To Spaine or Greece, and with your mony bought
The head of all the vintage, and that brought,
At your owne charge home to his Celler dore,
You had done much; but this is much much more:
You brought him sack even from a god like giver,
Such, and so blest, as it shall last for ever,
As if the Fates, being pleas'd, would now designe,
To the immortall Muses pretious wine;
So that your Poet to the last of dayes,
Is bound loud Sir, to singe your lasting prayse;
Thus have you built your self brave Sir, a tombe,
That neither time nor envie can consume.
        And if you want an Epitaph, you must dye,
        When as Parnassus burns, and Helicon is dry.

[*Poems* (1658), pp. 23–24. This miscellaneous collection is often catalogued as John Eliot's, because one poem in the volume is signed by him.]

ANONYMOUS, 1658

An Epigram, To his Friend Ben Johnson, *upon his
Libellous Verses against the Lords of the
Green-Cloath concerning his Sack.*

You swore dear *Ben* you'ld turn the green cloth blew,
If your dry Muse might not be bath'd in sack,
Nay drunk with choller you protested too,
Their white stains you would smoke till they were black.
This with those fearless Lords nothing prevailing,
The Scean you alterd and you smooth'd your pen,
You left* your bitter and your fruitless rayling,
And basely flatter'd e'en the worst of men;
Then give me leave henceforth good Ben to think,
You drunkest are when you the most want drink.

* Misprinted "lest."

[*Ibid.*, p. 26. On authorship see above.]

ANONYMOUS, 1658

To Ben Johnson *again, upon his verses dedicated to the Earl of* Portland, *Lord* Treasurer.

Your verses are commended and tis true,
That they were very good, I mean to you;
For they return'd you *Ben* as I was tould,
A certain sum of forty pound in gold:
  The verses then being rightly understood,
  His Lordship not *Ben Johnson* made them good.

[*Ibid.*, p. 27. On authorship see above.]

ANONYMOUS, 1658

To the Lord Chamberlain.

. . . . yet with any pain
Or honest industry, Could I obtain
A noble favourer, I might write, and do
  Like others of more name, and get one too,
Or else my *Genius* is false, I know
  That *Iohnson* much of what he has does owe
To you, and to your *Familie*, and is never
  Slow to professe that, nor had *Fletcher* ever
Such reputation, and Credit won
  But by his honour'd Patron *Huntington.*
Inimitable *Spencer* ne'r had been
  So famous for his matchless *fairie Queene*,
Had he not found a *Sidny* to preferr
  His plain way in his shepherds *Callender.*

[*Ibid.*, p. 110. On authorship see above.]

RICHARD BROME, 1658

And do not weeds creep up first in all Gardens? and why not then in this? which never was a Garden until now; and which will be the Garden of Gardens, I foresee't. And for the weeds in it, let me alone for the weeding of them out. And so as my Reverend Ancestor *Jus-*

tice Adam Overdoe, was wont to say, *In Heavens name and the Kings*, and for the good of the Commonwealth I will go about it.

[*The Weeding of Covent Garden* (1658), Act I, scene 1, sig. B₁ᵛ, printed in *Five New Plays* (1659). Since Cockbrain, the Justice of the Peace who makes this speech, is obviously modeled on Jonson's Justice Adam Overdo of *Bartholomew Fair*, this passage is an unusually frank admission of source.]

ASTON COKAYNE, 1658

To my noble Friend, Mr. Marmaduke Wivel.

After so many in the *English* tongue,
Whose happy Muses, Epigrams have sung,
I have too boldly done, and writ in vain
To get repute by following that strain.
When I bethink me that great *Johnson* (he
Who all the ancient wit of *Italy*
And learned *Greece* (by his industrious Pen)
Transplanted hath for his own Countreymen,
And made our *English* tongue so swell, that now
We scarce an equal unto it allow)
Writ Epigrams, I tremble, and (instead
Of praise) beseech a pardon when I'm read.

[*A Chain of Golden Poems* (1658), No. 60, p. 166.]

ASTON COKAYNE, 1658

To my especial Friend Mr. Henry Thimbleby.

Platonick Love must needs a Friendship be,
Or els *Platonick* Love's a Gullery:
Love is (as *Johnson* in's *New Inne* hath prov'd)
Desire of union with the belov'd:
And cannot onely be a gazing at;
But a strong Appetite t'incorporate.

[*Ibid.*, No. 77, p. 175.]

ASTON COKAYNE, 1658

Iohnson, Chapman, and *Holland* I have seen,
And with them too should have acquainted been.

What needs this Catalogue? Th' are dead and gone;
And to me you are all of them in one.

[*Ibid.*, No. 99, p. 134 (for 234).]

RICHARD FLECKNOE, 1658

Of one that imitates the good companion another way.

He is on, who now the stage is down Acts the *Parasites* part at Table; and since *Tailors* death, none can play *Mosco's* part so well as he.

[*Enigmaticall Characters* (1658), p. 10.]

WILLIAM LONDON, 1658

B. *Iohnson's* Playes. 2. vol. *folio.*

. . . .

The Widow, a Comedy, by Mr *Johnson*, and Mr *Fletcher.*

[*A Catalogue of the most vendible Books in England* (1658), sig. Ff₁^{r & v}, in the section entitled "Playes."]

[SIR JOHN MENNIS AND JAMES SMITH], 1658

Pompey that once was Tapster of *New-Inne*,
And fought with *Cæsar* on th' *Æmathian* plaines,
First with his dreadfull *Myrmidons* came in
And let them blood in the Hepatick veines.

["*Ad* Johannuelem Leporem, *Lepidissimum, Carmen Heroicum*," *Wit Restor'd* (1658), published in *Facetiae* (1874), I, 154.]

[EDWARD PHILLIPS], 1658

Q. One askt Ben. Johnson *what reparation he would tender to his honor for spitting in his face?*
A. He answered, if he pleased, he would tread it out again.

[*The Mysteries of Love and Eloquence* (1685), p. 208; first edition, 1658.]

J. S., 1658

'Tis true quoth he,[9] Loves troubles make me tamer,
Res est Soliciti plena timoris Amor.

. . . .

[9] There the Author translates out of Ovid, as Ben Johnson do's in Sejanus out of Homer.

["The Innovation of Ulysses and Penelope," *Wit Restored* (1658), published in *Facetiae* (1874), I, 276.]

JAMES SMITH, 1658

I grudge thee not; for if I met
Vulpone's potion, or could get
Nectar, or else dissolv'd to dew
Th'Elixir, which the gods n'ere knew:
'Twere thine, ...

["*The same, to the same,*" i.e., "*Mr.* Smith, to *Captain* Mennis," *Wit Restor'd* (1658), published in *Facetiae* (1874), I, 125.]

E. WILLIAMSON, 1658

To the Discerning Reader.

Worthy Friend, there is a saying, *Once well done, and ever done:* the wisest men have so considerately acted in their times, as by their learned Works, to build their own monuments, such as might eternize them to future Ages: our *Johnson* named his, *Works,* when others were called *Playes,* though they cost him much of the Lamp and oyl; yet he so writ, as to oblige posterity to admire them.

["To the Discerning Reader," *J. Cleaveland Revived: Poems, Orations, Epistles* (1668), sig. A₃. This Foreword is dated "*Newark, Nov.* 21.·1658."]

IMPRINT, 1659

Printed for *R. Pollard,* and *Tho. Dring,* and are to be sold at the *Ben Johnsons* Head, behind the *Exchange,* and the *George* in *Fleet-street,* near Saint *Dunstans* Church. 1659.

[John Day's *The Blind-Beggar of Bednal-Green* (1659).]

HENRY BOLD, 1659

To W. M. *Esq; I being in a Course of Physick
and newly recovered of a Squinancy*, February,
1659.

For *Burr* of *Ear*, and *Burr* in *Throat*,
'Tis better with me, then ith' Moat-
Ed-*Chamber*, when for fear of *Squincy*.
Toung was *worm'd*, and *Woolsie Lincy*,
Hooded *Head* like *Hawke* with *Muzzle*,
(A *Sight*, would put one, to the *Puzzle*)
Not unlike *Ben. Johnsons Morose*,
That was *wrapt* and *wrapt* before us.

[*Poems* (1664), p. 149.]

EDMUND GAYTON, 1659

Of Drinks, and first of Wine

Whilest I do write thy profits, and the good
Thou dost confer (plump Grapes most noble blood)
I neither have nor call for helps from thee,
Thou voucht infuser of high Poetry;
It is enough for those who write thy praise,
Such as my Father *Ben*, whose head with bayes,
Scarce yet inherited, thou justly crown'dst,
To be *Silenus* like, well souc'd and plounc'd
In essences of Sack, whence spirits follow,
Richer and higher than his own *Apollo*.
Let those thy brave and warm contagions boast,
Who do recite to th' profit of their hoast
And club-delight, whate're th' hesternall fire,
(Not at next meeting quencht) did fore-inspire:
A long forgetfulnesse hath seiz'd my soul,
Nor have I felt thy flames since *Henham* Bowl;
The cooler *Hypocrene* is spurn enough,
And the cleer liquor headed from the hoof
Of the wing'd *Courser*, serves for such poor stuff,

As humbly now comes forth his Muses Cell,
Is sutable, and hath its name from *Well*.

[*The Art of Longevity* (1659), chap. vi, p. 14.]

EDMUND GAYTON, 1659

Of Ale

Dr[i]nk famous, infamous, prais'd and disprais'd,
From stygian lakes, that's muddy harbours rais'd
From common shores and father Ben's adventures,
How dar'st thou boiled bog or muzzles enter?

[*Ibid.*, chap. viii, p. 19.]

EDMUND GAYTON, 1659

. . . . first *Avicen*

Sayes, Pork's most naturall to men, so *Ben;*
Hogs flesh is likest mans, saith *Isaak;*
The same again saith *Ben*, but adds, that Sack,
A Hogshead full, for a *vehiculum*,
Will spoile its grumbling in our *medium*,
(Or middle Region of our Trunk) for Swine,
Alive or dead, will be still laid with Wine.
Indeed my Father *Ben* doth there produce
A reason why they were denied the Jews;
Because that Nutrimentall Animall
Of a provoking sap, and *Hogon* all,
Would have disorder'd and o're-pamper'd those
Who newly come from *Egypts* hard dispose:
Rebels in rough *Mosaick* Discipline,
How much more Rebels, had they eaten Swine?

["*Of the Flesh of Swine*, Deer, Hares *and* Bears," *ibid.*, chap. xv, p. 31. These
lines immediately follow those quoted in *The Jonson Allusion-Book*, pp. 317–18.]

HUMPHREY MOSELEY, 1659

We have also in Print (written by the same hand [i.e., Jonson's])
the very Beginning only (for it amounts not to one full *Scene*) of a
Tragedy call'd *MORTIMER*. So that we find the same fate to have

hapned in the Works of two of the most celebrated and happy Wits
of this Nation.

[From the address to the reader printed by Moseley before *The Sad One* in *The
Last Remains of Sir John Suckling* (1659) and immediately following the reference
to *The Sad Shepherd* which is in *The Jonson Allusion-Book*.]

E. WILLIAMSON, 1659

Forbear hereafter, *Vice*, to paint so well,
Such draughts may hap t'enlarge the pow'r of hel.
Since writ by *Ben*, inspir'd by lusty wine,
We love *Sejanus*, and bold *Cataline*.

[From the anonymous poem, "*An Elegy on Mr.* Cleaveland, *and his Verses on*
Smectimnus," *J. Cleaveland Revived: Poems, Orations, Epistles* (1668; first ed., 1659),
sig. B₁.]

E. WILLIAMSON, 1659

[Jasper Mayne's poem on Jonson, first printed in *Jonsonus Virbius*, is reprinted
in *J. Cleaveland Revived* (1668; first ed., 1659), pp. 35–40.]

E. WILLIAMSON, 1659

[Richard West's poem "On Master Ben Jonson" in *Jonsonus Virbius* is reprinted
anonymously in *J. Cleaveland Revived* (1668; first ed., 1659), pp. 57–61.]

E. WILLIAMSON, 1659

[The anonymous poem in *Jonsonus Virbius* which begins "The Muses' fairest
light in no dark time" is printed in *J. Cleaveland Revived* (1668; first ed., 1659), pp.
80–81, with the title "*An Epitaph on* Ben. Johnson."]

ANONYMOUS, 1660

These are Ben Johnson's *Workes*, the Printer says:
Printer thou ly'st, They are Ben Johnson's Plays.

[Number 258 of *A Choice Banquet of Witty Jests* (1660) tells of the gentleman who
drew his pencil through the title of the folio edition of Jonson's works and added
the above couplet (Thornton S. Graves, "Jonson in the Jest Books," in *Manly Anniversary Studies*, p. 132).]

Anonymous, 1660

These two notable and famous Poets endeavoured to out-vy each other in the making onely one (and that best and truest) Verse, which was thus ended:

> I Silvester lay with thy Sister.
> I Ben Johnson lay with thy wife.

Whereupon Silvester told him that was not a right Verse. O! quoth Ben. Johnson, but it is true.

[Number 336 in *A Choice Banquet of Witty Jests* (1660), quoted by Graves, *loc. cit.*, pp. 129–30. The story also occurs as No. 179 in H. C.'s *England's Jests Refin'd and Improv'd* (1693).]

Anonymous, 1660

The *Alchemist;* Fire, breeding Gold, our *Theme:*
Here must no Melancholie be, nor Flegm.
Young *Ben*, not Old, writ this, when in his Prime,
Solid in Judgement, and in Wit sublime.
　　The *Sisters*, who at *Thespian* Springs their Blood
Cool with fresh Streams, All, in a Merry Mood,
Their wat'ry Cups, and Pittances declin'd,
At *Bread-Street's Mer-maid* with our *Poët* din'd:
Where, what they Drank, or who plaid most the Rig,
Fame modestly conceals: but He grew big
Of this pris'd Issue; when a *Jovial* Maid,
His Brows besprinkling with *Canarie*, said.
　　Pregnant by Us, produce no Mortal Birth;
Thy active Soul, quitting the sordid Earth,
Shall 'mongst Heav'ns glitt'ring *Hieroglyphicks* trade,
And *Pegasus*, our winged Sumpter, jade,
Who from *Parnassus* never brought to *Greece*,
Nor *Romane* Stage, so rare a Master-piece.
　　This Story, true or false, may well be spar'd;
The *Actors* are in question, not the *Bard:*
How they shall humour their oft-varied Parts,
To get your Money, Company, and Hearts,
Since all Tradition, and like Helps are lost.

Reading our Bill new pasted on the Post,
Grave Stagers both, one, to the other said,
The ALCHEMIST? What! are the Fellows mad?
Who shall *Doll Common* Act? Their tender Tibs
Have neither Lungs, nor Confidence, nor Ribs.

Who *Face*, and *Subtle?* Parts, all Air, and Fire:
They, whom the *Authour* did Himself inspire,
Taught, Line by Line, each Tittle, Accent, Word,
Ne're reach'd His Height; all after, more absurd,
Shadows of fainter Shadows, wheresoe're
A *Fox* be pencil'd, copied out a *Bear.*

Encouragement for young Beginners small:
Yet howsoe're we'll venture; have at All.
Bold Ignorance (they say) falls seldome short
In *Camp*, the *Countrey*, *City*, or the *Court.*

Arm'd with the Influence of your fair Aspects,
Our Selves we'll conquer, and our own Defects.
A thousand Eyes dart raies into our Hearts,
Would make Stones speak, and Stocks play well their Parts:
Some few Malignant Beams we need not fear,
Where shines such Glory in so bright a Sphere.

[A broadside in Worcester College Library entitled "Prologue to the Reviv'd Alchemist," quoted by C. H. Wilkinson, "Worcester College Library," *Oxford Bibliographical Society Proceedings and Papers* (1927), I (1922–26), 281–82. Wilkinson thinks the verses are probably by Davenant. "It is certain from the pieces among which it was bound that it was published in 1660, and this early revival throws an interesting light on the popularity of the play."]

BENJAMIN FRANCIS, 1660

Hence to our Inn: noyse flies about the Town,
Gallants are come, mongst whom *Ben Johnson's* one,
(so *Spurstow* call'd me) how! a third replyes,
If *Ben* be there 'tis time for us to rise
He'l scare them from their witts where e're they go,
Then sure 'tis he; for they'r already so.

["A Relation of a mad merry Ramble, merrily begun, and as madly concluded," *Poems by Ben. Francis* (1660), p. 30.]

Elizabeth Bodvile(?), 1661

I was to aquant you that to morrow att ten you are expected; likewis, I would have you belive to that you will not bee worst lookt one by y^r friends for y^r father's not being Lord Privi Seall. Good night, and pray sleep never the les. I hope y^r good fortune is still to come; and pray bee well to morrow, or I shall bee Mrs. Otter.

[*Correspondence of the Family of Hatton, A.D. 1601–1704* (1878), ed. Edward Maunde Thompson, I, 22. The letter is dated "[A.D. 1661.]" and is supposedly from Elizabeth Bodvile.]

Robert Boyle, 1661

Ben. Johnson passionately complaining to a learned Acquaintance of mine, that a Man of the long Robe, whom his Wit had rais'd to great Dignities and Power, had Refus'd to grant him some very valuable thing he had Begg'd of him, concluded with saying with an upbrading Tone and Gesture to my Friend; *Why the ungratefull Wretch knows very well, that before he came to Preferment, I was the Man that made him Relish* Horace.

["Epistle Dedicatory," *Some Considerations Touching the Style of the H. Scriptures* (1661), sig. a₃; quoted in Herford and Simpson, *Ben Jonson*, I, 184.]

Alexander Brome, 1661

Those *politick would-bees* do but shew themselves asses,
    That other mens calling invade,
We only converse with pots and with glasses;
    Let the *Rulers* alone with their trade.

[Song XXV, "*The Prisoners*. Written when *O. C.* attempted to be King," *Songs and other Poems* (1664; first ed., 1661), p. 95.]

Alexander Brome, 1661

Ben. Johnsons *sociable rules for the* Apollo.

Let none but *Guests* or *Clubbers* hither come;
Let Dunces, Fools, sad, sordid men keep home;
Let learned, civil, merry men b'invited,
And modest too; nor the choice *Ladies* sleighted:
Let nothing in the *treat* offend the Guests,
More for delight then cost prepare the feasts:

The *Cook* and *Purvey'r* must our palats know;
And none contend who shall sit high or low:
Our waiters must quick-sighted be and dumb,
And let the *drawers* quickly hear and come:
Let not our wine be mixt, but brisk and neat,
Or else the dinkers [*sic*] may the *Vintners* beat.
And let our only emulation be,
Not drinking much, but *talking* wittily:
Etc.

[*Ibid.*, p. 325.]

Sir Henry Herbert, 1661

That King James made the like grante to Benjamin Johnson,
5. October, in the 19th yeare of his Reigne.

["Breviat, Sir Henry Herbert versus Sir William Davenant," *The Dramatic Records of Sir Henry Herbert*, ed. John Quincy Adams (1917), p. 103.]

Barten Holyday, 1661

864.

Paul the Third and *Morone* (they so compact)
At *Rome* and *Trent*, *Volpone* and *Mosca* act.

["Book IX. Of Polititians," *A Survey of the World in Ten Books* (1661), p. 103.]

Sir Henry Herbert, *ca.* 1662

That King James made the like Grante to Beniamin Johnson,
5 October, In the 19 yeare of his Reigne.

[Another breviat, Herbert versus Davenant, *The Dramatic Records of Sir Henry Herbert*, p. 104.]

John Evelyn, 1661/62

This night [January 16, 1661/62] was acted before his Ma^tʸ
"The Widow," a lewd play.

[*Diary of John Evelyn*, ed. William Bray (1879), II, 143.]

Anonymous, 1662

I mean to speak of *Englands* sad fate,
To help in mean time the King, and his Mate,

That's ruled by an Antipodian State,
　　　　Which no body can deny.

But had these seditious times been when
We had the life of wise Poet *Ben,*
Parsons had never been Parliament men,
　　　　Which no body can deny.

["Englands Woe," *Rump: or an Exact Collection of the Choycest Poems and Songs Relating to the Late Times* (1662), p. 39.]

ANONYMOUS, 1662

Tread softly through, least *Scyllah's* ghost awake,
And us i'th' roll of his *Proscriptions* take.

["The Times," *ibid.*, p. 198.]

MARGARET CAVENDISH, DUCHESS OF NEWCASTLE, 1662

Likewise my Playes may be Condemned, because they follow not the Antient Custome, as the learned sayes, which is, that all Comedies should be so ordered and composed, as nothing should be presented therein, but what may be naturally, or usually practiced or Acted in the World in the compass of one day; truly in my opinion those Comedies would be very flat and dull, and neither profitable nor pleasant, that should only present the actions of one day; for though *Ben. Johnson* as I have heard was of that opinion, that a Comedy cannot be good, nor is a natural or true Comedy, if it should present more than one dayes action, yet his Comedies that he hath published, could never be the actions of one day; for could any rational person think that the whole Play of the Fox could be the action of one day? or can any rational person think that the Alchymist could be the action of one day? as that so many several Cozenings could be Acted in one day, by Captain *Face* and *Doll Common;* and could the Alchymist make any believe they could make gold in one day? could they burn so many Coals, and draw the purses of so many, or so often from one person, in one day? and the like is in all his Playes, not any of them presents the actions of one day, although it were a day at the Poles, but of many dayes, nay I may say some years.

[The third "To the Readers," *Playes* (1662), sigs. A₄–A₄ᵛ.]

MARGARET CAVENDISH, DUCHESS OF NEWCASTLE, 1662

.... for to go away before a Play is ended, is a kind of an affront, both to the Poet and the Players; yet, I believe none of my Playes are so long as *Ben. Johnson's* Fox, or Alchymist, which in truth, are somewhat too long; but for the Readers, the length of the Playes can be no trouble, nor inconveniency, because they may read as short or as long a time as they please, without any disrespect to the Writer; but some of my Playes are short enough, etc.

[The second "To the Readers," *ibid*. [sig. A$_4$+^{v}].]

MARGARET CAVENDISH, DUCHESS OF NEWCASTLE, 1662

A General Prologue to all my Playes.

NOBLE Spectators, do not think to see
Such Playes, that's like *Ben. Johnsons* Alchymie,
Nor Fox, nor Silent Woman: for those Playes
Did Crown the Author with exceeding praise;
They were his Master-pieces, and were wrought
By Wits Invention, and his labouring thought,
And his Experience brought Materials store,
His reading several Authors brought much more:
What length of time he took those Plays to write,
I cannot guess, not knowing his Wits flight;
But I have heard, *Ben. Johnsons* Playes came forth,
To the Worlds view, as things of a great worth;
Like Forein Emperors, which do appear.
Unto their Subjects, not 'bove once a year;
So did *Ben. Johnsons* Playes so rarely pass,
As one might think they long a writing was.

[*Ibid*., sig. A$_7$, ll. 1–16.]

JOHN EVELYN, 1662

[October] 16th [1662]. I saw "Volpone" acted at Court before their Maties.

[*Diary of John Evelyn*, II, 153.]

Sir Henry Herbert and Symon Thelwall, 1662

And whereas alsoe King James, by his other Letters Patents, the 5th of October, in the 19th year of his Reigne, graunted the said office to Beniamin Johnson, gentleman, for his life, from the death of the said George Bucke and John Ashley, or assoon as the said office by resignacion or surrender or other lawfull manner should become void, after which graunt, to witt the 20th of September, 1623, the said George Bucke dyed, after whose death John Ashley, by vertue of the said graunt of the office, was seized thereof as of his freehold for his life. And being soe seized, and the said Beniamin Johnson then alive, the late King Charles, by his Letters Patents vnder the great seale, the 22th of August, in the 5th year of his Reigne, ... did give and graunt to the plaintiffs the said office Habendum to them for their lives, and the life of the longer liver of them after the death of the said John Ashley and Beniamin and assoon as the said office . . . . should become void, ... And that afterwards, to witt the 20th of November, 1635, Beniamin Johnson dyed, and on the 13th of January 1640 the said John Ashley dyed, after whose deaths the plaintiffs tooke vpon them the said office, ...

["Declaration, May 6, 1662, Herbert and Thelwall versus Betterton," *The Dramatic Records of Sir Henry Herbert*, ed. John Quincy Adams, p. 109.]

Robert Hobbes, 1662

Nov. 1 [1662]. 15. Ro. Hobbes to Sec. Bennet. Congratulates his increase of honour; as to his own little ambition, rolls himself upon his word, as Sir Epicure Mammon says in the Alchymist.

[*Calendar of State Papers, Domestic, 1661–62* (1861), p. 540.]

E. M., 1662

Ben's Auditours were once in such a mood,
That he was forc't to swear his *Play* was good;
Thy Play then his, doth far more currant go,
For without swearing, wee'l beleeve thine so.

[Commendatory verses prefixed to Robert Neville's *The Poor Scholar* (1662), sig. A₂.]

T. S., 1662

King James.

King *James* first coined his 22 shillings peice of Gold called *Jacobusses* where on his head he wore a Crown, after that he coined his 20. shillings and wore the Lawrel in stead of the Crown, upon which mutation *Ben. Johnson* said pleasantly. That *Poets* being alwayes poor Bayes were rather the Embleme of Wit then wealth *since King James no sooner began to wear them, but he fell two shillings in the pound in publique valuation.*

[*Fragmenta Aulica* (1662), pp. 41-42.]

T. S., 1662

One was friendly telling *Benjamin Johnson* of his great and excessive drinking continually. Heres a greivous clutter and talk quoth *Benjamin* concerning my drinking, *but heres not a word of that thirst which so miserably torments me day and night.*

[*Ibid.*, pp. 99-100, quoted by Thornton S. Graves, "Jonson in the Jest Books," in *Manly Anniversary Studies,* p. 134.]

EDWARD BROWNE(?), 1662-64

At the Cock Pit in Drewry Lane.

	s.	d.	
Silent woman	2	0	K. P.

[In the list of plays in Brit. Mus. Sloane MS 1900, entitled "Sir Edw. Browne's Memorandum Book, 1662." See W. W. Greg, "Theatrical Repertories of 1662," *Gentleman's Magazine,* CCCI (new ser.; July–December, 1906), 69, 71.]

EDWARD BROWNE(?), 1662-64

At the New Theatre in Lincolnes Jnne fields.

Alchymist	. . . . .	2	6	K. P.
Widdow	. . . .	1	0	
Bartholomew faire	. . .	1	6	
The Fox	. . . . .	2	6	

[*Ibid.*]

THOMAS JORDAN, 166-?

An Acrostical Encomium, Composed on . . . .

Sir FRANCIS ENGLEFIELD . . . .

. . . .

E very favour in your Gifts or Letters,
L eaves the Receiver bound in Golden Fetters:
D on, *Johnson*, *Fletcher*, and (your name-sake) *Francis*
B *eaumont* in you might find new Theams for *Fancies*.

[*Jewels of Ingenuity, Set in a Coronet of Poetry* (n.d.).]

THOMAS JORDAN, 166-?

On Ben Johnson *and a Country man.*

Ben. Johnson in a Tavern once began
Rudely to talk to a plain Country man.
And thus it was, Thou dull laborious Moyle
That I beleeve wert made for nought but toyle;
For every *Acre* of thy *Land* I have
Twenty of wit: Such *Acres* Sir, are brave,
Replyed the *Country man:* What great Mistakers
Have we been of your wealth, *Mr. Wise Acres.*

[*Ibid.*]

ANONYMOUS, 1663

[The words of the song "Still to be neat" from *Epicoene* were printed in *The Academy of Complements* (1663), p. 205. Robert Gale Noyes, *Ben Jonson on the English Stage 1660–1776* (1935), p. 181, n. 5.]

ANONYMOUS, 1663

["The Post of the Signe," a ballad printed in *Recreation for Ingenious Headpeeces* (1663), sigs. Z₃ᵛ–Z₅, is really "John Urson's Ballad" from Jonson's *The Masque of Augurs*, as the Simpsons have pointed out (Herford and Simpson, *Ben Jonson*, VII, 627).]

ANONYMOUS, 1663

How I shall hurle *Protosebastus's* panting brain
Into the Air in mites as small as Atomes.

[*The Unfortunate Usurper* (1663), I, 4. The lines are a quotation of *Sejanus*, I, 1, 255–57:

> "and with my hand
> I'ld hurle his panting braine about the ayre,
> In mites, as small as *atomi*."

Pointed out by W. D. Briggs, "The Influence of Jonson's Tragedy in the Seventeenth Century," *Anglia*, XXXV (1912), 281.]

ANONYMOUS, 1663

> I hope I am so wrought into your trust,
> And woven to your design. . . . .

[*The Unfortunate Usurper* (1663), I, 4. The lines are a quotation of *Sejanus*, Act III, ll. 625–26:

> "Thou know'st how thou art wrought into our trust;
> Wouen in our designe."

Pointed out by Briggs, *loc. cit.*, pp. 282–83.]

ABRAHAM COWLEY, 1663

Worm. I'll have her; I'm the better scholar; and we're both equal soldiers, I'm sure.

Cutter. Thou, Captain Bobadill? What with that Ember-week face o' thine? that Rasor o' thy nose?

[*Cutter of Coleman Street* (1663), Act I, scene v. Noted by C. B. Graham, "Jonson Allusions in Restoration Comedy," *Review of English Studies*, XV (1939), 202.]

JAMES HOWELL, 1663

Vpon a Rare and Recent Persian TRAGY-
HISTORY. 1655.

. . . .

Nor is it *Europe* onely that doth breed
Such Monsters, but the Asian Regions feed
As bad; witness this *Persian* Tragedy,
Compil'd with so much Art and Energy:
As if the Soul of *Ben*, of *Pond'rous Ben*,
Did move in you, and guide both Brain and Pen:

You make the Actors with such passion speak,
As if the very Lines with Blood did reak.

[*Poems* (1663), sig. D₂ᵛ. Obviously, the tragi-history was Robert Baron's *Mirza*, the second edition of which was published in 1655. There are a dozen evidences of the commendatory relations between Howell and Baron.]

ANONYMOUS, 1663/64

1664 February 2 Epicoene King's Company at the Inner Temple

[Robert Gale Noyes, *Ben Jonson on the English Stage 1660–1776*, p. 320. Noyes gives only his general sources for all performances, not individual documentation. I have not seen the original records of these performances.]

ANTHONY WOOD, 1663/64

January.—1, Th., given to see Volponey acted at the town hall by prentices and tradesmen, 6*d*. . . . .
       6, T., given to see Volponey acted againe, 6*d*.

[Andrew Clark, *The Life and Times of Anthony Wood* (1891–1900), I, 467.]

ANONYMOUS, 1664

1664 June 1 Epicoene Theatre Royal in Bridges St.

[Noyes, *Ben Jonson*, p. 320.]

HENRY BOLD, 1664

To *R. B.* Esq; having Read his *Mirza*.

Thy scene was *Persia*, but too like our own,
Only our *Soffie* has not got the *Crown*,
Me-thinks it so concernes us, as it were
A Romance there, but a true story here.
Had *Johnson* liv'd t'have seen this work h'ad sed
Th'adst been his bravest Boy! strok't thee oth' head
Given thee his blessing in a bowle of Wine
Made thee's Administrator, or Assign.
But father *Ben.* I think was too much Poet,
To have much wealth (one need not care who owe it)
Besides had Elder Sons, yet, where there's merit,

Or custom, Yonger brothers oft inherit.
What though of's Gold th'ast got the Devil a bit,
I'm* sure th'art heir apparent to his Wit
Which thou hast in that vigour, and high shine
As when he wrote his *Strenuous Cateline.*
Hence be't observ'd 'mongst our Chronologers,
Since *Johnson* inspir'd *Baron*—Years.
You are so much each other (no dispraise)
Robin and *Ben.* are now synonoma's
    Nor can time blast a Wit: thine's ripe as His
    That Age, a *Johnson* crown'd, a *Baron* this.

* Misprinted "I'ne."

[*Poems* (1664), pp. 196–97.]

RICHARD FLECKNOE, 1664

Beaumont and *Fletcher* were excellent in their kinde, but they often err'd against *Decorum*, seldom representing a valiant man without somewhat of the *Braggadoccio*, nor an honourable woman without somewhat of *Dol Common* in her.

[*A Short Discourse of the English Stage* (1664), reproduced by J. E. Spingarn, *Critical Essays of the Seventeenth Century* (1908), II, 94.]

ANONYMOUS, 1640–90

The first that breake silence was good ould Ben
prepared before with Cannary Wyne
And he tould them playnly he deserved the Bayes
for his were cal'd workes whereas others were cald playes

And bid them Remember how he had purg'd the stage
Of Errours that had lasted many an age
And he hoped they did think the Silent woman
The Fox and the Alchymist out done by noe-man.

[Quoted from "A Long Poem, 14 stanzas of 8 lines, and one stanza of 6 lines, in seventeenth century handwriting," in P. J. and A. E. Dobell, *A Catalogue of Autograph Letters and MSS*, No. 72 (October, 1942) # 107. The poem is Suckling's "Session of the Poets," normally printed as twenty-eight four-line stanzas.]

Thomas Jordan, *ca.* 1665

I am not so extravagant as once a presented Poetaster (in a good Comedy) said, *Who loves not Verse is damn'd:* nor so rapt with a vain-glorious humour and self-admiration as old *Ben* was when he made this *Distick*, the Theam being *Poets.*

> *When God begins to do some* exc'lent *thing,*
> *He makes a* Poet *or, at least, a* King.

[The address, "To all Noble, Learned, and Ingenious Lovers, of Poets, and Poetry," prefixed to *A Nursery of Novelties* (n.d.), sig. A₄.]

Thomas Jordan, *ca.* 1665

The Players Petition to the Long Parliament,
after being long Silenc'd, that they
might Play again, 1642.

. . . .

> We will not dare at your strange Votes to jeer,
> Or personate King *Pym* with his State fleire:
> Aspiring *Cataline* shall be forgot,
> Bloody *Sejanus,* or who ere could plot
> Confusion 'gainst a State.

[*Ibid.*, p. 79.]

E. Bostocke, 1665

> . . . . and I come
> Amongst my Friends, to fill a vacant Room.
> But pray below, above, I fear the Air
> Suits not the Climate of my Hemisphere.
> *Scoggin* and *Ben* late in conjunction met,
> Such strange effects have wrought upon thy Pate.
> Makes me afraid near that hot seat to sit.
> Lest I be Carbonado'd by thy Wit.

[Commendatory verses prefixed to Matthew Stevenson's *Poems* (1665).]

David Lloyd, 1665

One great argument for his [Fulke Greville, Lord Brooke's] worth, was his respect for the worth of others, desiring to be known to posterity under no other notions than of *Shakespeare's* and *Ben Johnson's* Master, Chancellor *Egerton's* Patron, Bishop *Overal's* Lord, and Sir *Philip Sidney's friend.*

[*Statesmen and Favourites of England since the Reformation* (1665), p. 504, quoted by E. K. Chambers in the Preface to *The Shakspere Allusion-Book*, p. xii.]

MATTHEW STEVENSON, 1665

I come not here to beg approbation; for those I writ it for, like it, and that's enough. Every Reader is not a competent Judge of Poesie, my Judges are in the following Pages, who are not afraid to call it good, and subscribe to it: I am for multitudes, *Vnus mihi pro populo*. If thou be'st of those Geese that hiss'd at *Johnsons* works, let mine alone, lest thou show thy self as much a fool in buying, as I in composing it.

[The address to the "Reader," prefixed to *Poems* (1665), sig. A₄ʳ & ᵛ.]

JOHN WILSON, 1665

Go—go down into the Country and awe your poor neighbours with my Lord's nod, or his whisper in your ear at parting—Studie Longitude and the Philosophers Stone; The North-West Passage, and the Square of a Circle—So brave a Sir *Poll*, trouble himself with trifles!—By no means—no—no—Embark for the *Indies* in a Cock-boat, or to *France* on a Mil-stone; Plant a Colonie in *Terra Incognita*, or settle an Intelligence with the Emperor of *Vtopia*—these were fit for Sir *Gudgeon!*

[*The Projectors* (1665), p. 58. Sir Poll is, of course, Sir Politic Would-Be of *Volpone*. The passage is quoted in part by C. B. Graham, "Jonson Allusions in Restoration Comedy," *Review of English Studies*, XV (1939), 203.]

ARTHUR CAPELL, 1650–83

[The commonplace book of Arthur Capell, Earl of Essex (1631–83), is preserved in Brit. Mus. Harl. MS 3511. Geoffrey Tillotson writes that the manuscript contains poems by "Sidney, Jonson, Bacon, Donne, Drayton, William Browne, Cartwright, Randolph, Cleveland, Carew, Quarles, Henry King, Habington, William, Earl of Pembroke, Corbet, Strode, Robert Gomersal, Henry Reynolds, Hugh Holland, Jasper Fisher, Henry Ventrice, William Lewis, and others." He does not specify what the poem or poems of Jonson are. See "The Commonplace Book of Arthur Capell," *Modern Language Review*, XXVII (1932), 381–91.]

ALEXANDER BROME, 1666

Sir, For my speedier *dispatch* and your *advantage*, I made bold to take in all such parts of HORACE, as have been *Englished* by the *Lord Embassadour Fanshaw;* and what were *omitted* by him, I *supplyed* with such as have been done by Sir *Thomas Hawkins*, or Dr. *Holiday*, or both, for they are both the same; and whether of the two is the *Author*, remains to me *undiscovered:* What were not touched by these, I gathered out of Mr. *Cowleys* and other Printed Books; and such as were not *Translated* by others, my self and several friends of mine at my request have attempted: *De Arte Poetica* being long since *Englished* by that great *Master* thereof B. *Johnson*, I have borrowed to *crown* the rest.

[Dedication, signed by Brome, to *The Poems of Horace . . . . Rendred in English and Paraphrased by Several Persons* (1666), sigs. A₅–A₅ᵛ.]

WARRANT, 1666

Dec: 10 1666 The Silent Weoman at Court £20

[Warrant dated August 29, 1668, for plays acted from December 10, 1666, to July 31, 1668 (L.C. 5/139, p. 129), quoted by Allardyce Nicoll, *A History of Restoration Drama* (3d ed., 1940), p. 305.]

[—— RAYMUND], 1667

A Ballad, To the Tune of *the Song in the play of* Bartholomew Fair.

[Title of a song in *Folly in Print* (1667), p. 101.]

WARRANT, 1667

[Ap:] 27 [1667] Bartholomew fayre at the Theatre. .   10
Aug: 28:   The fox at Court.   20

[Warrant of August 29, 1668, for plays acted from December 10, 1666 to July 31, 1668 (L.C. 5/139, p. 129), quoted by Nicoll, *A History of Restoration Drama*, pp. 305–6.]

WILLIAM WINSTANLEY, 1667

Tho. Randolph the wit of *Cambridge* coming to *London*, had a great mind to see Master *Johnson*, who was then drinking at the Devil-Tavern near *Temple-bar*, with Master *Drayton*, Master *Daniel*, and Master *Silvester*, three eminent poets of that age; he being loath to intrude into their company, and yet willing to be called, peeped in several times at the door, insomuch that Master *Johnson* at last took notice of him, and said, Come in *John Bopeep*. Master *Randolph* was not so gallant in cloathes as they, however he sat down amongst them; at last when the reckoning came to be paid, which was five shillings, it was agreed, that he who made the best extempore verse should go Scot-free, the other four to pay it all: whereupon every one of them put out their verses; at last it come to Master *Randolph's* turn, whose lines were these:

> *I John Bo-peep, to you four sheep,*
> *With each one his good fleece:*
> *If you are willing to pay your five shilling,*
> *'Tis fifteen pence apiece.*

[*Poor Robins Jests* (1667), p. 78; quoted by Bernard H. Newdigate, *Michael Drayton and His Circle* (1941), p. 139 and n. 1. The anecdote also occurs in Winstanley's *Lives of the Poets* (1687), pp. 143–44.]

JOHN DENHAM, 1668

Going this last Summer to visit the *Wells*, I took an occasion (by the way) to wait upon an Ancient and Honourable Friend of mine, whom I found diverting his (then solitary) retirement with the Latin Original of this Translation, which (being out of Print) I had never seen before: when I looked upon it, I saw that it had formerly passed through two Learned hands, not without approbation; which were *Ben Johnson*, and *Sir Kenelme Digby;* but I found it, (where I shall never find my self) in the service of a better Master, the *Earl* of *Bristol*.

[*Poems and Translations* (1668), Preface to a translation from the Latin of Mancini, p. 145.]

JOHN DRYDEN, 1668

For two Actions equally labour'd and driven on by the Writer, would destroy the unity of the Poem; it would be no longer one Play, but two: not but that there may be many actions in a Play, as *Ben. Johnson* has observ'd in his discoveries; but they must be all subservient to the great one, which our language happily expresses in the name of under-plots.

[*Of Dramatick Poesie* (1684), p. 9 (1st ed., 1668).]

John Dryden, 1668

Next, for the Plot, ... it has already been judiciously observ'd by a late Writer, that in their [Greek and Roman] Tragedies it was only some Tale deriv'd from *Thebes* or *Troy*, or at least some thing that happen'd in those two Ages; which was worn so thred bare by the Pens of all the Epique Poets, and even by Tradition it self of the Talkative Greeklings (as *Ben. Johnson* calls them) that before it came upon the Stage, it was already known to all the Audience.

[*Ibid.*, p. 12.]

John Dryden, 1668

That is, those actions which by reason of their cruelty will cause aversion in us, or by reason of their impossibility unbelief, ought either wholly to be avoided by a Poet, or only deliver'd by narration. To which, we may have leave to add such as to avoid tumult, (as was before hinted) or to reduce the Plot into a more reasonable compass of time, or for defect of Beauty in them, are rather to be related than presented to the Eye. Examples of all these kinds are frequent, not only among all the Ancients, but in the best receiv'd of our English Poets. We find *Ben. Johnson* using them in his Magnetick Lady, where one comes out from Dinner, and relates the quarrels and disorders of it to save the undecent appearance of them on the Stage, and to abreviate the Story: and this in express imitation of *Terence*, who had done the same before him in his Eunuch, where *Pythias* makes the like relation of what had happen'd within at the Soldiers entertainment. The relations likewise of *Sejanus's* death, and the prodigies before it are remarkable; the one of which was hid from sight to avoid the horrour and tumult of the representation; the other to shun the introducing of things impossible to be believ'd.

[*Ibid.*, pp. 24–25.]

John Dryden, 1668

Corneille himself, their Arch-Poet, what has he produc'd except *the Lier*, and you know how it was cry'd up in *France;* but when it came upon the English Stage, though well translated, and that part of *Dorant* acted to so much advantage as I am confident it never receiv'd in its own Country, the most favourable to it would not put it in competition with many of *Fletchers* or *Ben. Johnsons*.

[*Ibid.*, p. 27.]

JOHN DRYDEN, 1668

'Tis evident that the more the persons are, the greater will be the variety of the Plot. If then the parts are manag'd so regularly that the beauty of the whole be kept intire, and that the variety become not a perplex'd and confus'd mass of accidents, you will find it infinitely pleasing to be led in a labyrinth of design, where you see some of your way before you, yet discern not the end till you arrive at it. And that all this is practicable, I can produce for examples many of our English Plays: as the Maids Tragedy, the Alchymist, the Silent Woman; I was going to have named the Fox, but that the unity of design seems not exactly observ'd in it; for there appear two actions in the Play; the first naturally ending with the fourth Act; the second forc'd from it in the fifth: which yet is the less to be condemn'd in him, because the disguise of *Volpone*, though it suited not with his character as a crafty or covetous person, agreed well enough with that of a voluptuary: and by it the Poet gain'd the end at which he aym'd, the punishment of Vice, and the reward of Virtue, both which that disguise produc'd. So that to judge equally of it, it was an excellent fifth Act, but not so naturally proceeding from the former.

[*Ibid.*, pp. 29–30.]

JOHN DRYDEN, 1668

We have borrowed nothing from them [the French]; our Plots are weav'd in English Looms: we endeavour therein to follow the variety and greatness of characters which are deriv'd to us from *Shakespeare* and *Fletcher:* the copiousness and well-knitting of the intrigues we have from *Johnson*, and for the Verse it self we have English Presidents of elder date than any of *Corneilles*'s Plays: (not to name our old Comedies before *Shakespeare*, which were all writ in verse of six feet, or *Alexandrin's*, such as the French now use) I can shew in *Shakespeare*, many Scenes of rhyme together, and the

like in *Ben. Johnsons* Tragedies: In *Catiline* and *Sejanus* sometimes
thirty or forty lines; I mean besides the Chorus, or the Monologues,
which by the way, shew'd *Ben.* no enemy to this way of writing,
especially if you read his Sad Shepherd, which goes sometimes on
rhyme, sometimes on blank Verse, like an Horse who eases himself
on Trot and Amble. You find him likewise commending *Fletcher*'s
Pastoral of the Faithful Shepherdess; which is for the most part
Rhyme, though not refin'd to that purity to which it hath since
been brought: And these examples are enough to clear us from a
servile imitation of the French.

[*Ibid.*, pp. 32–33.]

JOHN DRYDEN, 1668

. . . . in most of the irregular Plays of *Shakespeare* or *Fletcher*,
(for *Ben. Johnson*'s are for the most part regular) there is a more
masculine fancy and greater spirit in the writing, than there is in
any of the French.

[*Ibid.*, p. 33.]

JOHN DRYDEN, 1668

Examen of the Silent Woman.

To begin first with the length of the Action, it is so far from exceeding the compass of a Natural day, that it takes not up an Artificial one. 'Tis all included in the limits of three hours and an half,
which is no more than is requir'd for the presentment on the Stage.
A beauty perhaps not much observ'd; if it had, we should not have
look'd on the Spanish Translation of five hours with so much wonder. The Scene of it is laid in *London;* the latitude of place is almost
as little as you can imagine: for it lies all within the compass of two
Houses, and after the first Act, in one. The continuity of Scenes is
observ'd more than in any of our Plays, except his own Fox and
Alchymist. They are not broken above twice or thrice at most in
the whole Comedy, and in the two best of *Corneille*'s Plays, the *Cid*
and *Cinna*, they are interrupted once. The action of the Play is
intirely one; the end or aim of which is the setling *Morose*'s Estate
on *Dauphine*. The Intrigue of it is the greatest and most noble of
any pure unmix'd Comedy in any Language: you see in it many persons of various characters and humours, and all delightful: As first,

Morose, or an old Man, to whom all noise but his own talking is offensive. Some who would be thought Criticks, say this humour of his is forc'd: but to remove that objection, we may consider him first to be naturally of a delicate hearing, as many are to whom all sharp sounds are unpleasant; and secondly, we may attribute much of it to the peevishness of his Age, or the wayward authority of an old Man in his own house, where he may make himself obeyed; and to this the Poet seems to allude in his name *Morose*. Beside this, I am assur'd from divers persons, that *Ben. Johnson* was actually acquainted with such a man, one altogether as ridiculous as he is here represented. Others say it is not enough to find one man of such an humour; it must be common to more, and the more common the more natural. To prove this, they instance in the best of Comical Characters, *Falstaffe:* .... The description of these humours, drawn from the knowledge and observation of particular persons, was the peculiar genius and talent of *Ben. Johnson;* To whose Play I now return.

Besides *Morose*, there are at least nine or ten different Characters and humours in the *Silent Woman*, all which persons have several concernments of their own, yet are all us'd by the Poet, to the conducting of the main design to perfection. I shall not waste time in commending the writing of this Play, but I will give you my opinion, that there is more wit and acuteness of Fancy in it than in any of *Ben. Johnson*'s. Besides, that he has here describ'd the Conversation of Gentlemen in the persons of *True-Wit*, and his Friends, with more gayety, air and freedom, than in the rest of his Comedies. For the contrivance of the Plot, 'tis extream elaborate, and yet withal easie; for the λύσις, or untying of it, 'tis so admirable, that when it is done, no one of the Audience would think the Poet could have miss'd it; and yet it was conceal'd so much before the last Scene, that any other way would sooner have enter'd into your thoughts. But I dare not take upon me to commend the Fabrick of it, because it is altogether so full of Art, that I must unravel every Scene in it to commend it as I ought. And this excellent contrivance is still the more to be admir'd, because 'tis Comedy where the persons are only of common rank, and their business private, not elevated by passions or high concernments as in serious Plays. Here every one is a proper Judge of all he sees; nothing is represented but that with which he daily converses: so that by consequence all faults lie open to discovery, and few are pardonable. 'Tis this which *Horace* has judiciously observ'd:

> *Creditur ex medio quia res arcessit habere*
> *Sudoris minimum, sed habet Comedia tanto*
> *Plus oneris, quanto veniæ minus.*——

But our Poet, who was not ignorant of these difficulties, has made use of all advantages; as he who designs a large leap takes his rise from the highest ground. One of these advantages is that which *Corneille* has laid down as the greatest which can arrive to any Poem, and which he himself could never compass above thrice in all his Plays, *viz.* the making choice of some signal and long-expected day, whereon the action of the Play is to depend. This day was that design'd by *Dauphine* for the setling of his Uncles Estate upon him; which to compass he contrives to marry him: That the marriage had been plotted by him long beforehand is made evident by what he tells *True-Wit* in the second Act, that in one moment he had destroy'd what he had been raising many months.

There is another artifice of the Poet, which I cannot here omit, because by the frequent practice of it in his Comedies, he has left it to us almost as a Rule, that is, when he has any Character or humour wherein he would shew a *Coup de Maistre*, or his highest skill; he recommends it to your observation by a pleasant description of it before the person first appears. Thus, in *Barthlomew-Fair* he gives you the Pictures of *Numps* and *Cokes*, and in this those of *Daw, Lafoole, Morose*, and the *Collegiate Ladies;* all which you hear describ'd before you see them. So that before they come upon the Stage you have a longing expectation of them, which prepares you to receive them favourably; and when they are there, even from their first appearance you are so far acquainted with them, that nothing of their humour is lost to you.

I will observe yet one thing further of this admirable Plot; the business of it rises in every Act. The second is greater than the first; the third than the second, and so forward to the fith. There too you see, till the very last Scene, new difficulties arising to obstruct the action of the Play; and when the Audience is brought into despair that the business can naturally be effected, then, and not before, the discovery is made. But that the Poet might entertain you with more variety all this while, he reserves some new Characters to show you, which he opens not till the second and third Act. In the second *Morose, Daw*, the *Barber* and *Otter;* in the third the *Collegiat Ladies:* All which he moves afterwards in by-walks, or under-Plots, as diversions to the main design, lest it should grow tedious, though they are still naturally joyn'd with it, and somewhere or other sub-servient to it. Thus, like a skilful Chest-player, by little and little he draws out his men, and makes his pawns of use to his greater persons.

If this Comedy, and some others of his, were translated into French Prose (which would now be no wonder to them, since *Moliere* has lately given them Plays out of Verse which have not displeas'd them) I believe the controversie would soon be decided betwixt the two Nations, even making them the Judges.

[*Ibid.*, pp. 35–39.]

JOHN DRYDEN, 1668

. . . . I confess I have a joynt quarrel to you both, because you have concluded, without any reason given for it, that Rhyme is proper for the Stage. I will not dispute how ancient it hath been among us to write this way; perhaps our Ancestours knew no better till *Shakespeare's* time. I will grant it was not altogether left by him, and that *Fletcher* and *Ben. Johnson* us'd it frequently in their Pas-torals, and sometimes in other Plays. . . . . I have therefore only to affirm, that it is not allowable in serious Plays. . . . . To prove this, I might satisfie my self to tell you, how much in vain it is for you to strive against the stream of the peoples inclination; the greatest part of which are prepossess'd so much with those excellent Plays of *Shakespeare, Fletcher*, and *Ben. Johnson*, (which have been writ-ten out of Rhyme) that except you could bring them such as were written better in it, and those too by persons of equal reputation with them, it will be impossible for you to gain your cause with them, who will still be judges.

[*Ibid.*, p. 40.]

John Dryden, 1668

In our own language we see *Ben. Johnson* confining himself to what ought to be said, even in the liberty of blank Verse; and yet *Corneile*, the most judicious of the *French* Poets, is still varying the same sense an hundred ways, and dwelling eternally on the same subject, though confin'd by Rhyme.

[*Ibid.*, p. 42.]

John Dryden, 1668

This way of writing in Verse, they have only left free to us; our age is arriv'd to a perfection in it, which they never knew; and which (if we may guess by what of theirs we have seen in Verse (as the *Faithful Shepherdess*, and *Sad Shepherd:*) 'tis probable they never could have reach'd.

[*Ibid.*, p. 46.]

John Dryden, 1668

Ovid whom you accuse for luxuriancy in Verse, had perhaps been farther guilty of it had he writ in Prose. And for your instance of *Ben. Johnson*, who you say, writ exactly without the help of Rhyme; you are to remember 'tis only an aid to a luxuriant Fancy, which his was not: As he did not want imagination, so none ever said he had much to spare. Neither was verse then refin'd so much to be an help to that Age as it is to ours.

[*Ibid.*, pp. 50–51.]

John Evelyn, 1668

Dec. 19th. I went to see yᵉ old play of "Cataline" acted, having ben now forgotten almost 40 yeares.

[*Diary of John Evelyn*, ed. William Bray, II, 233.]

[Francis Kirkman and Richard Head], 1668

My Wife acted the *Silent Woman* to the life, whilest in a single state; for before we were married all her answers were very short, comprehended within the two Monosyllables of *I*, and *No;* and those two must be forcibly extracted from her; But now her tongue **wagg'd** in a perpetual motion, and her voice so shrill and loud, that it would be heard distinctly, though a piece of Ordnance were discharged near her at the same time.

[*The English Rogue Described in the Life of Meriton Latroon* (1668), ⟨Part I⟩, p. 200; quoted by Robert Gale Noyes, *Ben Jonson on the English Stage, 1660–1776*, p. 179.]

[FRANCIS KIRKMAN AND RICHARD HEAD], 1668

She retrived my intentions, clasping me in her arms; I should rather have chosen the imbraces of a she-Bear, as thinking her breath far sweeter; and truly I have often wondred at my recovery in so impure and unwholsom air. Being on Horse-back she so bathed her Cheeks with tears (wanting no moisture, derived from an everlasting spring of humours distilling from her head) that you would have sworn she was the representation of the Pig-woman in *Ben's Bartholomew*-Fair.

[*The English Rogue*, ⟨Part I⟩ (1668), pp. 228–29, quoted in *ibid.*, pp. 226–27 and n. 1.]

DAVID LLOYD, 1668

. . . . *Selden* went away with the character of Deep and Learned, *Hillingworth* was reckoned Rational and Solid, *Digby* Reaching and Vigorous, *Sands* and *Townsend* Smooth and Delicate, *Vaughan* and *Porter* Pious and Extatical, *Ben. Johnson* Commanding and Full, *Carew* Elaborate and Accurate, ...

[*Memoires of the Lives . . . . of Those . . . . Personages That Suffered . . . . for the Protestant Religion* (1668), p. 159.]

DAVID LLOYD, 1668

So just a Poet [was Cartwright] that *Ben. Johnson* our ablest Judge and Professor of Poetry, said with some Passion; *My Son* Cartwright *writes all like a man.* (What had *Ben.* said, had he read his own Eternity in that lasting Elegy given him by Mr. *Cartwright*, or that other by his good friend Mr. *Robert Waring*, neither of which pieces are easily to be imitated.)

[*Ibid.*, p. 423.]

DAVID LLOYD, 1668

His [John Selden's] industry was great, in the mornings attending his Philosophy, and in the afternoons Collecting Materials for such subjects as he would receive satisfaction in; his body strong, his natural and artificial memory exact, his fancy slow, though yet he made several sallies into Poetry and Oratory, both to relieve his severer thoughts, and smooth and knit his broken and rough stile (made so by the vast matter it was to comprehend) (being taught by *Ben Johnson*, as he would brag, *to rellish Horace*).

[*Ibid.*, p. 519.]

THOMAS SHADWELL, 1668

Lovel. Let's in and see when the Fury of this *Dol Comon* will be at an End.

[*The Sullen Lovers* (1668), Act II, p. 20.]

THOMAS SHADWELL, 1668

Ninny. I was with my Bookseller, Madam . . . . he has got some hundreds of pounds by some plays and poems of mine which he has printed. And let me tell you, some under the Names of Beaumont and Fletcher and Ben Jonson too. . . . .

[*The Sullen Lovers* (1668), ed. Montague Summer (1927), Vol. I, Act II, scene 2; noted by C. B. Graham, "Jonson Allusions in Restoration Comedy," *Review of English Studies*, XV (1939), 200–201.]

THOMAS SHADWELL, 1668

Sir Pos. Hear it you Rascals, I'le rout an Army with my single valour: I'le burn a whole fleet at three Leagues distance; I'le make ships go all over the world without sayles: I'le plow up rocks steep as the Alps in dust, and lave the Tyrrhene Waters into Clouds (as my friend *Cateline* sayes.)

Ninn. P'sh[a]w! you! I'le pluck bright honour from the pale fac'd Moon (as my friend Hot-spur sayes) what do you talk of that?

[*The Sullen Lovers* (1668), Act V, p. 80.]

ROBERT WARING, 1668

AMORIS | EFFIGIES: | Sive, | *Quid sit Amor?* | Efflagitanti | RESPONSUM | ROBERTI WARING | ex *Æde Christi* OXON. Art. | Mag. & Academiæ | Procuratoris. | Huic quartæ editioni præfigi- | tur ejusdem Autoris | CARMEN LAPIDARIUM |

Memoriæ | Vatum Principis, | BEN: JONSONI, | sacratum. | LONDINI, | Excudebat *J. Redmayne*, | 1668.

. . . .

Nec tamen aspernandum, credito *Lector* habes & Auctariolum, *Carmen* scilicet *Lapidarium*, quo & BEN. JONSONI Poetarum nostratium facilè Principis litavit Memoriæ, utique & propriā. Sibi eodem reddidit immortalem: quod tamen in Libro, cui *Jonsonus Viribius* titulo est, miserè discerptum adeò reperiens Autor, vix sine novo partûs nixu pristino tandem restituit nitori, *Apollo* factus. . . . . .

[Title-page and excerpt from the "Præloquium Guilhelmi Griffithii ad Lectorem," sig. a₆.]

WARRANT, 1668

The Poetaster

[In the list of plays allotted to Davenant, August 20, 1668 (L.C. 5/139, p. 375), quoted in Allardyce Nicoll, *A History of Restoration Drama*, p. 315.]

WARRANT, 1668-69

[Dec:] 18: [1668]	Cattalines Conspiracie Knig (sic) here.	10
Jan: 2ᵈ:	Cattalines Conspiracie King & Queene here	20

. . . .

13	Cattalines Conspiracie King here.	10

. . . .

[ffeb:] 22	Bartholomew ffayre at Court.	20

. . . .

Ap. 17: 1669	The Alchymist The King here.	10

[Warrant for plays to May 6, 1669 (L.C. 5/12, p. 17), quoted in *ibid.*, p. 306.]

ANONYMOUS, 1668/69

Everyman in his Humour
Everyman out of his Humour
Cyntheas Revells
Sejanus
The ffox
The Silent Weoman
The Alchymist
Catalin

Bartholomew ffayre
Staple of Newes
The Devills an Asse
Magnitick Lady
Tale of a Tubb
New Inn

[In the list of plays allotted to Killigrew about January 12, 1668/69 (L.C. 5/12, p. 212), quoted in *ibid.*, p. 315.]

SAMUEL PEPYS, 1668/69

[January] 15ᵗʰ . . . . he told me of the great factions at Court at this day, even to the sober engaging of great persons, and differences, and making the King cheap and ridiculous. It is about my Lady Harvy's being offended at Doll Common's acting of Sempronia, to imitate her; for which she got my Lord Chamberlain, her kinsman, to imprison Doll: when my Lady Castlemayne made the King to release her, and to order her to act it again, worse than ever, the other day, where the King himself was: and since it was acted again, and my Lady Harvy provided people to hiss her and fling oranges at her: but it seems the heat is come to a great height, and real troubles at court about it.

[*The Diary of Samuel Pepys*, ed. Wheatley (1893–99), VIII, 188. Wheatley points out in a note that Mrs. Corey played both Doll Common in *The Alchemist* and Sempronia in *Catiline*.]

ANONYMOUS, 1664–74

Memorandum of his [Jonson's] Plays, 2nd part, bought for seven shillings by a Fellow of Sidney-Sussex College, Cambridge [1664–1674]. 3780, f. 5.

[Edward J. L. Scott, *Index to the Sloane Manuscripts in the British Museum* (1904), p. 284.]

ANONYMOUS, 1669

A PROLOGUE To *CATILINE*, To be Merrily
spoke by Mrs. *Nell*, in an *Amazonian* Habit.

A Woman's Prologue! This is vent'rous News;
But we, a *Poet* wanting, Crav'd a *Muse*.
Why should our Brains lye Fallow, as if they

Without His fire, were meer *Prometehan* (*sic*) Clay?
In Natur's Plain-Song we may bear our parts;
Although We want choice Descant from the Arts.
Amongst *Musicians;* so the *Philomel*
May in Whild-Notes, though not in Rules excell.
And when i'th weaker Vessel Wit doth lye;
Though into Froth it will work out, and flye.
But Gentlemen, You know our formal way,
Although we're sure 'tis false, yet we must say,
Nay Pish, Nay Fye, in troth it is not good,
When we the while, think it not understood:
Hither repair all you that are for *Ben;*
Let th' House hold full, We're sure to carry't then.
Slight not this Femal Summons; *Phœbus-rayes,*
To Crown his *Poets,* turn'd our Sex to *Bayes.*
And Ladies sure you'l vote for us entire,
(This Plot doth prompt the Prologue to conspire)
Such inoffensive Combination can
But show, who best deserve true worth in Man.
And You, with Your great Author taking Part;
May chance be thought, like him to know the Art,
Vouchsafe then, as you look, to speak us fair,
Let the Gallants dislike it, if they dare:
They will so forfeit the repute of Judges,
You may turn *Am'zons,* and make them Drudges,
Man's claim to Rule is, in his Reason bred;
This Masculine Sex of Brain may make you Head.
'Tis real Skill, in the Right place to praise;
But more, to have the Wit, not to Write Playes.

[*Catiline* (1674). First edition with this prologue, 1669.]

ANONYMOUS, 1669

THE EPILOGUE

By the same [Mrs. Nell].

No *Dance,* no *Song,* no *Farce?* His lofty Pen,
How e're we like it, doubtless Wrote to Men.

Height may be his, as it was *Babel's* fall;
There *Bricklayers* turn'd to Linguists, ruin'd all.
I'de ne're spoke this, had I not heard by many,
He lik't one silent Woman, above any:
And against us had such strange prejudice;
For our Applause, he scorn'd to Write amiss.
For all this, he did us, like Wonders, prize;
Not for our Sex, but when he found us Wise.
A *Poet* runs the Gantlet, and his slips,
Are bare expos'd to regiments of Whips;
Among those, he to *Poetick* Champions Writ;
As We to gain the Infancy of Wit.
Which if they prove the greatest Number, then
The House hath cause to thank *Nell*, more than *Ben.*
Our *Author* might perfer (*sic*) your praise, perhaps,
Wee'd rather have your Money, that (*sic*) your Claps.

[*Ibid.* First edition with this epilogue, 1669.]

Hesychius Pamphilus [Richard Brathwaite], 1669

Rabbi *Ben-Johnson* was highly in their Books, and they more versed in his Writings, then either Rabbi *Ben-Syrach*, or Rabbi *Solomon.*

[*The History of Moderation* (1669), sig. F₄.]

Thomas Shadwell, 1669

I have endeavour'd to carry on these few Humors, which were but begun by him [the author of the play on which this one was based]; and (to satisfie the Concupiscence as Mr. *Johnson* call's it, of Jigge and Song) I designed as fit occasions for them as I could, there being in the former Play but one short Song which is the last but one.

["The Epistle to the Reader," *The Royal Shepherdess* (1669), sig. A₂ᵛ.]

Robert Bowyer, 1670

1670, December 27. [Dublin] "Yesterday there being very many people at the playhouse the lofts fell down, three or four killed dead

in the house, whereof a maid of Mr. Savage's was one. My Lord
Lieutenant was hurt a little, one of his son's much hurt, the Countess of Clanbrasill ill hurt, very many wounded, some of which it is
said cannot live. The play that was acted was Bartholomew Fair,
in which it seems there is a passage that reflects upon a profession
of holiness, and it is said when they were entering upon that part
the scaffold fell."

[Letter to Robert Southwell, Historical Manuscripts Commission, *Manuscripts
of the Earl of Egmont*, II (1909), 24.]

Matthew Medbourne, 1670

EPILOGUE

Many have been the vain Attempts of Wit,
Against the still-prevailing Hypocrite.
Once (and but once) a Poet got the day,
And vanquish't *Busy* in a Puppet-Play.
But *Busy* rallying, Arm'd with Zeal and Rage,
Possest the Pulpit and pull'd down the Stage.
To laugh at English Knaves is dangerous then,
Whilst English Fools will think 'em honest Men.
But sure no zealous Rabby will deny us
Free leave to act our Monsieur *Ananias*.

[*Tartuffe* (1670).]

Anonymous, 1671

That of wch learned Johnson did complain,
And often wisht to see, but wisht in vain,
Fate has bestow'd on us: he wisht to see
A learned, a selected company
To sit in judgemt on ye playes he writ
And give em ye imortall stamp of witt.

["An Epilogue to ye University at ye same time" (i.e., probably for the production of *Cambyses* [1671]), *Rare Prologues and Epilogues, 1642–1700*, ed. Autrey Nell
Wiley (1940), p. 119.]

Anonymous, 1671

Song 43.

Shall *I* lye wasting in despair,
Die because a womans fair?
Etc.

[*The New Academy of Compliments* (1671), pp. 111–13, sigs. E₉-E₁₀. Wither's poem and Jonson's reply are printed in alternate stanzas as if they were all one poem. See Newdigate, *The Poems of Ben Jonson*, pp. 300–302 and 372.]

Anonymous, 1671

Song 261.

Cook *Laurel* would have the Devil his Guest,
And bade him home to *Peak* to Dinner,
Where Fiend had never such a Feast.
Prepared at the Charge of a Sinner.
With a Hey Down, Down, a Down, Down.
Etc.

[*Ibid.*, pp. 260–62, sigs. M₁₁ᵛ-M₁₂ᵛ. All but the last three stanzas of the gypsies' song from *The Gypsies Metamorphosed* are quoted. The fourteenth stanza is not from the folio but is the first of the additional stanzas printed in Bishop Percy's folio. See Newdigate, *The Poems of Ben Jonson*, p. 374.]

Anonymous, 1671

[The words of the song "Still to be neat" from *Epicoene* were printed in *Westminster-Drollery* (1671), Part I, pp. 107–8. See Robert Gale Noyes, *Ben Jonson on the English Stage, 1660–1776*, p. 181, n. 5.]

Aphra Behn, 1671

Beyond the merit of the Age
You have adorn'd the Stage
So from rude farce to Comick order brought
Each action and each thought
To so sublime a Method as yet none
But mighty *Ben* alone
Durst ere compare, and he at distance too;
Were he alive, he would resign to you
Thou hast outdone even what He writ,

In this last great Example of thy wit.
Thy *Solymour* does his *Morose* destroy,
And thy *Black Page* undoes his *Barbers Boy:*
His whole College of Ladies must retire
Whilst we thy braver Heroins do admire.

. . . .

The Modern Poets have with like success
Quitted the Stage, and salli'd from the Press.
   Great *Johnson* scarce a Play brought forth
But *Monster*-like it frighted at its birth;
   Yet he continu'd still to write
And still his Satyre did more sharply bite
      He writ though certain of his doom
      (Knowing his Power in Comedy)
      To please a wiser Age to come;
And though he weapons wore to justifie
The reason of his Pen; he could not bring
Dull souls to sence by Satyre nor by Cudgelling.

[Commendatory verses prefixed to Edward Howard's *The Six Days Adventure,*
or The New Utopia (1671), sig. a₂ʳ ᵃ ᵛ.]

SAMUEL CLYAT, 1671

8.

Unwearied *Ben* in the ungrateful Age
Propt up the stooping ruins of the Stage;
He bravely finish'd what he knew was good
Scorning the envy of the multitude;
Rebuk'd, and then sustain'd with patience
      The poor and rude
      Revilings of the Croud,
And whipt the foolish world at last to sence.

9.

Cease not to do undauntedly the same
And you'l succeed that great man in his fame.
Bea[u]mont and witty *Fletcher* then as due

Will yield their Antient glories up to you.
Go on, your help you may too long defer
    And then this Age must give to you
    What that to *Ben* did owe;
And call you the supporter of the sinking Theater.

[*Ibid.*, sig. b₁ᵛ.]

JOHN DRYDEN, 1671

I am oblig'd my Lord, to return you not only my own acknowl-
edgements; but to thank you in the name of former Poets, The
manes of *Johnson* and *D'avenant* seem to require it from me, that
those favours which you plac'd on them, and which they wanted
opportunity to own in publick, yet might not be lost to the knowledge of Posterity, with a forgetfulness unbecoming of the Muses,
who are the Daughters of Memory. And give me leave, my Lord,
to avow so much of vanity, as to say, I am proud to be their Re-
membrancer: for, by relating how gracious you have been to them,
and are to me, I, in some measure, joyn my name with theirs: and
the continu'd descent of your favors to me is the best Title which
I can plead for my succession.

[Dedication to the Duke of Newcastle, prefixed to *An Evening's Love* (1671),
sig. A₃ᵛ.]

JOHN DRYDEN, 1671

And some perhaps, wou'd be apt to say of *Johnson*, as it was said
of *Demosthenes; Non displicuisse illi jocos, sed non contigisse*, I will
not deny but that I approve most the mixt way of Comedy; that
which is neither all Wit, nor all Humour, but the result of both.
Neither so little of Humor as *Fletcher* shews, nor so little of Love
and Wit, as *Johnson*. Neither all cheat, with which the best Plays
of the one are fill'd, nor all adventure, which is the common practice of the other. I would have the characters well chosen, and kept
distant from interfaring with each other; which is more than
Fletcher or *Shakespear* did: but I would have more of the *Urbana,
venusta, salsa, faceta* and the rest which *Quintilian* reckons up as the
ornaments of Wit; and these are extremely wanting in *Ben.
Johnson*.

[Preface to *An Evening's Love* (1671), sig. B₁ᵛ.]

JOHN DRYDEN, 1671

A witty Coward, and a witty Brave must speak differently. *Falstaffe* and the *Lyar*, speak not like *Don John* in the *Chances*, and *Valentine* in *Wit without Money*, and *Johnson*'s *Truwit* in the *Silent Woman*, is a Character different from all of them. Yet it appears that this one character of Wit was more difficult to the Author, than all his images of Humor in the Play: For those he could describe and manage from his observation of Men; this he has taken, at least a part of it, from Books: witness the Speeches in the First Act, translated *verbatim* out of *Ovid de Arte Amandi*. To omit what afterwards he borrowed from the sixth Satyre of *Juvenal* against Women.

[*Ibid.*, sig. B₂.]

JOHN DRYDEN, 1671

'Tis charg'd upon me that I make debauch'd persons (such as they say my Astrologer and Gamester are) my Protagonists, or the chief persons of the *Drama;* and that I make them happy in the conclusion of my Play; against the Law of Comedy, which is to reward Virtue, and punish Vice. I answer first, that I know no such Law to have been constantly observ'd in Comedy, either by the antient or Modern Poets. . . . . *Ben. Johnson* himself, after whom I may be proud to erre, has given me more than once the example of it. That in the *Alchimist* is notorious, where *Face*, after having contriv'd & carried on the great cozenage of the Play, and continued in it, without repentance, to the last, is not only forgiven by his Master, but inrich'd by his consent, with the spoils of those whom he had cheated. And, which is more, his Master himself, a grave man, and a Widower, is introduc'd taking his Man's counsel, debauching the Widow first, in hope to marry her afterward. In the *Silent Woman*, *Dauphine* (who with the other two Gentlemen, is of the same Character with my *Celadon* in the *Maiden Queen*, and with *Wildblood* in this) professes himself in love with all the Collegiate Ladies: and they likewise are all of the same character with each other, excepting only Madam *Otter*, who has something singular:) yet this naughty *Dauphine*, is crown'd in the end with the possession of his Vncles Estate, and with the hopes of enjoying

all his Mistresses. And his friend Mr. *Truwit* (the best Character of
a Gentleman which *Ben. Johnson* ever made) is not asham'd to
pimp for him.

[*Ibid.*, sig. B₂ᵛ.]

EDWARD HOWARD, 1671

. . . . besides a Satyr cannot be poetically expressed but it must
be highly Hyperbolical, as may be seen in those of *Juvenal's*, as also
in most of the comedies of *Ben Jhonson* in which are very many
characters of no being amongst men, as in his *Devil's an Ass*, *Cin-
thio's Revels*, and others; nay in his more exact one of the silent
Woman, I doubt not to affirm that there was never such a man as
Morose who convers'd by a whisper through a Trunk, but the Poets
authority in that case is sufficient for what is not probable, because
it was an extravagancy well applyed to the humour of such a person, which is sufficient to direct us that things may be allow'd in a
Poetical sence which are not naturally so.

[Preface to *The Six Days Adventure, or The New Utopia* (1671), sig. A₄ʳ ᵃ ᵛ.]

EDWARD HOWARD, 1671

Peac. And art thou the sprightly Black the Lady of Night And
beautiful blossom of darkness?
Merid. Ha, ha, ha, blossom of darkness.
Peac. The Bride of this Gravity's, and Sister of *Hymens*.
Frank. He has rais'd her descent, Sir, something for your sake.
Soly. O the perplexity I am in—a night of *Cynthia's* Revels In
which all the Lunaticks are at liberty.

[*Ibid.*, Act IV, p. 64.]

EDWARD HOWARD, 1671

And for my greater Authority I will adde these few excellent
Verses of our Famous *Johnson* on this subject, which he calls a fit
Rhime against Rhime.

> *Rhime the rack of finest Wits*
> *That extracteth but by fits*
> *True conceipts,*

Spoiling senses of their treasure,
Couzening judgment with a measure,
But false weights.
Soon as lazie thou wert known,
All good Poetry hence was flown, &c.

And as I doubt not well enough to wave any oblique exception that any man can throw on my Opinion (since patronized by his) so I do not detract from the deserts of any who have done well in this kind, otherwise then by declaring, that as I find it not used by our former Poets, I likewise do not approve it, or have made use of it in this Play of mine.

[Preface to *The Womens Conquest* (1671), sig. a₁.]

EDWARD HOWARD, 1671

They allow'd them the names of Tragi-Comedies, & I do not find but the highest of our English Tragedies (as *Cataline, The Maids Tragedy, Rollo, The Cardinal and Traytor*) considerable enough to be rank'd with the best of these.

[*Ibid.*, sig. A₃ᵛ.]

EDWARD HOWARD, 1671

. . . . and whensoever Verse was us'd by *Ben. Johnson,* as it is in *Sylla's Ghost,* or scatter'd in some places in *Sejanus;* I cannot but observe his Art and Nature together, in not confining periods of sense and Rhime together (as is too much us'd now) but most commonly by carrying the sense of one verse into part of another, which elevates the stile of Verse (as is to be seen in *Virgil*) and without which it will never shew so like Prose, and proper for Dialogue, as it ought to do; an example to be worthily imitated by such as will write in Verse, to whose consideration I presume to commend it.

[*Ibid.*, sigs. a₁-a₁ᵛ.]

EDWARD HOWARD, 1671

As it is the duty of Comedy to do the same, in those that come nearest our Moralities, though it must be granted that the representation of Tragedy, cannot be so universally practicable (and

consequently not of that benefit to mankind) because its concernments, and actions, are more sublime, and separated from the uni-
versality of men, rather fit only for the ear of Princes, (who are very
often the greatest number of characters in a Tragical Fable) then
for a lower degree of Persons; which shews us, that Comedy hath
some merit above it, in that it is of a more universal nature. Upon
which occasion our famous *Johnson* well observes, that *Lysippus*
was not able to form with his Graver, or *Apelles* to Paint with his
Pencil, those life stroaks and touches, that true Comedy represents,
in respect of the various affections of the mind, in beholding the
insolence of some in joy, the melancholy fretings of others, the rag-
ing madness of such as are undone with love, avarice, riot, tortur'd
with expectation, consum'd with fear, &c. as he gives the example,
and to whom we are obliged for so many excellent Dramatick Characters to this purpose.

[*Ibid.*, sig. b₁ᵛ.]

EDWARD HOWARD, 1671

. . . . wherefore I wonder to find it affirmed, that extravagancies
of actions should be fixed on Farce, (which is rather an entertainment of Mimikry, than a Play in any kind) since Plays must not be
so even, as to represent nothing above nature, which were to make
them more reasonable, then Poetical; besides, it is a commendable
license (especially in Poetry) to represent what is rather useful to
know, (as it seems actually done) then the possibility of it, so it
provide well for our manners; as we see in Comedies, where we are
taught from the mouths of Fools, and by such extravagancies as
are in some kind impossible to be supposed, how we may become
the wiser; why else did our learned *Johnson* compleat that great
work of his Alchymist, with such persons that continue a prosecu-
tion of extravagancy of humour or impossibility together, (except
the making of the Philosophers Stone be held a known truth) or
that his *Dol Comon* representing the Queen of Fairies, was not to
pass upon the weak capacity of *Dapper* deceived by it? The same
may be affirmed of his *Cynthias Revells*, where *Cupid*, *Mercury*, and
Eccho have parts, or somewhat more extraordinary in his *Devil's
an Ass*, where the grand Demon, and a lesser, are made characters,

as Satyrical Reflections on Vanity and Vice, to be corrected by them; which shews, that the truth or possibility of the characters, is less to be considered, then the Morality they aim at.

[*Ibid.*, sigs. b₂ᵛ–b₃.]

EDWARD HOWARD, 1671

. . . . here I cannot chuse but reflect on our mean imitation of *French* Plays, by introducing of servants and waiting women to have parts, without being essential characters; an error well avoided by our former writers, who never admitted any, otherwise then as messengers and attendants, except on the account of being characters, as is to be seen by *Numphs* in *Bartholomew Fair*, and *Face* in the *Alchymist;* the latter of which (notwithstanding what can be objected against him) may deservedly be granted one of the best parts on our English Stage.

[*Ibid.*, sig. b₄ʳ⁻ᵛ.]

THOMAS JORDAN, 1671
THE SPEECH TO THE KING.

Pardon, not praise, great monarch! we implore,
For shewing you no better sights, nor more:
The Greek and Roman wits (we must confess)
Shew'd greater fancy, but their theams were less;
For we more excellence in you behold,
Than they in all their emperours of old.
We hope your majesty will not suppose
You're with your Johnsons or your Inigoes.

[*London's Resurrection to Joy and Triumph* (2d ed., 1671), quoted by Frederick W. Fairholt, *Lord Mayors' Pageants*, Part II (1844), pp. 203–4. Fairholt points out that this passage appears in the second edition only and has been lifted from Tatham's *London's Triumphs* (1664), *q.v.*]

FRANCIS KIRKMAN, 1671

It is now just ten years since I Collected, Printed, and Published, a Catalogue of all the *English* Stage-Playes that were ever till then Printed; I then took so great care about it, that now, after a ten years diligent search and enquiry I find no great mistake; I only

omitted the Masques and Entertainments in *Ben. Johnsons* first
Volume. There was then in all, 690. several Playes; and there hath
been, since that time, just an hundred more Printed; so, in all, the
Catalogue now amounts to (those formerly omitted now added)
806. I really believe there are no more, for I have been these
twenty years a Collector of them, and have conversed with, and
enquired of those that have been Collecting these fifty years.

["An Advertisement to the Reader," following Kirkman's "exact Catalogue" of
all English plays printed "till this present year 1671" in John Dancer's translation
of Corneille's *Nicomede* (1670), p. 16.]

FRANCIS KIRKMAN, 1671

First, I begin with *Shakespear*, who hath in all written forty
eight. Then *Beaumont* and *Fletcher* fifty two, *Johnson* fifty, *Shirley*
thirty eight, *Heywood* twenty five, *Middleton* and *Rowley* twenty
seven, *Massenger* sixteen, *Chapman* seventeen, *Brome* seventeen,
and *D'Avenant* fourteen; so that these ten have written in all, 304.
The rest have every one written under ten in number, and therefore
I pass them as they were in the old Catalogue, and I place all the
new ones last. I have not only seen, but also read all these Playes,
and can give some account of every one; but I shall not be so presumptuous, as to give my Opinion, much less, to determine or
judge of every, or any mans Writing, and who writ best.

[*Ibid.*]

EDWARD RAVENSCROFT, 1671

How happy, Sir, was the last age
When learned *Johnson* rul'd the Stage
That strict observer of mankind.
Men were the Books he read, and he
Made the whole town his Librarie;
Theatres were then the Schools
Of good morality, where Knaves and Fools
Their follies saw, and vices acted so,
Shame, those made honester, these, wiser grow.

In every Scene he writ we find
With Pleasure Profit joyn'd,
And every Comedie
He did intend
An *Errata* Page should be,
To show men faults and teach 'em how to mend.

. . . .

Great *Ben* thought it enough to swear
That his were good
Believe me so they are,
Could we but find a man had as much wit
To read and judg of them as he that writ.

[Commendatory verses prefixed to Edward Howard's *The Six Days Adventure, or The New Utopia* (1671), sig. a₄ʳ ᵃ ᵛ.]

ELKHANAH SETTLE, 1671

Like the Issue of the Dragons teeth, one brother
In a poetick fury falls on t'other.
'Tis thought you'll grow to that excess of Rage,
That *Ben* had need come guarded on the Stage.
Nay, you have found a most compendious way
Of Damning, now, before you see the Play.
But maugre all your spight, Poets of late
Stand stoutly unconcern'd at their Play's Fate;
Provided, 'tis their destiny to gain,
Like the fam'd Royal Slave, a third dayes Reign.

[Epilogue to *Cambyses King of Persia* (1671), p. 87.]

THOMAS SHADWELL, 1671

If this argument (that the Enemies of Humor use) be meant in this sense, that a Poet, in the writing of a Fools Character, needs but have a Man sit to him, and have his Words and Actions taken; in this case there is no need of Wit. But 'tis most certain that if we should do so, no one Fool (though the best about the Town) could appear pleasantly upon the Stage, he would be there too dull a Fool, and must be helped out with a great deal of Wit in the Author. I

scruple not to call it so, First, because 'tis not your down-right Fool
that is a fit Character for a Play, but like Sir *John Dawe* and Sir
Amorous la Foole, your witty, brisk, airy *Fops* that are *Entrepren-
nants*.

[Preface to *The Humorists* (2d ed., 1691), sig. B₂ (1st ed., 1671).]

ANONYMOUS, *ca.* 1672

Extract from the Tragedy of Catiline with a prologue by Mrs.
Nell Guin, and from Sejanus, *circ.* 1672. 161, ff. 22–28.

[Edward J. L. Scott, *Index to the Sloane Manuscripts*, p. 284.]

ANONYMOUS, 1660–85

Prologue and epilogue to 'The Sad Shepherd,' spoken by ——
Portlock, *temp.* Chas. II. 1009, f. 373.

[*Ibid.*]

ANONYMOUS, 1672

[The words of the song "Still to be neat" from *Epicoene* were printed in *Windsor-
Drollery* (1672), No. 189. See Robert Gale Noyes, *Ben Jonson on the English Stage*,
1660–1776, p. 181, n. 5.]

ANONYMOUS, 1672

Lastly, Their characters they quite mistake,
Whilst they their valiant Man, a *Hector* make.
Their Prince the Fool o' th' Play, and Noble Woman
As Ranting and Ramping as *Dol Common*.

[Prologue to *Emilia* (1672), sig. A₃.]

JOHN DRYDEN, 1672

But *Almanzor* is tax'd with changing sides: And what tye has he
on him to the contrary? he is not born their Subject whom he
serves: and he is injur'd by them to a very high degree. he threatens
them, and speaks insolently of Sovereign Power: but so do *Achilles*
and *Rinaldo;* who were Subjects and Soldiers to *Agamemnon* and
Godfrey of *Bulloign*. he talks extravagantly in his Passion: but, if I
would take the pains to quote an hundred passages of *Ben. Johnson's Cethegus*, I could easily shew you that the *Rhodomontades* of
Almanzor are neither so irrational as his, nor so impossible to be put

in execution. for *Cethegus* threatens to destroy Nature, and to raise a new one out of it: to kill all the Senate for his part of the action; to look *Cato* dead; and a thousand other things as extravagant, he sayes, but performs not one Action in the Play.

["Of Heroique Playes," prefixed to *The Conquest of Granada*, Part I (1672), sig. b₂.]

JOHN DRYDEN, 1672

Catiline sayes of *Cethegus*, that for his sake he would

> *Go on upon the Gods; kiss Lightning, wrest*
> *The Engine from the Cyclops, and give fire*
> *At face of a full clowd, and stand his ire.*

To *go on upon*, is onely to go on twice. to give fire at face of a full cloud, was not understood in his own time: (and stand his *ire*) besides the antiquated word *ire* there is the Article His, which makes false construction: and Giving fire at the face of a cloud, is a perfect image of shooting, however it came to be known in those daies to *Catiline*.

> ——— ——— *others there are*
> *Whom Envy to the State draws and pulls on,*
> *For Contumelies receiv'd; and such are sure ones.*

Ones in the plural Number: but that is frequent with him; for he sayes, not long after.

> *Caesar and* Crassus; *if they be ill men,*
> *Are Mighty ones.*
> *Such Men they do not succour more the cause, &c.*

They redundant.

> *Though Heav'n should speak with all his wrath at once;*
> *We should stand upright and unfear'd.*

His is ill Syntax with Heaven: and by Unfear'd he means Unaffraid. words of a quite contrary signification.

> *The Ports are open,*

He perpetually uses Ports for Gates: which is an affected error in him, to introduce *Latine* by the loss of the *English* Idiom: as in the Translation of *Tully's* Speeches he usually does.

Well placing of Words for the sweetness of pronunciation was not known till Mr. *Waller* introduc'd it: and therefore 'tis not to be wonder'd if *Ben. Johnson* has many such lines as these

But being bred up in his father's needy fortunes, Brought up in's sister's Prostitution, &c.

But meaness of expression one would think not to be his error in a Tragedy, which ought to be more high and sounding than any other kind of Poetry. and yet amongst many others in *Catiline* I find these four lines together:

> *So Asia, thou art cruelly even*
> *With us, for all the blows thee given:*
> *When we, whose Vertues conquer'd thee,*
> *Thus, by thy Vices, ruin'd be.*

Be there is false *English,* for *are:* though the Rhyme hides it.

["Defence of the Epilogue," appended to *The Conquest of Granada*, Part II (1672), pp. 166–67.]

JOHN DRYDEN, 1672

I think few of our present Writers would have left behind them such a line as this,

> *Contain your Spirit in more stricter bounds.*

But that gross way of two Comparatives was then, ordinary: and therefore more pardonable in *Johnson.*

[*Ibid.*, p. 168.]

JOHN DRYDEN, 1672

By this graffing, as I may call it, on old words, has our Tongue been Beautified by the three fore-mention'd Poets, *Shakespear, Fletcher* and *Johnson:* whose Excellencies I can never enough admire. and in this, they have been follow'd especially by Sir *John Suckling* and Mr. *Waller,* who refin'd upon them. neither have they, who now succeed them, been wanting in their endeavours to adorn our Mother Tongue: but it is not so lawful for me to praise my living Contemporaries, as to admire my dead Predecessors.

[*Ibid.*, p. 169.]

JOHN DRYDEN, 1672

Asper, in which Character he personates himself, (and he neither was, nor thought himself a fool.) exclaiming against the ignorant Judges of the Age, speaks thus.

> *How monstrous and detested is't, to see*
> *A fellow, that has neither Art nor Brain,*
> *Sit like an* Aristarchus, *or* Stark-Ass,
> *Taking Mens Lines, with a* Tobacco-Face,
> *In Snuffe, &c.*

And presently after

I mar'le whose wit 'twas to put a Prologue in yond Sackbut's *mouth? they might well think he would be out of Tune, and yet you'd play upon him too.* Will you have another of the same stamp?

O, I cannot abide these limbs of Sattin, *or rather* Satan.

But, it may be you will object that this was *Asper, Macilente,* or, *Carlo Buffone:* you shall, therefore, hear him speak in his own person: and, that, in the two last lines, or sting of an Epigram; 'tis Inscrib'd to *Fine Grand:* who, he says, was indebted to him for many things, which he reckons there: and concludes thus;

> *Forty things more,* dear Grand, *which you know true,*
> *For which, or pay me quickly, or I'le pay you.*

This was then the mode of wit, the vice of the Age and not *Ben. Johnson*'s. for you see, a little before him, that admirable wit, Sir *Philip Sidney*, perpetually playing with his words.

[*Ibid.,* p. 171.]

JOHN DRYDEN, 1672

That the wit of this Age is much more Courtly, may easily be prov'd by viewing the Characters of Gentlemen which were written in the last. First, for *Jonson, True-Wit* in the *Silent Woman,* was his Master-piece. and *True-wit* was a Scholar-like kind of man, a Gentleman with an allay of Pedantry: a man who seems mortifi'd to the world, by much reading. The best of his discourse, is drawn, not from the knowledge of the Town, but Books. and, in short, he would be a fine Gentleman, in an University.

[*Ibid.,* p. 172.]

John Dryden, 1672

I cannot find that any of them were conversant in Courts, except *Ben. Jonson:* and his *genius* lay not so much that way, as to make an improvement by it. greatness was not, then, so easy of access, nor conversation so free as now it is.

[*Ibid.*, p. 173.]

Sir George Etherege(?), 1672

["Epilogue to *Every Man in his Humour,* [in] *A Collection of Poems* (1672), mostly by Etherege, says Langbaine, MS. notes in *Dramatick Poets* in the Bodleian, Malone 129 (1691), p. 290" (*Rare Prologues and Epilogues, 1642–1700,* ed. Wiley, pp. 324–25).]

John Lacy, 1672

Nib. You mean down right pimping, Nurse, that's a little against the hair methinks for a husband. *Ben. Johnson* says, fathers and mothers make the best bauds.

Nur. Bauds! your *Johnson's* an ill bred foul-mouth'd fellow to call them so; besides he is a fool, for a husband's worth a hundred fathers and mothers for that office; for then the wife's unstain'd, the world cannot taint her, when the husband gives her countenance.

[*The Dumb Lady* (1672), IV, 1, p. 58. Noted by C. B. Graham, "Jonson Allusions in Restoration Comedy," *Review of English Studies,* XV (1939), 201, where he observes that "the statement to which Mrs. Nibby refers is to be found in Sir Epicure Mammon's speech, *The Alchemist,* II, 1."]

Andrew Marvell, 1672

And, as I think, he [Bayes] hath disobliged the Clergy of *England* in this matter; so I believe the favour that he doth his Majesty is not equivalent to that damage. For (that I may, with Mr. *Bays* his leave, prophane *Ben. Johnson,*) *though the gravest Divines should be his Flatterers;* he hath a very quick sense, and (shall I prophane *Horace* too in the same period?)

Hunc male si palpere recalcitrat undiq; tutus.

[⟨Andrew Marvell⟩, *The Rehearsal Transpros'd* (1672), pp. 109–10.]

ANDREW MARVELL, 1672

They are the *Politick would-be's* of the Clergy. Not Bishops, but men that have a mind to be Bishops, and that will do any thing in the World to compass it.

[*Ibid.*, p. 238.]

ANONYMOUS, 1673

To which purpose, his dealing with *Ben Johnson* (though dead, and of Immortal Fame with the judicious) was very observable, in that Mr. *Dryden*, who had at one time thought fit to call his Comedy, with the rest of his Time, mean, low, or as you have it in this hobling Verse of his mentioned by the *Rota*,

> *Then Comedy was faultless, but 'twas course,*

(not to examine the consistency of *course* and *faultless*,) At another time had otherwise sung a Parallel of his Muses Fame with *Ben. Johnson*'s, as in his Prologue to the *Maiden Queen*, where he vaingloriously enough calls that Play

> . . . . *a mingled Chime*
> *Of* Johnsons *humour, and* Corneille's *Rhime.*

But how *Johnsons* humour, could make such Musick with *Corneille's* rhyme, is not to be understood otherwise, than as Mr. *Dryden* hath made his own Commendation and it chime together. Which may be called another *Bizarre* in Mr. *Dryden*.

[*The Friendly Vindication of Mr. Dryden from the Censure of the Rota by His Cabal of Wits* (1673), pp. 11–12.]

ANONYMOUS, 1673

. . . . it was to be told Mr. *Dryden* that he in the sense of some, with no less Arrogance and Ignorance, taxed *Virgil* the Prince of *Latine* Poets, then he had injured *Ben Johnson* the best of *English*.

[*Ibid.*, p. 13.]

ANONYMOUS, 1673

Epilogue to Tartuffe
Spoken by Himself

Many have been the vain attempts of Wit
Against the still-prevailing Hypocrites

Once, and but once, a Poet got the day
And vanquished *Busy* in a Puppet-play:

[*A Collection of Poems written upon Several Occasions* (1673), p. 59. The epilogue is that for Medford's translation of *Tartuffe*; it was printed in the 1670 edition. There are further references to Rabbi Zeal-of-the-Land Busy in the epilogue; see under Medford, 1670.]

ANONYMOUS, 1673

He begins to apprehend that his Wit and Invention may *fail* him, and therefore thinks necessary to provide himself early of a *Nick-name* to take breath withal against he comes to be *Jaded*. Just (methinks) like *Bartholomew-Cokes—Who sate in the Stocks Numps, Ha!* Who, with that one word only *Rehearsed* again and again absolutely *ranspros'd Numps*. But if this does not give satisfaction, he will derive his *Authority* (which *Resolute Bat* would have *scorn'd* now) out of St. *Thomas*, who (says *Trans*) says, that *not only Governors, but any thing else, may give Names.*

[*S'too him Bayes: Or Some Observations upon the Humour of Writing Rehearsal's Transpros'd* (1673), p. 12.]

ANONYMOUS, 1673

Your next Expression of a *Daw-Divine* derides the *Faculty* (what needs that?) not the *person*. Can't you call whom you please Sir *Roger* without calling whoever is a *Divine* a Sir *John Daw*? One should make fine work, if as you compare a *Divine* to a *Daw*, I should compare the *Throne*, or *Chair* of *Infallibility* to his Nest.

[*Ibid.*, pp. 33–34.]

ANONYMOUS, 1673

Here follows a whole leaf that belongs to *Ursula;* & so he brings you to *Astrologie*, & *Comets*, & says you can't by a *Tellescope*, but you may with a *Microscope* see the Author in *Heaven-Inn*, *Calvins* head. I never saw anything so like *Doll in her Fit*.

[*Ibid.*, p. 35. There are a surprising number of allusions in this time to Doll Common's tantrums in *The Alchemist*.]

ANONYMOUS, 1673

But thou art more refractory than *Dame Plyant*, that *would not* understand the *Count* when he spoke *Spanish*.

[*Ibid.*, p. 119. The reference is to *The Alchemist*, IV, 4.]

J. B., 1673

She went indeed sometimes to see a Play and sometimes she would read Romances; but all this onely augmented her calamity, and these pretty divertisements were the greatest plagues in nature to her. At a Play she would fain get *Celadon* from *Florimel*, or *Dauphire* from the Collegiate Ladies, and could not endure to hear Romeo compliment his *Iuliet*.

[*The Drudge: or The Jealous Extravagant. A Piece of Gallantry* (1673), p. 17. The book is a translation of R. Le Pays' *Zelotyde* (1666), but both the *Romeo and Juliet* allusion and the allusion to Dauphine and the Collegiate ladies of *Epicoene* are substitutions for the French characters of the original. Taken from *The Shakspere Allusion-Book*, II, 190.]

APHRA BEHN, 1673

We all well know that the immortal *Shakespears* Playes (who was not guilty of much more of this than often falls to womens share) have better pleas'd the World than *Johnsons* works, though by the way 'tis said that *Benjamin* was no such Rabbi neither, for I am inform'd his Learning was but Grammer high; (sufficient indeed to rob poor *Salust* of his best Orations) and it hath been observ'd, that they are apt to admire him most confoundedly, who have just such a scantling of it as he had; and I have seen a man the most severe of *Johnsons* Sect, sit with his Hat remov'd less than a hairs breadth from one sullen posture for almost three hours at the Alchymist; who at that excellent Play of *Harry* the Fourth (which yet I hope is far enough from Farce) hath very hardly kept his Doublet whole.

["An Epistle to the Reader," *The Dutch Lover* (1673), sig. a₁.]

EDMUND HICKERINGILL, 1673

Is't not a *marvel* who this same Gregory Father-Greybeard is? The thing should be female by the *Billings-gate* Oratory of scolding; But then—*whoop Holla; Holla whoop;* some ridiculous *common Hunt;* by fears and jealousies, by his apology for I. O. and the brethren, it should be some R. B. or snivelling *whining Black-cap* underlay'd with *white;* by its busie intermedling with State-affairs, some Sir *Politick would be;* by its half Jests, quarter Jests, and half-quarter Jests, it would be thought to be some *little Droll*, and by its plea for Corporations, some candidate against the next vacation for a Burgess place in Parliament.

[*Gregory, Father-Greybeard, with his Vizard off: Or, News from the Cabal in some Reflexions upon a Late Pamphlet Entituled, The Rehearsal Transpros'd* (1673), pp. 37–38.]

EDMUND HICKERINGILL, 1673

I can scarce forbear smiling to my self to see how prettily he sets his face, and makes up his mouth, with such caution and gravity before he begins to read to Princes his *Politick would-bees*.

[*Ibid.*, p. 173.]

BARTEN HOLYDAY, 1673

Wherefore in Hope and Zeal I ventur'd on this work, not doubting but that a man may, not without success, though without custome, Preach in Verse. Which purpose being understood by some worthy friends, was not condemn'd but incourag'd by a free and happy supply of diverse excellent Manuscripts of our Author. My honour'd friend Mr. *John Selden* (of such eminency in the Studies of Antiquities and Languages) and Mr. *Farnaby* (whose learned Industry speaks much for him in a little) procur'd me a fair Manuscript Copy from the famous Library at St. *James*'s, and a Manuscript Commentary from our Herald of Learning, Mr. *Cambden*. My dear friend, the Patriarch of our Poets, *Ben. Johnson* sent-in also an ancient Manuscript partly written in the *Saxon* Character.

["The Preface to the Reader," *Decimus Junius Juvenalis, and Aulus Persius Flaccus Translated and Illustrated as well with Sculpture as Notes* (1673), sig. a₂ᵛ.]

BARTEN HOLYDAY, 1673

And this Reading, *Junio*, is confirm'd by two of the Copies, which I use (*Corpus-Christi & Ben Jonson's Manuscripts.*)

[*Ibid.*, p. 274.]

BARTEN HOLYDAY, 1673

Two of the Manuscripts (*Corpus Christi* and *Ben Jonson's*) alleadge partly the like reason.

[*Ibid.*, p. 277.]

[RICHARD LEIGH], 1673

Such has been the good fortune of your eminent Preachers, that their Sermons have been *Acted* with the same applause at the Theatre, which they have had in the Church, and been at the same time diversion to the Court, and edification to the Saints. But yet what the Play-house gives us, is but *Repetition* of their excellent *Notes*, and we must confess, *Ananias* and *Tribulation* are *Copies* short of their *Originals*. The exploits of a *Thanksgiving-Romance* have far exceeded the boldest of our *Heroick-Plays*, and no Farce yet was ever comparable to one with *Doctrines* and *Vses*.

["A Postscript etc.," *The Transproser Rehears'd* (Oxford, 1673), p. 14.]

[RICHARD LEIGH], 1673

Some therefore there were that spoke of the *unhoopable* Tun of *Heidelberg*, some of Sir *Politick*'s comprehensive *Tortoise*, and some of Sir *John Falstaff*'s more capacious Buckbasket.

[*Ibid.*, pp. 22–23.]

[RICHARD LEIGH], 1673

You see Sir, that I am improved too with reading the Poets, and though you may be better read in Bishop *Dav'nants Gondibert;* yet I think this *Schismatick* in *Poetry*, though *noncomformable* in point of Rhyme, as authentick ev'ry jot, as any *Bishop Laureat* of them all. Tell not me now, of turning over the moth-eaten Criticks, or the mouldy Councils: the *Gazetts* and the *Plays* are fitter Texts for the *Rehearsal*—Divines (men more acutely learned than Parson *Otter* and Doctor *Cutberd* the Canonist) than a company of dry Fathers and Schoolmen, that write in *Latin* and *Greek;* Romances are thumb'd more than St. *Thomas* and *Gondibert* is Dogs-ear'd, while the *Rabbies* are untoucht.

[*Ibid.*, p. 43.]

[RICHARD LEIGH], 1673

Well, I see it now all along this can be no less a man than Sir *Politique Would-bee* himself, his Reasonings, his Debates, and his Projects are the same, both for Possibility and Use. And what does more abundantly confirm it, his *Diary* proclaims him right Sir *Pol*.

There is nothing so low or trivial that escapes a Place either in his Memory or Table-book. Every Action of his Life is quoted.

[*Ibid.*, p. 121.]

[RICHARD LEIGH], 1673

. . . . the Answer is easie, if they cannot write their Names, they may set their Mark, (this I conceive was the *first Essay* towards *the Art* of *Writing*, as that in *single Characters upon Iron*, was towards that other of *Printing*) and to authenticate this, I remember Sir *Politick Would-bee* (that worthy Predecessor of this Gentleman) tells us of a Letter he receiv'd from a High and Mighty Cheese-monger, one of the Lords of the *States General*, who could not Write his Name (at least at length, and with all his Titles) and therefore had set his Mark to it. Not but that he had *Secretaries* under him (*Latin* or no, I know not) that could do it. But this was for the greater Majesty.

[*Ibid.*, pp. 124–25.]

[HENRY NEVILLE PAYNE], 1673

Mer[ry]. *Rose, Rose*, I tell thee, *Rose*, I would follow with this noise of Fiddles at my heels, and drive him back to Town, or never let him sleep but in shelter of as many Night-Caps as *Morose* in the Silent Woman hath.

[*The Morning Ramble* (1673), I, 3.]

[CHARLES SACKVILLE, EARL OF DORSET], 1673
Epilogue
To every Man in his humour.

In treaty shall not serve nor violence,
To make me speak in such a Playes defence.
A Play where Wit and Humour do agree
To break all practis'd Laws of *Comedy*:
The Scene (what more absurd) in *England* lies,
No Gods descend, nor dancing Devils rise,
        Etc.

[*A Collection of Poems* (1673), pp. 29–32. The epilogue, with numerous minor variants, is that printed in *The Jonson Allusion-Book*, pp. 380–81, from a later collection of 1675.]

Thomas Shadwell, 1673

Bev. Pray forbear, Sir, you are not to see her; she recovers.

Mrs. Wood. Give her more air, quoth a'? how he frighted me?

Wood. Good, Sir *Pol*, make a secret on't no longer; she may as well unmask, she and I are no strangers to one another.

[*Epsom Wells* (1673), III, 1, ed. Montague Summers, *The Complete Works of Thomas Shadwell* (1927), II, 143. As Summers points out in the notes, the reference is to Sir Politic Would-Be.]

Thomas Shadwell, 1673

Clodp. Oh miserable man! I have not only married a *Londoner*, and consequently a Strumpet, and consequently one that is not sound, but the most audacious of her Sex, a *Moll*-Cutpurse, a *Doll* Common.

[*Ibid.*, V, 1.]

Thomas Shadwell, 1673

Clodp. Oh, oh, oh, Udsooks there's my Gag broke at length, thanks to the strength of my teeth; unmerciful Rogues, if it had been like *Dappers* Gag of Ginger-bread, it would have melted in my mouth.

[*Ibid.* Clodpate refers to the end of Act III, scene 5, in *The Alchemist.*]

Anonymous, 1674

Catalogus Librorum; Or, Books worth buying.

Plutarchus Redivivus, in a parallel between Mall Cutpurse and Madam Moders, with a new invention to cheat Cutpurses by carrying no money in ones pocket.

Mercurius Fumigosus, the excellent worth of a pipe of Tobacco in the morning, being the plat-form of a design to make Physicians work for their living; by T. F.

The Seven Champions of Christendom translated out of Prose, into English Heroical (Latine) Verse, By P. F.

Coriatus Lithligonius, a discourse of Travel, with golden Cuts, prescribing a way of Transportation by an Engine of Clock-work.

The Ballad of Chevy Chase in large Folio.
Likewise the famous Play called the London Puritan, written by
Ben. Johnson in the Elizium shades, over a pint of Canary.

[*Poor Robin* (1674), sig. C₈ᵛ.]

ANONYMOUS, 1674

And now all Masons were, and Bricklayers made,
Or like the Theban Poet, they cou'd bring
The stones to follow the harmonious string,
Good lines, and brick, and verse do well agree,
Johnson did famous grow for all the three:

[*Troia Rediviva, or the Glories of London Surveyed in an Heroick Poem* (1674),
ll. 30–34, as quoted by Robert Arnold Aubin, *London in Flames, London in Glory*
(1943), pp. 210–11.]

ELKANAH SETTLE, 1674

*In the next Page I find him strutting, and impudently comparing
himself to* Ben Johnson. [I knew that to write against him was to
do him too much honour: But I consider'd *Ben Johnson* had done
it before to Deeker our Authors Predecessor, *&c.*]

[Preface to *Notes and Observations on the Empress of Morocco Revised* (1674).]

ELKANAH SETTLE, 1674

. . . . suppose here agen, she says more than she can do: So did
*Catiline. I'le Plough the Alps to dust, and lave the Tyrrhene Ocean
into Clouds*, &c. And yet *Ben* did not write nonsence in this expression. But 'tis possible that his *Empress* might *murder* and *damn* too;
but not *innocent people*, as commentator thrusts in to help on with
the *Impossibility*.

[*Ibid.*, p. 40 (sig. L₂ᵛ).]

ELKANAH SETTLE, 1674

I wonder how *Ben* and *Shakespear* ventured in several of their
Tragedies, as one for example in *Macbeth*, to write [*enter Murther-
ers*] at the beginning of a Scene, when the *Murder* for which they
were so call'd was not committed till after their entrance.

[*Ibid.*, p. 85.]

WARRANT, 1674

Nouember 12: The Alchymist.......... £10

. . . .

30 Bartholomew fayre....... 10

[Taken from a list of plays in a warrant dated January 27, 1674/75, for plays acted from November 12, 1674, to January 15, 1674/75 (L.C. 5/141, p. 116), quoted in Allardyce Nicoll, *A History of Restoration Drama*, p. 307.]

WARRANT, 1674/75

March 8 Catalins Conspiracye the Kings Ma^te.... £10

[L.C. 5/141, p. 215, from a warrant dated June 14, 1675, quoted in *ibid*.]

ANONYMOUS, 1675

1675 n.d. Every Man out of his Humour   Theatre Royal in DL

[Robert Gale Noyes, *Ben Jonson on the English Stage, 1660–1776*, p. 320. Noyes gives only his general sources for all performances, not individual documentation. I have not seen the original records of these performances.]

ANONYMOUS, 1675

Trup. Fough, I hate it.—Why, did you never hear the Song?
Clar. The Song, what Song?
Trup. Why this 'tis to be an ignorant *Londoner*.—I'll tell ye, Mr. *Spruce*, for you are my friend, and an understanding person. It was made by a very honest fellow in our Country that chanc'd to be at *Bartholomew*-fair once, and had his pocket pickt.
Clar. Aye, aye, I knew him very well; his name was *Bartholomew Cokes*.
Trup. No, Sir, he was none of your *Cokes*, I assure ye, but a Kinsman of mine at *Mansfield*. To see how your'e mistaken with your *Cokes's*.—

[*The Woman Turn'd Bully* (1675), Act IV, scene 3, p. 63.]

THOMAS DUFFET, 1675

Prologue to Ev'ry Man out of his Humour,
Spoken by Mr. Hayns, July, 1675

So fast from Plays approv'd and Actors known,
To drolling, stroling Royal Troop you run,

That *Hayns* despairing is Religious grown.
So Crack enjoy'd, the queazy Gallants slight,
And she, though still her beauty's in its height,
In rage turns Nun and goes to Heav'n in spight.
O Novelty, who can thy pow'r oppose!
Polony Bear or strange Grimace out-goes
Our finest language and our greatest shows.

As thick-scul'd Zealots, who from Churches fly,
Think doleful nonsense good that makes them cry;
Y'are pleas'd and laugh because—you know not why.
There ign'rant crouds round travel'd Gallants sit,
As am'rous youths round Vizards in our Pit,
And by their motions judg the Farces Wit.

If they but grin, a jest is understood,
All laugh outright and cry—I'gad that's good;
When will our damn'd dull silly rogues do so?
Y'are very complaisant, I fain would know
Where lies the wit and pow'r of (*il ohe*).

The modish Nymphs now ev'ry heart will win,
With the surprising ways of *Harlequin*.
O the fine motion and the jaunty mene,
While you Gallants—
Who for dear Missie ne'r can do to much,
Make Courtships *alamode de Scarramouch*.
Ha — ha —
I could have taught you this, but let that pass,
Y'have heard I've wit, now you shall know I've grace,
I will reform—
But what Religion's best in this, lewd Town,
My friends I'm yet like most of you, of none.
If I commence, I fear it will not do,
Religion has its *Scarramouchys* too,
Whose hum's and ha's get all the praise and pence,
For noise has still the upper hand of sense.
Well since 'tis so—
I'll keep my Station till your humors come,
Though like the longing woman, now you rome,
And leave all dainties for the Butchers thumb.

You and vile husbands equally proceed
Like rambling Bees, you quit your balm to feed
On ev'ry gaudy flow'r and painted weed.
When Winter comes you will again grow wise,
And visit home the wife that you despise,
With empty purses and with laden thighs.

Epilogue to Ev'ry Man out of his Humor

How crossly and how kindly things do go!
Though Forreign troop does very pow'rful grow,
Kind Justice beats down our domestick foe.
Th'inchanted Castle's once more overthrown,
That nursery where all the youth in Town,
Such deeds of Valour and of Love have shown.
Britains Low Countreys, where at mighty rates,
The younger Brothers urg'd their needy Fates,
And th' Elder got diseases for Estates.

See how the scatter'd Cracks in parties fly,
How like a nest of Wasps disturb'd they ply,
And fiercely fix on any Fop that's nigh.
I warn you, though your presence theirs will bring,
Be not too eager for the pretty thing.
The bag of Hony's sweet, but 'ware the sting.
Play round the light, but from the heat retire;
For if y'are joyn'd between hot Love and Ire
Like *Samsons* Foxes you'l set all on fire.
Reform your selves, Reformers of the Stage,
Blame not my Zeal, who can suppress their rage?
When Love and Wrath spare neither Sex nor Age.
For our Play we say nothing.—
The merit of it will your plaudits gain,
Or else new Wit would strive to prop in vain,
When *Johnsons* sacred mem'ry can't sustain.

[Quoted by Robert Gale Noyes, *Ben Jonson on the English Stage, 1660–1776*, pp. 297–99, from *New Poems, Songs, Prologues & Epilogues* (1676), pp. 72–76; *New Songs and Poems, a-la-mode both at Court and Theatres* .... By P. W. Gent. (1677), pp. 72–76.]

William Seymar (i.e., Ramsey), 1675

All that our [x] *Poets*, both Ancient and Modern have wrote in this kind, tend only to explain unto us what this *Love burning Lust* is, The Lives and Deaths of these *Hair-brain'd Fools;* And so are most of our Romances.

[x] They are the Priests of *Cupid; Homer*, ... And our new *Ariostoes, Boyerds*, Sir *Philip Sydney*, Sir *John Sucklin, Benjamin Johnson, Shakespear, Beaumont and Fletcher, Cleaveland, Cowley, Dreyden*, &c., and all Authors of *Uranias, Romances, Fairy* Queen, &c.

[*Conjugium conjurgium, Or, some Serious Considerations on Marriage* (1675), pp. 74-75.]

William Wycherley, 1675

The late so bafled Scribler of this day,
Though he stands trembling, bids me boldly say,
What we before most Playes are us'd to do,
For Poets out of fear, first draw on you;
In a fierce Prologue, the still Pit defie,
And e're you speak, like *Castril*, give the lye.

[Prologue to *The Country Wife* (1683; 1st ed., 1675).]

Warrant, 1675, 1675/76

Octo: 26 The Alchymist £10

. . . .

[Jan:] 17 The ffox 10

[Taken from a list of plays in a warrant dated February 16, 1675/76, for plays acted from June 19, 1675, to January 29, 1675/76 (L.C. 5/141, p. 359), quoted in Allardyce Nicoll, *A History of Restoration Drama*, pp. 307-8.]

Elisha Coles, 1676

Ben. Johnson.

Much phrase that now is dead, shall be reviv'd;
And much shall dye, that now is nobly liv'd,
If Custom please; at whose disposing Will
The pow'r and Rule of Speaking resteth still.
Hor. de Arte Poet.

[From the title-page of *An English Dictionary* (1676).]

ROBERT GOULD(?), 1676

Vpon Ben. Johnson's *Picture.*

Thus look'd, the Guide, and Raiser of the stage,
Whom, *first* the Age saw Great, *then* he the Age;
Johnson: in whom, those *distant Parts* (ne'r great
But when divided) *Judgment* and *Fancy* met.
All was not *Rapture;* Nor (to shun that) *Supine,*
(Like their dull works who put their *Prose* in Rime)
But a just, *Equal Heat,* Each part inform'd
Which, both at once, Beauty and strength adornd.

   Thy plaies were not only ith' *Action* seen,
As when St. *George,* and Dragon *Both,* came in;
And good Sr. *Lancelot* with his trenchard Blade,
Broke the Gyants Head *in earnest,* and made
The Boyes, and (wiser than the Boyes) the *Men,*
Laugh, and cry out, *Let's ha' that Jest agen!*
No; by itself, we could approve thy play,
Though *Bevis* and the Champions were away.

   No *General Muster* came upon thy stage,
No *Piques,* nor *Errant Prentises* did rage;
No *Batteries* were made, nor did the Drum
With direful Noise, *Summon* the Tyring Room,
'Twas *Peace* in thy time *Ben!* Some Messenger
Brought in th'*Event,* but carried *off* the *War.*

   Thou ne'r such Tragique words, or sense, didst choose
Which did the People, and *thy self* amuse;
No Caytiff vile was plung'd in *speckling Troubles*
Of Sinking Grief, rowld up in sevenfold Doubles
Of plagues unvanquishable: Though thy Muse flew high
And *lessen'd* to the City, *some* might descry,
Thou, didst not alter Nature; Things came in
Such as th' are Born, no Outrage wrong'd the scene:
No Ship was cast away in *Open Field;*
No fort, in *Person,* did come in, and yield;
Nor was't all One to thee, *which* crost the Seas,
The sad *Ambassadour,* or *Tripoles;*

Things had their just proportion, Colour, Light,
Nature ne'r fell, nor Reason, both kept their Fight.*
   The Poets Fictions, though [thou] didst resign
To Boyes, and Pedants; Thou didst not vex Each line
With Harpyes, Gorgons, Hydra's, Bears, and Goddesses,
Beyond *Tim Corgats* works; or *Homer's Odysses;*
Such Antique draughts ne'r Issued from thy Pen,
Thou *turnd'st* the Centaurs *Out*, and *brought'st in* Men.
   But he was *slow*, and *heavy*, a year scarce brings
One play forth! Fools! The *wary growth* of things
Precludes to their *Continuance;* delays
Crown Poems, the price, and emblem of the Bays:
Plants that live Ages, creep *slowly* from the Earth;
They came forth *late*, and *Aged* in the *Birth;*
So steddy, careful, and (*So*) *slow*, grew thine,
Perfect, *Full-tim'd*, and truly Masculine;
Born to Posterity, and the long stay
Of Ages; such, as shall ne'r decay
Till time fall with e'm, till the Muses grace
Prin's Poems, Or nice Ladyes court thy Face.

* A former reader of the passage has changed "Fight" to "Right."

[*Ludus Scacchiae: A Satyr against Unjust Wars* (1676), pp. 22–23.]

Thomas Shadwell, 1676

Sir Sam. . . . . Ha! what's here, a Rope? I am deliver'd as *Rabby Busie* was by Miracle. I'll slide down from the window into the garden.

[*The Virtuoso* (1676), Act IV, p. 65. Sir Samuel refers to the end of scene vi of Act IV in *Bartholomew Fair.*]

Anonymous, 1677

[The words of the song, "Still to be neat," from *Epicoene*, were printed in *Wit's Academy; or, The Muses Delight* (1677), p. 79. Noted by Robert Gale Noyes, *Ben Jonson on the English Stage, 1660–1776*, p. 181, n. 5.]

JOHN DRYDEN, 1677

And Poets may be allow'd the like liberty, for describing things which really exist not, if they are founded on popular belief: of this nature are Fairies, Pigmies, and the extraordinary effects of Magick: for 'tis still an imitation, though of other mens fancies: and thus are *Shakespeare's Tempest*, his *Midsummer nights Dream*, and *Ben. Johnson's Masque of Witches* to be defended.

[Preface to *The State of Innocence, and Fall of Man* (1677), sig. c₁.]

JOHN DRYDEN, 1677

Poetique Licence I take to be the Liberty, which Poets have assum'd to themselves in all ages, of speaking things in Verse, which are beyond the severity of Prose. . . . . This is that Birthright which is deriv'd to us from our great Forefathers, even from *Homer* down to *Ben.* and they who would deny it to us, have, in plain terms, the Foxes quarrel to the Grapes; they cannot reach it.

[*Ibid.*, sigs. c₁ᵛ–c₂.]

THOMAS D'URFEY, 1677

Fumble. Pish, the Devil's an Ass, I ha' seen't in a Play.

[*A Fond Husband* (1677), V, 1. Noted by C. B. Graham, "Jonson Allusions in Restoration Comedy," *Review of English Studies*, XV (1939), 201–2.]

THOMAS D'URFEY, 1677

Sir Arthur Oldlove. . . . . . I am nothing, a man of ignorance, a meer Reptile in these rarities.

Jollyman. Every man in his humour, and let the world rub.

[*Madam Fickle* (1677), III, 1. Noted by Graham, *loc. cit.*, p. 201.]

APHRA BEHN, 1678

Witt. Good morrow to the day, and next the Gold, open the Shrine, that I may see my Saint—hail the Worlds Soul—

[*Sir Patient Fancy* (1678), V, 1, p. 88. Taken almost without change from the opening lines of *Volpone*:

"Good morrow to the day, and next, my gold!
Open the shrine, that I may see my saint.
Hail the world's soul, and mine!"

Recorded by C. B. Graham, "An Echo of Jonson in Aphra Behn's *Sir Patient Fancy*," *Modern Language Notes*, LIII, 278–79.]

JOHN DRYDEN, 1678

In my Stile I have profess'd to imitate the Divine *Shakespeare;* . . . . Words and Phrases must of necessity receive a change in succeeding Ages: but 'tis almost a Miracle that much of his Language remains so pure; and that he who began Dramatique Poetry amongst us, untaught by any, and, as *Ben Johnson* tells us, without Learning, should by the force of his own Genius perform so much, that in a manner he has left no praise for any who come after him.

[Preface to *All for Love* (1678), sig. b₄ᵛ.]

EDWARD HOWARD, 1678

Luce. (To Sir Ralph Nonsuch, "a publick, ridiculous pretender, and a Luxuriast.") And next Sir Amorous, I add not fool and knave —here's your money, you may take it, Sir. . . . . .

[*The Man of Newmarket*, V, 1. Noted by C. B. Graham, "Jonson Allusions in Restoration Comedy," *Review of English Studies*, XV (1939), 203.]

[THOMAS RAWLINS, THE YOUNGER], 1678

Vain. I apprehend the Gentleman's very quarrelsome.

Owm. The veriest Wasp in *Europe;* he beat a modish Fop for discharging a Volley of crittical non sence upon *Ben Johnsons* Fox, and kickt a Vallet de Chambre in the pride of his Lords cast Suit, disputing precedence with a Ballad-maker.

[*Tunbridge-Wells, or a Days Courtship* (1678), Act I, sig. C₁ᵛ.]

SIR ROBERT SOUTHWELL, 1678

After this preamble give me leave to bemoan with hearty trouble the crazy state of your health. This, Deare Cosen, and the care of it, must now be the Great Thought and business of your Life. Tis truly that which Ben Johnson called it, 'the Riches of the Poore and the Blessing of the Rich.'

[The Marquis of Lansdowne, *The Petty-Southwell Correspondence 1676–1687* (1928), p. 53 (Letter 27, March 30, 1678).]

ANONYMOUS, 1679

[According to John Munro, "More Shakspere Allusions," *Modern Philology*, XIII (1915–16), 162–63, there is a reference to Jonson in *The Country Club: A Poem* (1679), p. 2.]

John Oldham, 1679

Nor do I mention these great Instances
For bounds and limits to your wickedness:
Dare you beyond, something out of the road
Of all example, where none yet have trod,
Nor shall hereafter: what mad *Cataline*
Durst never think, nor's madder *Poet* feign.

[Satyr I, *Satyrs upon the Jesuits: Written in the Year 1679* (1681), sig. C₁.]

Sir Carr Scroop(?), 1679

A Very Heroical Epistle from my Lord
All-Pride to Doll-Common.

The Argument.

Dol-Common being forsaken by my Lord *All-Pride*, and having
written him a most lamentable Letter, his Lordship sends her the
following answer.

[Joseph Woodfull Ebsworth, *The Roxburghe Ballads*, IV (1883), 575.]

Thomas Shadwell, 1679

Lump. I myself have brought in *Ananias*, and he will send
Money to you, to put out for him.

[*A True Widow* (1679), III, i, p. 32. Noted by C. B. Graham, "Jonson Allusions
in Restoration Comedy," *Review of English Studies*, XV (1939), 203.]

Edward Sherburne, 1679

Horace (*de Art. Poet.*) has drawn his Picture to the Life in these
Verses.
> *Scriptor honoratum si forte reponis Achillem,*
> *Impiger, iracundus, inexorabilis, acer,*
> *Jura neget sibi nata, nihil non arroget armis.*

Which *Ben. Johnson* hath thus Copied.
> ———*If again*
> *Honour'd* Achilles *chance by thee be seiz'd,*
> *Keep him still active, angry, unappeas'd;*
> *Sharp and contemning Laws, which at him aim,*
> *And daring any thing by Arms to claim.*

[*Troades* .... *by* .... *Seneca* (1679), p. 32, n. 1.]

Robert Wild, 1679

Poets, who others can Immortal make,
When they grow Gray, their Lawrels them forsake;
And seek young Temples, where they may grow Green;
No Palsie-hands may wash in *Hypocrene;*
'Twas not Terce Clarret, Eggs, and Muskadine,
Nor Goblets Crown'd with *Greek* or *Spanish* Wine,
Could make new Flames in Old *Ben Johnsons* Veins,
But his Attemps prov'd lank and languid strains:
His *New Inn* (so he nam'd his youngest Play,
Prov'd a blind Ale-house, cry'd down the first Day:
His own dull Epitaph—*Here lies Ben Johnson,*
(Half drunken too) He Hickcupt—*who was once one.*
Ah! this sad *once one! once* we *Trojans* were;
Oh, better never, if not still we are.
Rhymes of Old Men, *Iliack* passions be, ⎫
When that should downward go, comes up we see, ⎬
And we are like *Jews*-Ears in an Elder-Tree; ⎭
When Spectacles do once bestride the Nose,
The Poet's Gallop turns to stumbling-Prose.

[*Dr. Wild's Poem In Nova Fert Animus, &c. or, a New Song to an Old Friend from an Old Poet upon the Hopeful New Parliament* (1679).]

[Robert Nightingale], 1680

The Effigies of Love: being a translation from the Latine of M[r]. R. W. [by R. Nightingale] . . . . To which is prefixt a tombstone encomium, by the same author, sacred to the memory of . . . . Ben Johnson; also made English by the same hand. *London,* 1680. 16°.

[Taken from the Brit. Mus. catalogue (under Robert Waring); I have not seen this book.]

Nathaniel Lee, 1681

No doubt that divine Poet imagined it might be too great for any People but his own, perhaps I have found it so, but *Johnsons Catiline* met no better fate as his Motto from *Horace* tells us.

— — His non plebecula gaudet &c.

Nay *Shakespear's Brutus* with much adoe beat himself into the

heads of a blockish Age, so knotty were the Oaks he had to deal
with.

["The Epistle Dedicatory," *Lucius Junius Brutus* (1681), sig. A₃.]

THOMAS OTWAY, 1681

Fourbin. The Devil's an Ass, Sir, and here's a Health to all
those who defy the Devil.

[*The Souldier's Fortune* (1681), IV, 1. Noted by C. B. Graham, "Jonson Allusions
in Restoration Comedy," *Review of English Studies*, XV (1939), 202.]

JOHN AUBREY, 1669–96

He [Sir Robert Aiton] was acquainted with all the witts of his
time in England. He was a great acquaintance of Mr. Thomas
Hobbes of Malmesbury, whom Mr. Hobbes told me he made use of
(together with Ben Johnson) for an Aristarchus, when he made his
Epistle Dedicatory to his translation of Thucydides.

["*Brief Lives*," *chiefly of Contemporaries, set down by John Aubrey, between the
Years 1669 & 1696*, ed. Andrew Clark (1898), I, 25–26.]

JOHN AUBREY, 1669–96

W. Shakespeare—quaere Mr. Beeston, who knowes most of him
from Mr. Lacy. He lives in Shoreditch at Hoglane within 6 dores
north of Folgate. Quaere etiam for *Ben Jonson*.

[*Ibid.*, p. 97.]

JOHN AUBREY, 1669–96

[In Aubrey's discussion of Elizabeth Broughton, a noted beauty and courtesan,
he says:]

In Ben Johnson's execrations against Vulcan, he concludes
thus:—

> Pox take thee, Vulcan! May Pandora's pox
> And all the ills that flew out of her box
> Light on thee. And if those plagues will not doe
> Thy wive's pox take thee, and *Bess Broughton's* too.

—In the first edition in 8vo her name is thus at length.

[*Ibid.*, p. 128.]

John Aubrey, 1669–96

[Sir Edward Coke] maried, his second wife, ... , the relickt of Sir . . . . Hatton, who was with child when he maried her[a].— ⟨from⟩ ⟨Elizabeth⟩ lady Purbec; vide B. Johnson's masque of the Gipsies.

[a] Three lines of the text are suppressed here.

[*Ibid.*, p. 179.]

John Aubrey, 1669–96

Richard Corbet, D.D., was the son of Vincent Corbet . . . . who was a gardner at Twicknam, as I have heard my old cosen Whitney say. Vide in B. Johnson's *Underwoods* an epitaph on this Vincent Corbet, where he speakes of his nurseries etc., p. 177.

[*Ibid.*, p. 184.]

John Aubrey, 1669–96

After the death of Ben Johnson he [Davenant] was made in his place Poet Laureat.

[*Ibid.*, p. 205.]

John Aubrey, 1669–96

[Davenant's] grave . . . . is in the south crosse aisle, on which, on a paving stone of marble, is writt, in imitation of that on Ben Johnson, '*O rare Sir Will. Davenant.*'

[*Ibid.*, p. 208.]

John Aubrey, 1669–96

Sir Kenelm Digby, knight: he was borne at ⟨Gotehurst, Bucks⟩ on the eleventh of June: see Ben: Johnson, 2d volumne:—

> 'Witnesse thy actions done at Scanderoon
> Upon *thy* birthday, the eleaventh of June.'

[Memorandum:—in the first impression in 8vo it is thus; but in the folio 'tis *my*, instead of *thy*.]

Mr. Elias Ashmole assures me, from two or three nativities by Dr. ⟨Richard⟩ Nepier, that Ben: Johnson was mistaken and did it for the ryme-sake.

[*Ibid.*, p. 224.]

JOHN AUBREY, 1669–96

Sir Kenelme had severall pictures of her [Venetia Stanley Digby] by Vandyke, &c. He had her hands cast in playster, and her feet, and her face. See Ben: Johnson's 2d volumne, where he hath made her live in poetrey, in his drawing of her both body and mind:—

> 'Sitting, and ready to be drawne,
> What makes these tiffany, silkes, and lawne,
> Embroideries, feathers, fringes, lace,
> When every limbe takes like a face!—&c.

[*Ibid.*, p. 231.]

JOHN AUBREY, 1669–96

In Ben. Johnson's 2d volumne is a poeme called 'Eupheme, left to posteritie, of the noble lady, the ladie Venetia Digby, late wife of Sir Kenelme Digby, knight, a gentleman absolute in all numbers: consisting of these ten pieces, viz. Dedication of her Cradle; Song of her Descent; Picture of her Bodie; Picture of her Mind; Her being chose a Muse; Her faire Offices; Her happy Match; Her hopefull Issue; Her 'ΑΠΟΘΕΩΣΙΣ, or Relation to the Saints; Her Inscription, or Crowne.

[*Ibid.*, p. 232.]

JOHN AUBREY, 1669–96

Old Serjeant Hoskins (the poet, grandfather to this Sir John Hoskins, baronet, my hon[d] friend) knew him (was well acquainted with him), by which meanes I have this tradicion which otherwise had been lost; as also his very name, but only for these verses in Ben Johnson's 2d volumine, viz.:—

. . . .

. . . .

[*Ibid.*, p. 319. Clark says in a note on p. 321: "Aubrey was most anxious to have these verses inserted, three times directing Anthony Wood to do so. MS. Aubr. 8, a slip at fol. 4:—'Past on Nicholas Hill, in his proper place in part 1st' ⟨i.e., MS Aubr. 6⟩, but no copy of the verses is there given. MS. Aubr. 8, fol. 7:—'Insert B. Johnson's verses of Nicholas Hill.' MS. Wood F. 39, fol. 351[v]: 13 Jan. 1680/1:—'B. Johnson speakes of N. Hill in his "Voyage to Holbourne from Puddle-dock in a ferry boate.

> A dock there is . . . . called *Avernus*
> . . . . concern us."' ']

Vide tom. I of Ben: Johnson's workes, pag. 48, epigram
CXXXIV, title 'The famous voyage' . . . .

Here sev'rall ghosts did flitt,
About the shore, of . . . , but late departed;
White, black, blew, greene; and in more formes out-started
Than all those *Atomi* ridiculous
Whereof old Democrite and Hill Nicholas,
One sayd, the other swore, the world consists.

[*Ibid.*, p. 321, note at the end of the account of Nicholas Hill.]

Vide Ben Jonson's *Underwoods*—that 'the most worthy men
have been rock't in meane cradles.'

[*Ibid.*, p. 356.]

[In Aubrey's discussion of Hobbes, in the "Catalogue of his learned familiar
friends and acquaintances," is:]

Sir William Davenant, Poet Laureat after B. Johnson, and generall of the ordinance to the duke of Newcastle.

[*Ibid.*, p. 370.]

The lady Elizabeth Hatton (mother to the lady Purb⟨ec⟩) was his
[Hugh Holland's] great patronesse (vide B. Jonson's masque of the
Gipsies for these two beauties).

[*Ibid.*, p. 406.]

Sir James Long, baronet:—I should now be both orator and sol-
dier to give this honoured friend of mine, 'a gentleman absolute in
all numbers,' his due character.

[*Ibid.*, II, 36. As Clark points out, the phrase is Jonson's and was quoted as Jonson's by Aubrey in his account of Venetia Digby (*ibid.*, I, 232).]

JOHN AUBREY, 1669–96

Ben Johnson dedicates his comoedie called the Poetaster to him [Richard Martin, recorder of London]:—

'A thankefull man owes a courtesie ever, the unthankefull but when he needes. For whose innocence, as for the author's, you were once a noble and timely undertaker to the greatest justice of this kingdome.'

[*Ibid.*, II, 49.]

JOHN AUBREY, 1669–96

[Thomas May] stood candidate for the laurell after B. Jonson; but Sir William Davenant caried it.

[*Ibid.*, p. 55.]

JOHN AUBREY, 1669–96

When the duke of Buckingham's great masque[b] was represented at court (vide Ben Jonson), anno . . . . (quaere), he [John Ogilby] was chosen (among the rest) to performe some extraordinary part in it, and high-danceing, i.e. vaulting and cutting capers, being then in fashion, he, endeavouring to doe something extraordinary, by misfortune of a false step when he came to the ground, did spraine a veine on the inside of his leg, of which he was lame ever after, which gave an occasion to say that 'he was an excellent dancing master, and never a good leg.'

[b] '. . . . Quaere nomen and time—vide B. Jonson.' MS. Aubr. 7. fol. 20.

[*Ibid.*, p. 100.]

JOHN AUBREY, 1669–96

'Tis a good testimoniall of his [Sylvanus Scory's] worth, that Mr. Benjamin Johnson (who ever scorned an unworthy patrone) dedicated his . . . . to him.

[*Ibid.*, p. 217.]

JOHN AUBREY, 1669–96

His [Selden's] great friend heretofore was Mr. . . . . Hayward, to whom he dedicates his *Titles of Honour;* also Ben Johnson.

[*Ibid.*, p. 220.]

JOHN AUBREY, 1669–96

He [Selden] was a poet°, and Sir John Suckling brings him in the 'Session of the Poets.'

° He haz a learned copie of verses before Hopton's 'Concordance of Yeares'; before Ben Jonson's Workes; &c.

[*Ibid.*, p. 223.]

JOHN AUBREY, 1669–96

He [Sir Francis Stuart] was a learned gentleman, and one of the club at the Mermayd, in Fryday street, with Sir Walter Ralegh, etc., of that sodalitie: heroes and witts of that time. Ben Jonson dedicates *The Silent Woman* to him.

'To the truly noble by all titles Sir Francis Stuart.

'This makes that I now number you not only in the names of favour but the names of justice to what I write, and doe presently call you to the exercise of the noblest and manliest vertue as coveting rather to be freed in my fame by the authority of a judge than the credit of an undertaker.'

[*Ibid.*, pp. 239–40.]

JOHN AUBREY, 1669–96

He [Edmund Waller] told me he was not acquainted with Ben. Johnson (who dyed about 1638), but familiarly with Lucius, lord Falkland; Sydney Godolphin, Mr. Hobbes; &c.

[*Ibid.*, p. 275.]

JOHN AUBREY, 1669–96

Riding at the quintin at weddings is now left in these partes but in the west of England is sometimes used yet. I remember when I learned to read English I saw one at Will Tanner's wedding sett up at the green by Bownet howse by the pounde. Vide the masque of Ben Johnson, wher is a perfect description of rideing at the quintin.

[*Ibid.*, p. 330.]

ANONYMOUS, 1682

Fur[nish]. By my Faith (as *Ben Johnson* says) a very high vapour, 'tis a strain beyond *Ela Man—*

[*The Factious Citizen, or, The Malancholy Visioner* (1685)—a reissue of *Mr. Turbulent or The Melanchollicks* (1682)—p. 27 (mispaged 21), sig. E₂.]

ANONYMOUS, 1682

1 M*ad man*. I say Mr. *Aristotle*, that the Poets of our Age, have nothing of Wit in them, and all their Peieces [*sic*] are false Draughts —O the wise *Sophocles*, the wise *Euripides*, the Oracles of their Age—

2 M*ad*. I say the *Baye's*, and the *Ninnies* of this Age are far beyond them, and they know more than they did, and write better Sence—

1 M*ad*. I say *Aristotle* thou lyest—The Ancient *Aristophanes*, and the witty *Menander*, were the only Persons that understood Comedy among the *Greeks—Terrence* had some Wit; but *Shakespear*, and *Ben. Johnson* were mere Oafs.

[*Ibid.*, Act V, p. 73, sig. K.₁]

ANONYMOUS, 1682

Did but *Ben. Johnson* know how Follies rise
Swell and look big, how Poets do despise
The lawful charms of wit, and spend their days
In bawdy Prologues and licentious Plays,
He'd bid adieu to th'*Elysian* Field,
Gay with the splendour that the Muses yield,
And to the dusky world again repair,
To suck the thicker blasts of earthly air,
He'd leave his softer Rhymes, and would dispense ⎫
A hoarser sound, he'd *Satirist* commence ⎬
And try to lash the Ideots into Sence. ⎭

[*The Tory-Poets* (1682), p. 9.]

ANONYMOUS, 1682

'Tis true quoth he,[s] Loves troubles make me tamer,
Res est Soliciti plena timoris Amor.

[s] *There the Author translates out of* Ovid, *as* Ben. Johnson *do's in* Sejanus *out of* Homer.

["The Invocation of Ulysses and Penelope," *Wit and Drollery* (1682), pp. 215 and 218.]

JOHN DRYDEN, 1682

Thou art my Blood where *Johnson* hath no Part,
What share have we in Nature, or in Art?
Where did his Wit or Learning fix a *Brand?*
Or rail at Arts he did not understand?
Where made he love in *Price Nycanders* Vain?
Or swept the Durst in *Psyches* humble Strain?
Where sold he Bargains? *Whip-stich, Kiss mine A—s,*
Promis'd a Play, and dwindled to a Farce.
Where did his Muse from *Fletchers* Scenes purloin,
As thou whole *Etheridge* dost transfuse to thine?
But so transfus'd as Oyls on Water Flow,
His always Floats above, thine Sinks Below.

[*MacFlecknoe* (1682), p. 12. The first two lines are quoted in *The Jonson Allusion-Book* with the four preceding lines, but this most illuminating part is omitted.]

W. R., 1682

His Ears, and Shoulders kiss'd, his Waste did shun
All Smiles b'ing swoln beyond *Ben-John-Sons* Tun.

[*The Christmas Ordinary* (1682), scene vii, p. 13.]

THOMAS SHADWELL, 1682

For my part, I am (as it is said of *Surly* in the *Alchymist*) some-what costive of belief. The evidences I have represented are natural, *viz.* slight, and frivolous, such as poor old Women were wont to be hang'd upon.

[*The Lancashire Witches* (1682), "To the Reader," sig. A₃.]

Thomas Shadwell, 1682

See the renown'd *Johnson* in the last Scene of the second Act of his sad Shepherd.

[*Ibid.*, p. 44, n. f.]

Sir Robert Southwell, 1682

Besydes how preposterous is it for the Iniquity of the present by-standers (which are but a handfull) to bespite the inoffensive generations that are to come? And how well did Ben Johnson defy their hissings when he declared that what he had written was for Posterity. A prophet has no honour in his owne time.

[The Marquis of Lansdowne, *The Petty-Southwell Correspondence*, p. 112 (Letter 63, November 28, 1682).]

E. W., 1682

To Mr. Creech on his Translation of *Lucretius*.

. . . . let not the Stage
The Idl'st Moment of thy hours engage.
Each Year that Place some wond'rous Monster breeds,
And the Wits Garden is or'erun with Weeds.
There *Farce* is *Comedy*, Bombast call'd Strong,
Soft words, with nothing in 'em, make a Song.
'Tis hard to say they steal 'em now adaies,
For sure the Ancients never wrote such Playes.
These Scribling Insects have what they deserve,
Not Plenty, nor the Glory for to Starve.
That *Spencer* knew, That *Tasso* felt before,
And Death found surly *Ben.* exceeding poor.
Heaven turn the Omen from their Image here,
May he with Joy the well plac'd Lawrel wear:
Great *Virgil*'s happier fortune may he find,
And be our *Cæsar*, like *Augustus*, kind.

[Commendatory verses by "E. W., London, *Feb.* 6," prefixed to [Thomas Creech's] *T. Lucretius Carus his six books de Natura rerum* (1683; first ed., 1682), sig. D₃.]

Anonymous, 1683

He takes great Advantage from the different accompts which *Oates* and *Dugdale* give of the various Discourses they heard of the management of the Design. We understand him,—he would have had all the several Gangs and Clubbs of Plotters have all just jumpt in one and the same sence and opinion, like the Translators of the *Septuagint*. As if he could be such a *Nicodemus*, so blockishly ignorant of the world, not to know that where several people are engag'd, there will be several Sir *Politick Woodbe's*, that will be putting their Oar i'th Boat where they are concern'd; one will be proposing this, another that, and many a Fool's Bolt will be shot, and this Discourse, though never so simple is Treason, and fit to be known by way of Circumstance.

[*Remarks upon E. Settle's Narrative* (1683), p. 13.]

John Crowne, 1683

'Tis said, I openly confest, who I meant by the principal Characters in the *Play*, particularly by that of *Bartoline*. That this is false, common sence, and the Character it self will prove. Is it possible, I shou'd be such a *Bartholomew-Cokes*, to pull out my Purse in a Fair, and as soon as ever a Knave tickled my Ear with a S[t]raw (a little silly Flattery) I shou'd let go my Discretion and perhaps my Fortune? (for Libels may prove costly things.)

["To the Reader," *City Politiques* (1683), sig. A₂.]

John Dryden, 1683

You then, that would the Comic Lawrels wear,
To study Nature be your only care:
Who e're knows Man, and by a curious art
Discerns the hidden secrets of the heart;
He who observes, and naturally can Paint
The Jealous Fool, the fawning Sycophant,
A Sober Wit, an enterprising Ass,
A humorous *Otter*, or a *Hudibras*;
May safely in these noble Lists ingage,
And make 'em Act and Speak upon the Stage:

Strive to be natural in all you Write,
And paint with Colours that may please the Sight.

[Sir William Soames and John Dryden, trans. Nicolas Boileau, *The Art of Poetry* (1683), pp. 49–50; quoted by Robert Gale Noyes, *Ben Jonson on the English Stage, 1660–1776*, pp. 182–83.]

JOHN DRYDEN, 1683

Observe the town, and study well the court;
For thither various characters resort.
Thus 'twas great Jonson purchased his renown,
And in his art had borne away the crown,
If, less desirous of the people's praise,
He had not with low farce debased his plays;
Mixing dull buffoonery with wit refined,
And Harlequin with noble Terence joined.
When in the Fox I see the tortoise hist,
I lose the author of the Alchemist.

[Soames and Dryden, trans. Boileau, *The Art of Poetry* (1683), quoted from Scott and Saintsbury's edition of *The Works of John Dryden* (1882–93), XV, 246–47. Dryden is said to have added the English illustrations.]

THOMAS WOOD, 1683

I know They all defiance do profess,
Stubborn and disobedient to my Lash;
But time there was when they observ'd my Nod,
And gratefully would *love* and *kiss* the Rod.
For *Johnson* his't at length a Poet was,
But th' HONOURABLE ESQUIRE's *still* an Ass.

[*Juvenalis Redivivus* (1683), pp. 28–29.]

THOMAS ANDREWS, 1684

But hold! methinks, great Shade, I see thee rove
Through the smooth Path of Plenty, Peace and Love;
Where *Ben.* salutes thee first, o'erjoy'd to see
The Youth that sung his Fame and Memory.

["On the Death of Mr. John Oldham. A Pastoral," *The Works of Mr. John Oldham* (7th ed., 1710), sig. A₇. First printed in the edition of 1684.]

JOHN LACY, 1684

Sir Hercules. . . . . we are an ancienter family than the La-Fools.

[*Sir Hercules Buffoon* (1684), I, 1. Noted by C. B. Graham, "Jonson Allusions in Restoration Comedy," *Review of English Studies*, XV (1939), 203.]

JOHN LACY, 1684

Sq[uire Buffoon]. Poets are esteem'd above Princes; I have a reverend author for it called *Taylor the Water-Poet;*

> *When Nature did intend some wond'rous thing,*
> *She made a Poet, or at least a King.*

Ben Johnson wou'd a given a hundred pounds (if he had had it, that is) to a been author of those two lines.

[*Ibid.*, III, 1, p. 22. Noted by Graham, *loc. cit.*, p. 201.]

JOHN LACY, 1684

> True English topers *Racy Sack* ne'er fail;
> With such *Ben Johnson*'s humming Plays prevail.

[*Ibid.*, Epilogue. Noted by Graham, *loc. cit.*, p. 201.]

SIR ROGER L'ESTRANGE, 1684

But you have done Something for your self, (I hope) For you have now so Impudently Own'd the *Popish Cause*, and in the Owning it, thrown such *Infamy* on the *Government*, that I Despair not of seeing thee *Whipt at a Carts Arse by an Order of Councel*, &c. Do our Statesmen think that because the *Capitol* was once Sav'd by the *Cackling* of a *Goose, Their Babel* must be preserv'd by the *Braying* of an *Asse?* such a Fellow as would make the Best Cause Scandalous; A *Play-house* will Teach 'em more Generosity. *Ben Johnson* thinks it fit, the *Romans* should Scorn (in the *Catiline Conspiracy*) to Owe their Preservation to *Sempronia*, A Poor Civil Gentlewoman that had no Fault but being too Charitable of her Own Proper Goods and Chattels. Yet what an Infamous, Stigmatiz'd Villain (Pardon my Freedom, Sr) have we found out to be the *Tutelar Saint*, &c.

[*The Observator*, Vol. II, No. 155 (October 23, 1684).]

JOHN OLDHAM, 1684

The *Satyr* and *Odes* of the Author, which follow next in order, I have translated after the same libertine way. In them also I labour'd under the disadvantages of coming after other persons. The *Satyr* had been made into a Scene by *Ben Johnson*, in a Play of his, called the *Poetaster*.

[*Poems and Translations* (1684), Advertisement.]

THOMAS OTWAY, 1684

Theod. Filthy, filthy, fulsom filthy! What, be a *Doll-Common*, follow the Camp! How lovelily would your fair Ladyship look, mounted upon a Baggage-Cart, presiding over the rest of the Captain's dirty Equipage!

[*The Atheist* (1684), Act V, p. 59.]

SIR WILLIAM PETTY, 1684

You have done your part; and now you mention charges, discharges, and surcharges, I could, like Dol Common in the 'Alchemist', run out into a new ocean of complaints that much of this hath been done, and other parts I have many times begged to have done.

[The Marquis of Lansdowne, *The Petty-Southwell Correspondence*, p. 121 (Letter 69, April 19, 1684).]

N. T., 1684

Enjoy thy Fate, thy Voice in Anthems raise;
So well tun'd here on Earth to our *Apollo*'s Praise:
Let me retire, while some sublimer Pen
Performs for thee what thou hast done for *Homer* and for *Ben*.

["In memory of the Author," *Remains of Mr. John Oldham in Verse and Prose* (1684), sig. A₂ᵛ.]

WILLIAM WINSTANLEY, 1684

But this our reverend Schoolmaster was of another temper, taking great pains for the well educating of his Scholars; as witnesseth these lines of Mr. *Benjamin Johnson*, once a Scholar under him.

Cambden, most reverend head to whom 1 owe
All that 1 am in Arts, all that 1 know.

How nothing's that to whom my Country owes
The great renown and name wherewith she goes? &c.

["The Life of Mr. William Cambden," *Englands Worthies* (1684), pp. 307-8.
Not in the first edition of 1660.]

WILLIAM WINSTANLEY, 1684

Many were the Wit Combats betwixt him and *Ben. Johnson*,
which two we may compare to a *Spanish great Gallion*, and an
English-man of War, Mr. *Johnson* (like the former) was built far
higher in Learning; Solled but slow in his performances: *Shakespeare* with the *English-man of War*, lesser in bulk, but lighter in
sailing, could turn with all Tides, tack about and take advantage of
all Winds, by the quickness of his Wit and invention.

["The Life of Mr. Wil. Shakespeare," *ibid.*, p. 346.]

WARRANT, 1684/85

Janu: 15 The King & Queene at the Silent Weoman   £05

[Taken from a list in a warrant dated December 28, 1685, for plays acted from
January 13, 1684/85, to December 14, 1685 (L.C. 5/147, p. 68), quoted by Allardyce Nicoll, *A History of Restoration Drama*, p. 312.]

ANONYMOUS, 1685

The *Dutch* and *Germans* (as though frozen up) have produced
little in this kind; yet we must confess that *Grotius*, *Heinsius*,
Scaliger, and *Vossius* were Learned *Criticks*. Some of the *English*
have indeed rais'd their Pens, and soar'd as high as any of the
Italians, or *French*; yet *Criticism* came but very lately in fashion
amongst us; without doubt *Ben. Johnson* had a large stock of
Critical Learning; *Spencer* had studied *Homer*, and *Virgil*, and
Tasso, etc.

["Preface to the Translation," *Mixt Essays upon Tragedies, Comedies, etc.* (1685);
written by the Sieur de Saint Euvremont.]

[C. CLEEVE], 1685

A Task too vast for any living Mortal Wight
Oh cou'd we call back from the shades again
Great *Oldham*, *Cowley*, or *Immortal Ben*,

Those happy Bards might something worthy thee indite;
And though these three to our assistance came,
With all their rich and shining Eloquence,
With all the gaudy Trappings of their sence,
The Dress wou'd prove too poor and scanty for thy Fame.

["A Poem on M^r. L'Estrange," *The Songs of Moses and Deborah Paraphrased*
(1685), p. 135.)

JOHN DRYDEN, 1685

. . . . as *Ben. Johnson* tells us in the Alchymist, when Projection
had fail'd, and the Glasses were all broken, there was enough however in the Bottoms of them to cure the Itch.

[Preface to *Albion and Albanius* (1685), sig. b₁.]

SIR ROGER L'ESTRANGE, 1685

Obs. As dead as a Herring; And, as a man may say; *Annihilated,
Evacuated, Defunct,* and *Vtterly Abolish'd;* Departed *in Fumo;* and
as *Honest Ben. Johnson* said of the Miscarriage of his *Great Med'-
cine,* not enough left on't to Cure the *Itch.*

[*The Observator,* Vol. III, No. 41 (May 13, 1685).]

NAHUM TATE, 1685

As you will find the following Scenes drawn from the Stores of
that great Master *Ben,* I hope you will think the Contrivance no
ill Imitation: . . . . When *Ben Johnson* was inform'd, that a certain
Person had done him Injury, he cry'd out with Indignation, *I made
the Ingrateful Man understand* Horace.

[Dedication to *Cuckolds-Haven* (1685). The play is almost entirely taken from
Eastward Ho, with one character (Clogg, drawn from Pug) and scenes 2 and 3 of
Act II of *The Devil Is an Ass* utilized in Act I, scene 2.]

NATHANIAL THOMPSON, 1685

But had you seen the *Skittish Jade,*
You would have thought her *Drunk or Mad;*
For at first dash *his Hand she seiz'd,*
Much was th' *Ambitious* Heroe *pleas'd.*

So sweetly did *Don Quixot* grin;
When the *Maid Marrian of the Inn*
He thought was some *Enchanted Queen;*
Askt his *Dead-doing Hand to Kiss;*
But what *White Devil danc'd in this?*
Some *Fly*, some *Rat*, or *Great old Pus*,
Or *Spirit Mephostophilus;*
Or *Pug* that *Paracelsus* wore
In *the Pomel of his Sword before;*
Or *Healing Virtue* that as Rare is,
Is sent *His Grace by's Aunt of* Fayries,
Who aids him thus in *Hugger Mugger*,
So did *Doll Common*, *Abel Drugger*.

["A Canto upon the Miraculous Cure of the K's Evil, perform'd by the D. of M. in 80," *A Collection of 86 Loyal Poems* (1685), pp. 21–22.]

FERRAND SPENCE, 1686

I now pass to *Comedy*, wherein my Author *seems* not to *take* the *same* measures, as he did in *Tragedy*, that *every thing* ought to be *referr'd* to one *principal event*, However, he *declares* not his *own Opinion* in *this point*, but with many *allowances*. He will only have it a *contest* depending on the *Genius* of the *two Nations*. He very *fairly* and *justly* allows *Ben. Johnson* to be an *Excellent Comic Poet*, *in depicting the several humours and manners of men*. Yet he thinks, *our humours are carried on too far*, which proceeds from our *too* much *thinking* on the *same thing*, and our too long *plodding* in the same *beaten* Tract of *Re-action*.

[Preface to *Miscellanea: or Various Discourses. . . . . By the Sieur de Saint Euvremont* (1686), sigs. b₈ᵛ–b₉.]

FERRAND SPENCE, 1686

So that, instead of representing an eminent and signal *Imposture*, carryed on by means that refer all to the same end, they [the English] represent a *Famous Cheat* with his *hundred* several *tricks*, every one of which produces its *particular* effect according to its proper *Constitution*. As they almost always renounce *Unity of Action* to represent a *principal* Person, who diverts 'em with *different* Actions; so they likewise forsake this Principal Person, to let you take a prospect *diverse* ways of what happens in *publick* places to *many* Persons: *Ben. Johnson* has taken this course in his *Bartholomew-Fair:* The same thing we see in *Epsoam Wells:* And in *both* Comedies are comically represented the ridiculous passages in both those places.

[*"Of the English Comedy," ibid.*, pp. 37–38.]

FERRAND SPENCE, 1686

The *French Moliere*, into whom the *Ancients* inspir'd the *true Spirit* of *Comedy*, equalls their *Ben. Johnson* in admirably representing the several *humors* and different *manners* of Men, both of them in their *respective* paintings, keeping a *just regard* to the *genius* of their Nation. I shou'd believe that, in this point, they were as much *out* as the *Antients:* But we cannot deny, but that they had more regard to the *Characters* than the *main subjects*, whose successive *Inferences* also might have been better *tyed* together, and the laying 'em out *naked* much more *natural*.

[*Ibid.*, p. 40.]

JOHN DRYDEN, 1687

When to her ORGAN, vocal Breath was giv'n
An Angel heard, and straight appear'd
Mistaking Earth for Heaven.

["A Song for St. Cecilia's Day, 1687," printed from the broadside edition of 1687 in Cyrus Lawrence Day, *The Songs of John Dryden* (1932), p. 77. As William Alfred Eddy points out, *Modern Language Notes*, XLVI (1931), 40–41, the last line is a verbatim quotation from Jonson's "The Musical Strife," stanza 6, l. 4. See Newdigate, *The Poems of Ben Jonson*, p. 99.]

CHARLES MONTAGU, EARL OF HALIFAX, 1687

Bayes. . . . . Well, but where were we? Oh! Here they are, just going up stairs into the *Apollo;* from whence my White takes occasion to talk very well of *Tradition*.

Thus to the place where *Johnson* sat we climb,
Leaning on the same Rail that guided him;
And whilst we thus on equal helps rely,

> Our Wit must be as true, our thoughts as high.
> For as an *Author* happily compares
> *Tradition* to a well-fixt pair of *Stairs*,
> So this the *Scala Sancta* we believe,
> By which his *Traditive Genius* we receive.
> Thus every step I take my Spirits soar,
> And I grow more a *Wit*, and more, and more.

There's humour! Is not that the liveliest Image in the World of a Mouses going up a pair of Stairs. *More a Wit, and more and more?*

[*The Hind and the Panther Transvers'd* (1687), pp. 22–23.]

SIR ROBERT SOUTHWELL, 1687

If you name 3 or 4 words ('Column' is one, the other 2 I can send you) Hee will, like Dol Common in the 'Alchemist,' fall into Extravagances.

[The Marquis of Lansdowne, *The Petty-Southwell Correspondence* (Letter 156, April 7, 1687, pp. 266–67.]

WILLIAM WINSTANLEY, 1687

[Drayton] was buried in *Westminster-Abbey*, near the South-door, by those two eminent Poets, *Geoffry Chaucer* and *Edmond Spencer*, with this Epitaph made (as it is said) by Mr. *Benjamin Johnson*.

> Do, pious Marble, let thy Readers know
>   What they, and what their Children ow
>   To *Drayton's* Name, whose sacred Dust
>   We recommend unto thy Trust
> Protect his Memory, and preserve his Story,
> Remain a lasting Monument of his Glory:
>   And when thy Ruines shall disclaim
>   To be the Treasurer of his Name,
>   His Name that cannot fade shall be
>   An everlasting Monument to thee.

[*The Lives of the Most Famous English Poets* (1687), pp. 107–8.]

WILLIAM WINSTANLEY, 1687

Joshua Sylvester, a very eminent Translator of his time, especially of the Divine *Du Bartus*, whose six days work of Creation, gain'd him an immortal Fame, having had many great Admirers even to these days, being usher'd into the world by the chiefest Wits of that Age; amongst others, the most accomplisht Mr. *Benjamin Johnson* thus wrote of him.

> If to admire, were to commend my Praise
> might then both thee, thy work and merit raise;
> But, as it is (the Child of Ignorance
> And utter stranger to all Ayr of *France*)
> How can I speak of thy great pains, but err;
> Since they can only judge that can confer?
> Behold! the reverend shade of *Bartus* stands
> Before my thought, and (in thy right) commands
> That to the world I publish, for him, this:
> *Bartus doth wish thy* English *now were his*,
> So well in that are his Inventions wrought,
> As his will now be the *Translation* thought,
> Thine the Original; and *France* shall boast
> No more those Maiden-Glories she hath lost.

[*Ibid.*, p. 108.]

WILLIAM WINSTANLEY, 1687

This reverend Doctor [Richard Corbet] was born at *Ewel* in *Surrey;* a witty Poet in his youth, witness his *Iter Boreale*, and other *facetious Poems*, which were the effects of his juvenal fancy; He was also one of those celebrated Wits, which with Mr. *Benjamin Johnson*, Mr. *Whitaker*, Sir *Joh. Harrington*, Dr. *Donne*, Mr. *Drayton*, Mr. *Davis*, whom I mentioned before, and several others, wrote those mock commendatory Verses on *Coriats Crudities*.

[*Ibid.*, p. 121.]

WILLIAM WINSTANLEY, 1687

Many were the Wit-combats betwixt him and *Ben Johnson;* which two we may compare to a *Spanish great Gallion*, and an *English Man of war:* Mr. *Johnson*, (like the former) was built far higher in Learning, solid, but slow in his performances; *Shakespear*, with the *English Man of war*, lesser in Bulk, but lighter in sayling, could turn with all Tides, tack about, and take advantage of all Winds, by the quickness of his Wit and Invention.

[*Ibid.*, pp. 132–33.]

WILLIAM WINSTANLEY, 1687

[Thomas Middleton] was Contemporary with *Johnson* and *Fletcher*, and tho' not of equal Repute with them, yet were well accepted of those times such Plays as he wrote.

[*Iibid.*, pp. 135–36.]

WILLIAM WINSTANLEY, 1687

We could also produce you *Ben. Johnsons* Verses [on Brome], with other of the prime Wits of those times; but we think these sufficient to shew in what respect he was held by the best Judgments of that Age.

[*Ibid.*, p. 151.]

ANONYMOUS, *ca.* 1688

These were follow'd by some of a more modern stamp, whose only pride was a large pair of Boot-hose & a well starch'd Ruff, & whose Style, as well as their Habit was something more elegant & refin'd than that of those antique Reformers of our inconstant Language: in the head of these advanc'd Will. Shakespear, & Ben. Johnson, whose unparallel'd worth never mett with any Rivals, but such as did not understand it, & consequently could not euqal it: these march'd forward with all the Modesty in their Garb, & the Majesty in their Deportment that befitted the Innocence & Learning of their Times.

[*A Journal from Parnassus*, ed. Hugh MacDonald (1937), pp. 5–6.]

ANONYMOUS, *ca.* 1688

Hereupon their Address was form'd into a Bill, & referr'd to a Committee of Greivances, in which every Member nominated had his peculiar province of inspecting & licensing the severall Species of Poetry.

The Examination of Heroics was assign'd to Spencer: of Epics & Pindarics to Mr Cowley: of Panegyrics to Mr Waller: of Satyrs to

Mr Oldham. For Stage-Poetry the supervising of Tragedies was committed to Shakespear; of Comedies to Ben. Johnson: of Tragic-Comedies to Beaumont & Fletcher: of Prologues, Songs & all the Garniture & Appurtenances of this sort of Poetry (especially Prefaces,) to Bays who it seems had been old Dog at them ever since Herringam hir'd him by the week to epistolize his Readers.

[*Ibid.*, pp. 37–38.]

ANONYMOUS, *ca.* 1688

And for the further discouragement of ignorant Pretenders, Apollo thought fit to give order to the Library-Keeper Ben. Johnson that no Book or Paper should be admitted into the Musæum till it had pass'd the Censure of the Committee aforesaid: for by these means, when the importunate Authors found their Access thither not so easy as formerly, they would either forbear coming, or come better prepar'd. Ben. reply'd he had done all this & more to litle purpose, as might appear by those monstrous heaps of Volumes that lay pil'd before the Library-door, waiting for admittance, thô waiting in vain; for he was resolv'd to leave them there to the mercy of the Moths.

[*Ibid.*, pp. 38–39.]

ANONYMOUS, *ca.* 1688

Ben answer'd he wou'd obey their Orders, & with submission to the House, propose an expedient which would not a little disappoint the ambitious expectations of these importunate intruders; this he would effect by choosing out of the Books that are brought hither the very worst, & placing it in the Library, not among the rest, but by itself on high in the middle of the Room, & there letting it remain till a worse came in it's place & releiv'd it. This Motion being approv'd & the Bill pass'd into a Law, the Clerk was order'd to proceed to the next.

[*Ibid.*, p. 40.]

ANONYMOUS, *ca.* 1688

Here Ben. Johnson interpos'd, & was seconded by Bays (both of whom thought themselves reflected upon for the freedome of the

one with the Roman & of the Other with the French Authors) that
Mr Waller was a litle too invective: & that some distinction ought
to be made between those modest Writers who by an ingenuous
Imitation & a happy Allusion to antient Authors did as it were natu-
ralize forreign Witt & make it deservedly their own, & those law-
less unmercifull Pirates that live upon the Spoil, & count all they
meet with lawfull Prize.

[*Ibid.*, p. 51.]

Anonymous, *ca.* 1688

The humble Address of his Maties. poor
Subjects the Company of Players.

. . . . We have exhausted Shakespear, Fletcher, & Johnson, are
now plundering Terence, & must shortly be forc'd to go higher &
borrow Plots from Plautus & Aristophanes. Nay for the better
maintaining the Trade we have not only reviv'd old Plays but acted
our own, & cannot but blush while we boast that our Burlesque has
succeeded better than many of our Poets labours.

[*Ibid.*, pp. 53, 54.]

Anonymous, *ca.* 1688

. . . . they are grown so fine that nothing will suit with their
Palate but Shakespear or Johnson, & a modern Author after nine
Months labour to elevate & surprize, must be forc'd to stand to
their Courtesy without Appeal.

[*Ibid.*, p. 56.]

Anonymous, *ca.* 1688

Here Bays . . . . cry'd, ... I shall, by the permission of the
House, entertain you with a reading of the whole Peice, & leave any
unprejudiced Hearer to judge of the unreasonableness of this Gentleman's Objections, & a thousand more that Readers of the Op-
posite party make against it, and of Ben. Johnson's injustice in the
exclusion of this Book from the Library, & the unkind separation
of it from the rest of my Works.

[*Ibid.*, p. 66.]

Anonymous, 1688

Here *Galatea* mourns; In such sad Strains
Poor *Philomel* her wretched Fate complains.
Here *Fletcher* and Immortal *Johnson* shine,
Deathless, preserv'd in his Immortal Line.

["On the Death of Mr. Waller," *Poems to the Memory of that Incomparable Poet Edmond Waller Esquire* (1688), p. 23.]

Thomas D'Urfey, 1688

For now-a-days poor Satyr hides his Head.
No wholsom Jerk dares lash fantastick Youth,
You wits grow angry, if you hear the Truth,
Old Fumble now, may at *Doll Commons* strip,
Without being flagn'd by a Poetick Whip.

[Prologue to *A Fool's Preferment* (1688), sig. A₄.]

Gerard Langbaine, 1688

The *first* Catalogue that was printed of any worth, was that Collected by *Kirkman*, a *London* Bookseller, whose chief dealing was in Plays; which was published *1671*, at the end of *Nicomede*, a Tragicomedy, Translated from the *French* of Monsieur *Corneille*. This Catalogue was printed *Alphabetically*, as to the Names of the *Plays*, but *promiscuously* as to those of the *Authors*, (*Shakspeare*, *Fletcher*, *Johnson*, and some others of the most voluminous Authors excepted).

[Preface to *Momus triumphans* (1688), sig. A₃.]

Gerard Langbaine, 1688

. . . . *and Mr.* Rymer, *whose Judgment of him is this;* I cannot (*says he*) be displeas'd with honest *Ben*, when he chuses rather to borrow a Melon of his Neighbour, than to treat us with a Pumpion of his own growth.

[*Ibid.*, sig. a₂. A marginal note says, "Tragedies of the last Age, *p.* 143."]

GERARD LANGBAINE, 1688

But at the same time I cannot but blame him [Dryden] for taxing others with stealing Characters from him, (as he does *Settle* in his *Notes on Morocco*) when he himself does *the same*, almost in all the Plays he writes; and for arraigning his Predecessours for stealing from the *Ancients*, as he does *Johnson;* which 'tis evident that he himself is guilty of the same.

[*Ibid.*, sig. a₂ᵛ.]

GERARD LANGBAINE, 1688

But in the mean time, would our *Nobility* and *Gentry*, who delight in Plays, but allow themselves so much time as to read over what is extant on this Subject in *English*, as, *Ben. Johnson*'s Discoveries; *Roscommon*'s Translation of *Horace*'s Art of Poetry; *Rapin*'s Reflections on *Aristotle*'s Treatise of Poetry; *Longinus* of the loftiness of Speech; *Boyleau*'s Art of Poetry; *Hedelin*'s Art of the Stage; *Euremont*'s Essays; *Rimer*'s Tragedies of the last Age considered; *Dryden*'s Drammatick Essay; and several others; though they understood none but their native Language, and consequently could not read what *Vossius, Heinsius, Scaliger, Plutarch, Athenaeus, Titius Giraldus, Castelvetro, Lope de Vega, Corneille, Menardiere*, and others which have written to the same purpose in several Languages; yet those which are to be met with in *English*, are sufficient to inform them, both in the *excellency* of the Poetick Art, and the Rules which Poets follow, with the Reasons of them: They would then find their Pleasure encrease with their Knowledge; and they would have the greater satisfaction in seeing a *correct Play*, by how much they were capable (by the help of these Rules) to discern the *Beauties* of it; and the greater value for a *good* Poet, by how much they were sensible of the Pains and Study requisite to bring such a Poem to perfection.

[*Ibid.*, sigs. a₃ᵛ–a₄.]

GERARD LANGBAINE, 1688

(*l*) Part of it from *Johnson*'s *New Inn*, Octavo, and the Plot from *Exemplary Novels*, Two Damsels.

[Note on Beaumont and Fletcher's *Love's Pilgrimage* in *ibid.*, p. 8.]

GERARD LANGBAINE, 1688

(†) *Benj. Johnson.*

Alchymist .... }	C. Fol.
Bartholomew-Fair. }	
Christmas's Masque .... }	M. Fol.
Cloridia .... }	
Cynthia's Revels	C. Fol.
Challenge at Tilt	M. Fol.
(*e*) Cataline's Conspiracy	T. Fol.
Devil's an Ass	C. Fol.
Every Man in his Humour .... }	C. Fol.
Every Man out of his Humour .... }	
(*f*) Entertainment at K. *James*'s Coronation	E. Fol.
Entertainments of the Q. and Prince, at *Althrop*	E. Fol.
Entertainments of the King of *England*, and the King of }	F. Fol.
Denmark, at *Theobalds* .... }	
Entertainment of K. *James*, and Q. *Ann*, at *Theobalds*	F. Fol.
Entertainment of the King and Queen, on *May*-Day, at }	E. Fol.
Sir *Wil. Cornwallis*'s House, at *High-gate* .... }	
Fortunate Isles	M. Fol.
Fox	C. Fol.
Golden Age restored	M. Fol.
Honour of Wales	M. Fol.
* Hymenes	M. Fol.
Irish Masque	M. Fol.
King's Entertainment at *Welbeck*	M. Fol.
Loves Triumph	M. Fol.
Love's Welcome	M. Fol.
Love Restored	M. Fol.
Magnetick Lady	C. Fol.
Masque of Auguurs	M. Fol.
Masque at the Lord *Hayes*'s House	M. Fol.
Masque at the Lord *Haddington*'s Marriage	M. Fol.
Masque of Owls	M. Fol.
* Masque of Queens	M. Fol.
Mercury Vindicated	M. Fol.
Metamorphosed Gipsies	M. Fol.
(*a*) Mortimer's Fall	T. Fol.
News from the New World in the Moon	M. Fol.
Neptune's Triumph	M. Fol.
* Oberon the Fairy-Queen	M. Fol.

(†) *All* Ben. Johnson'*s except the four last, are Printed with other Poems in two Volumes, Folio,* London, 1640.

(e) *Plot from* Salust'*s History.*

(f) *From several Authours quoted in the Margin throughout.*

* *All marked with this* * *are in the first Volume, and Quotations are Cited by the Authour in the Margin throughout.*

(a) *An Imperfect Piece just begun.*

GERARD LANGBAINE, 1688—*Continued*

Pleasure reconciled to Virtue......................... M. Fol.
Pan's Anniversary.................................... M. Fol.
(*b*) Poetaster....................................... C. Fol.
* Queen's Masque of Blackness....................... M. Fol.
*—Her Masque of Beauty............................ M. Fol.
Speeches at Pr. H. Barriers.......................... M. Fol.
Staple of News...................................... C. Fol.
(*c*) Silent Woman.................................. C. Fol.
(*d*) Sad Shepherd.................................. T. Fol.
(*e*) Sejanus....................................... T. Fol.
Tale of a Tub....................................... C. Fol.
Time Vindicated.................................... M. Fol.
Vision of Delight................................... M. Fol.
Case is altered..................................... C. 4°
New-Inn... C. 4°
(*f*) Eastward Hoe.................................. C. 4°
(*g*) Widow.. C. 4°

(b) *From Ovid's Elegies; and from* Horace's Satyrs, *Book the Ninth,* Satyr *the first Part.*

(c) *Borrowed part of it from* Ovid de Arte Amandi, *and* Juvenal's *Sixth Satyr.*

(d) *This Play left Imperfect.*

(e) *Plot,* Tacitus, Suetonius, Seneca, *&c. There is an Edition of this Play,* 4°, *Printed* Lond. 1605, *by the Authour's own Orders, with all the Quotations from whence he borrowed any thing of his Play.*

(f) *Joyn'd in this with* Chapman.

(g) *Joyn'd in this with* Fletcher *and* Middleton.

[*Ibid.*, pp. 12–13.]

ROBERT GOULD, 1689

Ben Johnson, *too, lets us know in his Elegie upon Divine* Shakespear,

> That, though the *Poet's Matter Nature* be,
> His *Art* must give the Fashion; and that *He*
> That means to write a *Living Line* must sweat,
> And (*without tiring*) strike the *second Heat*
> Upon the *Muses Anvil,*——
> Or for the *Lawrel* he may purchase *scorn;*
> For a *good Poet's made* as well as *born.*

[Preface to *Poems Chiefly consisting of Satyrs and Satyrical Epistles* (1689), sig. a₃ᵛ.]

ROBERT GOULD, 1689

Here *Fletcher* and Immortal *Johnson* shine,
Deathless, preserv'd in his Immortal Line.

["*To the Memory of* Edmund Waller *Esq;*" in *ibid.*, p. 69.]

ROBERT GOULD, 1689

Thee, mighty *Ben!* we ever shall affect, ⎫
Thee ever mention with profound Respect; ⎬
Thou most Judicious *Poet!* most correct! ⎭
I know not on what single Play to fall;
Thou did'st arrive t' an Excellence in all.
Yet we must give thee but thy just desert;
Thou'd'st less of *nature*, though much more of *Art:*
The Springs that move our Souls thou did'st not touch:
But then thy *Judgment, care* and *pains* were such,
We ne'r yet, nor e'r shall an *Author* see,
That wrote so many *perfect Plays* as thee:
Not one vain humour thy strict view escapes,
All Follies thou hadst drest in all their proper shapes.
Hail, sacred *Bards!* Hail, you Immortal *three!*
Y'ave won the Goal of vast Eternity,
And built your selves a Fame, where you will live
While we have *Wits* to read, and they have *praise* to give.

["The Play-house. A Satyr. Writ in the Year 1685," in *ibid.*, pp. 178-79.]

ROBERT GOULD, 1689

Flush't with success, full *Gallery, Box*, and *Pit*,
Thou branded'st all Mankind with want of Wit,
And in short time wer't grown so vain a Ninny,
As scarce t' allow that *Ben* himself had any.

["The Laureat. A Satyr," in *ibid.*, p. 229.]

[ROBERT GOULD], 1689

Flush'd with success, full Gallery, and Pit,
Thou bravest all Mankind with want of Wit.

Nay, in short time, wer't grown so proud a Ninny,
As scarce t'allow that *Ben* himself had any.

["The Laureat," *The Muses Farewel to Popery and Slavery, or, a Collection of Miscellany Poems, Satyrs, Songs, &c.* (1689), pp. 27–28.]

THOMAS SHADWELL, 1689

Old. No Wit! Ounds, now you provoke me. Shall I, who was *Jack Fletcher's* Friend, *Ben Johnson's* Son, and afterward an Intimate Crony of *Jack Cleaveland*, and ·*Tom Randal*, have kept Company with Wits, and been accounted a Wit these Fifty Years, live to be Depos'd by you?

L. Fan. Ha, ha, ha.

Old. Ha, ha, ha. I, that was a Judge at *Blackfriers*, writ before *Fletcher's* Works and *Cartwright's*, taught even *Taylor* and the best of them to speak. I cannot go to *London* yet, but the Wits get me amongst them, and the Players will get me to Rehearsal to teach them, even the best of them: and you to say I have no Wit, I say, you have not, nor ever had, any Beauty.

[*Bury-Fair* (1689), II, i, p. 16.]

THOMAS SHADWELL, 1689

Where is my *Jezebel*, my Cockatrice, my Clogdogdo, as honest *Tom Otter* says? A senceless Jade, with her Wit, and her Breeding.

[*Ibid.*, III, i, p. 39. The allusion is to the statement of Captain Otter in *The Silent Woman*, IV, ii, 75.]

ANONYMOUS, 1690

Jon. [Simper:] Have not I been as silent as a *Turkish* Mute, or as *Epicœne* in the *Silent Woman*, lest my Voice should betray my Sex.

[*The Folly of Priest-Craft* (1690), IV, i, p. 36.]

[THOMAS BROWNE], 1690

But alas poor Gentlewoman! She had scarce travell'd half way, when *Cupid* served her as the Cut-Purse did the Old Justice in *Bartholomew*-Fair, tickled her with a Straw in her Ear, and then she could not budge one foot further, till she had humbly requested her Maker to grant her a private Act of Toleration for a little Harmless Love, otherwise called Fornication.

[*The Late Converts Exposed: or the Reasons of Mr. Bays's changing his Religion, Part the Second* (1690), p. 3.]

THOMAS D'URFEY, 1690

For as, when *Cataline* a League
Had made the Senators to fegue,
And strumpet had told *Marcus Tully*,
The close intentions of that Bully,
He not so much the cause revenging
O'th'State, as t'hinder his own swinging,
Made the best speech to quell that strife,
(Tis said) that e're he made in's Life,
Since when, 'tis found upon Record,
In th' (m) Tragedy, writ word for word:
So thou since frighted by the Rabble,
Hast spoke like him most admirable.

(m) In *Ben Johnsons* Tragedy of *Catiline*, *Cicero's* Oration to the Senate, and several other Speeches are translated from his own Latin, and that of *Salust* Word for Word.

[*Collin's Walk through London and Westminster* (1690), pp. 84–85 and 199.]

THOMAS D'URFEY, 1690

Loud Musick sounding through his Ears,
That were more sanctified than theirs,
Made him a great while doubting stand,
Till seeing Brother *Zeal o'th Land*,
Give to his Canting Sister Greeting,
Confirm'd him this must be a Meeting;
With Eyes turn'd up and shake of Head,
He now repeated all was said;
Admir'd the Habit of the Prig,
And wink'd at stealing of the Pig,
As wisely knowing all those Slips,
Natural to their Apocalips;
And that the Brethren may Steal,

As well as Lie, to shew their Zeal;
He had not long been in this Rapture,
Which pleas'd him more than any Chapter;
But by the Nature of the Play,
His Mood was turn'd another way;
For finding that a little after,
Meerly to urge the Peoples Laughter,
The Rabbi with loud Shouts and Mocks,
Was for Slight reason set ith' Stocks;
In *Breast* a suddain Anger glow'd,
And instantly revenge he vow'd,
As thinking this a base affront,
To the whole Tribe of those that Cant;
This Maggot working in his Pate,
He starts from off the Bench he sate;
And getting near half choak'd with Rage,
Thus spoke to those upon the Stage.

[*Ibid.*, pp. 149–50. The fourteen lines preceding these are quoted in *The Jonson Allusion-Book*, p. 420, but the editors seem not to have noted that the lines quoted above are a description of *Bartholomew Fair*.]

GEORGE POWELL, 1690

The time has been when as old *Ben* ended his Grace with God bless me, and God bless *Ralph*, *viz.* the honest Drawer that drew him good Sack. So some Modern Authors with the same Equity, might full as Pathetically have furnish'd out one Article of their Prayers, (not forgetting the present Props of the Stage) with God bless Mohun, and God bless Hart, the good Actors that got 'em their good third Days, and consequently more substantial Patrons then the greatest gay Name, in the Frontispiece of the proudest Dedication.

["The Epistle Dedicatory," *The Treacherous Brothers* (1690), sig. A₂ʳ.]

ANONYMOUS, 1691

He who can calmly hear his own Countrymen so vilified, without some Emotion, deserves better to be toss'd in a Blanket, than the Mayor

of Scarbrough. For, with Asper, in a Play of Ben Johnson's, *it becomes every English Man to say,*

> Who can behold such Prodigies as these,
> And have his Lips seal'd up? Not I. My Soul
> Was never ground into such Oily Colours,
> To Flatter Vice, and Daub Iniquity.
> But with an armed and resolved Hand,
> I'll strip the ragged Follies of the Times
> Naked, as at their Birth.

["The Epistle Dedicatory," *A Satyr against the French* (1691), sig. A₃.]

ANONYMOUS, 1691
The feasting of the Divel by Ben Johnson

[Under this title is printed Jonson's "Gypsies' Song" from *The Masque of Gypsies*
in *Merry Drollery* (1691), ed. Ebsworth, pp. 214-17.]

ANONYMOUS, 1691

A Session was held the other day,

. . . .

The first that broke the silence was good old *Ben*,
Prepar'd before with Canary wine.

["A Sessions of Wit," *ibid.*, p. 73.]

ANONYMOUS, 1691
In praise of Sack

Fetch me *Ben Johnsons* scull, and fill't with Sack,
Rich as the same he drank, when the whole pack
Of jolly sisters pledg'd, and did agree
It was no sin to be as drunk as he.

[*Ibid.*, p. 293. The verses were first printed in *Wits Recreation* (1640).]

SAMUEL BUTLER, 1691

. . . . therefore you [J. Cooke, author of *King Charles His Case*
(1649)] do ill to accuse him of reading *Johnsons* and *Shakespears*
Plays, which should seem you have been more in yourself to much

worse purpose, else you had never hit so right upon the very Dialect of their railing Advocates, in which (believe me) to have really out-acted all that they could fansie of passionate and ridiculous Outrage.

[*The Plagiary exposed: or an Old answer to a Newly revived Calumny against the memory of King Charles I* (1691), p. 2, as quoted in *The Shakspere Allusion-Book*, I, 525.]

Thomas D'Urfey, 1691

Meriton. . . . . Now am I wishing for one of Morose's nightcaps only to defend my ears against him, for I see he has us in the wind.

[*Love for Money* (1691), I, 1. Noted by C. B. Graham, "Jonson Allusions in Restoration Comedy," *Review of English Studies*, XV (1939), 203.]

Thomas D'Urfey, 1691

Sir Rowland. . . . . Oh rare Sir Rowland it shall be; I intend to have it for an epitaph upon my tomb as well as Ben Jonson. . . . . I can drink sack as well as he, tho' I cannot write so well in praise of it.

[*Ibid.*, II, 1. Noted by Graham, *loc. cit.*, p. 201.]

Gerard Langbaine, 1691

This Play [Brome's *Northern Lass*] is commended not only by the above-mentioned *Ben Johnson*, but by Five other Copies of Verses printed before the Play.

[*An Account of the English Dramatic Poets* (1691), p. 37.]

Gerard Langbaine, 1691

This Play [*Cola's Furie*] was never acted, but introduc'd into the world by two Recommendatory Copies of Verses, written by his Friends: both which may seem to the Reader, to be too partial in their Judgments; as may be judg'd by the following Lines, which are part of a Copy writ by Mr. *Paul Aylward*.

> *What tho' of Terence, Seneca, we hear,*
> *And other modern Scenicks, in our Sphere;*
> *You I prefer.* Johnson *for all his Wit*
> *Could never paint out Times as you have hit*

> *The Manners of our Age: The Fame declines*
> *Of ne're enough prais'd* Shakespear *if thy lines*
> *Come to be publisht:* Beaum^t *&* Fletcher'*s skill*
> *Submits to yours, and your more learned Quill.*

[*Ibid.*, pp. 41-42.]

GERARD LANGBAINE, 1691

The Author [Henry Burnel] it seems, miscarried in a former Play, and therefore in imitation of *Ben Johnson* (whom he stiles *The Best of English Poets*) he has introduc'd his Play, by a Prologue spoken by an *Amazon*, with a Battle-Ax in her Hand; which succeeded to the Author's satisfaction.

[*Ibid.*, p. 42. The reference is to the Prologue to *Poetaster.*]

GERARD LANGBAINE, 1691

Amongst his [Cartwright's] Poems, there are several concerning the Dramatick Poets and their Writings, which must not be forgot: . . . . and One in Memory of *Ben Johnson*, which are so Excellent that the Publisher of Mr. *Carthwright*'s Poems speaks as in a Rapture in the Preface; *viz.* What had *Ben* said, had he read his own Eternity in that lasting Elegy given him by our Author.

[*Ibid.*, p. 55.]

GERARD LANGBAINE, 1691

I find them [Chapman's translations] highly extoll'd in an Old Copy call'd *a Censure of the Poets:* which having spoke of the Eminent Dramatick Poets, as *Shakespear, Johnson, Daniel,* &c. it adds of Translators as follows.

[*Ibid.*, p. 67.]

GERARD LANGBAINE, 1691

I hope it will not be thought Foreign to my purpose, to transcribe part of that Copy which he writ on this Admirable Poets [Cowley's] Death and Burial amongst the Ancient Poets. The whole Copy deserves to be engraved in Brass; but I shall here transcribe only what is to our purpose;

> *Old Mother Wit, and Nature gave*
> Shakespear, *and* Fletcher, *all they have;*

In Spencer, *and in* Johnson, *Art,*
Of slower Nature got the start;
But both in him so equal are,
None knows which bears the happy'st share;
To him no Author was unknown,
Yet what he wrote was all his own;
He melted not the ancient Gold,
Nor with Ben Johnson *did make bold*
To plunder all the Roman *Stores*
Of Poets, and of Orators:
Horace *his Wit, and* Virgil's *State,*
He did not steal, but emulate,
And when he would like them appear,
Their Garb, but not their Cloaths, did wear.

[*Ibid.*, pp. 82–83.]

GERARD LANGBAINE, 1691

He [Shakespeare] was as much a Stranger to French as Latine, (in which, if we believe *Ben Johnson*, he was a very small Proficient;).

[*Ibid.*, pp. 141–42.]

GERARD LANGBAINE, 1691

There are many other Hints from this Poem, that are inserted in this Play by Mr. *Dryden*, and which I should not have laid to his Charge had he not accus'd *Ben Johnson* of the same Crime [*i.e.*, borrowing].

[*Ibid.*, p. 157.]

GERARD LANGBAINE, 1691

Faithful Shepherdess, a Pastoral, writ by Mr. *Fletcher*, and commended by two Copies written by the Judicious *Beaumont*, and the Learned *Johnson*, which the Reader may read at the end of the Play.

[*Ibid.*, p. 208.]

GERARD LANGBAINE, 1691

Knight of the burning Pestle, a Comedy. This Play was in vogue some years since, it being reviv'd by the King's House, and a new Prologue (instead of the old One in prose) being spoken by Mrs. *Ellen Guin*. The bringing the Citizen and his Wife upon the Stage, was possibly in imitation of *Ben Johnson*'s *Staple of News*, who has introduc'd on the Stage Four Gossips, Lady-like attir'd, who remain during the whole Action, and criticise upon each Scene.

[*Ibid.*, p. 210.]

GERARD LANGBAINE, 1691

Our Author [Fletcher] joyn'd with the Famous *Johnson*, and *Middleton*, in a Comedy called *The Widow*. Of this Play, see more under the Name of *Ben. Johnson*.

[*Ibid.*, p. 218.]

GERARD LANGBAINE, 1691

Our Author [Heywood] in the Epistle both to this Play, and *The English Traveller*, pleads Modesty, in not exposing his Plays to the publick view of the World, in numerous Sheets and a large Volume, under the Title of *Works*, as others: By which he would seem tacitly to arraign some of his Cotemporaries for Ostentation, and want of Modesty. I am apt to believe, that our Author levell'd his Accusation at *Ben Johnson*: since no other Poet that I know of, in those day, gave his Plays, the pompous Title of *Works*; of which Sir *John Suckling* has taken notice in his *Sessions of the Poets*.

> *The first that broke silence was good Old* Ben,
> *Prepar'd before with* Canary *Wine;*
> *And he told them plainly that he deserv'd the Bays,*
> *For his were call'd* Works, *where others were but* Plays.

This puts me in mind of a Distick directed by some Poet of that Age, to *Ben Johnson;*

> *Pray, tell me* Ben, *where does the myst'ry lurk?*
> *What others call a* Play, *you call a* Work.

Which was thus answer'd by a Friend of his;

> *The Author's Friend thus for the Author say's,*
> Ben's *Plays are Works, when others Works are Plays.*

[*Ibid.*, pp. 263–64.]

GERARD LANGBAINE, 1691

His [James Howell's] *Letters*, which were formerly in four distinct Volumes, and are reduc'd into one; amongst which are several to *Ben. Johnson*, which speak their Intimacy.

[*Ibid.*, p. 279.]

GERARD LANGBAINE, 1691

[*The Conspiracy*, by Henry Killigrew] was afterwards acted on the *Blackfryars* Stage, and found the approbation of the most Excellent Persons of this kind of Writing which were in that time, if there were ever better in any time; *Ben Johnson*, being then alive, who gave a Testimony of this Peice even to be envy'd.

[*Ibid.*, p. 310.]

GERARD LANGBAINE, 1691

He [Thomas Killigrew, in *Thomaso or The Wanderer*] has made use of *Ben Johnson* considerably, for not only the Character of *Lopus*, but even the very Words are copied from *Johnson's Fox*, where *Vulpone* personates *Scoto* of *Mantua:* as the Reader will see by comparing Act 4. Sc. 2. of this Play, with that of the *Fox*, Act 2. Sc. 2. I do not believe that our Author design'd to conceal his Theft, since he is so just to acknowledge a Song against Jealousy, which he borrow'd, and was written by Mr. *Thomas Carew*, Cupbearer to King *Charles* the First; and sung in a Masque at *Whitehall*, *An.* 1633. 'This *Chorus* (says he) I presume to make use of here, because in the first design, 'twas writ at my request, upon a Dispute held betwixt Mrs. *Cicilia Crofts* and my self, where he was present; she being then Maid of Honor: this I have set down, lest any man should believe me so foolish as to steal such a Poem from so famous an Author; or so vain as to pretend to the making of it my self.' Certainly therefore, if he scrupled to rob Mr. *Carew*, he would much more Mr. *Johnson*, whose Fame as much exceeded the others, as his Writings and Compositions are better known: However it be, I am sure he is not the only Poet that has imp'd his Wings with Mr. *Johnson*'s Feathers, and if every Poet that borrows, knew as well as Mr. *Killegrew* how to dispose of it, 'twould certainly be very excusable.

[*Ibid.*, pp. 313–14.]

GERARD LANGBAINE, 1691

An Author [Christopher Marlowe] that was Cotemporary with the Incomparable *Shakespear*, and One who trod the Stage with Applause both from Queen *Elizabeth*, and King *James*. Nor was he accounted a less Excellent Poet by the Judicious *Johnson*.

[*Ibid.*, p. 342.]

GERARD LANGBAINE, 1691

Male Content, a Tragicomedy, the first Design being laid by Mr. *Webster*, was corrected and augmented by our Author [Marston], printed 4°. *Lond.* 1604. and dedicated in the following Stile to *Ben Johnson*: *Benjamini Johnsonio, Poetæ Elegantissimo, Gravissimo, Amico suo candido & cordato, Johannes Marston, Musarum Alumnus, asperam hanc suam Thaliam D. D.* Notwithstanding our Authors profession of Friendship, he afterwards could not refrain from reflecting on Mr. *Johnson*, on Account of his *Sejanus*, and *Catiline*, as the Reader will find in the perusal of his Epistle to *Sophonisba*: 'Know (says he) that I have not labour'd in this Poem to relate any thing as an Historian, but to enlarge every thing as a Poet. To transcribe Authors, quote Authorities, and translate *Latin* Prose Orations into *English* Blank-Verse, hath in this Subject been the least aim of my Studies.' That Mr. *Johnson* is here meant, will I presume be evident to any that are acquinted with his Works, and will compare the Orations in *Salust*, with those in *Catiline*. On what provocations our Author thus censured his Friend I know not, but this Custom has been practic'd in all Ages; the Old Proverb being verify'd in Poets as well as Whores, *Two of a Trade can never agree.*

[*Ibid.*, pp. 349–50.]

GERARD LANGBAINE, 1691

Mr. *Fitz-Geoffry* above-mention'd, in the Account of *Daniel* and *Johnson*, writ in their Commendation the following Hexastick.

[*Ibid.*, pp. 351–52.]

GERARD LANGBAINE, 1691

. . . . however pompous and splendid the *French* version . . . . , our *English* Translation [May's translation of Lucan's *Pharsalia*] is little inferiour to it; and is extreamly commended by our Famous *Johnson*, in a Copy of Verses prefix'd before the Book well worth the Reader's perusal.

[*Ibid.*, p. 364.]

GERARD LANGBAINE, 1691

I cannot refrain from trespassing yet further, by transcribing an Epigram writ to the Duke, on this Subject; but it being the produc-tion of the Immortal *Johnson*[e] I hope that alone will attone for the Digression.

[e] *Underwood, p. 223.*

[*Ibid.*, p. 389. The epigram quoted is Jonson's to the Earl of Newcastle on his horsemanship (Newdigate, *The Poems of Ben Jonson*, p. 166).]

GERARD LANGBAINE, 1691

As a proof of my Assertion [of the merits of the plays of Margaret Duchess of Newcastle], it may be proper in this place, before I give an Account of her Plays, to transcribe part of that general Prologue, the whole being too long to be here inserted.

> But Noble Readers, do not think my Plays
> Are such as have been writ in former Days;
> As Johnson, Shakespear, Beaumont, Fletcher writ;
> Mine want their Learning, Reading, Language, Wit;
> The Latin Phrases I could never tell,
> But Johnson could, which made him write so well.

[*Ibid.*, p. 391.]

GERARD LANGBAINE, 1691

There was another Copy of Verses writ by Mr. *Carew* to Mr. *Johnson*, on occasion of his Ode of Defiance, annexed to his Play of the *New-Inn:* See his Poems, 8°. p. 90.

[*Ibid.*, p. 414.]

GERARD LANGBAINE, 1691

As to the *Magick* in the Play [Shadwell's *Lancashire Witches*], our Author has given a very good Account in his Notes, from the Writings of *Delrio, Bodinus, Wierus, &c.* and I know nothing that we have in this Nature, in Dramatick Poetry, except *Ben. Johnson's Masque of Queens*, which is likewise explained by Annotations.

[*Ibid.*, p. 448.]

GERARD LANGBAINE, 1691

. . . . as no Man ever undertook to discover the Frailties of such Pretenders to this kind of Knowledge, before Mr. *Shadwell;* so none since Mr. *Johnson's* Time, ever drew so many different Characters of Humours, and with such Success.

[*Ibid.*, pp. 451–52.]

GERARD LANGBAINE, 1691

I hope now, our Author [Shadwell] is advanced to a Station, wherein he will endeavour to exert his *Muse;* and having found Encouragement from Majesty it self, aim at writing Dramatick Pieces, equal to those of Antiquity: which however applauded, have been paralelled (I was about to say excelled) by the Comedies of the Admirable *Johnson*.

[*Ibid.*, p. 452.]

GERARD LANGBAINE, 1691

The whole Book [the Shakespeare Folio] is dedicated to the Earls of *Pembroke* and *Montgomery:* being usher'd into the World with several Copies of Verses; but none more valued than those Lines made by *Ben Johnson;* which being too long to be here transcribed, I shall leave them to be perus'd by the Reader, with his Works.

[*Ibid.*, pp. 454–55.]

GERARD LANGBAINE, 1691

Sr. *John Sucklin* had so great a Value for our Author, that (as Mr. *Dryden* observes in his *Dramatick Essay*) he preferred him to *Johnson:*

[*Ibid.*, p. 467.]

GERARD LANGBAINE, 1691

He [James Shirley] had a great Veneration for his Predecessors, as may be seen by his Prologue to the *Sisters;* and particularly for Mr. *Johnson*, whom in an Epistle to the Earl of *Rutland*, he stiles, *Our acknowledg'd Master, the Learned* Johnson.

[*Ibid.*, pp. 474–75.]

GERARD LANGBAINE, 1691

B. J.

The Author of a Tragedy, call'd *Guy of Warwick*, which I have once seen in quarto *Lond.*—and the Gentleman that shew'd it me, told me it was writ by *Ben Johnson;* tho' by that little I read, I guess'd it to be writ by a Pen far inferiour to that Great Master in *Poetry.*

[*Ibid.*, p. 519.]

GERARD LANGBAINE, 1691

Marcus Tullius Cicero, that Famous *Roman* Orator, his Tragedy; printed quarto *Lond.* 1651. I know not whether ever this Play was acted; but it seems to me to be written in Imitation of *Ben. Johnson*'s *Cataline.*

[*Ibid.*, p. 540.]

THOMAS SHADWELL, 1691

Sir Will. He'll be worse to us two than *Doll Common* to Face and Subtile: But something must be done to deliver these pretty Rogues.

[*The Scowrers* (1691), IV, i, p. 33.]

[WILLIAM WALSH], 1691

You would think it very hard, that *Alexander* and *Caesar* should quit the Art of War, because some *Thrasoes* and bragging Bullies pretended to it as well as they; and *Virgil* and *Horace* would take it very ill, that you shou'd damn all sorts of Poetry, because of the *Bavius's* and *Maevius's*, who set up for it; and whatever reason you wou'd give against the being a Minister of State, I dare say Sir *Politick Woudbee's* aiming at it, wou'd be none.

[*A Dialogue concerning Women, Being a Defence of the Sex* (1691), p. 63.]

ANTHONY À WOOD, 1691

Afterwards he [Thomas Randolph] commenced Master of Arts, in which Degree he was incorporated at *Oxon*, became famous for his ingenuity, an adopted Son of *Benj. Johnson*, and accounted one of the most pregnant wits of his age.

[*Athenae Oxonienses* (1691–92), I, 196.]

ANTHONY À WOOD, 1691

This is all, of truth, that I know of *Nich. Hill*, only that his name is mentioned by[(o)] *Ben. Johnson* thus.

——— *Those Atomi ridiculous,*
Whereof old Democrite, and Hill Nicholis,
One said, the other swore, the World consists.

(o) In his *Epigrams* numb. 134.

[*Ibid.*, p. 313.]

ANTHONY À WOOD, 1691

Which book [Coryate's *Crudities*, 1611] was then usher'd into the world by an *Odcombian banquet*, consisting of near 60 copies of excellent verses made by the Poets of that time: (which did very much advantage the Sale of the book) Among them were *Ben. Johnson*, Sir *Jo. Harrington* of *Kelston* near *Bathe*, *Dudl. Digges* afterwards Master of the *Rolls*, *Rich. Martin* Recorder of *London*, *Laur. Whittaker*, *Hugh Holland* the traveller, *Jo. Hoskyns* Sen. *Inigo Jones*, the surveyour, *Christop. Brook*, *Rich. Corbet* of *Ch. Ch. Joh. Chapman*, *Thom. Campian* Dr. of Phys. *Jo. Owen* the Epigrammatist, *Sam. Page* of *C. C. C. Tho. Bastard* of *New* coll. *Tho. Farnaby* sometimes of *Mert.* coll. *Jo. Donne, Mich. Drayton, Joh. Davys* of *Hereford, Hen. Peacham,* &c.

[*Ibid.,* p. 359.]

ANTHONY À WOOD, 1691

There was no person in his time more celebrated for ingenuity than *R. Martin,* none more admired by *Selden,* Serjeant *Hoskins, Ben. Johnson,* &c. than he; the last of which dedicated his Comedy to him called *The Poetaster.*

[*Ibid.,* p. 374.]

ANTHONY À WOOD, 1691

Our author *Daniel* had also a good faculty in setting out a Mask or a Play, and was wanting in nothing that might render him acceptable to the great and ingenious men of his time, as to Sir *Joh. Harrington* the Poet, *Camden the learned,* Sir *Rob. Cotton,* Sir *H. Spelman, Edm. Spencer, Ben. Johnson, John Stradling,* little *Owen* the Epigrammatist, &c.

[*Ibid.,* p. 379.]

ANTHONY À WOOD, 1691

The second part, or book [of *Britannia's Pastorals*], was printed at *Lond.* 1616. fol. and then commended to the World by various copies made by *John Glanvill,* (whom I shall mention elsewhere, for his sufficiences in the Common Law), *Joh. Davies* of *Hereford, George Wither* of *Linc.* Inn, *Ben. Johnson, Thom. Wenman* of the *Inner Temple,* &c.

[*Ibid.,* p. 419.]

ANTHONY À WOOD, 1691

He [John Davies] was held in great esteem by the noted Scholars of his time, among whom were *Will. Camden,* Sir *Jo. Harrington* the Poet, *Ben. Johnson, Jo. Selden, Facete Hoskyns, R. Corbet* of Ch. Ch. and others.

[*Ibid.,* p. 431.]

ANTHONY À WOOD, 1691

All which [John Beaumont's works] were collected together, after the authors death by his Son, Sir *Joh. Beaumont*, Bt. and were printed with the former Poems in 1629. being then usher'd into the world by the commendation-Poems of *Tho. Nevill, Tho. Hawkyns, Benj. Johnson, Mich. Drayton, Philip King*, Son of the B. of *London*, &c.

[*Ibid.*, pp. 446–47.]

ANTHONY À WOOD, 1691

In all which, being eminent, he [Donne] was therefore celebrated, and his memory had in great veneration by the Wits and Virtuosi of his time, among whom were *Ben. Johnson*, Sir *Lucius Cary* afterwards L. *Faulkland, Sydney Godolphin, Jasp. Mayne, Edward Hyde* afterwards L. Chancellour, *Endymion Porter, Arthur Wilson*, &c.

[*Ibid.*, p. 474.]

ANTHONY À WOOD, 1691

Afterwards he [Robert Hayman] retired to *Lincolns* Inn without the honour of a degree, studied for a time the municipal Law, but his Genie being well known to be poetical, fell into acquaintance with, and received encouragement to proceed in his studies from, *Mich. Drayton, Ben. Johnson, John Owen* the Epigrammatist, *George Wither* the puritanical Satyrist, *John Vicars* of *Ch. Ch.* Hospital, &c.

[*Ibid.*, p. 494.]

ANTHONY À WOOD, 1691

His [Henry Cary's] first years of reason were spent in Poetry and polite learning, into the first of which he made divers plausible sallies, which caused him therefore to be admired by the Poets of those times, particularly, first by *Ben. Johnson*, who hath an Epigram on him in his *Underwood*, in the second vol. of his works.

[*Ibid.*, p. 501.]

ANTHONY À WOOD, 1691

'Twas he [John Hoskyns] that polish'd *Ben. Johnson* the Poet and made him speak clean, whereupon he ever after called our au-

thor *Father Hoskyns*, and 'twas he that view'd and review'd the
History of the World, written by Sir *W. Raleigh*, before it went to
the Press.

[*Ibid.*, p. 523.]

ANTHONY À WOOD, 1691

Virgin Martyr, Tr. *Lond.* 1631. 1661. qu. In this Trag. he [Philip
Massinger] was assisted by *Tho. Dekker* a high flier of wit, even
against *Ben Johnson* himself in his Com. called *The untrussing of
The humerous Poet.*

[*Ibid.*, p. 536.]

ANTHONY À WOOD, 1691

[1616] Jul. 9. *Francis Stewart* of *Ch. Ch.* (Knight of the *Bath*) one
of the Sons of the Earl of *Murrey*, was actually created Master of
Arts.—He was a learned Gentleman, was one of Sir *Walt. Raleigh*'s
Club at the *Meremaid* Tavern in *Friday* street in *London*, and much
venerated by *Ben. Johnson*, who dedicated to him his Comedy
called *The silent Woman.*

[*Ibid.*, p. 824.]

ANTHONY À WOOD, 1691

[Christopher Brooke] setled in *Lincolns* Inn, purposely to advance himself in the municipal Law, where he became known to,
and admired by, *Joh. Selden, Ben. Johnson, Mich. Drayton, Will.
Browne, George Withers* and *Joh. Davies* of *Hereford*, especially after
he had published *An Elegy consecrated to the never dying memory of
Henry Prince of Wales.* Lond. 1613. qu.

[*Ibid.*, p. 841.]

ANTHONY À WOOD, 1691

To the said Edition [the third edition of Robert Waring's *Effigies
Amoris*] is joyned our Authors *Carmen Lapidorium*, written to the
memory of *Ben. Johnson*, which *Griffith* finding miserably mangled
in *Jonsonus virbius*, or *Verses on the death of Ben. Johnson*, he, with
his own hand, restored it to its former perfection and lustre, by
freeing it from the errors of the Press.

[*Ibid.*, II, 143.]

ANTHONY À WOOD, 1691

KENELME DIGBY, the magazine of all Arts, ... was born at *Gothurst* on the eleventh day of *July* 1603, (1 *Jac.* 1.) yet *Ben. Johnson* for rhyme sake will have[f] it *June*, thus;

> *Witness thy action done at Scanderoon*
> *Upon thy birth day the eleventh of June.*

.... In the year 1628 being then Admiral of a Fleet going to the *Levant* .... he acquired great honour by his gallant comportment at *Algier*, in reescating many English Slaves, and by bearing up so bravely in the resolute Onset on the Venetian Fleet in the Bay of *Scanderoon*, and making the *Pantolini* to know themselves and him better. This Onset was made (as 'tis reported) on the eleventh of *June* (his birth-day, as *Ben. Joh.* will have it) yet a Pamphlet that was publish'd the same year, giving an account of all the Transactions of that Fight, tells us it was on the 16 of the same month; which if true, then the fortune of that day is again mar'd.

[f] In his *Underwoods*, pag. 243.

[*Ibid.*, pp. 238-39.]

ANTHONY À WOOD, 1691

After the death of *Ben. Johnson* he [Davenant] was created Poet Laureat, *an.* 1637.

[*Ibid.*, p. 293.]

ANTHONY À WOOD, 1691

The verses in the said book called *Annalia Dubrensia* were composed by several Poets, some of which were then the chiefest of the Nation, as *Mich. Drayton* Esq. *Tho. Randolph* of *Cambridg, Ben. Johnson, Owen Feltham* Gent. Capt. *Joh. Mennes, Shakerley Marmion* Gent. *Tho. Heywood* Gent, &c. Others of lesser note were *Joh. Trussell* Gent. who continued *Sam. Daniel's History of England, Joh. Monson* Esq. *Feryman Rutter* of *Oriel* Coll, *Will. Basse* of *Moreton* near *Thame* in *Oxfordshire*, sometimes a Retainer to the Lord *Wenman* of *Thame Parke. Will. Denny* Esq. &c.

[*Ibid.*, p. 614.]

ANONYMOUS, 1692?

Clients, Precarious Titles May Debate;
The Lawyer only Thrives, grows Rich and Great:
The Golden Fee alone is his Delight;
Gold makes yᵉ Dubious Cause go wrong or Right.
Nay; rather than his Modesty he'll hide,
He'll take a Private Dawb o' t'other side:
Heraldry ne'er Devis'd a fitter Crest,
Than Sly Volpone so demurely drest:
Lawyers by subtle querks, their Clients fleece,
So when old Reynard Preaches, 'ware yᵉ Geese.

[Printed below an engraving of 1692(?) called *The Lawyers Arms. Catalogue of Prints and Drawings in the British Museum, Division I, Political and Personal Satires* (1873), II, 42. Quoted by Robert Gale Noyes, "Volpone; or, the Fox—the Evolution of a Nickname," *Harvard Studies and Notes in Philology and Literature*, XVI (1934), 164–65.]

ANONYMOUS, 1692

Shakespear (Will) B. at Stratford in Warwick-Sh. was in some sort a Compound of three eminent Poets, Martial, Ovid and Plautus the Comedian. His Learning being very little, nature seems to have practised her best Rules in his Production. The Genius of this our Poet was Jocular, by the quickness of his wit and Invention; so that *Heraclitus* himself might afford a smile at his comedies. Many were the Witty Combats between him and Ben. Johnson. He died 1616 and buried at Stratford.

[*An Historical History of England and Wales in Three Parts* (1692), quoted by John Munro, "More Shakspere Allusions," *Modern Philology*, XIII, 169–70. The passage is based on Fuller's *Worthies*.]

NICHOLAS BRADY, 1692

But why should *English*, who in both excel,
And always us'd to feed, and judge so well,
Be now content on Snails or Herbs to dine;
And for light Kick-Shaws quit the lusty Chine?
Were our great *Ben* alive, how would he rage!
How would he scourge the folly of this Age,
And lash the Vermine who infect the Stage!

Who with so little Nature, and less Art,
A Theater would to a Booth convert:
For shame redeem your Credit, and forbear
To favour Drolls, such Piteous *Smithfield* Ware:
Try if to Night you can digest a Play
Cook'd in the plain, but wholesom *English* way.

["Prologue, Spoke by Mr. Betterton," *The Rape, or, The Innocent Impostors* (1692).]

THOMAS D'URFEY, 1692

Sir *Law*. Well, for my part, since chance must rule the Roast, in spite of all Endeavours, I'll be a fond doting Fool no longer,—Let my Son *Bias* be pox'd if he pleases; my hopeful Son *Solon* hang himself in his hopeful Wifes Garters, And let my Daughter turn *Doll* Common to the Army.

[*The Marriage-Hater Match'd* (1693; 1st ed., 1692), V, 3, p. 52.]

SIR ROBERT HOWARD, 1692

The manner of the Stage-Entertainments have differ'd in all Ages; and as it has encreas'd in use, it has enlarg'd it self in business: The general manner of Plays among the Ancients we find in *Seneca*'s Tragedies for serious Subjects, and in *Terence* and *Plautus* for the Comical; in which latter we see some pretences to Plots, though certainly short of what we have seen in some of Mr *Johnson*'s Plays; and for their Wit, especially *Plautus*, I suppose it suited much better in those days than it would do in ours; for were their Plays strictly Translated, and Presented on our Stage, they would hardly bring as many Audiences as they have now Admirers.

["To the Reader," *Five New Plays* (1692), sig. A₂^v.]

SIR ROBERT HOWARD, 1692

If these Premises be granted, 'tis no partiality to conclude, That our *English* Plays justly challenge the Preheminence; yet I shall as candidly acknowledge, That our best Poets have differed from other Nations (though not so happily) in usually mingling and interweaving Mirth and Sadness through the whole Course of their

Plays, *Ben Johnson* only excepted, who keeps himself entire to one Argument; and I confess I am now convinc'd in my own Judgment, That it is most proper to keep the Audience in one entire disposition both of Concern and Attention; for when Scenes of so different Natures immediately succeed one another, 'tis probable the Audience may not so suddenly recollect themselves, as to start into an enjoyment of the Mirth, or into a concern for the Sadness:

[*Ibid.*, sig. A₃.]

Sir Robert Howard, 1692

. . . . and when I consider how severe the former age has been to some of the best of Mʳ *Johnson*'s never to be equal'd Comedies, I cannot but wonder why any Poet should speak of former times, but rather acknowledge that the want of Abilities in this Age is largely supply'd with the Mercies of it.

[*Ibid.*, sig. A₄ᵛ.]

Thomas Rymer, 1692

It was then a strange imagination in *Ben. Johnson*, to go stuff out a Play with *Tully*'s Orations. And in *Seneca*, to think his dry Morals, and a tedious train of Sentences might do feats, or have any wonderful operation in the *Drama*.

[*A Short View of Tragedy* (1693, for 1692), p. 6.]

Thomas Rymer, 1692

Amongst the Moderns, our *Rehearsal* is some resemblance of his *Frogs*: The *Vertuoso*'s Character, and *Ben Johnson*'s *Alchymist* give some shadow of his *Clouds*; but nowhere, peradventure wanders so much of his Spirit, as in the *French Rabelais*.

[*Ibid.*, p. 24.]

Thomas Rymer, 1692

Ben. Johnson, knew to distinguish men and manners, at an other rate. In *Catiline* we find our selves in *Europe*, we are no longer in the *Land of Savages*, amongst Blackamoors, Barbarians, and Monsters. The Scene is Rome and first on the Stage appears *Sylla*'s Ghost.

Dost thou not feel me, Rome? Not yet?

One would, in reason, imagine the Ghost is in some publick open place, upon some Eminence, where Rome is all within his view: But it is a surprizing thing to find that this ratling Rodomontado speech is in a dark, close, private sleeping hole of *Catliine*'s [*sic*],

Yet the *Chorus*, is of all wonders the strangest. The *Chorus* is always present on the Stage, privy to, and interested [*sic*] in all that passes and thereupon make their Reflections to Conclude the several *Acts*.

Sylla's Ghost, tho' never so big, might slide in at the Key-hole; but how comes the *Chorus* into *Catilins* Cabinet?

Aurelia is soon after with him too, but the Poet had perhaps provided her some Truckle-bed in a dark Closet by him.

In short, it is strange that *Ben*, who understood the turn of Comedy so well; and had found the success, should thus grope in the dark, and jumble things together without head or tail, without any rule or proportion, without any reason or design. Might not the *Acts of the Apostles*, or a Life in *Plutarch*, be as well Acted, and as properly called a Tragedy, as any History of a Conspiracy?

Corneille tells us, in the *Examen* of his *Melite*, that when first he began to write, he thought there had been no Rules: So had no guide but a little *Common sence*, with the Example of Mr. *Hardy*, and some others, not more regular than he. This *Common sence* (says he) *which was all my rule, brought me to find out the unity of Action to imbroyl four Lovers by one and the same intreague. Ben. Johnson*, besides his Common sence to tell him that the *Vnity of Action* was necessary; had stumbl'd (I know not how) on a *Chorus;* which is not to be drawn through a Key-hole, to be lugg'd about, or juggl'd with an *hocus pocus* hither and thither; nor stow'd in a garret, nor put into quarters with the *Breentford* Army, so must of necessity keep the Poet to *unity of place;* And also to some Conscionable *time*, for the representation: Because the *Chorus* is not to be trusted out of sight, is not to eat or drink till they have given up their Verdict, and the *Plaudite* is over.

One would not talk of rules, or what is regular with *Shakespear*, or any followers, in the Gang of the *Strouling* Fraternity; but it is lamentable that *Ben. Johnson*, his Stone and his Tymber, however otherwise of value, must lye a miserable heap of ruins, for want of

Architecture, or some Son of *Vitruvius*, to joyn them together. He had red *Horace*, had Translated that to the *Pisones:*

> *Nec verbum verbo curabis reddere, fidus interpres.—*

Ben.—*Being a Poet, thou may'st feign, create,*
      Not care, as thou wouldst faithfully translate,
      To render word for word—

And this other precept.

> *Nec circa vilem, patulumque morabe is Orbem.*

Ben.—*The vile, broad-trodden ring forsake.*

What is there material in this *Catiline*, either in the *Manners.* in the *Thoughts*, or in the *Expression*, (three parts of Tragedy) which is not word for word translation? In the *Fable*, or Plot (which is the first, and principal part) what see we, but the *vile broad trodden ring?* *Vile*, *Horace* calls it, as a thing below, and too mean for any man of wit to busie his head withal. *Patulum*, he calls it, because it is obvious, and easie for any body to do as much as that comes to. 'Tis but to plodd along, step by step in the same tract: 'Tis drudgery only for the blind Horse in a Mill. No Creature sound of Wind and Limb, but wou'd chuse a nobler Field, and a more generous Career.

Homer, we find, slips sometime into a *Tract* of *Scripture*, but his *Pegasus* is not stabl'd there, presently up he springs, mounts aloft, is on the wing, no earthly bounds, or barriers to confine him.

For *Ben*, to sin thus against the clearest light and conviction, argues a strange stupidity: It was bad enough in him, against his Judgment and Conscience, to interlard so much fiddle-faddle, Comedy, and *Apocryphal* matters in the History: Because, forsooth,

> *—his nam plebecula gaudet.*

Where the Poet has chosen a subject of importance sufficient and proper for Tragedy, there is no room for this petty interlude and diversion. Had some Princes come express from *Salankemen* (remote as it is) to give an account of the battel, whilst the story was hot and new, and made a relation accurate, and distinctly, with all the pomp, and advantage of the Theatre, wou'd the Audience have suffer'd a Tumbler or Baboon, a Bear, or Rope dancer to have withdrawn their attention; or to have interrupted the Narrative; tho' it had held as long as a Dramatick Representation. Nor at that time wou'd they thank a body for his quibbles, or wit out of season: This mans Feather, or that Captains Embroidered Coat might not be touched upon but in a very short *Parenthesis*.

[*Ibid.*, pp. 159–64.]

[JOHN DUNTON], 1691-96

'Tis said, our Nation is *richer* in *Humour* than any in *Europe;* and tho the Stage has large *Supplies* from it, yet it can never be *exhausted*. If it be so, *Ben. Johnson* stands fairest for *Treasurer*, tho he need not have gone farther than any one of his *Merry Wives of* Windsor to have employ'd him all his Life: He needed but have *shown one Face* in one *Play* to have had sufficient *Variety*.

[*Athenian Sport* (1707), pp. 93–94; the book is a condensation of *Athenian Mercury*, published between 1691 and 1696.]

[JOHN DUNTON], 1691-96

Tho I'm the *softest Creature in Nature*, yet am I bad Company for Ladies, for they'l sit a whole day in talking of nothing but the *newest Fashions* (and how much they're admir'd by this Beau and t'other Beau)—How can I have Patience to hear this, when I'm positive *there's nothing new?* And when they ask me when I saw any *new Play*, I bluntly tell 'em, there is no such thing: For you know, Madam, and so wou'd they, if they'd look into old Authors, that *Dryden* stole from *Shakespear*, and *Shakespear* from *Ben. Johnson;* and they all so steal from one another, that there's no Wit in any *Play*, but what we had fifty years ago.

[*Ibid.*, p. 335.]

[JOHN DUNTON], 1691-96

All this is no *new Thing*, ... *To swear and forswear*, and to play at fast and loose with a Crown (as a late Author observes) *is no new thing*. Neither is it any *new thing* for Men to cheat, slander, duel, whore; and to pick a Pocket under the Gallows, is a *Custom as old as* Tyburn.—Neither is it a *new thing to see a Man accuse himself* (for a guilty Conscience e'nt easy without it) or for Men of a mean

Birth to grow proud, if they grow rich, and to forget their Duty both to God and Man: This is but *Shakespear* and *Ben. Johnson* brought again upon the Stage.

[*Ibid.*, p. 337.]

ANONYMOUS, 1693

. . . . many of the Spectators took several of the Bones and carried them away, some of which are now to be seen at the *Ben-Johnson*'s Head, near St. *Brides* Church by *Fleetstreet*.

[*The Cruel Midwife* (1693), p. 6, from *The Pepys Ballads*, ed. Hyder Edward Rollins (1931), VII, 9.]

H. C., 1693

[The jest printed under Anonymous, 1660, from *A Choice Banquet of Witty Jests* is reprinted in H. C.'s *England's Jests Refin'd and Improv'd* (1693); see Thornton S. Graves, "Jonson in the Jest Books," in *Manly Anniversary Studies*, p. 130, n. 1.]

H. C., 1693

Coming up to London, Randolph entered the Devil Tavern, where Jonson was drinking in the company of Daniel, Drayton, and Sylvester. "Come in, John Bopeep," exclaimed Ben, who saw Randolph hesitating to enter. Shortly afterward Randolph evened scores by reciting the following lines in compliance with the agreement that the composer of the best extempore verses should be excused from paying his part of the bill:

> *I* John Bopeep, *to you four Sheep,*
> *With each one his good Fleece:*
> *If you are willing to pay your five Shilling,*
> *'Tis fifteen Pence apiece.*

[*England's Jests Refin'd and Improv'd* (1693), No. 178, from Graves, *loc. cit.*, p. 133.]

THOMAS D'URFEY, 1693

Sophronia. Instead of heiresses and blooming Brides of fifty thousand pounds, stick to your old Doll Commons of the Town, and cater as you used for half a crown.

[*The Richmond Heiress* (1693), V, v. Noted by C. B. Graham, "Jonson Allusions in Restoration Comedy," *Review of English Studies*, XV (1939), 203-4.]

WILLIAM FREKE, 1693

After all, Mr. Johnson, *and Mr.* Rimer's *Mettled* Stiles *to me*, *look with full as much Native Beauty as ever a slow-pac'd Don's in the Vniverse: Every thing in its way;* '*tis as natural for the Cholerick, and the Sanguine, to be daring and sprightly, as 'tis for the* Melancholy *and* Phlegmatick *to be heavy and dull.*

[Preface to *Select Essays Tending to the Universal Reformation of Learning* (1693), sig. A6.]

JOHN HACKET, 1693

But what the Region wants in Fatness of Soil, is requited by the Generous Spirits of the Inhabitants, a far greater Honour than much Clay and Dirt. I light upon it in the Invention of a Masque, Presented before King *James* at *Whitehall, An.* 1619. that our Laureat-Poet *Ben. Johnson* hath let some weighty Words drop from him, to the Honour of that Nation, and I take them as a serious Passage, and will own them, That the Country is a Seed-Plot of honest Minds and Men. What Lights of Learning hath *Wales* sent forth for our Schools? What Industrious Students of our Laws? What Able Ministers of Justice? Whence hath the Crown in all times better Servitors, more Liberal of their Lives and Fortunes? And I know I have their good Leave to say, That the Honour of *Wales* shin'd forth abroad in the Lustre of such a Native as this; and I add what *Pliny* writes to *Sabinus* of the *Firmians*, among whom he was born, *Credibile est optimos esse inter quos tu talis extiteris,* Lib. 6. Epist.

[*Scrinia reserata: A Memorial Offer'd to the Great Deservings of John Williams, D. D.* (1693), Part I, p. 5. The lines are quoted from *For the Honour of Wales,* ll. 392–97.]

JOHN HACKET, 1693

So if all Counsels, offer'd to Princes, were spread out before many Witnesses, Ear-Wiggs that buzz what they think fit in the retir'd Closet, durst not infect the Royal Audience with pernicious Glozing, for fear of Scandal or Punishment. Well did the Best of our

Poets, of this Century, decipher a Corrupt Court, in his *Under-woods*, Pag. 227.

> *When scarce we hear a publick Voice alive;*
> *But whisper'd Counsels, and those only thrive.*

[*Ibid.*, p. 85.]

JOHN HACKET, 1693

As our Poet Mr. *Johnson* says upon Prince *Henry's* Barriers, *He doth but scourge himself his Sword that draws. Without a Purse, a Counsel, and a Cause.*

[*Ibid.*, Part II, p. 13.]

JOHN HACKET, 1693

At last the difficulty was overcome; the Petitioners had one Answer from the King, and look'd for a fuller, and had it in the end: So much sooner had been so much better; as our Poet *Johnson* writes to *Sir E. Sackvile*, of some mens Good-turns, *They are so long a coming, and so hard.* When any Deed is forc'd, the Grace is marr'd.

[*Ibid.*, p. 77.]

JOHN HACKET, 1693

With such Diversions our *Job* compounded with his Sorrows, to pay them not the half he owed them: And whatsoever Face thy Fate puts on, shrink not, nor start not, but be always one, as Laureat *Johnson* sings it in his *Underwoods*.

[*Ibid.*, p. 127.]

JOHN HACKET, 1693

And some of the chief Lords of that Knot made him such Offers of Honour and Wealth for his share, if he would give way to their Alterations, that they would buy him, if his Faith had been salaeble [*sic*], with any Price. The worst Requital that could be propounded to an honest man, and of the narrowest, to scantle their Blessing to him alone, that labour'd for a Publick Good: As *Ben. Johnson* hath put it finely into his *Underwoods*, p. 117.

> ———*I wish the Sun should shine*
> *On all mens Fruits and Flowers, as well as mine.*

[*Ibid.*, p. 144.]

John Hacket, 1693

But where were those Earls and Barons that sided with the Bishops before? Shrunk, absent, or silent.

> ———*They that are wise,*
> *Leave falling Buildings, fly to them that rise.*

Or as *Plautus* in *Stych.* as neat in his Comick Phrase as *Johnson*, *Si labant res lassae, itidem amici collabajcunt.*

[*Ibid.*, p. 181.]

John Hacket, 1693

It is fit to serve Kings in things lawful with undiscoursed Obedience, which *Climachus* calls *Sepulchrum voluntatis:*

> ———*For we deny*
> *What Kings do ask, if we ask why,*

says our Master Poet *Johnson.*

[*Ibid.*, p. 217.]

Henry Higden, 1693

I may well say [the play was] *Vnadorn'd*, for there was nothing done for the advantage or decoration of this Play: not a farthing expended. When I had given them leave to Act it, I was told it was theirs, and they would Cooke it according to their own humour. Some of the *Politick would be* of the Coffee-house had given it an ill Name and Caracter and were glad to see it succeed accordingly.

[Preface to *The Wary Widdow* (1693).]

Henry Higden, 1693

Nur[*se*]. It will be dangerous in you to oppose the Currant of your Fathers humour and cross his design: and you will find him *Resolute Batt* when he sets upon it. Therefore it will be best to comply with his humour and dissemble obedience.

[*Ibid.*, Act II, p. 11. See *Bartholomew Fair*, III, 4, ll. 40–41: "*Cok*[*es*.] Good *Numps*, hold that little tongue o' thine, and saue it a labour. I am resolute *Bat*, thou know'st."]

[Sir William Temple], 1693

Mr. *Dryden*, I remember, amongst several other judicious Remarks that so frequently occur in his *Essay upon Dramatick Poetry*, has this of the famous *Johnson*, which in my Opinion (and I think I have not lost all my Taste in my Old Age) is admirable. *Ben*, says he, never introduces any Person upon the Stage, but first of all informs his Reader of his Character, and by that means bespeaks his attention. As for instance if a *La-fool* is to be brought in, he makes a Foot-boy tell *True-wit*, that one Monsieur *La-fool* is coming to pay him a Visit; and before he makes his appearance, *True-wit* lets his Friends know, and consequently, by them, the Audience, what sort of a Gentleman *La-fool* is, and what are his best Qualities.

[*An Answer to a Scurrilous Pamphlet* (1693), p. 32.]

Thomas Wright, 1693

Sir Maur. But I tell you Lady, that I will have a Reformation in my House, that this Plague of Wit has infected all my Servants, even my little Boy, forsooth, cannot turn the Spit now without a *Pharamond*, or a *Cassandra* in his hand; if I call for Drink, the Butler brings me a *Spencer*, or a *Ben Johnson*.

[*The Female Vertuoso's* (1693), Act III, p. 26.]

Anonymous, 1694

Something beyond the uncall'd drudging Tribe,
Beyond what BEN cou'd write, or I describe.

["A Satyr against *Poetry*," in Charles Gildon's *Chorus Poetarum* (1694), p. 122.]

Sir Thomas Pope Blount, 1694

I think, says *Dryden*, there's no folly so great in any *Poet* of our Age, as the Superfluity and Waste of *Wit* was in some of our *Predecessors:* particularly we may say of *Fletcher* and of *Shakespear*, what was said of *Ovid*, *In omni ejus ingenio, faciliùs quod rejici, quàm quod adjici potest, invenies.* The contrary of which was true in *Virgil*, and our Incomparable *Johnson*. Dryd. *Pref. to the* Mock-Astrologer.

[*De re poetica: or Remarks upon Poetry* (1694), p. 20.]

SIR THOMAS POPE BLOUNT, 1694

The *Poetick Licence*, says *Dryden*, in his *Apology for Heroick Poetry*, is that *Birthright*, which is deriv'd to *Poets*, from their great *Fore-fathers*, even from *Homer* down to *Ben*.

[*Ibid.*, p. 31.]

SIR THOMAS POPE BLOUNT, 1694

When Shakespear, Johnson, Fletcher, *rul'd the Stage,*
They took so bold a Freedom with the Age,
That there was scarce a Knave, *or* Fool, *in Town,*
Of any Note, but had his Picture *shown.*

. . . .

Earl of Rochester in Defence of *Satyr*

[*Ibid.*, p. 44. Blount probably took the passage from the 1680 Antwerp edition of Rochester's poems, where it occurs on p. 45. Wood says, however (Bliss ed. *Fasti* [*Athenae Oxonienses*, Vol. IV] II, 294), that the lines are by Sir Carr Scrope.]

SIR THOMAS POPE BLOUNT, 1694

They who have best succeeded on the Stage,
Have still conform'd their Genius to their Age.
Thus Johnson *did* Mechanick *Humour show,*
When Men were dull, and Conversation low.
Then, Comedy *was faultless, but 'twas course:*
Cobb's *Tankard was a Jest, and* Otter's *Horse.*
And as their Comedy, *their* Love *was mean:*
Except, by chance, in some one labour'd Scene,
Which must atone for an ill-written Play.
They rose; *but at their height could seldom stay.*
Fame *then was cheap, and the first Comer sped;*
And they have kept it since, by being dead.
But were they now *to write when Criticks weigh*
Each Line, and ev'ry Word, throughout a Play,
None of 'em, no not Johnson, *in his height*
Could pass, without allowing Grains for weight.

. . . .

Dryd. Epilogue to the 2d Part of *Granada*.

[*Ibid.*, p. 88.]

Sir Thomas Pope Blount, 1694

Dryden tells us, That *Johnson*, *Fletcher*, and *Shakespear*, are honour'd, and almost ador'd by us, as they deserve; Neither do I know (*says he*) any so presumptuous of themselves as to contend with them; Yet give me leave to say thus much, without Injury to their Ashes, that not only *we* shall never equal *them*, but *they* could never equal *themselves*, were they to rise and write again.

[*Ibid.*, p. 89.]

Sir Thomas Pope Blount, 1694

This way of Writing in *Verse*, says *Dryden*, they have only left free to us; our Age is arriv'd to a perfection in it, which *they* never knew; and which (if we may guess by what of theirs we have seen in *Verse*; as the *Faithful Shepherdess*, and *Sad Shepherd:*) 'tis probable they never could have reach'd. For the *Genius* of every Age is different; and though *ours* excel in *this*, I deny not, says *Dryden*, but that to imitate Nature in that Perfection which they did in *Prose*, is a greater Commendation, than to write in *Verse* exactly. Dryd, *Essay of* Dram. Poesie, *pag.* 45, 46.

[*Ibid.*, pp. 89–90.]

Sir Thomas Pope Blount, 1694

I will not (says *Burnet*) provoke the present Masters of the Stage, by preferring the Authors of the last Age to them: for though they all acknowledge that *they* come far short of *Ben. Johnson*, *Beaumont*, and *Fletcher*, yet I believe they are better pleas'd to say this *themselves*, than to have it observ'd by *others*.

[*Ibid.*, p. 91.]

Sir Thomas Pope Blount, 1694

At this time with us many great Wits flourish'd, but *Ben Johnson*, I think, says *Rimer*, had all the *Critical* Learning to himself; and till of late Years *England* was as free from *Criticks*, as it is now from Wolves.

[*Ibid.*, pp. 113–14.]

SIR THOMAS POPE BLOUNT, 1694

The *Anonymous Translator* of St. *Euvremont*'s mixed Essays, in his Preface, speaking of Epick Poems, observes, That . . . . Criticism came but very lately in fashion amongst us; without doubt *Ben. Johnson* had a large stock of *Critical* Learning; *Spencer* had studied *Homer*, and *Virgil*, and *Tasso*, yet he was mis-led, and debauch'd by *Ariosto*, as Mr. *Rimer* judiciously observes; *Davenant* gives some stroaks of great Learning and Judgment, yet he is for unbeaten Tracks, new Ways, and undiscover'd Seas; *Cowley* was a great Master of the *Ancients*, and had the true *Genius* and Character of a *Poet*; yet this nicety and boldness of *Criticism* was a stranger all this time to our Climate.

[*Ibid.*, p. 114.]

SIR THOMAS POPE BLOUNT, 1694

Winstanley tells us, That *Beaumont* and *Fletcher* joyned together, made one of the happy *Triumvirate* (the other two being *Johnson* and *Shakespear*) of the chief *Dramatick* Poets of our Nation, in the last foregoing Age; among whom there might be said to be a *Symmetry* of *Perfection*, while each excell'd in his peculiar way: *Ben. Jonson* in his elaborate Pains and Knowledge of Authors; *Shakespear* in his pure Vein of Wit, and natural *Poetick* Height; *Fletcher* in a Courtly Elegance, and Genteel Familiarity of Style, and withal a Wit and Invention so overflowing, that the Luxuriant Branches thereof were frequently thought convenient to be lopt off by *Beaumont*.

["Characters and Censures," *ibid.*, p. 22.]

SIR THOMAS POPE BLOUNT, 1694

Dryden says, That *Beaumont* and *Fletcher* had, with the advantage of *Shakespear*'s Wit, which was their *precedent*, great Natural Gifts, improv'd by Study. *Beaumont* especially being so accurate a Judge of *Plays*, that *Ben. Johnson*, while he liv'd, submitted all his Writings to his Censure, and, 'tis thought, us'd his judgment in Correcting, if not contriving all his Plots. What value *he* had for him, appears by the Verses he writ to him; and therefore (says *Dryden*) I need speak no farther of it. The first Play that brought *Fletcher* and *him* in esteem, was their *Philaster;* for before that, they had written two or three very unsuccessfully: As the like is reported of *Ben. Johnson*, before he writ *Every Man in his Humour.* Their *Plots* were generally more regular than *Shakespear*'s, especially those which were made before *Beaumont*'s death; and they understood and imitated the Conversation of *Gentlemen* much better; whose wild Debaucheries, and quickness of Wit in *Repartees*, no Poet before them could paint as *they* have done. *Humour*, which *Ben Johnson* deriv'd from particular Persons, *they* made it not their business to describe: *They* represented all the *Passions* very lively, but above all, *Love*. I am apt to believe, says *Dryden*, the English Language in *them* arriv'd to its highest perfection; what words have since been taken in, are rather superfluous than ornamental. *Their* Plays are now the most pleasant and frequent Entertainments of the Stage; *two* of *theirs* being acted through the Year for *one* of *Shakespear*'s or *Johnson*'s: The reason is, says *Dryden*, because there is a certain *gayetie* in *their* Comedies, and *Pathos* in their more serious Plays, which suits generally with all Mens Humours. *Shakespear*'s Language is likewise a little obsolete, and *Ben. Johnson*'s Wit comes short of *theirs*. Dryd. *Essay* of *Dramatick Poesie, pag.* 34.

[*Ibid.*, pp. 22–23.]

Sir Thomas Pope Blount, 1694

But of all *Poets*, this Commendation is to be given to *Ben. Johnson*, that the *Manners* even of the most inconsiderable Persons in his Plays are every where apparent. Dryd. *Pref.* to *Troilus* and *Cressida*.

[*Ibid.*, pp. 23–24.]

Sir Thomas Pope Blount, 1694

How *I do love thee* Beaumont, *and thy Muse,*
That unto Me *do'st such Religion use!*
. . . .
For Writing better, I must envy Thee.

Ben. Johnson.

[*Ibid.*, p. 25.]

Sir Thomas Pope Blount, 1694

When Johnson, Shakespear, *and thy self did sit,*
And sway'd in the Triumvirate *of* Wit—
Yet what from Johnson's *Oil, and Sweat did flow,*
Or what more easie Nature *did bestow*
On Shakespear's *gentle Muse, in Thee full grown*
Their Graces both appear, yet so, that none
Can say here Nature *ends, and* Art *begins,*
But mixt like th' Elements, *and born like* Twins.

[*Ibid.*, p. 26, from "J. Denham on Fletcher's Works."]

Sir Thomas Pope Blount, 1694

Old Mother Wit, and Nature gave
Shakespear *and* Fletcher *all they have;*
In Spencer, *and in* Johnson, *Art*
Of slower Nature got the Start;

. . . .

He [Cowley] *melted not the ancient Gold,*
Nor with Ben. Johnson *did make bold*
To plunder all the Roman *Stores*
Of Poets, and of Orators.

[*Ibid.*, p. 52, from "Denham's Poems, *pag.* 90, 91. of the 3*d* Edition."]

Sir Thomas Pope Blount, 1694

He has writ Fifty Plays in all, whereof Fifteen are *Comedies*, Three are *Tragedies*, the rest are *Masques* and Entertainments: And besides these, (for he is not wholly *Dramatick*,) there are his *Vnderwoods, Epigrams, &c.*

Winstanley, in *The Lives of the most Famous English Poets*, says, That *Ben. Johnson* was paramount in the *Dramatick* part of *Poetry*, and taught the Stage an exact conformity to the Laws of *Comedians*, being accounted the most Learned, Judicious, and Correct of all the *English Poets;* and the more to be admir'd for being so, for that neither the height of Natural Parts, for he was no *Shakespear;* nor the Cost of extraordinary Education, but his own proper

Industry, and Application to Books, advanc'd him to this perfection.

He likewise *tells* us, That *Johnson's* Plays were above the Vulgar Capacity, and took not so well at the *first Stroke*, as at the *rebound*, when beheld the second time; yea, that they will endure Reading, and that with due Commendation, so long as either Ingenuity or Learning are fashionable in our Nation. And altho' all his *Plays* may endure the Test, yet in Three of his *Comedies*, namely, *The Fox*, *Alchymist*, and *Silent Woman*, he may be compar'd, in the Judgment of Learned Men, for *Decorum*, *Language*, and *Humour*, as well with the Chief of the *Ancient Greek* and *Latin Comedians*, as the Prime of *Modern Italians*, who have been judg'd the best of *Europe* for a happy Vein in *Comedies;* Nor is his *Bartholomew-Fair* much short of them. As for his other Comedies, *Staple of News*, *Devil's an Ass*, and the rest, if they be not (says *Winstanley*) so sprightful and vigorous as his *first Pieces*, all that are Old, *will*, and all that desire to be Old, *should* excuse him therein; and therefore let the Name of *Ben. Johnson* shield them against whoever shall think fit to be severe in Censure against them. The truth is, says *Winstanley*, his Tragedies, *Sejanus*, and *Cataline* seem to have in them more of an *Artificial* and *Inflate*, than of a *Pathetical* and *naturally Tragick Height;* yet do they far excel any of the *English* ones, that were writ before him; so that *He* may be truly said, to be the *first Reformer* of the *English* Stage.

In the rest of his *Poetry*, (for he is not wholly *Dramatick*,) as his *Vnderwoods*, *Epigrams*, &c. He is (says *this Author*) sometimes bold and strenuous, sometimes Magisterial, sometimes lepid and ful enough of Conceit, and sometimes a Man as other Men are.

Dryden tells us, [here follows a quotation from *Of Drammatick Poesie*, pp. 34–35].

Dryden, in his *Postscript* to *Granada*, calls *Ben Johnson*, *The most Judicious of Poets* and *Inimitable Writer*, yet, he says, his Excellency lay in the low Characters of Vice, and Folly. When at any time (says he) *Ben*. aim'd at Wit in the stricter Sense, that is sharpness of Conceit, he was forc'd to borrow from the *Ancients*, (as to my knowledge he did very much from *Plautus:*) Or When he trusted himself alone, often fell into meanness of Expression. Nay, he was not free from the lowest and most groveling kind of *Wit*, which we call *Clenches:* Of which *every Man in his Humour* is infinitely full, and which is worse, the Wittiest Persons in the *Drama* speak them.

Dryden, in another place, allows, [here he quotes from the Preface to *An Evening's Love, or The Mock-Astrologer*, sigs. B₁-B₁ᵛ].

Shadwell, in his Dedication before the *Vertuoso*, says, That *Johnson* was incomparably the best *Dramatick Poet* that ever was, or, he believes, ever will be; and that he had rather be Author of one Scene in his best *Comedies*, than of any Play this Age has produc'd.

Notwithstanding the general Vogue of *Ben. Johnson*, yet we finde a most severe *Satyr* against his *Magnetick Lady*, Writ by Dr. *Gill*, Master of *Pauls* School, or at least his *Son:* Part of which I shall take the pains to Transcribe: [Here Blount quotes the last twelve lines of Alexander Gill's "To B. Johnson on his Magnetick Lady" and all of Jonson's answer.]

The haughty Humour of *Johnson* was blam'd, and Carpt at by several, but by none more Ingeniously, than by Sir *John Suckling*, who arraign'd him at the *Sessions* of *Poets* in this manner: [He quotes stanzas 5-8.]

Ben. Johnson died *Anno Dom.* 1637. in the Sixty Third Year of his Age, and was buried in St. *Peters* Church in *Westminster*, on the West-side near the *Belfry;* having only a plain Stone over his *Grave*, with this *Inscription*,

> *O Rare BEN. JOHNSON.*

[*Ibid.*, pp. 106-12.]

Sir Thomas Pope Blount, 1694

Langbaine tells us, for his part he esteems *Shakespear's* Plays beyond any that have ever been Publish'd in our Language: And though he extreamly admires *Johnson*, and *Fletcher;* yet (*says he*) I must still aver, that when in Competition with *Shakespear*, I must apply to them, what *Justus Lipsius* Writ in his Letter to *Andræas Schottus*, concerning *Terence* and *Plautus*, when Compar'd; *Terentium amo, admiror, sed Plautum magis.*

[*Ibid.*, p. 202.]

Sir Thomas Pope Blount, 1694

The consideration of this (as *Dryden* observes) made Mr. *Hales* of *Eaton* say, That there was no Subject of which any *Poet* ever Writ, but he would produce it better done in *Shakespear;* and however others are now generally preferr'd before him, yet the Age wherein he liv'd, which had Contemporaries with him, *Fletcher* and *Johnson*, never equal'd them to him in their esteem: And in the last Kings Court, when *Ben*'s Reputation was at highest, Sir *John Suckling*, and with him the greater part of the *Courtiers*, set our *Shakespear* far above him.

[*Ibid.*, pp. 203–4.]

Sir Thomas Pope Blount, 1694

But of all *Poets* (says *Dryden*) this Commendation is to be given to *Ben. Johnson*, that the *Manners* even of the most inconsiderable Persons in his *Plays* are every where apparent.

[*Ibid.*, p. 204.]

John Crowne, 1694

As to the wanton part of an Intrigue,
I think young Fellows have th' advantage of us;
And yet in that I'le vie with any of you.
I'm like *Ben Johnson*'s *Ursly*, the Pig-Woman,
'Gad, I roast Pigs as well as e're I did.
There's a sweet Pig, I'le make her crackle quickly.

[*The Married Beau* (1694), p. 20.]

John Dryden, 1694

Firm *Dorique* Pillars found Your solid Base:
The Fair *Corinthian* Crowns the higher Space;
Thus all below is Strength, and all above is Grace.
In easie Dialogue is *Fletcher*'s Praise:
He mov'd the mind, but had not power to raise.
Great *Johnson* did by strength of Judgment please:
Yet doubling *Fletcher*'s Force, he wants his Ease.
In differing Tallents both adorn'd their Age;

One for the Study, t'other for the Stage.
But both to *Congreve* justly shall submit,
One match'd in Judgment, both o'er-match'd in Wit.

[Dedicatory poem to Congreve, *The Double Dealer* (1694), sig. a₂ᵛ.]

[LAURENCE EACHARD], 1694

I speak of his Puns, Quibbles, Rhimes, Gingles, *and his several ways of playing upon words; which indeed were the Faults of his Age, as it was of ours in* Shakespear's *and* Johnson's *days.*

[Preface to *Plautus's Comedies, Amphitryon, Epidicus, and Rudens, made English* (1694), sig. b₁ᵛ.]

[JAMES WRIGHT], 1694

Our Poets, continued he, represent the Modern little Actions of Debauchees, as *Ben Johnson* presented the Humours of his Tankard Bearer, his Pauls Walkers, and his Collegiate Ladies, &c. things then known and familiar to every Bodies Notice; and so are these now, and consequently delightful to the times, as Pictures of Faces well known and remarkable. These, Answered *Julio*, were *Ben Johnsons* Weaknesses, and have been as such sufficiently exploded by our New fashion'd Wits, and therefore methinks they should not be imitated by them of all Men Living. Such Representations are like a Painters taking a Picture after the Life in the Apparel then Worn, which becomes Ungraceful or Ridiculous in the next Age, when the Fashion is out.

[*Country Conversations* (1694), pp. 9–10.]

[JAMES WRIGHT], 1694

Julio, either out of Complaisance to *Belamy*, being a stranger, or minded to Rally *Mitis*, highly applauded *Belamy*'s Version; saying, it shew'd the very Spirit of *Ben. Johnson*, when indulging his Genius in the *Apollo*.

[*Ibid.*, p. 27.]

EDWARD RAVENSCROFT, 1695

I' th' latter Age, ere Criticks dar'd to Damn,
Or Censure rashly, what deserv'd a Name;

When Bully *Ben* lugg'd out in *Cat'line's* Cause,
And huff'd his duller Audience to Applause,
Then if the Poet swore 'twas good, each Guest
Believ'd the Author, and approv'd the Feast:
But now in humble Prologue, the poor Muse
Implores your favour, and for mercy sues.
To day the ty'rd Satyr takes his rest,
And has at last himself a Fool confest.

[Prologue to *The Canterbury Guests, Or, A Bargain Broken* (1695).]

WILLIAM CONGREVE, 1696

What if we should get a Quantity of the Water privately con-
vey'd into the Cistern at *Will's* Coffee-House, for an Experiment?
But I am Extravagant—Thô I remember *Ben. Johnson* in his
Comedy of *Cynthia's* Revels, makes a Well, which he there calls
the Fountain of Self-Love, to be the Source of many Entertaining
and Ridiculous Humours. I am of Opinion, that something very
Comical and New, might be brought upon the Stage, from a Fic-
tion of the like Nature.

["*Mr.* Congreve, *to Mr.* Dennis," John Dennis, *Letters upon Several Occasions*
(1696), pp. 101–2.]

JOHN DENNIS, 1696

If there be any Diversion in Quibbling, it is a Diversion of which a
Fool and a Porter is as capable as is the best of you. And therefore
Ben. Johnson, who writ every thing with Judgment, and who knew
the Scum of the People, whenever he brings in a Porter or Tankard-
Bearer, is sure to introduce him Quibbling.

[*Ibid.*, p. 76 (i.e., p. 67), from the letter "*To Mr.* —— *at* Will's *Coffee-house in*
Covent-Garden."]

JOHN DENNIS, 1696

Dear Sir,

I Have now read over the Fox, in which thô I admire the strength
of *Ben. Johnson's* Judgment, yet I did not find it so accurate as I
expected. For first the very thing upon which the whole Plot turns,

and that is the Discovery which *Mosca* makes to *Bonario;* seems to me, to be very unreasonable. For *I* can see no Reason, why he should make that Discovery which introduces *Bonorio* into his Masters House. For the Reason which the Poet makes *Mosca* give in the Ninth Scene of the third Act, appears to be a very Absurd one. Secondly, *Corbaccio* the Father of *Bonario* is expos'd for his Deafness, a Personal defect; which is contrary to the end of Comedy Instruction. For Personal Defects cannot be amended; and the exposing such, can never Divert any but half-witted Men. *I*t cannot fail to bring a thinking Man to reflect upon the Misery of Human Nature; and into what he may fall himself without any fault of his own. Thirdly, the play has two Characters, which have nothing to do with the design of it, which are to be look'd upon as Excrescencies. Lastly, the Character of *Volpone* is Inconsistent with it self. *Volpone* is like *Catiline, alieni appetens, sui profusus;* but that is only a double in his Nature, and not an Inconsistence. The Inconsistence of the Character appears in this, that *Volpone* in the fifth Act behaves himself like a Giddy Coxcombe, in the Conduct of that very Affair which he manag'd so Craftily in the first four. In which the Poet offends first against that Fam'd rule which *Horace* gives for the Characters.

Servetur ad imum,
Qualis ab incepto processerit, et sibi constet.

And Secondly, against Nature, upon which, all the rules are grounded. For so strange an Alteration, in so little a time, is not in Nature, unless it happens by the Accident of some violent passion; which is not the case here. *Volpone* on the sudden behaves himself without common Discretion, in the Conduct of that very Affair which he had manag'd with so much Dexterity, for the space of three Years together. For why does he disguise himself? or why does he repose the last Confidence in *Mosca?* Why does he cause it to be given out that he's Dead? Why, only to Plague his Bubbles. To Plague them, for what? Why only for having been his Bubbles. So that here is the greatest alteration in the World, in the space of twenty-four hours, without any apparent cause. The design of *Volpone* is to Cheat, he has carried on a Cheat for three years together, with Cunning and with Success. And yet he on a sudden in cold blood does a thing, which he cannot but know must Endanger the ruining all.

I am, / *Dear Sir,* / *Your most Humble* / *Servant.*

[*Ibid.*, pp. 73–75.]

JOHN DENNIS, 1696
To Mr. Congreve.

Dear Sir,

I will not augment the Trouble which I give you by making an Apology for not giving it you sooner. Thô I am heartily sorry that I kept such a trifle as the inclos'd, and a trifle writ Extempore, long enough to make you expect a labour'd Letter. But because in the Inclos'd, I have spoken particularly of *Ben. Johnson*'s Fox, I desire to say three or four words of some of his Plays more generally. The Plots of the Fox, the Silent Woman, the Alchimist, are all of them very Artful. But the Intrigues of the Fox, and the Alchimist, seem to me to be more dexterously perplexed, than to be happily disentangled. But the Gordian knot in the Silent Woman is untyed with so much Felicity, that that alone, may Suffice to show *Ben Johnson* no ordinary Heroe. But, then perhaps, the Silent Woman may want the very Foundation of a good Comedy, which the other two cannot be said to want. For it seems to me, to be without a Moral. Upon which Absurdity, *Ben Johnson* was driven by the Singularity of *Moroses* Character, which is too extravagant for Instruction, and fit, in my opinion, only for Farce. For this seems to me, to Constitute the most Essential Difference, betwixt Farce and Comedy, that the Follies which are expos'd in Farce are Singular; and those are particular, which are expos'd in Comedy. These last are those, with which some part of an Audience may be suppos'd Infected, and to which all may be suppos'd Obnoxious. But the first are so very odd, that by Reason of their Monstrous Extravagance, they cannot be thought to concern an Audience; and cannot be supposed to instruct them. For the rest of the Characters in these Plays, they are for the most part true, and Most of the Humorous Characters Master-pieces. For *Ben Johnson*'s Fools, seem to shew his Wit a great deal more then his Men of Sense. I

Admire his Fops, and but barely Esteem his Gentlemen. *Ben* seems
to draw Deformity more to the Life than Beauty. He is often so
eager to pursue Folly, that he forgets to take Wit along with him.
For the Dialogue, it seems to want very often that Spirit, that
Grace, and that Noble Railery, which are to be found in more Modern Plays, and which are Virtues that ought to be Inseparable from
a finish'd Comedy. But there seems to be one thing more wanting
than all the rest, and that is Passion, I mean that fine and that
delicate Passion, by which the Soul shows its Politeness, ev'n in
the midst of its trouble. Now to touch a Passion is the surest way
to Delight. For nothing agitates like it. Agitation is the Health
and Joy of the Soul, of which it is so entirely fond, that even then,
when we imagine we seek Repose, we only seek Agitation. You know
what a Famous Modern Critick has said of Comedy. . . . .
I leave you to make the Aplication to *Johnson*—Whatever I
have said my self of his Comedies, I submit to your better Judgment. For you who, after Mr. *Wicherly*, are incomparably the best
Writer of it living; ought to be allowed to be the best Judge, too,
    I am, / Yours, &c.

[*Ibid.*, pp. 76–79.]

THOMAS DILKE, 1696

Bellair. . . . . Mr. Sapless, you were upon the brink of Ruine,
and going to marry a Doll Common.

[*The Lover's Luck* (1696), V, 1. Noted by C. B. Graham, "Jonson Allusions in
Restoration Comedy," *Review of English Studies*, XV (1939), 204.]

JOSEPH HAYNES, 1696

A dull World, want of Business, and much Idleness, with not
overstockt a Pocket, you see, Gentlemen, may do much. But now,
after exposing (to use *Ben Johnson*'s Title) my Works in Print,
what success I am like to meet, now hang me, as great a Fortune-
Teller as I have been, all my Prognosticks can no more foretell, than
Lily (with Reverence be it spoken) could divine who shit at his
Door.

[*A Fatal Mistake* (1696; 1st ed., 1692), "To the Reader," sig. A₂ᵛ.]

Anonymous, 1697

'Tis said, our Nation is *richer in Humour* than any in *Europe*, and tho' the Stage has large *Supplies* from it, yet it can never be *exhausted*. If it be so, *Ben Johnson* stands fairest for *Treasurer*, tho' he need not have gone farther than any one of his *Merry Wives of Windsor* to have employ'd him all his Life: He needed but have *shown one* Face in one *Play*, to have had sufficient *Variety*.

[*The Challenge, Sent by a Young Lady to Sir Thomas—&c. Or, The Female War* (1697), pp. 92–93 (second pagination). From G. Thorn-Drury, *More Seventeenth Century Allusions to Shakespeare and His Works Not Hitherto Collected* (1924), p. 40.]

Thomas Brown, 1697

But *Paul*'s will be built in a short time; and then a *Low-Country* Captain will make as busie a Figure in the middle Isle, as ever his Predecessors did in the Days of *Ben Johnson*.

[Thomas Brown to Dr. Baynard, *Familiar Letters Written by the Earl of Rochester* (4th ed., 1705), I, 209-10. The first volume first appeared in 1697.]

John Dennis, 1697

Not let me see a little whither they have brought me whither this is *Newgate* or *Bedlam*. (*He runs to the Door and looks out*) Death and the Devil! I have been all this while in my own house. But tho I am not at present in *Bedlam*, I am not like to be long out of it. Was ever man serv'd as I have been? I have been us'd like a *Bartholomew* Cokes; I have been cheated of five thousand pound, have been made to pass for a mad man: And my Son in all likelihood is marry'd to the worst of the Drabs. But hold, let me consider a little.

[*A Plot and No Plot* (n.d. [1697]), Act V, pp. 76 [i.e., 75]–76, sigs. L₂–L₂ᵛ.]

Thomas Dilke, 1697

Luc. Don't your Genius lead you to Ode and Elegy?
Ped. I have done very pretty things that way too; but for Anagrams, Acrosticks, and Extempore Distichs, *Ben. Johnson* was a Fool to me: E'gad I'll turn my back to no body.

[*The City Lady* (1697), Act III, p. 31.]

ANONYMOUS, 1698

Here again he's put to't to confess where he borrow'd the word
Whoreson; from *Shakespear* and *Johnson.* Well, but he has us'd it so
lately, that I shan't dispute his Title to't by any means.

[*Animadversions on Mr. Congreve's Late Answer to Mr. Collier in a Dialogue between Mr. Smith and Mr. Johnson* (1698), p. 53.]

ANONYMOUS, 1698

PROLOGUE.

OF old, in *England*'s Golden Age of Wit,
When Godlike *Ben,* and Lofty *Shakespear* Writ;
Hard was the Poets Task, and great their Toil,
Who strove to Cultivate the Muses Soil.

[*Feign'd Friendship, or the Mad Reformer* (1698), sig. A₂ᵛ.]

ANONYMOUS, 1698

His Envy shou'd at powerful *Cowley* rage,
And banish Sense with *Johnson* from the Stage:
His Sacrilege should plunder *Shakespear*'s Urn,
With a dull Prologue make the Ghost return
To bear a second Death, and greater Pain,
While the Fiend's Words the Oracle prophane.

["A Satyr on the Modern Translators . . . . By Mr. P——r," *Money Masters All
Things* (1698), p. 119.]

ANONYMOUS, 1698

WHO is't wou'd be a Poet in our days,
When e'ery Coxcomb crowns his Head with Bays,
And stands a sawcy Candidate for Praise?
The Stage is quite debauch'd, for every Day
Some new-born Monster's shown you for a Play;
Art Magick is for Poetry profest,
Horses, Asses, Monkeys, and each obscener Beast,
(To which Egyptian *Monarch once did bow)*

Vpon our English Stage are worship'd now.
Fletcher's despis'd, your Johnson's out of fashion,
And Wit's the only Drug in all the Nation.

[Prologue to *The Unnatural Mother* (1698).]

JEREMY COLLIER, 1698

Ben. Johnson is much more reserv'd in his *Plays*, and declares plainly for Modesty in his *Discoveries*, some of his Words are these. A just Writer whom he calls a *True Artificer*, will avoid *Obscene* and *Effeminate Phrase. Where Manners and Fashions are Corrupted, Language is so too.* [In margin: *Discov.* p. 700.] *The excess of Feasts and Apparel, are the Notes of a Sick State, and the Wantonness of Language of a sick Mind.* [In margin: p. 701.] A little after he returns to the Argument, and applies his Reasoning more particularly to the Stage. *Poetry* (says he) *and Picture, both behold Pleasure, and profit, as their common Object, but should abstain from all base Pleasures, least they should wholly Err from their End; And while they seek to better Men's Minds, Destroy their Manners, Insolent and obscene Speeches, and Jests upon the best Men, are most likely to excite Laughter. But this is truly leaping from the Stage to the Tumbrill again, reducing all Wit to the Original Dung-Cart.* [In margin: p. 706.] More might be cited to this purpose, but that may serve for an other Occasion.

[*A Short View of the Immorality and Prophaneness of the English Stage* (1698), pp. 50–51. Only the first two lines are given in *The Jonson Allusion-Book.*]

JEREMY COLLIER, 1698

Shakespear is comparatively sober, *Ben Jonson* is still more regular; And as for *Beaument* and *Fletcher*, In their *Plays* they are commonly Profligate Persons that Swear, and even those are reprov'd for't. Besides, the Oaths are not so full of Hell and Defiance, as in the Moderns.

[*Ibid.*, p. 57, from the section on cursing and swearing.]

JEREMY COLLIER, 1698

At the end of this *Act Bull* speaks to the Case of *Bigamy*, and determines it thus. *I do confess to take two Husbands for the Satisfac-*

tion of—is to commit the Sin of Exorbitancy, but to do it for the peace of the Spirit, is no more then to be Drunk by way of Physick; besides to prevent a Parents wrath is to avoid the Sin of Disobedience, for when the Parent is Angry, the Child is froward: The Conclusion is insolently Profane, and let it lie: The spirit of this Thought is bor-row'd from Ben *Johnsons Bartholomew-Fair,* only the Profaness is mightily improved, and the Abuse thrown off the *Meeting House,* upon the *Church.* The Wit of the *Parents being angry,* and the *Child froward,* is all his own.

[*Ibid.,* p. 109, from the discussion of the abuse of the clergy in *The Relapse.*]

JEREMY COLLIER, 1698

Towards the End of the *Silent Woman, Ben Johnson* brings in a *Clergyman,* and a *Civilian* in their *Habits.* But then he premises a handsom Excuse, acquaints the *Audience,* that the *Persons* are but borrow'd, and throws in a *Salvo* for the Honour of either profession. In the Third *Act,* we have another *Clergy-man;* He is abused by *Cutberd,* and a little by *Morose.* But his Lady checks him for the ill Breeding of the Usage. In his *Magnetick Lady, Tale of a Tub,* and *Sad Sheapherd,* there are *Priests* which manage but untowardly. But these *Plays* were his *last Works,* which Mr. *Dryden* calls *his Dotages.*

[*Ibid.,* p. 126.]

JEREMY COLLIER, 1698

Mr. *Dryden* makes Homewards, and endeavours to fortifie him-self in Modern Authority [for presenting immoral characters as protagonists]. He lets us know that *Ben Johnson after whom he may be proud to Err, gives him more than one example of this Conduct; That in the* Alchemist *is notorius,* where neither *Face* nor his *Master* are corrected according to their Demerits. But how Proud soever Mr. *Dryden* may be of an Errour, he has not so much of *Ben Jon-son*'s company as he pretends. His Instance of *Face &c.* in the *Alchemist* is rather *notorious* against his Purpose than for it.

For *Face* did not Council his Master *Lovewit* to debauch the Wid-dow; neither is it clear that the Matter went thus far. He might gain her consent upon Terms of Honour for ought appears to the contrary 'Tis true *Face* who was one of the Principal Cheats is Pardon'd and consider'd. But then his Master confesses himself kind to a fault. He owns this Indulgence was a Breach of Justice, and unbecoming the Gravity of an old Man. And then desires the Audience to excuse him upon the Score of the Temptation. But *Face continued in the Cousenage till the last without Repentance.* Under favour I conceive this is a Mistake. For does not *Face* make an Apology before he leaves the *Stage?* Does he not set himself at the *Bar*, arraign his own Practise, and cast the Cause upon the Clemency of the Company? And are not all these Signs of the Dislike of what he had done? Thus careful the *Poet* is to prevent the Ill Impressions of his *Play!* He brings both Man and Master to Confession. He dismisses them like Malefactours; And moves for their Pardon before he has given them their Discharge. But the *Mock-Astrologer* has a gentler Hand: *Wild-Blood* and *Jacinta* are more generously used: There is no Acknowledgment exacted; no Hardship put upon them: They are permitted to talk on in their Libertine way to the Last: And take Leave without the least Appearance of Reformation. The *Mock-Astrologer* urges *Ben Johnson's Silent Woman* as an other *Precedent* to his purpose. For *there* Dauphine *confesses himself in Love with all the Collegiate Lady's. And yet this naughty* Dauphine *is Crowned in the end with the Possession of his Vncles Estate, and with the hopes of all his Mistresses.* This Charge, as I take it, is somewhat too severe. I grant *Dauphine* Professes himself in Love with the Collegiate Ladies at first. But when they invited him to a private Visit, he makes them no Promise; but rather appears tired, and willing to disengage. *Dauphine* therefore is not altogether so naughty as this Author represents him.

Ben Johnson's Fox is clearly against Mr. *Dryden.* And here I have his own Confession for proof. He declares the *Poets end in this Play was the Punishment of Vice, and the Reward of Virtue. Ben* was forced to strain for this piece of Justice, and break through the *Vnity of Design.* This Mr. *Dryden* remarks upon him: How ever he is pleased to commend the Performance, and calls it an excellent *Fifth Act.*

Ben Johnson shall speak for himself afterwards in the Character of a Critick.

[*Ibid.*, pp. 151–53.]

JEREMY COLLIER, 1698

1st. Monsieur *Rapin* affirms 'That Delight is the End that Poetry aims at, but not the Principal one. For Poetry being an Art, ought to be profitable by the quality of it's own nature, and by the Essential Subordination that all Arts should have to Polity, whose End in General is the publick Good. This is the Judgment of *Aristotle* and of *Horace* his chief Interpreter.' *Ben Johnson* in his Dedicatory Epistle of his *Fox* has somewhat considerable upon this Argument; And declaims with a great deal of zeal, spirit, and good Sense, against the Licentiousness of the *Stage*. He lays it down for a Principle, 'That 'tis impossible to be a good *Poet* without being a good *Man*. That he (a good Poet) is said to be able to inform Young Men to all good Discipline, and enflame grown Men to all great Virtues &c.—That the general complaint was that the *Writers* of those days had nothing remaining in them of the Dignity of a *Poet*, but the abused Name. That now, especially in Stage Poetry, nothing but Ribaldry, Profanation, *Blasphemy*, all Licence of Offence to God and Man, is practised. He confesses a great part of this Charge is over-true, and is sorry he dares not deny it. But then he hopes all are not embark'd in this bold Adventure for Hell. For my part (says he) I can, and from a most clear Conscience affirm; That I have ever trembled to think towards the least Profaness, and loath'd the Use of such foul, and unwash'd Bawdry, as is now made the Food of the *Scene*. The encrease of which Lust in Liberty, what Learned or Liberal Soul does not abhor? In whole *Enterludes* nothing but the Filth of the Time is utter'd—with Brothelry able to violate the Ear of a *Pagan*, and Blasphemy, to turn the Blood of a Christian to Water. He continues, that the Insolence of these Men had brought the *Muses* into Disgrace, and made *Poetry* the lowest scorn of the Age. He appeals to his Patrons the *Vniversities*, that his Labour has been heretofore, and mostly in this his latest Work, to reduce not only the antient Forms, but Manners of the *Scene*, the Innocence and the Doctrine, which is the *Principal End* of Poesy, to inform Men in the best Reason of Living. Lastly he adds, that 'he has imitated the Conduct of the Antients in this *Play*, The goings out (or Conclusions) of whose *Comedies*, were not always joyful but oft-times the Bawds, the Slaves, the Rivals, yea and the

Masters are multed, and fitly, it being the Office of a *Comick Poet* (mark that!) to imitate Justice, and Instruct to Life &c.' Say you so! Why then if *Ben Johnson* knew any thing of the Matter, Divertisement and Laughing is not as Mr. *Dryden* affirms, the *Chief End* of *Comedy*. This Testimony is so very full and clear, that it needs no explaining, nor any enforcement from Reasoning, and Consequence.

[*Ibid.*, pp. 157–59.]

JEREMY COLLIER, 1698

Thus *Shakespear* makes *Hector* talk about *Aristotles* Philosophy, and calls Sr. *John Old Castle*, *Protestant*. I had not mention'd this Discovery in Chronology, but that Mr. *Dryden* falls upon *Ben Johnson*, for making *Cataline give Fire at the Face of a Cloud*, before Guns were invented.

[*Ibid.*, pp. 187–88.]

WILLIAM CONGREVE, 1698

For a Dispute about this word, would be very like the Controversie in *Ben. Johnson's Barthol. Fair*, between the *Rabbi* and the *Puppet*; it *is* profane, and it *is not* profane, is all the Argument the thing will admit of on either side.

[*Amendments of Mr. Collier's False and Imperfect Citations* (1698), pp. 45–46.]

WILLIAM CONGREVE, 1698

Ben. Johnson is much bolder in the first Scene of his *Bartholomew Fair*. There he makes Littlewit say to his Wife—*Man and Wife make one Fool;* and yet I don't think he design'd even that, for a Jest either upon *Genesis* 2. or St. *Matthew* 19. I have said nothing comparable to that, and yet Mr. *Collier* in his penetration has thought fit to accuse me of nothing less.

[*Ibid.*, p. 47.]

WILLIAM CONGREVE, 1698

For the word *Whoreson*, I had it from *Shakespear* and *Johnson*, who have it very often in their Low Comedies; and sometimes their

Characters of some Rank use it. I have put it into the Mouth of a Footman. 'Tis not worth speaking of.

[*Ibid.*, p. 50.]

WILLIAM CONGREVE, 1698

Such a Character neither does nor can asperse the sacred Order of Priesthood, neither does it at all reflect upon the persons of the pious and good Clergy: For as *Ben. Johnson* observes on the same occasion from St. *Hierome, Ubi generalis est de vitiis disputatio, Ibi nullius esse personæ injuriam*, where the business is to expose and reprehend Folly and Vice in general, no particular person ought to take offence. And such business is properly the business of Comedy.

[*Ibid.*, pp. 63-64.]

WILLIAM CONGREVE, 1698

Ben Johnson, in his Discoveries, says, *There be some Men are born only to suck the Poison of Books.* [In margin: *Johns. Disc.* P. 702.] Habent venenum pro victu imo pro deliciis. *And such are they that only relish the obscene and foul things in Poets; which makes the Profession tax'd: But by whom? Men that watch for it,* &c. Something farther in the same Discoveries, He is speaking again very much to our purpose; for it is in justification of presenting vicious and foolish Characters on the Stage in Comedy. It seems some People were angry at it then; let us compare his Picture of them, with the Characters of those who quarrel at it now. *It sufficeth* (says he) [In margin: *Johns. Disc.* P. 714.] *I know what kind of Persons I displease, Men bred in the declining and decay of Vertue, betrothed to their own Vices; that have abandoned, or prostituted their good Names; hungry and ambitious of Infamy, invested in all Deformity, enthrall'd to Ignorance and Malice, of a hidden and conceal'd Malignity, and that hold a concomitancy with all Evil.*

'Tis strange that Mr. *Collier* should oversee these two Passages, when he was simpling in the same Field where they both grow. This is pretty plain; because in the 51st Page of his Book he presents you with a Quotation from the same *Discoveries*, as one intire Paragraph, tho' severally collected from the 706 and 717th Pages of the

Original; so that he has read both before, and beyond these Passages. But a Man that looks in a Glass often, walks away, and forgets his resemblance.

[*Ibid.*, pp. 97–98.]

Thomas D'Urfey, 1698

Besides I do assure you, spite of your Ghostly Authority, and Uncharitable Position, that we are not fit, we will come in, and not only imbibe the Mystery of *Divinity* from the Pulpit, but unriddle the Mystery of *Iniquity*, if we can find any there. *Ben Johnson* found out *Ananias* and *Rabby Buisy; Fletcher, Hypocritical Roger, Shakespear,* Sir *John* of *Wrotham; Congreve, Say-grace; Vanbrook, Bull; Shadwell, Smirk;* and if *D'urfey* can find out a proud, stubborn, immoral *Bernard,* one, that when he was a Country Curate, *would not let the Children be brought to Church to be Christned for some odd Jesuitical Reasons* best known to himself, he shall presume to draw his Picture, tho' the *Absolver* drop another Chapter of Abuse upon him for so doing.

[Preface to *The Campaigners* (1698), pp. 14–15.]

Thomas D'Urfey, 1698

The *Absolver,* to turn back a little, affirms indeed, That *those that bring Devils upon the Stage, can hardly believe them any where else;* but I can give an instance, that our famous *Ben Johnson,* who I will believe had a Conscience as good as the Doctors, and who liv'd in as Pious an Age, in his Comedy call'd the *Devil's an Ass,* makes his first Scene a Solemn Hell, where *Lucifer* sits in State with all his Privy-Council about him: and when he makes an under Pug there beaten and fool'd by a Clod-pated Squire and his wanton Wife, the Audience took the Representation morally, and never keck'd at the matter.

[*Ibid.*, p. 20.]

Anonymous, 1699

That our Plays are not more dissolute than those of *Fletcher's* and *Ben,* may easily be made evident by consulting the several

Poets. There has been nothing so lewd as the bringing in *Bawdy-Houses*, and the *Stallions* of *Fletcher;* no not in the Plays in the two late Reigns; some of which indeed ought to be banish'd the Stage, tho even those are not without their *useful* Morals to the more staid and better Judges.

[*The Stage Acquitted* (1699), pp. 10–11.]

ANONYMOUS, 1699

[According to Robert Gale Noyes, *Ben Jonson on the English Stage 1660–1776*, p. 181 and n. 5, the music for the song from *Epicoene* beginning "Still to be neat" appeared in *Select Ayres and Dialogues to Sing to the Theorbo-Lute or Basse-Viol. Composed by Mr. Henry Lawes, : . . . and other Excellent Masters* (1699), Book II, p. 51.]

JEREMY COLLIER, 1699

Mr. *Congreve* says, *Ben. Johnson is much bolder in the first Scene of his Bartholomew Fair.* Suppose all that. Is it an excuse to follow an ill Example and continue an Atheistical practice? I thought Mr. *Congreve in his penetration* might have seen through this Question. *Ben. Johnson* (as he goes on) *makes Littlewit say, Man and Wife make one Fool. I have said nothing comparable to that.* Nothing comparable! Truly in the usual sense of that Phrase, Mr. *Congreve,* 'tis possible, has said nothing comparable to *Ben. Johnson,* nor it may be never will: But in his new Propriety he has said something more than comparable, that is a great deal worse. For though *Littlewit's* Allusion is profane, the words of the *Bible* are spared. He does not Droll directly upon *Genesis,* or St. *Matthew;* Upon God the Son, or God the Holy Ghost: Whereas Mr. *Congreve* has done that which amounts to both. And since he endeavours to excuse himself upon the Authority of *Ben. Johnson,* I shall just mention what Thoughts this Poet had of his profane Liberties, at a time when we have reason to believe him most in earnest. Now Mr. *Wood* reports from the Testimony of a great Prelate then present. "That when *Ben. Johnson* was in his last Sickness, he was often heard to repent of his profaning the Scriptures in his Plays, and that with Horrour."

Now as far as I can perceive, the Smut and Profaneness of Mr. *Congreve's* Four Plays out-swell the Bulk of *Ben. Johnson's* Folio.

I heartily wish this Relation may be serviceable to Mr. *Congreve*, and that as his Faults are greater, his Repentance may come sooner.

[*A Defence of the Short View of the Profaneness and Immorality of the Stage* (1699), pp. 53–54.]

JEREMY COLLIER, 1699

2*ly*. He [the Vindicator] mistakes the *Nature* of *Comedy*. This we may learn from *Ben. Johnson*, who acquaints [In margin: Fox Ep. Ded.] the *Vniversity*, *That he has imitated the Conduct of the Antients: In whose Comedies the Bawds*, &c. *yea and oft-times the Masters too, are multed, and that fitly, it being the Office of a* Comick Poet *to imitate Justice, and instruct to Life.* Is it the Office of a Comick Poet to *imitate Justice*, &c. then certainly Rewards and Punishments ought to be rightly apply'd: Then a Libertine ought to have some Mark of Disfavour set upon him, and be brought under Discipline and Disgrace.

[*Ibid.*, p. 125.]

JOHN DUNTON, 1699

Gentlemen!

I Told you in my *First Letter*, That I had brought into this Kingdom, *A General Collection of the most Valuable Books, Printed in* England, *since the Fire in* London *in 66. to this very time; to which, I told you, was added,—Great Variety of Scarce Books.* . . . Ben Johnsons *Works*—Shakespears *Works*—Beaumont *and* Fletchers *Works* —Cowleys *Works*—Oldhams *Works*—Drydens *Works*—Congreves *Works.* . . . .

[*The Dublin Scuffle* (1699), pp. 108–9.]

[CHARLES GILDON], 1699

Robert Armin

. . . . This Author lived in the Reign of King *James* I. and in the Title Page discovers himself to be one of his Majesty's Servants, and was, I believe, of the then Company of Actors, for I find his Name Printed in the *Drama* of *Ben. Johnson's Alchymist*, among the rest of the eminent Players of that Age; and indeed the Preface of his Play seems to intimate as much.

[*The Lives and Characters of the English Dramatick Poets* (1699), p. 5.]

[CHARLES GILDON], 1699

Robert Baron, Esq:

. . . . for most of the Scenes and Language [of *Mirza*] he seems to have Consulted *Ben. Johnson's Catiline.*

[*Ibid.*, p. 8.]

[CHARLES GILDON], 1699

Richard Brome.

He Liv'd in the time of King *Charles* I. was servant to *Ben. Johnson*, and writ himself into Reputation by his Comedies; was Complimented with Copies of Verses, from most of the Poets of his time, and even from his Master *Ben*.

[*Ibid.*, p. 13.]

[CHARLES GILDON], 1699

William Cartwright

. . . . He was expert in the *Latin*, *Greek*, *French*, and *Italian* Tongues; was extream modest, as well as handsome; and admired, not only by his Acquaintance but Strangers. *Ben. Johnson* among the rest writ in his Praise.

[*Ibid.*, p. 16.]

[CHARLES GILDON], 1699

George Chapman.

. . . . He joyn'd with *Ben. Johnson* and *Marston*, in the Composing one Play call'd *Eastward Hoe*. . . . . *Eastward Hoe*, a Comedy, 4 *to* 1605. This was his but in part, *Ben Johnson* and *Marston* having joyned with him in it.

[*Ibid.*, pp. 18 and 19.]

[CHARLES GILDON], 1699

Sir *William D'avenant*,

. . . . In the Year 1637. he succeeded *Ben. Johnson* as Poet *Laureat.*

[*Ibid.*, p. 33.]

[CHARLES GILDON], 1699

Thomas Deckar.

This Author was a Contemporary of *Ben. Johnson*'s, in the Reign of K. *James* I. and his Antagonist for the Bays.

[*Ibid.*, p. 36.]

[CHARLES GILDON], 1699

Thomas Deckar.

. . . . *Ben Johnson's Poetaster* (wherein he is severe on this our Author) occasioned the Writing of this Play.

[*Ibid.*, p. 37.]

[CHARLES GILDON], 1699

John Fletcher, and Francis Beaumont.

. . . . *The Faithful Shepherdess;* a Pastoral, *fol.* This was entirely *Fletcher's,* and commended by Copies of Verses by Mr. *Beaumont* and *Ben. Johnson.*

[*Ibid.*, p. 58.]

[CHARLES GILDON], 1699

John Fletcher, and Francis Beaumont.

. . . . part of the Play [*Love's Pilgrimage*] taken from *Johnson's New Inn.*

[*Ibid.*, p. 59.]

[CHARLES GILDON], 1699

John Fletcher, and Francis Beaumont

. . . . Mr. *Fletcher* join'd with *Ben. Johnson* and *Middleton*, in one other Comedy, call'd, *The Widow,* placed under *Johnson.*

[*Ibid.*, p. 61.]

[CHARLES GILDON], 1699

Peter Hausted.

. . . . he was impatient of Censure, as well as his admired *Ben.*

[*Ibid.*, p. 68.]

[CHARLES GILDON], 1699

Peter Hausted

. . . . The Scene betwixt *Love-all* and *Hamershin, Act* 3. *Scene* 7.
[of *The Rival Friends*] from that betwixt *True-wit, Daw,* and *La-Fool,* in *Ben's Silent Woman.*

[*Ibid.,* p. 68.]

[CHARLES GILDON], 1699

Benjamin Johnson.

Westminster gave him Birth, and the First Rudiments of his
Learning, under *Mr. Cambden;* which St. *John's-College* of *Cambridge,* and *Christ-Church* of *Oxon* finish'd, where he took his Master
of Arts Degree; Necessity drove him thence, to follow his Father-
in-Law's Trade of a *Bricklayer;* working at *Lincolns-Inn,* with a
Trowel in his Hand, and *Horace* in his Pocket, he found a Patron
that set him free from that Slavish Employment. He was of an
open, free Temper; blunt and haughty to his Antagonists and Criticks; a Jovial and Pleasant Companion; was Poet Laureat to *James*
and *Charles* the First. He died in the Sixty Third Year of his Age,
An. Dom. 1637. and is buried in *Westminster-Abby,* near the Belfry,
with only this Epitaph:

O RARE BEN. JOHNSON.

His Dramatick Pieces, about Fifty in Number, follow:
The Alchymist, a Comedy, Acted by the King's Majesty's Servants, first, 1610. and afterwards printed, *viz.* 1640. and 1692.
Bartholomew-Fair, a Comedy, *Fol.* 1640. and 1692. Acted first at
the *Hope,* on the *Bank-side,* 1614. by the Lady *Elizabeth's* Servants,
and Dedicated to King *James* the First; and Acted with good Applause, since King *Charles* the Second's Restauration.
Cateline his Conspiracy, a Tragedy, *Fol.* 1640. and 1692. and in
4*to* 16 . [*sic*] Acted first by the King's Majesty's Servants, 1611. and
sometimes since the Restauration, with good Applause. Is Dedicated to *William,* then Earl of *Pembrock.* Plot from *Salust. Hist. Plutarch in Vit. Cic.*
Challenge at Tilt, at a Marriage, a Masque, *Fol.* 1640. and 1692.

Christmas's Masque, Fol. 1640. and 1692. This was first Presented at Court, 1616.

Cloridia, or, *Rites to Cloris,* a Masque, *Fol.* 1692. presented by the Queen's Majesty, and her Ladies at Court, at *Shrovetide,* 1630. Mr. *Inigo Jones* assisted in the Invention hereof.

Cynthia's Revels, or, *the Fountain of Self-Love;* a Comedy, *Fol.* 1640. and 1692. Acted by the Children of Queen *Elizabeth's* Chappel. 1600.

Devil's an Ass, a Comedy, *Fol.* 1641. and 1692. Acted by his Majesty's Servants, 1616. See *Boccace's Novels, Day 3. Nov. 5.*

Entertainment at King James the First his Coronation. Fol. 1692. This contains only Gratulatory Speeches at the said *Coronation,* with a Comment by the Author to illustrate the same.

Entertainment of King *James* and Queen *Ann,* at *Theobalds, Fol.* 1640. and 1692.

Entertainment of the King of *England,* and the King of *Denmark,* at *Theobalds, July* 24. 1606. *Fol.* 1640. and 1692.

Entertainment of the King and Queen on *May-Day,* at Sir *William Cornwallis's* House at *High-gate,* 1604. *Fol.* 1640. and 1692.

Entertainment of the Queen and Prince at *Althrop;* this was the 25th of *June,* 1603. at the Lord *Spencer's* House there, at their coming First into the Kingdom. *Fol.* 1640. and 1692.

Every Man in his Humour, a Comedy, *Fol.* 1640. and 1692. Acted first in the Year 1598. by the then Lord *Chamberlain's* Servants, and Dedicated to Mr. *Cambden, Clarenceux.* It has been reviv'd and Acted since the Restauration, with good Applause, and a new Epilogue writ for the same, part of it spoken by *Ben. Johnson's* Ghost.

Every Man out of his Humour, a Comedy, *Fol.* 1640. and 1692. Acted by the then Lord *Chamberlain's* Servants. This was also revived and Acted at the Theatre Royal, 1675. with a new Prologue and Epilogue, writ by Mr. *Duffet,* and spoken by *Joseph Haynes.*

Fortunate Isles, a Masque, *Fol.* 1641. and 1692. design'd for the Court on *Twelfth Night,* 1626.

Golden Age Restored, a Masque, *Fol.* 1641. and 1692. This was presented at Court by the Lords and Gentlemen, the King's Servants 1626.

Hymnæi, or, *The Solemnities of a Masque and Barriers at a Marriage, Fol.* 1692. See the Learned Marginal Notes, for the Illustration of the *Greek* and *Roman Customs*.

Irish Masque at Court *Fol.* 1692. presented at Court by Gentlemen, the Kings Servants.

King's Entertainment, at *Welbeck*, in *Nottinghamshire, Fol.* 1692. This Entertainment was at the then Earl, since Duke of *Newcastle's* House, 1633.

Love freed from Ignorance and Folly, a Masque, *Fol.* 1692.

Love Restored, a Masque, *Fol.* 1692. presented at Court by Gentleman the King's Servants.

Love's Triumph thro' Callipolis, a Masque *Fol.* 1692. perform'd at Court by his late Majesty King *Charles* the First, with the Lords and Gentlemen assisting, 1630. Mr. *Johnson* and Mr. *Inigo Jones* join'd in the Invention.

Love's Welcome, an Entertainment for the King and Queen, at the then Earl of *Newcastle's* at *Bolsover*, 1634. and Printed *Fol.* 1692.

Magnetick Lady, or, *Humours Reconciled*, a Comedy, *Fol.* 1640. and 1692. Acted at the *Black Fryars*. This Play occasioned some Difference or Jarring, between Dr. *Gill*, Master of *Paul's* School, and our Author *Ben.* as appears by a Satyrical Copy of Verses writ by the former, and as sharp a Repartee by the latter.

Masque at the Lord Hadington's Marriage, presented at Court on *Shrove-Tuesday-Night*, 1608. Printed *Fol.* 1692.

Masque of Augurs, Fol. 1692. This was presented on *Twelfth-Night*, 1622. with several Anti-masques.

Masque of Owls, at *Kenelworth, Fol.* 1692. In this Presentation there was the Ghost of Captain *Cox*, mounted on his Hobby-Horse.

Masque of Queens, celebrated from the House of Fame, by the Queen of *Great Britain*, with her Ladies, at *White-Hall, Feb.* 2. 1609. *Fol.* 1692. See the Marginal Notes. The Author was assisted by Mr. *Inigo Jones*, in the Invention and Architecture of the Scenes belonging thereto.

Masque at the Lord Hayes House, Fol. 1692. This was presented by divers Noblemen, for the Entertainment of Monsieur *Le Baron de Tour*, Ambassador Extraordinary from the French King. 1617.

Metamorphosed Gipsies, A Masque, *Fol.* 1692. presented to King *James* the First, at *Burleigh on the Hill*, at *Belvoyr*, and at *Windsor-Castle.* 1621.

Mercury Vindicated from the Alchymists at Court, a Masque, *Fol.* 1692. presented by Gentlemen, the King's Servants.

Mortimer's Fall, a Tragedy, *Fol.* 1640. and 1692. This was not quite finish'd by the Author, but left imperfect, by reason of his Death.

Neptune's Triumph for the Return of Albion, a Masque, *Fol.* 1692. presented at Court on *Twelfth-Night*, 1624.

News from the New World discovered in the Moon, a Masque, *Fol.* 1692. presented also before King *James* the First, 1620.

Oberon, the Fairy Prince, a Masque of Prince *Henry's*, *Fol.* 1692. The Author has divers Annotations on this Play.

Pan's Anniversary, or, *The Shepherds Holyday*, a Masque, *Fol.* 1692. This was presented at Court before King *James* the First. Mr. *Inigo Jones* assisted our Author in the Decorations.

Pleasure reconciled to Vertue, a Masque, *Fol.* 1692. This was also presented at Court, before King *James* the First, 1619. Hereto were some Additions for the Honour of *Wales*.

Poetaster, or, *His Arraignment*, a Comedy, *Fol.* 1692. Acted by the Children of his Majesty's Chappel, 1601. This Play is adorned with several Translations from the Ancients. See *Ovid's Elegies*, *Lib.* I. *Eleg.* 15. *Horat. Sat. Lib.* 2. *Sat.* 9. and *Lib.* 2. *Sat.* 1. *&c.*

Queen's Masque of Blackness, *Fol.* 1692. This was Personated at the Court at *White-Hall*, on *Twelfth-Night*, 1605.

—Her *Masque of Beauty*, *Fol.* 1692. This also was presented at the same Court, at *White-Hall*, on *Sunday-Night* after the *Twelfth-Night*, 1608.

Sad Shepherd, or, *A Tale of Robin Hood*, a Pastoral, *Fol.* 1692. This Play has but Two intire Acts, finish'd, and a Third left imperfect.

Sejanus's Fall, a Tragedy, *Fol.* 1692. first Acted by the King's Majesties Servants, 1603. Plot from *Tacitus, Seutonius, Seneca, &c.* There is an Edition of this Play 4*to* 1605. by the Author's own Orders, with all the Quotations from whence he borrowed any thing of his Play.

Silent Woman, a Comedy, *fol.* 1692. Acted First by the Children of her Majesty's Revels, 1609. Act. I. Scene I. borrowed from *Ovid de Arte Amandi:* Act II. Scene II. Part from *Juvenal, Sat.* 6. Act II. Scene V. from *Plaut Auricular, Act 3. Scene 5, &c.* This Play has been in good Esteem, and for a farther Commendation you are refer'd to Mr. *Dryden's Examen.*

Speeches at Prince Henry's Barriers, Fol. 1692. These are indeed Printed among his Masques, but cannot be accounted one; only reckoned so in former Catalogues.

Staple of News, a Comedy, *Fol.* 1692. Acted by his Majesty's Servants. In this Play Four Gossips appear on the Stage, criticising on the same, during the whole Action.

Tale of a Tub, a Comedy, *Fol.* 1692.

Time vindicated to himself and his Honors, a Masque, *Fol.* 1692. This was presented at Court on *Twelfth-Night*, 1623.

Vision of Delight, a Masque, *Fol.* 1692. This was also presented at Court in *Christmas*, 1617.

Vulpone, or, *The Fox*, a Comedy, *Fol.* 1692. Acted by the King's Majesty's Servants. This is writ in Imitation of the Comedies of the Ancients.

The before mentioned Plays, and other Poems, &c. were formerly printed together in Two Volumes, *Fol.* 1640, and 1641. but Three other Plays which are there omitted, are hereunder mentioned, and may be found in the late Edition, printed 1692.

The Case is Altered, a Comedy, 4to 1609. and *fol.* 1692. This was sundry times Acted by the Children of the *Black Fryars.* See *Plautus's Comed. &c.*

The Widow, a Comedy, 4to. 1652. and *fol.* 1692. Acted at the Private House in *Black Fryars*, by his late Majesty's Servants, with good Applause. *Fletcher* and *Middleton* joyn'd with the above Author in this Play, which has been reviv'd since the Restauration, at the King's House, with a new Prologue and Epilogue.

The New-Inn, or, *The Light Heart*, a Comedy, 8vo. 1631. This Play (says our Author's Title) was never Acted, but most negligently play'd, by some of the King's Servants, and more squeamishly beheld, and censured by others, the King's Subjects, 1629. Now at last set at Liberty to the Readers, his Majesty's Servants and Subjects, to be judged.

These last, with all the beforegoing Plays, Masques and Entertainments, with an English Grammar, are now published together in one large Volume, *fol.* 1692. ·

[*Ibid.*, pp. 77–81.]

[CHARLES GILDON], 1699
Henry Killigrew.

. . . . At the first Acting of the aforegoing Play [*The Conspiracy*], it met with some few Cavillers against some part thereof; but that was soon over, when *Ben. Johnson,* and the Lord Viscount *Falkland* gave it another Encomium.

[*Ibid.*, p. 82.]

[CHARLES GILDON], 1699
Tho. Killegrew,

. . . . *Thomaso;* or, *The Wanderer,* in Two Parts, a Comedy, *fol.* The Author has here borrowed, not only a Story from *Fletcher's Captain,* but several things from *Johnson's Fox.*

[*Ibid.*, p. 83.]

[CHARLES GILDON], 1699
Tho. Middleton

This Author liv'd in the Time of King *James* and King *Charles* the First; was Contemporary and Associate with *Deckar, Rowley, Massinger, Fletcher* and *Johnson.* Under the title of *Johnson,* you have an Account that he join'd with him and *Fletcher,* in one Play, call'd, the *Widow.*

[*Ibid.*, p. 98.]

[CHARLES GILDON], 1699
Thomas Randolph

. . . . He was an adopted Son of *Ben. Johnson;* and dyed Young.

[*Ibid.*, p. 115.]

[CHARLES GILDON], 1699

William Shakespear.

. . . . He was both Player and Poet; but the greatest Poet that ever trod the Stage, I am of Opinion, in spight of Mr. *Johnson*, and others from him, that though perhaps he might not be that Critic in Latin and Greek as *Ben*.

[*Ibid.*, p. 126.]

[CHARLES GILDON], 1699

Nahum Tate

. . . . *The Cuckold's Haven* . . . . Plot from *Eastward Hoe*, and *The Devil's an Ass*.

[*Ibid.*, p. 139.]

[CHARLES GILDON], 1699

UNKNOWN AUTHORS

. . . . There are some Authors that have quoted several Lines out of this Play, *viz. Ben. Johnson* in *Every Man in his Humour*, *Shirley* in his *Bird in a Cage*, &c.

[*Ibid.*, p. 162.]

[CHARLES GILDON], 1699

UNKNOWN AUTHORS

. . . . *Marcus Tullius Cicero*, that famous Orator, his Tragedy, 4*to*. 1651. writ in Imitation of *Catiline's Conspiracy*, by *Johnson*.

[*Ibid.*, p. 164.]

JAMES WRIGHT, 1699

Lovew. To wave this Digression, I have Read of one *Edward Allin*, a Man so famed for excellent Action, that among *Ben. Johnson's* Epigrams, I find one directed to him, full of Encomium, and concluding thus

> *Wear this Renown, 'tis just that who did give*
> *So many Poets Life, by one should Live.*

[*Historia Histrionica* (1699).]

ANONYMOUS, 1700

anno 1700

May   2^d [Lady Morley and] three [in the Box at] the ffox
[16 s.]

. . . .

[Dec^r]   21th [Lady Morley] one in the Box at the Silent Woman
[4 s.]

"   27th [Lady Morley] one [in the Box at] the ffox   [4 s.]

[Leslie Hotson, *The Commonwealth and Restoration Stage* (1928), p. 378, from C10 364/8, an account used in the suit *Morley* v. *Davenant*.]

ANONYMOUS, 1700

Sive tibi placuit cato sermone jocari
Comœdum, & parvâ ante oculos quasi picta tabellâ,
Sistere discursus varios, vitaeq; tumultum:
Ceu gravior tragicos admisit Musa dolores,
Syrma trahens longum, cultosq; accincta cothurnos:
Cedat in hoc tibi Shaksperus, Jonsonus in illo.

[*Luctus Britannici: Or the Tears of the British Muses*; *For the Death of John Dryden, Esq.* (1700), Part II, pp. 4–5.]

W. B., 1700

Ben Johnson the Famed Poet, being in very ordinary Company, and poor too, as it seems, for they could not pay the Reckoning (which was but small) though they muster'd all their Forces, so *Ben.* made a Proposal to them, that he who should make the worst Verse or Rhimes amongst them, should pay the whole, thinking by this he had made a pretty good Bargain, at least for himself, because he was in his Profession, and they all plain honest Country Fellows, so they began; *Ben.* first, who [*sic*] Poetry pleased them all, says the next.

We eat, we Drink, we . . . . , we Stink, and all to Ease us,
Then Sits Ben. Johnson, and Swears 'tis good by Jesus.

Which being *Ben's* Oath, and the Rhime good, so pleas'd the Old Blade, that he swore by Jesus he would pay all the Reckoning, and so he did.

[*Ingenii fructus; or the Cambridge Jests* (1700), quoted by Thornton S. Graves, "Jonson in the Jest Books," in *Manly Anniversary Studies*, p. 133.]

SAMUEL COBB, 1700

This Congreve follows in his deathless Line,
And the tenth hand is put to the Design.
The happy boldness in his finish'd toil,
Smells more than *Sh-r's* Wit, or *J-n's* Oil.

[*Poëtae Britannici. A Poem, Satyrical and Panegyrical* (1700), p. 22; from G. Thorn-Drury, *More Seventeenth Century Allusions to Shakespeare*, p. 50.]

WILLIAM CONGREVE, 1700

Mira[bell]. . . . . I wou'd not tempt my Servant to betray me by trusting him too far. If your Mother, in hopes to ruin me, shou'd consent to marry my pretended Uncle, he might like *Mosca* in the *Fox*, stand upon Terms; so I made him sure beforehand.

[*The Way of the World* (1706), Act II, p. 1 (1st ed., 1700).]

JOHN DRYDEN, 1700

If this were wit, was this a time to be witty, when the poor wretch was in the agony of death? This is just John Littlewit, in "Bartholomew Fair," who had a conceit (as he tells you) left him in his misery; a miserable conceit.

[Preface to *Fables Ancient and Modern* (1700), *The Works of John Dryden*, ed. Scott, Saintsbury (1885), XI, 222.]

UNDATED SEVENTEENTH-CENTURY ALLUSIONS

ANONYMOUS

[A manuscript of Jonson's *Entertainment of the King and Queen at Theobalds* is in the Library of All Souls College, Oxford, MS No. clv, fols. 319–21a; it ends at l. 125 (Herford and Simpson, *Ben Jonson*, VII, 153).]

ANONYMOUS

["Transl. of Hor. *Ars Poet. (copy)*, **261**, 104." William Dunn Macray, *Catalogi Codicum Manuscriptorum Bibliothecae Bodleianae Partis Quintae Fasciculus Quintus* (1900), p. 644, col. 2, under Jonson.]

ANONYMOUS

["Epitaph on Q. Eliz., **1092**. 267[b]." *Ibid.*]

[1] These items are all taken from manuscripts; they are listed alphabetically under the library in which the manuscript is located.

ANONYMOUS

OF OTHES.

In other tyme an auncient custome was
To sweare in weighty matters By the Masse,
But when the Masse wente downe, as old men cuote
Then did they sweare by Crosse of this greye grote;
Now when the Crosse likewise was held in skorne,
Then By my fayth, the common othe was sworne,
But havinge sworne awaye all faythe and trothe
Only god damme me is the common othe.

Thus Custome by Decorum kept gradacion,
Lost beinge masse, crosse, fayth, they finde Damnacion.

Authore BEN: JONSONIO.

[These lines are found in Bodleian, Add. MS B 97, fol. 39, and Ashm. MS 47, fol. 47. They are quoted from Newdigate, *The Poems of Ben Jonson*, pp. 336–37.]

ANONYMOUS

Mr Ben: Jonson *and* Mr Wm Shake-speare *being Merrye att a Tavern*, Mr Jonson *haveing begune this for his Epitaph*

Here lies Ben Johnson that was once one

he gives ytt to Mr Shakspear *to make upp, who presently wrightes*

Who while hee liv'de was a sloe thinge
And now being dead is Nothinge.

[Newdigate, *The Poems of Ben Jonson*, p. 340, from Bodleian, Ashm. MS 38, fol. 181.]

ANONYMOUS

[Jonson's poem, "To the Ladies of the Court," from *Neptune's Triumph*, is listed in William Henry Black, *Catalogue of the Ashmolean Manuscripts* (1845), col. 18, as "34. *Come noble nymphes, and doe not hide.* (7 l[ines].) [folio] 29."]

ANONYMOUS

["62. 'Ode on the death of Sr Henry Morison, to the noble Sr Lucius Cary. *Brave infant of Siguntum cleare.*' By 'BEN JOHNSON.' [folio] 49," is listed in *ibid.*, col. 20.]

ANONYMOUS

["119. 'A speach presented unto King James at a tylting, in the behalfe of the two noble brothers S^r. Robert and S^r. Henry Rich, now Earles of Warwick and Hol-

land. *Two noble knightes whome true desire and zeale.*' (16 l.) 103," is listed in *ibid.*,
col. 44, from MS 38. The poem is Jonson's, and, according to Bernard H. Newdigate,
The Poems of Ben Jonson, p. 280, it is signed "Ben Johnson" in this manuscript.]

ANONYMOUS

["253. (124) 'An epitaph on a gentelwoman whose name was Elizabeth. *Wouldst
thou heare what man can say.*' (12 l.) 168," is listed in *ibid.*, cols. 50–51, from MS 38.
The poem is No. CXXIV in Jonson's "Epigrammes," "Epitaph on Elizabeth,
L. H."]

ANONYMOUS

["371. (129) 'Uppon a virgine wch lived and died att courte. *Staye viewe this stone.*'
(14 l.) 187," is listed in *ibid.*, col. 56, from MS 38. The poem is Jonson's "Epitaph
on Mrs. Celia Boulstred"; it was not published with his works, but is known to be
his because of a signed copy in his autograph in the Harvard College Library. See
Newdigate, *The Poems of Ben Jonson*, pp. 285 and 369.]

ANONYMOUS

["64. 'To William Earle [of] Pembrooke. *I doe but name thee.*' (4 l.) 44^b," is listed
in *ibid.*, col. 75, from MS 47. This is Jonson's poem, "CII. To William Earle of
Pembroke" in "Epigrammes."]

ANONYMOUS

["146. 'BEN JOHNSON to King James. *From ye goblin and ye spectar.*' (5 st. of
8 and 1 of 6.) 90," is listed in *ibid.*, col. 79, from MS 47.]

ANONYMOUS

["150. 'B: JOHN: on a fayre gent: voyce. *Bee silent you still musicke of ye spheres.*'
(12 l.) 92^b," is listed in *ibid.*, col. 79, from MS 47. Published by Newdigate, *The
Poems of Ben Jonson*, pp. 290–91.]

ANONYMOUS

["172. 'A letter to Ben Johnson. *Did Johnson crosse not our religion so.*' (58 l.)
107," is listed in *ibid.*, col. 80, from MS 47.]

ANONYMOUS

["174. 'An answer to Ben Johnson's ode in dislike of his New Inne. *Come leave
this sawcy way.*' 108^b," is listed in *ibid.*, col. 80, from MS 47.]

ANONYMOUS

["175. 'M^r. RANDOLLS answer in defence of Ben Johnson. *Ben, doe not leave y^e
stage.*' (6 st. of 10.) 110," is listed in *ibid.*, col. 80, from MS 47.]

ANONYMOUS

A Forme of a Grace.

The Kinge, the Queene, the Prince God blesse:
The Palsgrave and the Lady Besse.
God blesse the Counsell and the State,
And Buckingham the fortunate.
God blesse every livinge thinge,
That the King loves, and loves the Kinge.
God blesse us all, *Bedford keepe safe:
God blesse mee, and God blesse #Rafe.

* Countesse of Bedford.   # The Countesse's man who wonne the race.

[Bodleian, Rawl. Poet. MS 26, quoted in Newdigate, *The Poems of Ben Jonson*, p. 284. Another version of the same poem is in Bodleian, Ashm. MS 38, 117.]

ANONYMOUS

Sent by Ben Johnson to Attorney William
Noy Who Was Feasting with Venison
in Another Room.

Before the world was drown'd no venison was found
(For why? there was never a Parke:
Now heer wee sit without ever a bit;
For Noy hath all in's Arke.

[Bodleian, Rawl. Poet. MS 26, fol. 143, quoted in Newdigate, *The Poems of Ben Jonson*, p. 337.]

ANONYMOUS

Ben Johnson upon His Brother William.

Instead of Distickes and Tetrastickes
And long breath Encomiastickes
Epigrams and Annagrames
Cronograms and All-such-hard-names
Because I will be short and somwhat hasten
On thy tombestone this Ile fasten
Nother truer nothing righter
William Johnson hic mentitur.

[Bodleian, Rawl. Poet. MS 26, fol. 162, quoted in Newdigate, *The Poems of Ben Jonson*, p. 337.]

Benjamin Johnson, upon His Freind Mr. Calvin.

If heaven be pleased when man doth cease to sinn,
If hel be pleas'd when it a soule doth winn,
If the Earth be pleas'd when 'tis red of a knave,
Then all be pleas'd, for Calvin is in his grave.

[Bodleian, Rawl. Poet. MS 26, fol. 162, quoted in Newdigate, *The Poems of Ben Jonson*, p. 337.]

ANONYMOUS

Scotch Verses Highly Commended
by King James.

With that a friend of his cry'd foy
And ferth an arrow drew;
Hee fitted it so featously the bow in
shivers flew.

It was the will of God trow I,
For had the tree been true,
Men said that kend his Archery
That he had slayn enew
Belive that day.

Answered by Ben: Johnson.

With that a ffriend of his cry'd foh,
A suddain fart out flew;
Hee foysted it so furiously,
The Tird in fitters flew.
The Deel was in his Arse trow I,
For had the touch been true
Men said that kend his arserie
That he had shitt enew
Belive that day.

[Bodleian, Rawl. Poet. MS 26, fol. 162ᵛ, quoted in Newdigate, *The Poems of Ben Jonson*, p. 338.]

ANONYMOUS

[A manuscript copy of the Song of Christmas from *Christmas His Masque* (ll. 71–78, 93–101, 172–79, 182–245) is to be found in Bodleian, Rawl. Poet. MS 160, fols. 173–74. See Herford and Simpson, *Ben Jonson*, VII, 434.]

ANONYMOUS

ON THE BIRTH OF THE LADY MARY

The 3d of November	Vandeljn crost the water
the 4th	the Queen had a daughter
5th	we scapt great slaughter
& the 6th	was the next day after.

BEN: JOHNSON.

[Bodleian, Rawl. Poet. MS 210, fol. 58^v, quoted in Newdigate, *The Poems of Ben Jonson*, p. 283.]

ANONYMOUS

[The poem "Charles Cavendish to His Posteritie" is attributed to Jonson in Bolsover Church MS M. 1. See Newdigate, *The Poems of Ben Jonson*, p. 288.]

ANONYMOUS

[A copy of "Ode to Himselfe" is to be found in Brit. Mus. Harl. MS. 4064, fol. 236. See Newdigate, *The Poems of Ben Jonson*, p. 357.]

ANONYMOUS

A Petition of Prince Charles.

Read royall father, and mighty kinge,
What my little hand doth bringe,
I whose happy birth imparts
Joy to all good subjects harts,
(Though ane Infant) doe not breake
Natures lawes nowe, if I speake
By this enterprize for one
Whose face doth blush and hart doth groane
For her acknowledged offence
That only found my Inocence
To gaine her mercy. Shee is bould;

Oh may itt some proportion hold
If to the father shee doth runn
By mediation of the sunn:
If therefore (oh my Royall Sir)
My first request may purchase her
Restoreinge to your grace, to mee
(Though Prince) yett shall an honor bee,
When in my Cradle itt is said
I master of Requests was made.

Ben Johnson.

[Brit. Mus., Harl. MS 6057, fol. 21*b*; Sloane MS 1792, fol. 128*b*; Add. MS 25707, fol. 154*b*; Add. MS 30982, fol. 137*b*. Each manuscript gives the poem a different title. See Newdigate, *The Poems of Ben Jonson*, pp. 282 and 369.]

ANONYMOUS

On the Birth Daie of Prince Charles.

The Gods greate Issue, our Jove's greate increase;
An Infant Embleme of his Grandsires peace;
A Prince, the happy mothers pretty smiller;
The fathers and the unkles reconciler;
In whome the highe blood to sovereignty designd
Of *Brittane, Fraunce*, and *Florence* are combinde
Of *Burbons, Medices*, blest *Stewards* stem,
Designd to weare a *Triple diadem;*
And where the Rose and Lilly rarely mixd,
Hath made both union and succession fix'd.
Him whome the yearth shall honor heaven shall blesse;
The improved hope of future happinesse,
The Joye of other States, the fruits of ours,
Is borne this day, this morne, this moneth of flowers.

Ben Johnson.

[Brit. Mus., Harl. MS 6057; Add. MS 15227. Quoted in Newdigate, *The Poems of Ben Jonson*, p. 281.]

ANONYMOUS

[Verses by Inigo Jones "To his false friend Mr. Ben Johnson" are to be found at fol. 30 of Harl. MS 6057. *A Catalogue of the Harleian Manuscripts* (1808), III, 314.]

ANONYMOUS

[Harl. MS 6917 contains poems by Jonson on pp. 117 and 159. See *ibid.*, p. 448.]

ANONYMOUS

["Verses intitled, 'The Goodwife's Ale,' 17th cent. 396, f. 3." Edward J. L. Scott, *Index to the Sloane Manuscripts* (1904), p. 284. According to Newdigate, *The Poems of Ben Jonson*, pp. 303 and 373, the name "Ben Jonson" appears at the end of the poem. Newdigate notes (p. 303) other manuscript copies of the poem in Sloane MS 1792, Egerton MS 2421, Harl. MS 6931, Add. MS 30982; and a printed copy in *Wits Recreations Augmented* (1641).]

ANONYMOUS

["Couplet on [Jonson], late 17th cent. 1009, f. 395." Scott, *Index to the Sloane Manuscripts*, p. 284.]

ANONYMOUS

[According to Scott's *Index*, p. 284, Sloane MS 1446, fols. 54*b*, 55, 71*b*, 89*b*, and 91 have copies of one or another of Jonson's poems, all unspecified.]

ANONYMOUS

[According to Scott's *Index*, p. 284, Sloane MS 1792 has copies of one or another of Jonson's poems, all unspecified, on fols. 55, 56, 56*b*, 59, 61, 101–4, and 119*b*.]

ANONYMOUS

[Epitaph for Richard Burbage.]
Epi: B: Jo:

Tell me who can, when a player dies,
In which of his shapes againe hee shall rise?
What need hee stand at the Judgement throne,
Who hath a heaven and a hell of his owne?
Then feare not Burbage heavens angry rodd,
When thy fellows are angells, and old Hemmings is God.

[Newdigate, *The Poems of Ben Jonson*, p. 338, from the Burley MS, printed in *The Poems of John Donne*, ed. H. J. C. Grierson (1912), I, 443.]

ANONYMOUS

["The concluding song 'O blessed change!' is in the Cecil Papers at Hatfield (volume 144, p. 271)." Herford and Simpson, *Ben Jonson*, VII, 153, from the discussion of the text of "The Entertainment of the King and Queen at Theobalds," first printed in the folio of 1616.]

John Faith

[In Corpus Christi MS CLXXVI, compiled by John Faith, is "15. On a gentle-woman sitting in a chair to have her picture drawn, by B. Jonson. fol. 17" (Henry Coxe, *Catalogus Codicum MSS Qui in Collegiis Aulisque Oxoniensibus Hodie ad Servantur* [1852], Part II, p. 71).]

William Fulman

[In Corpus Christi MS CCCIX, compiled by William Fulman, is "3. Memorials and remains of English poets, namely, ... i. Ben. Jonson. fol. 24" (*ibid.*, p. 149).]

William Fulman

[In Corpus Christi MS CCCIX, compiled by William Fulman, is "On Ben. Jonson's Magnetic Lady. fol. 67" (*ibid.*, p. 149).]

William Fulman

[In Corpus Christi MS CCCXXVIII, probably compiled by William Fulman, are "1. The good wives all, by B. Jonson. fol. 5" and "31. Ben Jonson's ode to himself. fol. 45 b. Printed at the end of his New Inne 1631" (*ibid.*, pp. 172–73).]

William Fulman

[In Corpus Christi MS CCCXXVIII, probably compiled by William Fulman, are "30. c. On Ben Jonson's book in folio. fol. 43b." and "33. Answer to Ben. Jonson, by Tho. Randolph. fol. 48b" (*ibid.*, p. 173).]

Anonymous, n.d.

The Fox, the Alchemist, and Silent Woman, Done by Ben Jonson, and outdone by no man.

[Quoted in C. F. Tucker Brooke and N. B. Paradise, *English Drama, 1580–1642*, p. 528. Suckling obviously had this jingle in mind when he made Jonson say, in *A Session of the Poets*:

"And he hoped they did not think the *Silent Woman*
The *Fox* and the *Alchemist*, outdone by no man."]

PART III

RELEVANT ALLUSIONS TO OTHER JACOBEAN AND CAROLINE DRAMATISTS

FRANCIS BEAUMONT AND JOHN FLETCHER

THOMAS JAY, 1633

> *You may remember how you chid me when*
> *I ranckt you equall with those glorious men;*
> Beaumont, *and* Fletcher: *if you loue not praise*
> *You must forbeare the publishing of playes.*

[From the commendatory verses published in the 1633 quarto of Massinger's *A New Way to Pay Old Debts*, signed "Thomas Iay. Miles."]

ANONYMOUS, 1640

20 *To Mr. Francis Beaumont and Mr.*
John Fletcher gent.

Twin-stars of poetry, whom we justly may,
Call the two-tops of learn'd Pernassus-Bay,
Peerlesse for freindship and for numbers sweet,
Whom oft the Muses swaddled in one sheet:
    Your works shall still be prais'd and dearer sold,
    For our new-nothings doe extoll your old.

["Epigrams," *Wits Recreations* (1640), sig. B₄.]

[CLEMENT BARKSDALE], 1651

XXIX. *An English Library.*
To Ri. Sackvill.

Sir, you'r my *Scholar*, and desire that I
Should choose you out an *English* Library:
Not that you doe despise *Latine* or *Greek*,
But Knowledge also in your own Tongue seek.
Too many Books *distract* the mind: a dozen

Are worth a Hundred, if they be well *chosen*.

. . . .

When weary you throw the Graver *Prose* away
Refresh your spirits with witty *Fletchers* play.

[*Nympha Libethris or the Cotswold Muse* (1651), pp. 65–66.]

SAMUEL SHEPPARD, 1651

On the two admirable witts,
Francis Beaumont, *and* John Fletcher.

Cease *Greece* to boast of *Aristophanes*,
Or of *Menander*, or *Euripides*,
The *Comick Sock*, and *Tragick Buskin* we
Weare neatest here, in forreigne *Brittanie*:
Or if you list to struggle for the Bayes,
Wee'l fight with *Beaumont's* and with *Fletchers* Playes.

[*Epigrams, Theological, Philosophical, and Romantic* (1651), p. 23.]

THOMAS PESTELL, 1652

Beaumont and *Fletcher* coyn'd a golden *Way*,
T'expresse, suspend, and passionate a *Play*.
Nimble and pleasant are all Motions there,
For two *Intelligences* rul'd the Spheare.

Both *Sock* and *Buskin* sunk with Them, and then
Davenant and *Denham* buoy'd them up agen.
Beyond these *Pillars* some think nothing is:
Great BRITAIN'S *Wit* stands in a Precipice.

[Stanzas 2 and 3 of "For the Author, Truly Heroick, by Bloud, Virtue, Learning," *The Poems of Thomas Pestell* (1940), ed. Hannah Buchan, pp. 83–84. The poem prefaces Edward Benlowes' *Theophila* (1652).]

JAMES SHIRLEY, 1652

You see
What audience we have, what Company
„*To* Shakespear *comes* . . . .

. . . .

He has but few friends lately, think o'that,

Hee'l come no more, and others have his fate.
„Fletcher *the Muses darling, and choice love*
„*Of* Phœbus, *the delight of every Grove;*
„*Vpon whose head the Laurel grew, whose wit*
„*Was the Times wonder, and example yet,*
'Tis within memory, Trees did not throng,
As once the Story said to *Orpheus* song.

[Prologue to *The Sisters, Six New Playes* (1653); the separate title-page is dated 1652.]

Anonymous, 1661

LONDON: Printed for *F. Kirkman* at the *John Fletcher* Head over against the *Angel-Inn* on the back side of *St. Clements* without *Temple-Bar*, 1661.

[Imprint for Sir William Lower's *Three New Plays* (1661).]

Thomas Shadwell, 1668

1. *Clerk.* }   I do acknowledge and firmly believe that the
  reads. }   Play of Sir *Positive Att-All* Knight, called the Lady
              in the Lobster, notwithstanding it was damn'd by
the Malice of the Age, shall not onely read, but it shall act with any
of *Ben Johnsons*, and *Beaumont*'s and *Fletcher*'s Plays.

[*The Sullen Lovers* (1668), Act III, in *The Complete Works of Thomas Shadwell*, ed. Montague Summers (1927), I, 53.]

Thomas Shadwell, 1679

Magg. The World will bear with you that have Estates, tho you have a little; but tis enough to undo a man that is to make his Fortune. My roguy Nephhew [*sic*] must leave *Cook* upon *Littleton* for *Beaumont* and *Fletcher*.

[*A True Widow* (1679), p. 11.]

Anonymous, 1683

Farewel! Thou Darling of *Melpomene;*
The *Best* but *Imitate, None Equal Thee;*
With Thee the Glory of the Stage is fled,
The *Heroe, Lover*, both with HART lie dead:

Of whom all speak, when of His Parts they tell,
Not as of *Man*, but some great *Miracle*.
Such Pow'r He had o'r the Spectators gain'd,
As forc'd a *Real* Passion from a *Feign'd*.
For when they saw AMINTOR bleed, strait all
The House, for every Drop, a Tear let fall;
And when ARBACES wept by sympathy,
A flowing Tide of Wo gush'd from each Eye.
Then, when he would our easie Griefs beguile
Or CELADON or PEREZ made us smile:
Thus our Affections He or *Rais'd*, or *Lay'd*,
Mirth, *Grief* and *Love* by wondrous Art He sway'd.

[From a broadside entitled "An Elegy on that worthy and famous actor, Mr. Charles Hart, who departed this life Thursday August the 18th, 1683," printed in Thorn-Drury's *Little Ark*, p. 48. Amintor is in *The Maid's Tragedy*, Arbaces in *A King and No King*, and Perez in *Rule a Wife*.]

ROBERT WILD, 1689

[Furor Poeticus and Invention have come to call upon a schoolmaster who is engaged in writing a play for Christmas. His boy says that "he hath all the Play Books in the Country to help him. Like the Cuckooe, he sucks other's Eggs: Here he steals a Word, and there he filches a Line, as we Boys do for Theams." They look over his library, commenting on Plautus, Jonson, Shakespeare, Beaumont and Fletcher, and Randolph.]

Beaumont and Fletcher.

Invent. The Muse's Twins; and in our English Sphere
Castor and *Pollux*, so they did appear.
'Tis thought, when they were Born, *Appollo*'s Will
Was to divide th'Two-top't *Parnassus* Hill,
That *Beaumont* (Lofty *Beaumont!*) might have one,
And *Fletcher* take the other for his Throne.

Fur. A pair of Journey-Men. They write both with a Quill.—
—Thus have I seen two Grey-hound Puppies play
With one another's itching Tails all day.

A couple of Cowards. Part them, and like two Worms, they would shrink in their Heads. Marry,—Take them together, and let them spit in one another's Mouths, and they would do smartly. They would Club for Verse. One find Rhyme, and another Reason.

[*The Benefice* (1689), p. 10.]

JOHN DRYDEN, 1700

There is more Baudry in one Play of *Fletcher*'s, call'd *The Custom of the Country*, than in all ours together. Yet this has been often acted on the Stage in my remembrance.

[Preface to *Fables Ancient and Modern* (1700), sig. *D₂ᵛ.]

RICHARD BROME

THOMAS RANDOLPH, 1638

[*The New Inn*] was made to entertaine,
    Guests of a nobler strain,
Yet if they will have any of thy store,
Give 'em some scraps, and send them from thy dore.

    And let those things in plush,
    Till they be taught to blush
Like what they will, and more contented be
    With what *Broome* swept from thee.

["*An answer to* Mr Ben Iohnson's *Ode to perswade him not to leave the stage*," *Poems* (1638), p. 72.]

WILLIAM CARTWRIGHT

E. G., 1646

To the Author.

If ever I beleiv'd Pythagoras,
(My dearest freind) even now it was,
While the grosse Bodies of the Poets *die,*
Their Soule doe onely shift. And Poesie
Transmigrates, not by chance, or lucke; for so
Great Virgils *soule into a* goose *might go.*
But that is still the labour of Joves *braine,*
And he divinely doth conveigh that veine:

So Chaucers *learned soule in* Spenser *sung,*
(Edmund *the quaintest of the Fairy throng.*)
And when that doubled Spirit quitted place,
It fill'd up Ben: *and there it gained grace.*
But this improved thing hath hover'd much,
And oft hath stoopt, and onely given a touch:
Not rested *untill* now, Randall *it brush'd,*
And with the fulnesse of its weight it crush'd,
It did thy Cartwright *kisse, and* Masters *court,*
Whose soules were both transfused in the sport.
Now more accomplish'd by those terse recruits,
It wooes thee (freind) with innocent salutes.

[Commendatory verses in M[artin] Ll[uelyn], *Men-Miracles with Other Poems*
(1646), sig. A₅.]

THOMAS WASHBOURNE, 1654

Cartwright is Wit throughout, but I read o're
More then his four playes, his last pious four;
And then his several Gratitudes unto
Him, whose head taught him, and purse fed him too;
Who gave him to buy books, and gave him skil
In each of them, to chuse out Well from Ill;
The Learned, Pious, Constant *Duppa;* he
Who was, and is stil Reverend in those three;
Whom these three, voice, and pen, and heart cannot
(No not *Cartwrights* own) enough celebrate;
In these he kept Christs law, lov'd God, and then
His next act was to pay his debt to men.
He did it here; for this one to him wou'd
Be Universal, ev'ry neighbourhood.
Though he out-sobers, out-words, out-wits all,
Grave *Virgil, Horace* nice, Salt *Martial,*
Yet more then in's (though unprofane) verse, wou'd
I drench my soul in his Diviner flood;
Those Sermons in which he did wind about
Our passions more then *Cicero* could do't,
In which he did out-sense deep *Plutarchs* skil,
And taught so wel, almost all else taught ill,

Unlesse when's Father *Duppa* 'gan to preach,
Who us to live, and taught him too to teach.
Oh, for that Text where he forbad to ly,
And prest home truth, in unbound Poetry?
Where *David* like, he did instil and charme
Us to be honest, though to our own harm,
Charg'd truths upon us, such as do shine here
In this smal volume, scorn'd and damn'd elsewhere;
O for his Passion-text, that we might buy
Th' inestimable price at Sixpence fee;
That we that winepresse which at *Edom* was,
And Christs Church trod, might taste from a new press!

[*Divine Poems* (1654), sigs. A₇ᵛ–A₈.]

GEORGE CHAPMAN

EDMOND BOLTON, 1626

[In a manuscript of Edmond Bolton, dated 1626 and formerly in the possession of Sylvanus Morgan, Bolton sets forth his proposals for the formation of the "Academ roial." He lists eighty-four "essentials," or able and famous laymen of the time, for membership in the academy, among them "George Chapman." Chapman and Jonson are the only dramatists listed (Ethel M. Portal, "The Academ Roial of King James I," *Proceedings of the British Academy, 1915–16*, pp. 189–208).]

WILLIAM HEMMINGE, 1632–33

Clowd grapling Chapman whose Aeriall mynde
Soares att philosophie and strickes ytt blynd.

[*William Hemminge's Elegy on Randolph's Finger*, ed. G. C. Moore Smith (1923), p. 13. The poem, which was written *ca.* 1632, is in Ashm. MS 38. These lines also occur in the section which was printed in *Choyce Drollery* (1656) under the heading "On the Time-poets."]

[JOHN PHILLIPS], 1656

Others again, there lived in my dayes,
That have of us deserved no lesse praise
For their Translations, than the daintiest wit,
That on *Parnassus* thinks he high doth sit,
And for a chaire may amongst the Muses call,
As the most curious maker of them all:

But as reverent *Chapman*, who hath brought to us
Musaeus, *Homer*, and *Hesiodus*,
Out of the Greek, and by his skill hath rear'd
Them to that height, and to our tongue indear'd,
That were those Poets at this day alive,
To see their Books, that with us thus survive,
They would think, having neglected them so long
They had bin written in the *English tongue*.

["A Censure of the Poets," *Sportive Wit*, Part II, "Wits Merriment: Or, Lusty Drollery," pp. 70–71.]

ANONYMOUS, 1682

Alas! says *Bays*, what are your Wits to me?
Chapman's a sad dul Rogue at Comedy;
Shirley's an Ass to write at such a rate
But I excel the whole *Triumverate*.

[*The Tory-Poets, a Satyr* (1682), p. 5.]

JOHN OLDHAM, 1684

At first the Musick of our Stage was rude,
Whilst in the *Cock-pit* and *Black Friars* it stood:
And this might please enough in former Reigns,
A thrifty, thin, and bashful Audience:
When *Bussy d' Ambois* and his Fustian took,
And men were ravish'd with Queen *Gordobuck*.

["Horace His Art of Poetry, Imitated in English," *The Works of Mr. John Oldham* (1686; 1st ed., 1684), Book II, p. 18.]

WILLIAM DAVENANT

C. G., 1640

But I commend the wisedome of thy Fate,
To sell thy labours at a better rate,
Then the contempt of the most squeamish age;
Or the exactest Roscij of the Stage:
Which might provoke our Laureat to repine,
That thine should rivall his brave *Albovine*.

[Second stanza of commendatory verses for Nabbes's *Unfortunate Mother* (1640).]

JOHN FORD

ANONYMOUS, 1640

56   *To Mr. John Ford.*

If e're the Muses did admire that well,
Of Hellicon as elder times do tell,
I dare presume to say upon my word;
They much more pleasure take in thee rare *Ford.*

["Epigrams," *Wits Recreations* (1640), sig. B₈ᵛ.]

THOMAS GOFFE

ANONYMOUS, 1666

Had *Goffe, Ben Johnson,* or had *Shakespear* been . . . .⎫
Spectators there, such *Acts* they should have seen, ...⎬
As they ne'r *acted* in an *English Scean.* . . . .⎭

[*The Dutch Gazette* (1666), quoted in *The Jonson Allusion-Book,* p. 335.]

THOMAS HEYWOOD

ANONYMOUS, 1640

58   *To Mr. Thomas Heywood.*

Thou hast writ much and art admir'd by those,
Who love the easie ambling of thy prose;
But yet thy pleasingst flight, was somewhat high,
When thou did'st touch the angels Hyerarchie:
Fly that way still it will become thy age,
And better please then groveling on the stage.

["Epigrams," *Wits Recreations* (1640), sig. B₈ᵛ.]

[ABRAHAM COWLEY], 1648

Go on brave *Heroes,* and perform the rest,
Encrease your fame each day a yard at least,
Till your high Names are grown as glorious full
As the four *London*-Prentices at the *Bull:*
So may your Goodly Ears still prickant grow,

And no bold Hair encrease, to mar the show;
So may your *Morefields*-pastimes never fail,
And all the Towns about keep mighty Ale;
Ale your own Spirits to raise, and Cakes t'appease
The hungry coyness of your Mistresses:
So may rare Pageants grace the Lord-Mayor's show,
And none finde out that those are Idols too.
So may you come to sleep in Fur at last,
And some *Smectymnuan* when your days are past,
Your Funeral-sermon of six hours rehearse,
And *Heywood* sing your Acts in lofty Verse.

["A Satyre against Separatists," *The Four Ages of England: or The Iron Age* . . . . *Written in the Year 1648* (1675).]

ANONYMOUS, 1654

Who More famous in that Quallity then . . . . *Christ. Whitehead*, who for agillity of body, and neatness in Dancing,

> *Doth in best judgements, as farr exceed the* Turks,
> *As* Shakspere Haywood *in his Commick Works.*

[*Mercurius Fumogosus*, August 23–30, 1654, p. 118, quoted by Hyder E. Rollins, "Shakespeare Allusions," *Notes and Queries, Twelfth Series*, X (March 25, 1922), 224.]

JOHN DRYDEN, 1682

Besides, his goodly Fabric fills the Eye,
And seems design'd for thoughtless Majesty;
Thoughtless as Monarch-Oaks that shade the Plain,
And spread in solemn State, supinely Reign;
Heywood and *Shirly* were but Types of Thee,
Thou last great Prophet of Tautology.

. . . .

Now Empress Fame had Publish'd the Renown
Of *Shad*—s Coronation through the Town;
Rous'd by report of Pomp, the Nations meet
From near *Bunhill*, to distant *Watlingstreet;*
No *Persian* Carpet spread th' *Imperial* way,
But scattered Limbs of Mangled Poets lay;
From Dusty Shops neglected Authors come,

Martyrs of Pies, and Reliques of the Bum;
Much *Heywood*, *Shirly*, *Ogilby*, there lay,
But Loads of *Shad*—almost Choak'd the way.

[*MacFlecknoe* (1682), pp. 4 and 8.]

THOMAS JORDAN

JOHN OLDHAM, 1684

Thou, who with spurious Nonsense durst profane
The genuine issue of a Poets Brain,
May'st thou hereafter never deal in Verse,
But what hoarse Bell-men in their Walks rehearse,
Or *Smithfield* Audience sung on Crickets hears:
May'st thou print *H——*, or some duller Ass,
Jordan, or Him, that wrote *Dutch Hudibrass*.

["Upon a Printer that exposed him by Printing a Piece of his grossly Mangled, and faulty," *The Works of Mr. John Oldham* (1686; 1st ed., 1684), Book II, p. 133.]

THOMAS RYMER, 1693

Yet this Cardinal with so nice a taste, had not many years before been several times to see acted the Tragedy of Sir *Thomas Moor*, and as often wept at the Representation. Never were known so many people crowded to death, as at that Play. Yet was it the Manufacture of *Jehan de Serre*, one about the form of our *Flekno*, or *Thomas Jordan*.

[*A Short View of Tragedy* (1693), p. 8.]

PHILIP MASSINGER

WILLIAM HEMMINGE, 1632–33

Messenger that knowes
the strength to wright or plott In verse or prose,
Whose easye pegasus Can Ambell ore
some threscore Myles of fancye In an hower.

[Ashm. MS 38, in *William Hemminge's Elegy on Randolph's Finger*, ed. G. C. Moore Smith, p. 13.]

Anonymous, 1640

53   *To Mr. Philip Massinger.*

Apollo's Messenger, who doth impart
To us the edicts of his learned art,
We cannot but respect thee, for we know,
Princes are honour'd in their Legats so.

["Epigrams," *Wits Recreations* (1640), sig. B₈.]

THOMAS RANDOLPH

G. W., 1638

Immortall BEN is dead; and as that ball
On *Ida* toss'd, so is his Crowne by all
The Infantry of wit. Vaine Priests! That chaire
Is only fit for his true Sonne and Heire.
Reach here the Lawrell: *Randolph*, 'tis thy praise:
Thy naked Scull shall well become the Bayes.
    See, *Daphne* courts thy Ghost: and spite of fate,
Thy *Poëms* shall be Poet *Laureat*.

                                        G. W. *Joan.*

[Commendatory verse prefixed to Randolph's *Poems* (1638).]

Anonymous, 1640

27   *To Mr. Thomas Randolph.*

Thou darling of the Muses for we may
Be thought deserving, if what was thy play
Our utmost labours can produce, we will
Freely allow thee heir unto the hill,
The Muses did assign thee, and think 't fit,
Thy younger yeares should have the elder-wit.

["Epigrams," *Wits Recreations* (1640), sig. B₅.]

[Edward Philips], 1658

Q. *when will Playes be in request?*
A. When *Tom Randals Muses Look-glass* may be acted.

[*The Mysteries of Love and Eloquence* (1685; 1st ed., 1658), p. 187.]

Rowland Watkyns, 1662

The Poet's Condition.

A poet, and rich? that seems to be
A paradox most strange to me.
A poet, and poor? that maxim's true,
If we observe the canting crue.
What lands had *Randolph*, or great *Ben*,
That plow'd much paper with his pen?

[*Poems without Fictions* (1662), quoted in *The Jonson Allusion-Book*, p. 325.]

JAMES SHIRLEY

William Hemminge, 1632–33

Shirlye the Morninge Childe the Muses Breed
and sent hyme vs wth Bayes borne on his head.

[Ashm. MS 38, in *William Hemminge's Elegy on Randolph's Finger*, ed. G. C. Moore Smith, p. 13. The section in which these lines occur was printed in *Choyce Drollery* (1656) under the heading "On the Time-poets."]

John Johnson, 1641

These, said *Cupid*, are not called Bookes, but Tomes, or Sections, for that our courtly Dames study onely to exect or cut off their thread-bare curtesans, and induce fresh and new furnished ones: And viewing these Tomes, saw chained up in golden linkes two Spanish Poets, *Dante* and *Cost*, and an English one called *Messenger*, which *Messenger* they entertaine, hoping still to see the good and gratefull newes of a well-filled purse, but if it prove contrary to their expectation, they command shaving *Shirly* to make him acquainted with Sir *Philip*, and so they flirt him into *Arcadia* to sing a lamentation of his lost Mistresse.

[*The Academy of Love* (1641), pp. 98–99.]

JOHN HALL, 1652

Yet this I dare assert, when men have nam'd
Iohnson (the Nations Laureat,) the fam'd
Beaumont, and *Fletcher*, he, that wo'not see
Shirley, the fourth, must forfeit his best ey.

[From commendatory verses prefixed to Shirley's *Cardinal* (1652).]

FRANCIS KIRKMAN, 1673

The most part of these Pieces were written by such Penmen as
were known to be the ablest Artists that ever this Nation produced, by Name, *Shakespear, Fletcher, Johnson, Shirley*, and others;
and these collections are the very Souls of their writings, if the
witty part thereof may be so termed.

[Preface to *The Wits or Sport upon Sport* (1673), as quoted in *The Shakspere Allusion-Book*, II, 199:]

ROBERT GOULD, 1685

Think ye vain *scribling Tribe* of *Shirley*'s fate,
You that write *Plays*, and you, too, that *translate;*
Think how he lies in *Duck-lane* Shops forlorn,
And ne'r so much as mention'd but with scorn;
Think That the end of all your boasted skill,
As I presume to prophesie it will,
Justly, for many of you write as ill.

["The Playhouse, a Satyr, Writ in the Year 1685," *Poems* (1689), pp. 179–80.]

JOHN SUCKLING

S. HALL, 1640

She'le out-blaze bright *Aglaura's* shining robe:
Her scene shall never change, the world's her *Globe*.

[From commendatory verses in the 1640 quarto of Harding's *Sicily and Naples*,
sig. A4.]

GEORGE POWELL, 1690

Poetry thrives so little now, that I much fear the famous *Suckling* himself was mistaken in his own Laureat; for there are those wou'd be glad to find that kind rich Alderman, his *Appollo* gave the Bays to, that out of all his heaped Coffers, wou'd either give or lend, to the fairest of the nine *Mendicant* Sisters.

["The Epistle Dedicatory," *The Treacherous Brothers* (1690), sig. A₂ᵛ.]

JOHN WEBSTER

ANONYMOUS, 1648

Let the whole crowd of Poets, SENECA
SOPHOCLES, SHAKSPEARE, IOHNSON now in clay.
EVRIPIDES, with famous WEBSTER, and.
SVCKLIN, and Goffe, leave the Elizian Land.

["To the Readers of my former Peece," *The Second part of Crafty Crvmwell, or Oliver in his Glory as King* (1648), by Mercurius Pragmaticus.]

INDEX

[Since there is no bibliography, all books, articles, and plays referred to in the text are listed in this index. The full title and date are given at first occurrence in the text.

Casual occurrences of the names of Jonson and Shakespeare appear on almost every page and are therefore not indexed, but all references to their works, the characters in their plays, and their personal affairs are listed.

Though items mentioning Beaumont or Fletcher as individuals are indexed separately, all plays written by either or both of the dramatists are indexed under the joint head of Beaumont and Fletcher, regardless of date.

Manuscripts are listed under provenance.]